LISTENING TO ANIMALS

WILDLIFE REHABILITATION,

EXOTIC PETS,

TELEPATHIC ANIMAL COMMUNICATION,

AND A REMARKABLE JOURNEY
FROM ATHEISM TO SPIRITUALISM

Adele Lewis Coon

DISCLAIMER

The purpose of this *Listening to Animals* book is to increase awareness of the deeper connections we can have with animals and other beings with whom we share our world. No information contained herein is intended as medical or care-giving advice, either for humans or animals, nor is it intended to be a training manual for wildlife rehabilitators. Handling wild animals can be dangerous without appropriate knowledge and equipment. There are many differing opinions on the ideas expressed herein, and regulations may vary greatly depending on location. In all cases of handling and/or caring for wild or domestic animals, advice from relevant government officials and medical or care providers with appropriate licenses and permits is recommended before any action is taken. The author and publisher are not responsible for any adverse effects or consequences resulting from the use of any ideas or activities included in this *Listening to Animals* book.

Printed by CreateSpace, an Amazon.com Company

FOR ALL ANIMALS
with gratitude, respect, awe, and love

"We (all animal species) are so excited to have people awaken
and know that we speak!"

*- Ara, reticulated python in her September 4, 2002,
communication with Lyn, Chapter 25.*

ACKNOWLEDGMENTS

My deep gratitude and appreciation goes to the following people who have helped me with this book and in more other ways than they know. Of course any errors are mine.

Judy Hoy, wildlife rehabilitator and pioneer environmentalist, has been a great mentor, teacher, information resource, and friend for over 20 years. I still frequently call on her for help with animals and am in awe of her ability to "figure things out," and to create perfect wing splints using Styrofoam meat trays and a pair of scissors, as well as of her determination to help animals through educating people about pesticide and other human-caused dangers.

Sarah Monson, an old soul with whom I've been connected for a very long time, wonderful friend and traveling and seminar companion, who dedicated her knowledge, artistic skills, and time to formatting and marketing my work.

Mary Wolf, fellow rehabber, parrot rescuer, and writer, read the book several times, provided a helpful sounding board, kept me from at least some of my tangents, and did it all with a wildlife rehabilitation insider's understanding, compassion, and sense of humor.

Becki Koon and Jack Rouse, familiar old souls but relatively new friends in this lifetime, both read and made helpful comments and suggestions for the book. They also share an interest in spirituality, which I love to discuss with them, and eagles, one of whom they rescued.

Marge Hulburt is a shamanic healer, shamanism teacher, author, and editor, all in a warm and caring personality. I've enjoyed and benefitted in several ways from each of her professional roles. After reading an early draft, Marge stopped me from considering this book done long before it really was. She made many helpful suggestions, most of which I followed.

Lyn Benedict is a professional animal communicator and shamanic healer whose knowledge and skills helped me and so many animals, as is shown throughout this book. I greatly appreciate her insight and generous sharing of messages she has received from animals.

Don Coon, my husband of over 20 years, has calmly accepted parrots, goats, fawns, eagles, owls, and many other critters in the house, on the front table, and underfoot. Some scream when he's on business phone calls; animal food includes mice in freezers and thawing in cups or bowls next to the kitchen sink; phone calls may be emergencies involving bringing in just the right enclosure, or driving somewhere to pick up an injured animal or to a store for specialized food. Don does most of the euthanasias, for which I am ever grateful. He babysits when I want to travel in the summer, builds pens, carries heavy bags of feed, and fills many other roles I could not do without him.

TABLE OF CONTENTS

LIST OF NAMED CHARACTERS

CHAPTER 1... 1
CHAPTER 2... 9
CHAPTER 3...13
CHAPTER 4...17
CHAPTER 5... 25
CHAPTER 6... 29
CHAPTER 7... 35
CHAPTER 8... 39
CHAPTER 9... 45
CHAPTER 10... 51
CHAPTER 11... 57
CHAPTER 12... 63
CHAPTER 13... 69
CHAPTER 14... 73
CHAPTER 15... 79
CHAPTER 16... 83
CHAPTER 17... 91
CHAPTER 18... 99
CHAPTER 19... 109
CHAPTER 20... 115
CHAPTER 21... 121
CHAPTER 22... 127
CHAPTER 23... 131
CHAPTER 24... 141
CHAPTER 25... 147
CHAPTER 26... 153
CHAPTER 27... 157
CHAPTER 28... 161
CHAPTER 29... 165
CHAPTER 30... 169
CHAPTER 31... 175
CHAPTER 32... 181
CHAPTER 33... 187

CHAPTER 34... 191
CHAPTER 35... 197
CHAPTER 36... 203
CHAPTER 37... 209
CHAPTER 38... 215
CHAPTER 39... 221
CHAPTER 40... 231
CHAPTER 41... 237
CHAPTER 42... 243
PHOTOS.. 246
CHAPTER 43... 261
CHAPTER 44... 267
CHAPTER 45... 271
CHAPTER 46... 275
CHAPTER 47... 283
CHAPTER 48... 289
CHAPTER 49... 293
CHAPTER 50... 297
CHAPTER 51... 301
CHAPTER 52... 305
CHAPTER 53... 307
CHAPTER 54... 313
CHAPTER 55... 319
CHAPTER 56... 325
CHAPTER 57... 331
CHAPTER 58... 337
CHAPTER 59... 341
CHAPTER 60... 345
CHAPTER 61... 349
CHAPTER 62... 353
CHAPTER 63... 357
CHAPTER 64... 363
CHAPTER 65... 367
CHAPTER 66... 373
CHAPTER 67... 377
CHAPTER 68... 381
CHAPTER 69... 387

CHAPTER 70.. 391
CHAPTER 71.. 395
CHAPTER 72.. 399
CHAPTER 73.. 403
CHAPTER 74.. 411
CHAPTER 75.. 419
CHAPTER 76.. 423
CHAPTER 77.. 429
CHAPTER 78.. 435
CHAPTER 79.. 443
CHAPTER 80.. 447
CHAPTER 81.. 453
CHAPTER 82.. 461
CHAPTER 83.. 471
CHAPTER 84.. 477
CHAPTER 85.. 487
REFERENCES
    Web Addresses... 497
    Books... 500
    Videos.. 511

LIST OF NAMED CHARACTERS
Animals and People

Anna DeGrauw: a friend from Oregon whom I met after she and my friend Ed married; nurse, artist, e-Bay guru, kind and loving person.

Ara (emu): female emu, obtained through a free newspaper ad in 1999 at about one year old.

Ara (reticulated python): purchased as a baby in Portland, Oregon, during the late 1970s and raised to be at least 16 feet long.

Aten: (pronounced AH-ten, named after an ancient Egyptian sun god) male emu purchased in 1998 from a breeder in Idaho at two or three days old.

Atlas: male reticulated python, purchased from a breeder in Portland, Oregon, in the late 1970s.

Big Jim: male African grey parrot, purchased as a potential mate for Tisha; his name became Mikey because he and Tisha liked that name better.

Bo: baby black bear, apparently orphaned; born in early 2007; short-term care with Adele before transfer to the Montana Wildlife Center in Helena; eventually transferred to Beartooth Nature Center in Red Lodge, Montana.

Bonnie: female baby beaver, sick and perhaps swept downstream away from her family.

Brian Hobbs: friend and part-time neighbor who sometimes helps with fawns.

Bucky: male white-tailed deer, orphaned in 2006, kept for a month by the people who found him.

Burt Lewis: first husband; married in June 1966, divorced in March 1973.

Casey: male wallaby purchased in spring 2001 from a breeder in Oregon.

Cinco: mature male bald eagle, nearly died from eating poisoned rodents.

Clover: female lab/shar pei cross rescued from a puppy mill in spring 2005.

Cricket (wallaby): female wallaby purchased in spring 2002 from a breeder in Oregon.

Cricket (dog): female griffon who belongs to my brother David and his wife Diana.

Dan Waldo: my brother, 18 years younger than I am; welder, truck driver, hunter.

David Waldo: my brother, born when I was 11, who passed in early 2015; health food store owner, volunteer fireman, hunter.

Deanna: a friend from Portland, Oregon, with whom I started cleaning and articulating skeletons. We traveled to Yellowstone National Park together when she visited me the summer Solo was a baby.

Diana: my sister-in-law and friend with whom I attended the first self-hypnosis classes.

Don Coon: second husband; married in June 1993.

Eagly Owl: baby great horned owl who almost died in a fire that burned his nest tree; raised and released with Star Owl.

Ed DeGrauw: a friend from Oregon whom I met when we were students in a Herpetology class – which he now teaches – at Portland State University many years ago.

Eden: female black lab purchased from friends in Idaho in 1998.

Fancy: orphaned female white-tailed deer, raised with Rosie and Lily in 2008.

Ginger: female yellow lab who lived with Don when we got married; she was Nicki's first dog so he calls all dogs Ginger.

Harold: my nephew by marriage who rescued Bo, the baby bear, and Wendy, the baby cougar, when he worked as a logger.

Hope: female white-tailed deer raised here. She still lives in our neighborhood and raises twins each year.

Jim Waldo; my brother, born when I was nearly 2 years old; teacher, EMT, gardener, hunter.

Jordan: female wallaby born here in late 2003.

Judy Hoy: the main wildlife rehabilitator in our valley (the Bitterroot Valley of Montana). She trained me and I am still one of her sub-permittees.

Lily: female mule deer born near a bike path in spring 2008 when Solo was a yearling. Her twin was killed by a dog and conditions were poor for her so she was brought here.

Linda: veterinarian and friend who helps with our exotic animals and sometimes wildlife. We traveled to Africa together.

Little Joe: male white-tailed deer, orphaned and injured in a car accident; born in spring 2007, raised with Solo and Velvet.

Lyn J. Benedict: professional telepathic animal communicator who first talked with Tisha and Simon in 2002.

Mary Wolf: a friend and fellow wildlife rehabilitator who helps me with animals, writing, and moral support.

Michael: male mule deer kidnapped and brought here by well-meaning people in spring 2008, when Solo was a yearling.

Mikey: male African grey parrot initially named Big Jim; purchased as a possible mate for Tisha in 2010.

Missy: female white-tailed deer, born in 2006, kept for seven weeks by people who didn't care for her properly.

Nicki: male yellow-backed chattering lory born in 1994; purchased from a breeder in Missoula, MT, at age two months.

Patrizia Mastne: a friend from Oregon whom I met in a Comparative Vertebrate Anatomy class at Portland State University; inspired teacher, mother, kind and compassionate person.

Rosie: female white-tailed deer who was orphaned in spring 2008 when Solo was a yearling.

Ross: raven, perhaps raven/crow cross, who came to me with a broken wing during the summer of 2002. He became one of my teachers and spirit guides.

Ruth Van Beber: a friend and fellow atheist in Portland, Oregon, who died in 1994 at the age of 92.

Sandy: a friend from high school, who lives in the same town and sometimes travels with me.

Sarah: energy intuitive, energy healer, psychic, friend, who often helps me with wildlife. We have traveled together several times, including to Reconnective Healing seminars in Arizona.

Simon: male African grey parrot born in 1994; purchased as a companion for Tisha in 2001.

Skipper: male mule deer, orphaned and raised a couple years before Solo was born.

Solo: male mule deer, apparently orphaned; born around June 1, 2007; stayed with us till summer 2008.

Sophia: female white-tailed deer fawn, born when her mother was hit and killed by a car.

Spirit: baby golden eagle kicked out of the nest by a sibling, raised here and released back to his parents when he could fly.

Star Owl: baby great horned owl who was bleeding due to eating poisoned rodents.

Sunny: female mule deer, apparently orphaned in 2006.

Tisha: female African grey parrot born in 1994; taken in as a rescue in 2001 from someone who could no longer care for her.

Toby: male wallaby born here at the end of 2002.

Tom Edmonds: friend, neighbor, and chef who helps with some of the babies. He cooks for us sometimes (not often enough), and is almost always available for a trip to town for chocolate.

Valerie: a friend I met in the late 1990s through Don's air purifier business. Val told me about Lyn and suggested I ask her to talk with my parrots.

Velvet: female elk calf, probably kidnapped; born in spring 2007 with an umbilical hernia; raised with Solo and Little Joe.

Wendy: owner/manager of the World Parrot Refuge on Vancouver Island, British Columbia.

Wendy: female baby cougar, apparently orphaned in spring of 2008.

Zebanessa: female emu purchased as a hatchling in 1998 from a breeder in Idaho.

CHAPTER 1

Less than a week after his birth, a tiny mule deer fawn, dehydrated and emaciated, stumbled along next to Highway 93 just south of Darby, Montana. Though scared and very much alone, he came into this lifetime with a mission and was determined to survive to accomplish it. Fortunately, he was spotted by a kind and compassionate woman named Jennifer, who gave him the opportunity to do so.

For one so young, he'd already had an amazing variety of experiences. His first two or three days were exciting and wonderful. His mother had found a quiet, secluded place in which to give birth, hidden from predators and even other deer. As soon as he was out in the world, she cleaned away birth fluids with her warm tongue as the two began to bond. She made soft, encouraging sounds to which he replied with baby cries similar to those of a lamb. In this way they learned to recognize each other's voice, just as we know the voices of our family and friends.

Within a few minutes of birth, the baby lifted his head, which wobbled on his long neck, then managed to fold his legs enough to roll up onto his chest. A short time later, after gaining a bit more control over his head and neck, he began learning to use his long legs. At first he just kicked randomly, tipping himself back onto his side. Soon he managed to plant both hind feet and push the back half of his body into an unsteady upright posture. After falling and regaining the half-standing position a few more times, both front legs were underneath and he was propped on all four, swaying from side to side as he practiced coordinating the many different muscles.

Then he began learning how to walk. His mom continued to nuzzle and encourage him, but his survival required his accomplishing this feat on his own as soon as possible. His next goal was to find his mother's udder so he could suckle, taking in the colostrum her body had prepared for him. This first milk provided warmth and nutrients, as well as antibodies to protect him from illnesses while his immune system continued to develop.

When the baby was dry and full of warm milk, his mother slowly led him to a different area, removing him from birth odors attractive to predators before leaving him to find food for herself. At first he tried to follow her, but was much too uncoordinated to go far; this time she moved too quickly for him. As soon as she was out of his sight, instinct directed him to find a sheltered place under a bush or in long grass where he could rest and wait for his mother to return. His safety depended on remaining unseen, because he was far too small, slow, and weak to escape any predator. His soft tan coat with its pure white spots helped him resemble sun-dappled ground cover such as old pine needles and leaves.

After awakening from his nap, the little deer began becoming familiar with the sounds, sights, and scents of the natural world around him. He learned the squirrels and small birds were safe, though sometimes noisy. Each time he heard something bigger moving through the forest or caught an unfamiliar scent, he flattened his head and neck against the ground and held still, not even moving his large ears. Predators use their senses of smell and vision to find prey. Baby deer have virtually no body odor for a while after birth and are well camouflaged to avoid being seen – as long as they remain still. Predators quickly spot movement as slight as the flick of an ear, even if the rest of the baby is hidden.

Within a few hours his mom came back, just as the fawn began feeling hungry again. He recognized her voice when she called softly to him, so he answered, then clambered to his feet and walked toward her, already stronger and more coordinated. Again he suckled as she nuzzled him. When he was full, he practiced using his legs by running around his mom, sometimes even hopping clumsily. He stumbled a few times, but continued improving as he became used to his muscles. His mom stayed with him for a while and even laid next to him on the ground, keeping him warm through part of the night. After he suckled once more, she left to feed again. This pattern continued for two or three days as he became stronger and more agile.

Then disaster struck. His mother failed to return after the usual interval and the tiny deer grew more and more hungry. For many hours he waited for her, possibly moving to a different bed once in a while, but mostly remaining hidden and still. Finally, after 24 or more hours, he was desperate enough to run around in circles crying for his mom. The circles became bigger as he searched a larger area. Still, she didn't come. His behavior was dangerous for the little deer because predators listen for cries of distress, but he would starve to death without a mother.

A day or two later, he took a further terrifying step and left the area. Traveling like this went against his instincts, but the fawn couldn't survive alone. He had to try something else. At some point, at least three days after his last contact with his mom, he came to Highway 93 where his rescuer saw him.

Jennifer called me, described the fawn, and asked what she should do. He was walking somewhat clumsily with his head hanging down and mouth slightly open. His back was curved in an unnatural position as though he had been injured. There had been a motorcycle-versus-deer accident in that area a few days before; Jennifer thought the fawn's mother might have been the deer who was killed. I told her she could bring the baby to our place in Hamilton, 20 miles north of Darby.

As a volunteer wildlife rehabilitator, I take care of injured and orphaned native animals and birds. This was the first fawn I'd received that season so nothing was set up for him. While we waited for Jennifer and the deer, my husband Don brought the playpen in from storage and took goat milk out of the freezer. I washed a baby bottle, mixed electrolytes in warm water, and put the jug of milk in a pan of hot water to thaw. Goat milk keeps well when frozen for two or three months. Longer storage sometimes causes it to separate into a thin, yellowish liquid with thick, white curds at the bottom when thawed. It can be shaken back into solution, but again soon separates into layers. Fortunately, we had taken care of an orphaned baby bear less than a month before, so we had left-over goat milk on hand for this first fawn of the season.

I set up the playpen in the kitchen, preparing it with sheets and towels for bedding and a crib sheet for the top. Even very young deer can jump quite high and healthy ones a week or two old are able to hop out of a playpen. Our floors are covered with smooth vinyl tiles, making them easy to clean but slippery for little animals with hooves. If they fall with their legs spread, they can tear ligaments, tendons, muscles, and/or nerves in the groin area and become permanently crippled. I use a fitted crib sheet over the top, putting wooden chopsticks behind the corner posts of the playpen through small holes in the sheet. This is strong enough to keep tiny fawns safe for a few days, until they are stable and can stay outside in one of the deer pens.

Jennifer soon arrived with the fawn lying on the floor of her car. He looked so limp and unresponsive we initially thought he had already died. This baby was thinner than any I had seen before. When I picked him up, he opened his big, dark eyes and I felt his heart beating. After thanking Jennifer for caring enough to bring the little guy, I took him into the house and put him in the playpen.

Surprisingly, he managed to stand up. I was concerned to see his back still curved in the same shape as when he was lying down. Manipulation showed it could straighten, and I was unable to find any injuries in his back or elsewhere. I was shocked, however, at his state of emaciation. It looked like his body was made out of a two- by six-inch piece of wood. Even his chest was no wider than his vertebrae! I couldn't understand how his lungs, heart, and stomach would fit in such a narrow space. All the bones of his spinal column and pelvis were visible under a thin layer of skin. Newborn deer are always slender, but this was extreme.

When animals or birds (or humans, for that matter) are nearly starved to death, our first instinct is to quickly get as much food into them as possible. It is also the worst thing to do and may actually kill them. Digestion requires energy, which they need to build slowly before being able to tolerate much food. Also, water and electrolytes are necessary to create digestive enzymes and stimulate kidney function.

I filled a syringe with electrolytes and, using a soft rubber tube, squirted the warm liquid slowly into the back of the fawn's mouth. If this is done through the side of the mouth (instead of the front), they will usually swallow without choking. I gave him 10

4

to 20 cc every 15 minutes till he had taken three doses. Half an hour later I let him suck an ounce of warm goat milk mixed with a small amount of whipping cream from a baby bottle. Fortunately, the fawn was strong enough to suckle and was quite enthusiastic about it. He didn't think an ounce of milk was enough.

For the next two hours I gave him some liquids every half hour, alternating between an ounce of milk and 10 cc of electrolytes. By then he was urinating, so I knew his kidneys were functioning, and he seemed a bit stronger. I quit giving him electrolytes, just letting him take two ounces of milk every hour. By 10:00 p.m. he was doing so well I let him drink three ounces of milk and went to bed for two hours. At midnight he took about four ounces, so I went back to bed until 4:00 a.m., fed him again, and then slept until about 6:00 a.m.

When his bowels began working normally that morning, I believed he was going to survive. For the next few days, I fed him every four hours around the clock, allowing him to eat as much as he wanted each time. He was soon taking six to eight ounces of the goat milk and whipping cream mixture each feeding, a normal amount for fawns that age.

We live on almost five acres, with a fenced back yard about an acre in size. Inside that space are two smaller enclosures, one of which is a winter pen for our pair of emus whose names are Aten and Ara. The other, called the deer pen, is mostly for baby deer, elk, and moose, though we've housed other wild animals and birds there at times. In the deer pen is a small chain link enclosure, with metal roofing on top and surrounded on two sides by the walls of a garage; the other two wire panels face into the central area. There is also a covered shed with two wire sides and two solid wood sides.

Large ponderosa pine trees in and near the deer pen provide shade, with access to patches of sunlight during part of the day. Most of the enclosure is open so babies have room to run and play. The fence is six feet high, made of woven wire with two- by four-inch openings. Newborn deer are so tiny they can squeeze through most other kinds of fencing; also they need to be protected from predators who may jump over shorter fences.

The weather was warm during the day, so I took the fawn outside to the chain link pen the second day he was here. He was already stronger and his back no longer remained curved when he stood up. Baby deer need to practice running and bouncing. The playpen is far too small, and earth and grass provide a much better surface for traction. For the first week or so, fawns are somewhat wobbly and uncoordinated, but they quickly gain control of their muscles. It's such fun to watch them play! They seem to be saying, "Look what I can do with my legs!" Mule deer not only run; they jump with all four legs stiff, as though they are made of springs, like pogo sticks. It always brightens my day to watch them run and jump. They are so full of joy and life and innocence! They often do this right after they eat. Their bellies are full of warm milk, Mom is there so they feel safe, and it's time to play.

I still believed the little mule deer was the sole survivor of a motorcycle/deer collision, so I began calling him Solo. A neighbor wanted to call him Miracle because it seemed miraculous he had survived that degree of starvation, but the name seemed too long and awkward for such a tiny fellow. When he came to me, he only weighed about five pounds; he should have weighed seven or eight. I later learned the doe killed in the accident had still been pregnant, so she was not Solo's mother. The name remained, however.

For a few days I brought Solo into the house at night, both because the night temperature was still quite cool (in the 40s and sometimes even the high 30s) and it made the 2:00 a.m. feeding easier for me. Fawns in the wild are able to survive cold temperatures, of course. They find sheltered places to hide when their mothers leave them to feed. Also, does lie next to their babies to help keep them warm during inclement weather, and their milk warms fawns from the inside. However, it is much more difficult to maintain a healthy body temperature when weight is below normal. I wanted Solo to use most of his energy for growing and gaining weight, rather than for staying warm.

While he was still in the playpen part of the time, I noticed Solo's little black nose was peeling in spots. At first I thought he might be rubbing it against the mesh sides of the playpen, but the pink places kept getting bigger. It was as though his whole nose was a blister, with dead, surface skin peeling off. Within a few days, he had no black skin on his nose and it looked raw. Fortunately, there was no bleeding. The condition may have been a result of dehydration and starvation or it could have been some kind of pressure injury, unlikely since he had no cuts or scrapes.

I was concerned Solo might have a permanently pink nose that would easily sunburn. I saw no sign of infection, but covered the raw area with emu oil after every feeding. Emu oil helps promote healing and prevent infection and it's safe for animals and birds if they lick it off. Within a few days, little black freckles started appearing on Solo's nose. The spots kept spreading till they grew together, finally giving him a perfect little black nose. Beads of moisture even appeared on it when he drank from his bottle, as on normal fawn noses. I was so glad the skin was healthy, rather than made of scar tissue, and that the glands were undamaged.

CHAPTER 2

My introduction to caring for animals began nearly 50 years before I became a wildlife rehabilitator and has continued as a theme expressed in a number of ways throughout my life. I was born with an interest in and an affinity for studying biology. Insects and single-celled creatures have always been as amazing and fascinating to me as the larger ones. As my knowledge, vocabulary, and reading skills grew, I studied books about them at different levels, from children's books to upper division biology texts. As a child, I read all the Edgar Rice Burroughs animal stories (sometimes with covers over my head using a flashlight, because I was supposed to be sleeping), as well as non-fiction books about different ecosystems and animals.

We lived on a small farm for five years while I was in grade school. When I was in fourth grade, my dad took my brother Jim and me into a neighbor's pasture to watch a calf being born. It was fascinating to me and awe-inspiring, the beginning of my interest in veterinary medicine. I wanted to be around that kind of experience as often as I could. I would sit patiently in the chicken coop to watch our hens lay eggs, even though tiny bird mites crawled on me. We had some ducks, too, one of which sat on eggs till they hatched, a process I was also patient enough to watch. Neighbors would call me when one of their animals (pigs, cats, dogs, cows) was having babies because I was interested but remained quiet and out of the way.

My grandfather owned a ranch where he raised sheep and cattle for meat and wool. Jim and I spent a lot of time there, occasionally helping during some livestock procedures. I loved calving and lambing time, with all the new babies and opportunities to watch some being born. My family raised a few bum lambs (orphans), who went with the others to be butchered in the fall. We also occasionally raised a calf, and then butchered it for meat.

Hunting was an accepted activity as I was growing up. Men and boys in most families I knew hunted and fished, as did some of the girls. Wild meat was always an important part of our diet, less expensive than beef, but hunting and fishing were also a sport for the hunters. Jim and I learned to smoothly pull the trigger on a rifle before we were big enough to hold the gun, and began shooting wild grouse and ground squirrels with a .22 when we were quite young. Shooting gophers (actually Columbia ground squirrels) was a common summer sport. I didn't hunt big game, but all three of my brothers did, and still do. Jim and I also used to trap ground squirrels on my grandfather's ranch, and we all fished.

I began working in a local veterinary clinic when I was 15 and loved everything about it. I'd have lived there if I could. Of course I was going to school, working at Tom's News, the bookstore/newsstand my parents owned at that time, and sometimes babysitting my little brother David while my parents worked.

The veterinarians mainly took care of livestock, but saw some pets as patients, too. At first I was just allowed to be there because of my interest, following them around and even going on ranch calls with them. Soon they began to pay me because I also helped by cleaning kennels and instruments, holding small animals for treatments and exams, autoclaving (sterilizing) surgery equipment, etc. I read their medical books, asked questions, and decided to become a veterinarian, even though I wasn't doing very well in high school. Grades in English, Spanish, literature, and biology were acceptable; chemistry, physics, and math other than geometry were not. I don't know why I loved geometry.

When I was 17 and 18, just before and after I graduated high school, I worked as an unpaid student at Rocky Mountain Laboratory, a National Institutes of Health research facility located here in Hamilton. In a small brick building built early in the twentieth century, scientists began studying Rocky Mountain spotted fever and the ticks that carry and transmit the rickettsial organism that causes it. They developed a vaccine which was administered in schools, as well as in doctors' offices. My mother remembers waiting in line when she was a small child (in the 1930s) to receive the vaccinations; they burned badly for a while and often caused a swollen, sore arm. That practice continued when I was in grade school, so my brother Jim and I also stood in those lines before they quit giving the injections in schools.

While I worked at the lab, I was vaccinated for tularemia, rabies, Q fever, spotted fever (again), and typhus to protect me from some of the diseases they were studying. Part of the time I was there I worked in different laboratories, injecting mice with disease organisms as well as cleaning instruments and glassware. I also went on some field trips to collect ticks from grasses, and from squirrels we live-trapped and released. Cleaning cages in the Mouse House, where they raised mice, rats, guinea pigs, hamsters, and rabbits used in experiments, was another job I did sometimes.

I am now saddened by my lack of concern about our cruelty to animals: those we raise as livestock; wild ones we consider prey, competition, or a threat (such as predators); so-called nuisance animals (e.g., rodents, some birds, large herbivores who sometimes eat crops); those used in experiments; even exotic animals kept as pets. I felt twinges about them as a child, of course, but didn't think about it enough to avoid shooting, fishing, and trapping. I remember my dad assuring me worms don't feel things like we do when we put them on a hook. Of course they certainly do, as do lambs and calves when they're castrated, branded, tail-docked, roped and thrown to the ground, and all the other horrific practices we force our livestock and other animals to endure. I remember being aware of their pain, but only on a superficial level. It was simply normal, a necessary part of life.

When I told my friend Patrizia many years later that hunters in my family care about wild animals, as in a way they do, her comment was, "Adele, they hunt and kill them!" Duh! Normally we don't consider killing to be kind or affectionate – at least when a human or pet is the victim. But when we, as children, raise baby animals and then help butcher or sell them for slaughter, we learn to believe it's acceptable to kill an animal we grew to love. We have to avoid feeling their fear and pain or stop loving those we consider livestock, prey, or research subjects.

Because I also participated in that behavior, I understand how we can fail to critically examine beliefs learned during childhood, making it easier for me to avoid being judgmental of others. When small children are told and shown it is normal, expected behavior, they frequently don't analyze it further to equate it with animal abuse, something most of us find offensive and even criminal. It wasn't until I started working with wild animals, becoming more aware of their energy and emotions, learning about telepathic animal communication, and developing spiritual beliefs based on love, all many years later, that I began to be deeply saddened by our treatment of them. Many of us are unaware of animals – and often even people of other cultures – as feeling beings with spirits like ours.

CHAPTER 3

I started college in a pre-veterinary medicine program at Washington State University in Pullman when I was 18, but was too busy meeting new people and enjoying campus life to spend much time studying. I quit school the next spring, married Burt Lewis a year later, and worked in a small animal veterinary clinic while he finished graduate school at the University of Montana in Missoula. We then moved to Creede, Colorado, where we lived until he was drafted into the Army, and, in 1969, went to Germany for a year while he completed his military obligations on an Army base there. Burt was one of the lucky draftees who was not sent to the war in Vietnam.

After Burt finished college, I seldom had contact with animals for quite some time. When we returned from Germany, I spent a number of years working in hospitals and doctors' offices, mostly in clerical positions (insurance billing clerk, emergency room receptionist). I divorced during those years, before gathering enough determination and courage to go back to school at age 27, this time in pre-nursing at Linn-Benton Community College in Oregon. I was so terrified I wouldn't do well that I even used grade school and high school texts as references for math, making sure I could complete the homework in algebra and chemistry. I was shocked and further motivated when my first report card showed a 4.0 grade point average. From then on I loved the learning aspects of school.

After two years at the community college, I was accepted into the University of Oregon School of Nursing four-year program in Portland, Oregon, of which I completed a year and a half. I had decided to work toward going to medical school, with perhaps a nursing job to help pay for it, so was taking some pre-med classes at Portland State University at the same time. However, working in hospitals as a student nurse, as well as in paid clerical jobs, was giving me a different perspective on the whole field of medicine. I found the political aspects of hospital regulations and even patient care, as well as that in the nursing school, so offensive that I dropped out toward the end of 1974.

Patients were often treated like children no matter how old or intelligent they were. It seemed the attitude was often that the patients didn't need to know details of their condition or care; they were simply to trust the medical staff to do what was best for them without complaining or questioning anything. The intentions of the medical personnel certainly included a desire to help and heal people, but the patients' emotional and intellectual needs were a nuisance to many of them. I believe medical and nursing schools are changing that attitude now, as the importance of patients' beliefs and emotions in health and healing are better understood.

However, at that time I no longer wanted to be a part of the whole system. I was definitely interested in learning as much as I could about anatomy, physiology, biochemistry, microbiology, pharmacology, and all the other areas of study involved in medicine, but was concerned about beliefs and feelings I'd have to suppress in order to complete school or work in any of those fields. I even considered obtaining advanced degrees in biology and going into research, but politics and inequities happen in universities and research facilities, too. I was afraid I would either wake up one morning no longer liking the person I had become after making too many small compromises over time, or I would continue increasing my student loan debts before I quit school, going back to work in clerical jobs to pay them off slowly over many years. Fighting to change what disturbed me was completely unappealing to me, as it still is. Now, however, I know other, more positive ways to make a difference.

Quitting school was a devastating decision, one which set me adrift with no sense of purpose for a number of years. Not necessarily in this order, but the following were some of the results:

I frequently changed jobs, mostly working in clerical positions in different fields, but one was as an assistant for two years in a Portland veterinary clinic.

I moved several times, including to Seattle, where I lived for two years.

I was caught in a suicide attempt and hospitalized in a mental institution for a week, where psychological evaluation showed I was normal. Despite their diagnosis, I was disappointed for quite some time that I failed the attémpt, deciding if I chose to do it again I would make sure my plan was foolproof.

I was beaten by a man I lived with for a short time in Seattle, resulting in broken ribs, clavicle, nose, and possibly wrist, untreated because I had no money or insurance. Also, I had only been working at the job I had then for two weeks so was afraid to take time off. I could tell the bones were not displaced, but was able to feel a couple of them grating. I was unable to lie down for at least a month. Broken ribs are difficult; it's hard to move any body parts without causing discomfort. Splinting my wrist with a wooden spoon and an ace bandage allowed me to type and use a calculator. I was horribly embarrassed about going to work with black eyes, looking as though I'd been in a bar room brawl, but no one mentioned it.

I was raped by the acquaintance who helped me move from the apartment where I was beaten into one in which I was cold and hungry. I couldn't afford much food or the deposit for natural gas for a couple of months. Seattle winters can be quite harsh. The hardships were worthwhile because I was living alone, safe from being beaten again. I could have asked for help from several different people in Portland, but chose not to; I had gotten myself into the position that allowed all the difficult experiences and I knew I could pull myself out of it. My family had no idea what was going on in my life at that time.

Once I settled into that apartment and had worked long enough to pay deposits and buy things I needed, like a winter coat, blanket, and alarm clock, I reconnected with animals in the form of a ball python, Aaron, purchased from a pet store. I built him a large, round cage out of plywood rounds and plexiglass, and my deeper healing began.

I eventually moved back to Portland with my snake, starting a new and much better period of time. In 1980, shortly before Mt. St. Helens erupted for the first time, I began a clerical job for an electrical supplies distributor and rented a two-bedroom duplex, both of which I kept until I moved again in 1992. During those 12 years, I lived with lots of snakes and other reptiles (some of their stories are later in this book); developed a hobby of cleaning and articulating (putting together) skeletons of mammals, birds, and reptiles; began occasionally taking classes again, this time only because I wanted to learn more with no intention of earning a degree; and bought my own microscopes and lab equipment so I could study at home. I was still more comfortable with animals and books than with people.

CHAPTER 4

I moved from Portland in August 1992, back to western Montana where I grew up, and married Don Coon in June 1993. We bought our home outside of Hamilton and plan to live here the rest of our lives. In 1994 I was able to quit working, giving me the freedom to become a volunteer wildlife rehabilitator. I wanted to do something I considered worthwhile without having to work away from home. Given my lifelong interest in animals and our home on a few acres outside of town, wildlife rehabilitation was a perfect choice. I envisioned caring for baby deer and other little mammals, learning more about them as well as giving something back.

Becoming a volunteer wildlife rehabilitator in our state requires working with an established person who has appropriate federal and state permits. After at least two years of this kind of apprenticeship, it is possible to apply for the permits; until then, the volunteer is a sub-permittee. I contacted Judy Hoy, the main rehabilitator in our valley, asking to begin helping and learning from her. I filled out the forms required for adding me to her permits, explained my qualifications including being retired, living on five acres west of Hamilton, and some veterinary medicine experience.

Judy, who is a few years older than I am, has been taking care of domestic and wild animals, sometimes in unorthodox but effective ways, since she was a child. She is amazingly creative about making splints for fractures in animals and birds of many different shapes and sizes, as well as determining what is wrong and what may help critters, usually without the advantage of western medicine tests and equipment. She has cared for and raised many individuals of nearly all the mammal and bird species native to this area. Her knowledge of their behavior and needs is vast. Now, 20 years after I started working with her, I still seek her advice with animals that come to me, and take more difficult ones to her for help with splints or diagnostic problems.

There are seven towns, some very small, none large, in our county, which is a valley between two mountain ranges. Judy, who lives about 20 miles north of us, tries to have a rehabber in most of the towns, but usually only two or three are volunteering in the valley at a time. Game wardens, police dispatch, and a local animal shelter call us when they receive reports of injured and orphaned wildlife, as do lots of residents who know at least one of us. We have people call the rehabber closest to them, reducing travel times and distances .

Education permits allow some qualified people to keep specific, unreleasable birds to use in demonstrations. Judy gives talks at schools and other places, usually taking some education birds. Her intention is to teach people about our amazing wildlife, hoping to instill the desire to protect and live cooperatively with animals. Educating children is perhaps the most effective way to increase public awareness and Judy has spoken to thousands of them. She has been a fixture here for a long time.

For at least 15 years, Judy has been documenting physical problems she is witnessing (birth defects, developmental abnormalities, and illnesses) in wild mammals and birds, which she connects to chemical pollution primarily in the form of pesticides. She has co-authored a couple of peer-reviewed papers and is writing two books about this and her experiences with the wild ones. Her contact information is in the references section of this book for those who want to share their observations or learn more about her studies.

During my first few years as a rehabber, I mostly just took care of birds, splinting broken wings and legs, giving antibiotics and electrolytes, and raising babies. My first test was to raise four orphaned house sparrows, an introduced species considered less important than native birds. Judy pronounced them fat and healthy when they fledged (first started to fly), so she began sending me more injured and orphaned birds. I occasionally took care of small mammals for short periods of time if my place was closer to the people who found them than Judy's. She would pick them up when she came to town or I'd take them to her to finish raising them. I didn't start raising bigger mammals such as fawns for several years.

I am in awe of bird parents, especially those with altricial babies (e.g., robins, finches, warblers, and many others) which are completely helpless when they hatch (unlike baby chickens and ducks who walk around and find their own food). Altricial babies are always hungry, needing to be fed every 20 to 30 minutes during daylight hours. Since most birds in our area hatch during late spring and early summer when days are long, there are a lot of hours of frequent feedings! Fortunately most of these babies are ready to fly and be released within a few weeks.

Altricial birds generally have a relatively short incubation time (e.g., 11 to 14 days in house sparrows and robins; 18 days in crows), and the babies are able to leave the nest quite quickly (e.g., 14 to 16 days in robins, about 35 days in crows). Their eyes are closed for several days after hatching, and they are unable to do much more than stretch their necks, open their mouths, and cry for food. Most are nearly naked with some tufts of fine down. Raptors (birds of prey) are considered semi-altricial, with eyes open at hatching, and a thicker covering of down. However, they are also confined to the nest till they're full-grown.

A concept difficult for many people to grasp is that, by the time they can leave the nest and fly, these babies are as big as adults of the species. In fact, they are frequently heavier than their parents because they sit in the nest eating voraciously while their parents fly around constantly gathering food for them. During their short time in the nest, they must increase their body size from one that fits into an egg to adult size in only a few weeks, as well as grow a full set of feathers. It's no wonder they have to eat so much! Most are fed insects by their parents, even when the adults are seed-eaters, in order to provide enough protein for growth.

When we raise orphaned altricial birds, we mostly use meal worms and a powdered diet made for baby songbirds. Crows, ravens, jays, and magpies also receive baby mice and sometimes soft dog or cat food. Raptors require whole animals which are provided by their parents or us. Just giving them steak or hamburger is insufficient; we feed them primarily mice (received frozen from a local research laboratory), including the bones, organs, skin, and hair.

In some species of birds, both mother and father take care of babies; in some only one parent, usually the mother, is the caregiver. A few others, such as cowbirds, are parasitic, laying their eggs in the nests of other birds, who then unwittingly raise the young cowbirds. This can result in foster parents losing their own young, because the cowbird may be much bigger and squash or out-compete the smaller ones, or even push them out of the nest.

When altricial babies are coordinated enough to balance and hold onto twigs and branches, they frequently leave the nest, even if their feathers haven't quite finished growing enough for flight. The nest is crowded by then because of their size, and the youngsters often become uncomfortably hot during summer weather. Their parents still feed them and can find them by their calls, even when babies travel some distance from the nest. This is a dangerous time for the young birds, because they are unable to fly and are still developing coordination, as well as just becoming aware of dangers. Many are caught by cats, dogs, or native predators, and most of those don't survive.

As a rehabber, I groan when I receive phone calls from people who want me to finish raising baby birds they are concerned will be caught by cats. I know their intentions are good, but feeding wild birds when they are that old is difficult for rehabbers and the babies. They are starting to become independent, often requiring force-feeding because they are terrified of a human foster parent. Also, they have less chance to survive to adulthood; their natural parents not only continue feeding them for a time, even after they can fly, but also teach them how to find food for themselves. Rehabbers are not nearly as good at that as parent birds, no matter how knowledgeable or well-intentioned we are. If cat owners were simply to keep their pets inside for a few days while the babies learn to fly, many more birds would survive. Cat collars with bells may help by alerting birds to their presence.

Birds who have been injured by cats require antibiotics almost immediately; if we don't receive them within a few hours of being bitten or scratched, many don't survive even seemingly minor injuries. Cat bites and scratches cause a serious infection which quickly becomes systemic (throughout the body instead of only in the wound area). This is nearly always fatal. Birds heal much faster than we do, often surviving injuries that seem deadly, but there is a limit to this process. Wings broken in or too near a joint are unlikely to heal well enough for flight. Severe blood loss or punctured organs may kill them, and it's easy for a cat to cause these injuries. One feral cat (or even a pet cat that is outside much of the time) can kill several hundred birds each year.

Many altricial babies are victims of kidnapping. Well-meaning people find them in bushes, low branches, or on the ground and assume they have fallen out of the nest. We ask lots of questions before letting would-be rescuers bring these babies to us. If they are uninjured and in good flesh, it is far better to leave them where they are. People can try putting them into a bush or on a low branch rather than leaving them on the ground, but otherwise they should just stay away and keep children, dogs, and cats out of the area for a few days. Even if people don't see parent birds, they are probably around and will respond to the cries of their young unless they are disturbed. Watching from inside a house is probably okay, but parents will often stay away if they know people are near their babies.

An incorrect old wives' tale is that parent birds won't accept the babies if they have been touched by humans. The truth is most birds have a limited sense of smell compared to mammals, recognizing their babies primarily by voice. Parents will find and feed babies even when they are returned several days later to the area in which they were picked up. Parents call and babies respond, or babies cry and parents respond. Parents continue looking for them for days after they have been lost to predation, accident, or kidnapping.

Precocial birds (e.g., chickens, ducks, geese, emus, snipe, etc.) develop differently and present other problems for the parents, foster or natural. Incubation time is relatively longer (e.g., 21 days for chickens, 30 days for geese, 48 to 53 days for emus), because babies are more developed when they hatch. Their eyes are open, they are covered with thick down, and healthy babies are able to run around with their parents by the time they are a couple days old. They primarily feed themselves, following the example of their parents in learning what to eat. Most respond to the quick movements of insects, catching them to provide extra protein for growth even when adults mainly eat some form of plants. These babies grow and mature more slowly than altricial babies, remaining smaller than the adults for a period of time after they are fully feathered and able to fly. For example, wild turkey babies can fly up into a tree to roost when they are only two weeks old, but continue growing for more than a year.

Birds that have precocial babies usually nest on the ground; however some ducks and geese build nests in trees or on platforms provided by people. Wood ducks, for example, nest in cavities high in trees, and Canada geese sometimes compete with ospreys for platforms on tall poles. A day or two after hatching, the babies jump out of the nest and tumble to the ground, most protected from injury on landing by their covering of thick down.

Precocial babies have some challenges different from those of altricials, like becoming separated from parents long before they can survive alone. A little duck or goose may be swept downstream, ending up too far from the others to be found by its family. Also, precocial babies scatter when startled by a predator or a person, popping off in all directions like popcorn, then freezing in an attempt to become invisible. This adaptive behavior reduces predation fatalities, but may cause a baby to be unable to find its mother again, even though she chirps to call them to her. People who surprise this kind of family should immediately leave the area, allowing them to quickly regroup before anyone gets too far away.

Occasionally, when Mom starts incubating eggs before the last one is laid, one or two babies hatch later than their siblings. Development begins at the start of incubation, so the last baby is in an earlier stage, not quite ready to hatch with the others. In precocial babies, this can result in a newborn escaping the shell a day or two after everyone else has left the nest, leaving it alone and unprotected.

I've watched magpies work together to catch baby chickens and guinea fowl, and assume they do this with other precocial babies. One magpie distracts the mother while another comes in from behind to grab a baby. This seems cruel, but of course the magpies have babies to feed as well; theirs are altricial so parents have the whole job of collecting enough food for them to grow up.

Little precocial birds can be a challenge for rehabbers to raise, but are less time-consuming than altricial babies. They need to learn to eat different food than what they find in the wild (we give them Purina Game Bird Startena ™, meal worms, and tiny insects we catch with a fine net). They have the instinct to peck at particles and especially small moving objects, so dropping pieces of Startena in front of them attracts their attention when it bounces on a towel or paper plate. In this way they soon learn to eat dry food even when it is not moving. Putting live tiny insects on the Startena helps as well because babies pick up feed when pecking at the moving insects.

Ducklings and goslings require water for swimming as well as drinking. They make a terrible mess, so their enclosure has to be cleaned frequently. The feed quickly becomes sour when it is damp, and must be removed from the pen to avoid gastrointestinal disorders in the babies. At first I usually sprinkle some Startena in their water, and as they drink and scrabble around in the water, they pick up food.

These babies also need extra warmth in the form of a heating pad under the pen or a heat lamp over it. Even those who don't swim and just require small water dishes, like chicks and quail, need extra warmth for a while. Baby waterfowl easily become chilled because their down gets wet rather than shedding water like feathers do.

Having more than one of the same or similar species of baby makes caring for them much easier. As soon as one learns how to eat or drink, others follow its example. Also, they will cry for hours when alone, but seem more content if they have companions. For single babies, I put a wind-up alarm clock that ticks under a soft blanket in the pen, which helps somewhat. Once they are eating well and begin growing feathers, precocial babies are not overly time-consuming, other than requiring frequent water changes in the case of waterfowl.

CHAPTER 5

The little black bear I cared for in spring 2007, a few months before Solo (the starving little mule deer) was born, was a special treat. Like Solo, he was apparently an orphan and extremely thin when he arrived here. My nephew Harold, who was a logger then, brought him to me. Harold and his co-workers had noticed the baby running around crying in the woods for two days. They thought the mother was probably dead because this is abnormal behavior, but they watched carefully for her. Female bears are extremely dangerous if they feel their babies are threatened.

The boss of the logging crew told the men to leave the baby alone, even if the mother was dead, because it is illegal to interfere with wildlife. Finally, though, the loggers were unable to stand it; they went back into the woods after work with the intention of rescuing the cub. When they were close to him and spoke encouragingly, he ran over to one of them and climbed his leg. That was the last straw for the men; there was no way they could leave the little guy to die.

Harold named him Bobo because he seemed like such a clown. He and his wife Stacey took care of Bo for a couple of days before calling me, knowing they couldn't raise a bear no matter how little and cute he was at the time. My nephew was concerned he might be in legal trouble for taking the cub, so I assured him the game wardens I work with are kind and caring people. As long as he brought the bear to me, a legal rehabber, and I reported it to the game wardens, nobody would be in trouble. He was still uncomfortable, but fortunately was more concerned about the bear, so he brought Bo to me.

I called a game warden right after I talked with Harold, told him the story, and said the bear would be at my place that afternoon. He would transfer Bo the next day to the state wildlife center in Helena. When Harold and Stacey arrived, I again called the game warden, introducing him to Harold on the phone. Harold told him what had happened, explaining in detail where the cub was found. He and another logger had gone back to the area again, searching for signs of the mother (dead or alive), another cub, and the den, but were unable to find anything. They hadn't seen or heard any sign of hunters while they were working. The game warden again assured Harold he had done the right thing. If he had killed the mom, taken cubs out of a den when they were not in distress, or tried to raise the cub himself, it would be a different matter.

There is a spring hunting season for bear in Montana, but it is illegal to kill a sow with cubs. Hunters are supposed to watch a bear long enough to determine whether it has babies before shooting it. Unfortunately, unless cubs are present, it is difficult to tell males from females until they are dead. Then it's easy to determine whether the bear is a nursing mother; she has two mammary glands between her front legs and evidence of lactation and nursing is readily visible. Bo's mom could have been killed by a hunter, another bear, or in some kind of accident. In any case, she was unable to get back to her baby and he would not have survived much longer without human intervention.

Bo was too thin but not dehydrated, due to Harold and Stacey's care. He may have consumed snow in the woods for moisture as well. This little bear only weighed about four pounds and was just a few months old. Baby black bears are born while the mothers are hibernating, usually in January or February in our area (the timing may be different in other regions). They weigh only seven to twelve ounces, with their eyes remaining closed until they are 25 to 30 days old. Bo's baby canine teeth were just starting to erupt and he had no molars yet. He was quite tame, seeming completely comfortable about being handled by people. I think he was so relieved to be warm, safe, and with someone big who would care for him that he loved everybody. He was the most adorable little guy!

I began feeding Bo goat milk with whipping cream from a baby bottle. He had some trouble at first with the nipple, so I usually had goat milk all over me after a feeding. A bowl of milk was a worse mess, with most of the milk on his big feet, his face, and the floor. I let Bo sleep in the bed with me that night, both because he cried when I put him in a dog carrier and because I wanted to make sure I woke up every time he wanted to eat. *He* slept great. I sleep lightly and only for short periods of time when a small animal is in the bed. I lie on my side with my back to the edge, encircling the baby with my body and bedding as much as possible to make sure it can't scoot away from me where it could fall on the floor.

Bo had his own ideas about how he wanted to sleep. He put both paws around my upper arm near the elbow, planted his back feet, and tugged on my arm, directing me where to put it until it was in just the right place. Then he grabbed my lower arm and pulled on it until my hand was resting on his bottom. The second he had his nest organized to his satisfaction, he dropped his head on my upper arm and went limp. I was terrified he had died because it was so sudden. I had to watch for his breathing to be convinced he was still alive. It was astounding how fast he went to sleep!

Whenever Bo got hungry that night, he alerted me by sucking on my arm. I kept the bottle by the bed so I could give it to him quickly. Feeding Bo was a struggle because he insisted on using his paws to try to hold the bottle; the result was often that he pushed it away. I had goat milk all over me and the bed. He also urinated on me and the bed (fortunately soaking towels and mattress pad, not mattress). When he got too warm, Bo scooted away from me and slept sprawled on his belly with all four feet stretched out, a breathing bear rug (the best kind!).

During the day Bo ran around the house, following me and exploring everything. When I gave him a pine cone to play with, he rolled over on his side and held it in his paws, acting more like a kitten than a puppy. If he wanted to be held, Bo grabbed the nearest human leg and climbed. I was afraid he'd fall, but Harold said he had been climbing trees in the forest and he seemed to know what he was doing. He slept often, voluntarily curling up in a dog carrier in the kitchen when he was tired.

By the time the game warden came to pick Bo up the next afternoon, my arms were a mess even though he had been with me less than 24 hours. He wasn't at all mean, but he used his feet a lot; even a baby bear has long, unretractable claws. He seldom drew blood with them and then just a few tiny drops, but my arms

27

were covered with red welts from being scratched. Every once in a while little Bo turned into a bear. He quickly became annoyed when he wanted down and, if I was too slow, he growled, grabbed my arm with his paws, and bit. His teeth were so short and small he could only cause tiny round bruises with them, but his claws were another matter. I'm not sure I could have handled him much in another week or two.

Volunteer rehabbers in Montana are not allowed to keep bears or wild cats other than for short-term emergency care, which is better for the animals. Don and I could build bear-proof cages, but these animals need to be raised by people who know what they're doing and in a place where there are other babies of the same kind. At the state rehabilitation center in Helena, bear cubs are raised with little or no human contact and fed natural foods they would find in the wild. This gives them a chance to be released when they are old enough to care for themselves. The intention is to teach them how to find their own food and to avoid people and livestock. If they become a threat to us or domesticated animals, bears have to be trapped and moved or euthanized. In the fall, after they are ready, orphan bears are placed in a den (artificial or natural) deep in the woods for their time of hibernation. When they awaken in the spring, they are on their own. A game warden told me up to 80% of those raised in the Helena center are successfully released, which is great.

Bo didn't follow the pattern. By that winter he had grown to about 60 pounds. However, the rehabbers in Helena found he had some learning difficulties, seeming slower to master new skills than others and, though he had been raised with other baby bears and without human contact after he was able to eat solid food, he remained too habituated to people. He was transferred to the Beartooth Nature Center, a sanctuary for such animals in Red Lodge, Montana. When I saw him there a couple years later, he was with a girlfriend named Bluebeary. I was told the two roll and tumble and play together. They even have a swimming pool. It sounds like a fairly good life to me and I'm glad I had the experience of caring for Bo for a short time.

CHAPTER 6

While Solo's nose was still healing, a baby elk was brought to me. A neighbor named her Velvet because her hair, especially on her head, felt so soft. She, like Solo, was up to a week old when she arrived. Velvet's circumstances were much different from Solo's in that she wasn't starving and her mother was probably still alive.

Unfortunately many people do not understand the natural behavior of these animals. Well-meaning folks frequently think a baby is in trouble when it is actually behaving normally. Sometimes I'm able to convince them on the phone that they should leave the baby alone or take it back and release it where they found it. Other times I have to raise babies who were essentially kidnapped. Velvet was a borderline baby, but it turned out to be best for her to come to me. She was found lying in the middle of a narrow dirt mountain road on a busy weekend. She wouldn't stand up so the people who found her believed she had been injured or was ill. Someone else was on the way here with her before I knew she'd been picked up; I didn't know her circumstances until after she arrived.

Before they are two or three weeks of age, deer fawns and elk calves do not travel far with their mothers. They are too small, weak, and uncoordinated to be able to run well for any length of time, nor can they jump over obstacles found in the woods. Their only chance for survival is to hide. Therefore, they lie down in tall grass or under a bush when available and don't move. If something unfamiliar approaches, they drop, flatten head and neck against the ground, and hold still, no matter what is going on around them. They don't try to run away because they are unable to escape predators and moving only draws attention to them. The more afraid they are the less they move. Sadly for the babies, this makes some people think they are injured, ill, or abandoned.

Deer fawns under a month old are smaller than many people expect. Newborns weigh about the same as human babies; six to eight pounds is average. They look too thin so people often think they are underfed when they are perfectly normal. Elk and moose calves are much bigger, of course, and appear less thin. All are wobbly at first because it takes a while to develop coordination and strength. Several years before, a couple brought me what they said was a baby mule deer with an injured leg. When they arrived, they had a normal, uninjured baby elk who had been kidnapped by mushroom pickers. He was so young he was still unstable when he stood. Unfortunately he was found in the mountains, exact location unknown, by people other than those who brought him to me, so this baby had to be raised by humans.

Deer and elk mothers do not usually fight for their babies when the threat is from humans, but they will kick or stomp dogs and coyotes. Their primary method of protecting babies is to leave the area, hopefully drawing attention away from the little ones who drop down and remain still. When she thinks the danger is gone, a mother goes back to check on her baby. She will notice a human in the area long before the person knows she is there. If someone is watching for the mother, she will probably stay away from her baby, waiting for the perceived threat to leave. The area where Velvet was found had just been opened as a recreation area, so there were suddenly lots of people where her mother was used to few or none. She would probably have found a more private place to deliver her calf had she known so many humans would be arriving.

The babies nurse quickly because their mothers leave if there is any kind of disturbance, such as people or predators in close proximity. People often think the mother doesn't stay long enough to feed her baby, but she always does if she feels safe. Also it is difficult to see a baby when it is under the mother in grass or brush. Sometimes a fawn or calf will try to follow its mother for a short distance, especially if feeding was interrupted, maybe crying for the mother for a few minutes under those circumstances. As soon as the mother is out of sight, however, the baby will find a place to lie down and again be still and quiet.

When it is only a few days old, a fawn or calf may try to follow a person or even a dog or horse, because it is unsure which large, moving animal is Mom. The best thing to do under those circumstances is to quickly go far enough away so the baby can no longer see the person. It will then lie down again and wait for its mom. The mothers keep their babies away from other deer and elk during the first few days to ensure appropriate imprinting occurs .

Mothers and babies recognize each other primarily through voice and scent. It is better for the fawns and calves to have no human scent on them, so people should avoid touching them unless rescue is necessary. However, unlike the old wives' tale, moms will still care for the little ones if someone does mistakenly handle them. When people call us about inadvertently kidnapping a baby, we suggest they take it back to the place where they found it, rub the baby with grass from that area, and immediately leave. Mom will find and care for her little one after people go away.

These animals are well-adapted to survive in their natural environment. Because our babies need to be kept warm, people are concerned about wild babies being too cold. Actually, the fawns and calves can survive inclement weather and much cooler temperatures than our babies, who do not have a fur coat and are less developed at birth. They become damp from dew, rain, and sometimes even snow, but their hair usually keeps moisture from touching their skin. If people leave them alone, their mothers lick them dry, let them drink warm milk, and lie down next to them, sharing their body heat. Babies are also somewhat protected from cold and rain because they usually curl up in sheltered places, and their shivering helps keep them warm enough to be safe. If weather changes or they become uncomfortable, they move to a different place that is better.

A baby elk, deer, or moose that has truly been abandoned or orphaned will run around crying much of the time for hours or even days. That behavior is dangerous because it attracts predators, so a fawn or calf will do it only if its mom has been gone at least 24 hours with newborns and up to several days for older ones. Losing a fawn or calf is also traumatic for the mother. She will go back to the area many times, trying to find her baby. She calls to it and searches over a large range, using her powerful senses of smell and hearing. White-tailed deer fawns have been successfully returned to their mothers as long as five days after being picked up by people. Mule deer and elk returns may be successful for a

31

shorter period of time, but they also go back to look for their lost babies for a while.

Wild animals raised by humans have a miserable time at first, because everything is foreign and unnatural to them. Unless they are actually starving when they are picked up, it usually takes up to several days for them to be hungry enough to accept goat milk from a rubber nipple. The older the baby is, the longer and more difficult this process becomes. By the time they are three weeks old, it is extremely hard on them – and on the foster parent. At that age they may never accept being fed goat milk from a bottle or a bowl. Consequently they do poorly and may not survive.

I've raised a couple of fawns who were older and so afraid that I had to consistently grab them, pin them to my side with an elbow, and force the nipple into their mouths for more than two weeks. After a few days they were hungry enough to suckle, taking nearly as much milk as a tamer one would, but the same procedure was necessary for the next feeding. I had bruises from their little hooves for weeks. Of course, being grabbed and held was terrifying for them, even when followed by feeding. Eventually they came to me voluntarily when I was feeding others, but always remained so wary that, if anything startled them, they immediately ran away no matter how hungry they were.

Deer and elk will only nurse their own babies, so it goes against the instinct of fawns and calves to accept another mother. Velvet refused to eat for two days, even though she was so young. As soon as I was out of her sight, she started crying for her mom; however, she wouldn't eat for me even when I forced a nipple covered with goat milk into her mouth. It was heartbreaking to hear her, but there was nothing I could do until she was wretched and hungry enough to accept the new conditions.

Wild babies raised by humans are at a disadvantage when they grow up as well. A wild mother teaches her young one how to survive by showing it what to eat, where water is, how to find food in the winter, which animals are dangerous, no doubt many other things about which we are unaware. Mom also teaches it how to notice and escape from humans, dogs, and natural predators. People, no matter how well-intentioned, are unable to teach a wild baby everything it needs to know. Most fawns raised by local rehabilitators go with wild deer after they are weaned, thus learning from us, but their training is delayed and they have less chance of surviving to adulthood than those raised naturally.

It is illegal for anyone without appropriate state and federal permits to keep native animals or birds, regardless of the circumstances. Raising wild fawns and calves can be rewarding for trained people, especially when they are truly orphaned or seriously injured and would not survive otherwise. However, it is a lot of work and quite expensive, requiring fresh goat milk, special facilities, and frequent feedings for several months. They generally will not eat for strangers so asking someone to babysit for a few days or even one feeding is harmful to the animals and frustrating for the would-be babysitter. Some babies are injured, starved, or ill, requiring intensive, around-the-clock care.

These are not domestic animals. Deer, elk, and moose raised as pets can be a nuisance and even dangerous to humans when they become adults. They try to treat people as they do each other and we are not built to be kicked or head-butted. When this happens, they are classified as problem animals and may have to be euthanized. Obviously this is unfair to the animals because the fault belongs not to them, but to the people who raised them. However, their behavior cannot be allowed to continue. Most rehabilitators know how to avoid these problems and don't treat them as pets. Solo, however, didn't follow the rules no matter what I did. He treated all people as though they were his friends, the only deer I've raised who acted that way after the 'teenage' months.

CHAPTER 7

I kept Velvet, the little elk, in the chain link pen for a few days until she was settled and, every time I went out there for at least two days, I found her in hiding position. She refused to stand up until I forced her, returning to her perceived safe position on the ground as soon as possible. After Velvet began eating well from the bottle, she stood up as soon as I spoke to her, running joyfully to me as she would have with her natural mother.

Before Velvet became settled and hungry enough to suck milk from the bottle, an injured baby white-tailed deer was brought to me. I put him in the playpen in the kitchen and began the process of helping him recover. He had been crossing a highway behind his mother; when she was hit by a car, he fell down an embankment next to the road. The top of his rostrum (between nose and eyes) was scraped and his hind feet were in an unnatural position; they folded too far so he was walking on the backs of his toes rather than up on his hooves. The tendons or ligaments may simply have been too weak from birth or they could have been stretched too far (hyper-extended) when he fell. I gave him electrolytes, dripped emu oil on his nose which wasn't seriously injured, and applied splints to hold his feet in normal position.

This baby had been away from his mom long enough by the time he came here, and was young enough, that he accepted the bottle fairly quickly. I called him Little Joe and was glad for Solo that he was here. It's much better for them to be raised with a companion of the same or similar species. By the time Velvet was eating and able to be out of the chain link pen, Little Joe was stable enough to go outside. I left all three of them in the deer pen together, where they got along fine. Velvet was huge compared to the little deer; they could literally walk under her belly with their legs straight, even though Velvet was younger than Solo.

Unfortunately, a few days after she arrived I discovered Velvet had an umbilical hernia, meaning the place where her umbilical cord had gone through her abdominal wall didn't completely close after birth, as is normal. There was a small pouch on her belly with a piece of omentum (a membrane from inside the abdomen) in the pocket. I could push it back into her abdomen and feel an opening in the abdominal wall about the size of the tip of my index finger. It was too small for intestine to protrude, but big enough to be of concern and, with omentum through the hole, it couldn't finish closing. I called Linda, our veterinarian, who came over to check it. She also thought the hole was too big to ignore, so she researched the problem on the Internet.

Linda normally cares only for dogs, cats, and exotic pets, such as birds, rodents, rabbits, and reptiles, but she is kind enough to help me with wild animals (and some of my exotic pets) that are out of her primary area of expertise. She practices mostly from a van stocked with instruments and medications, which I find to be much more comfortable for the animals than going to a veterinary clinic. Even our dogs love to see her when she comes here, as opposed to their fear reactions in a clinic. She sits on the floor to play with them, behavior they remember more than injections or physical exams. Medical care at home is especially less stressful for exotics, who are often hard to transport and extremely anxious in unfamiliar surroundings. Linda has access to a veterinary clinic for services such as major surgeries and x-rays. Wound care, including sutures and removing porcupine quills from dogs, can be done with sedation at home, I know from experience.

I first met Linda when she was working in research at Rocky Mountain Laboratory shortly after I became a rehabber and before she began her veterinary practice. She had somehow obtained an injured bat, which she transferred to me with appropriate medication. We later became friends, even traveling together on an amazing two-week trip to Kenya and Tanzania in 2008. We went with a tour group of veterinarians so the main focus was seeing wildlife on reserves, as well as learning about some of their veterinary medical problems. It was the trip of a lifetime for me.

Through her Internet search, Linda found an appropriate anesthetic and dosage for elk. We were hesitant about major surgery because Velvet was so young; many wild animals respond poorly to anesthesia, with young ones perhaps being more fragile. She could die from the drugs, but it was certain she would die eventually from the hernia. Linda devised a plan to sedate her

36

for transport to a clinic and then to anesthetize her for surgery. Everything had to be fast because the sedative would wear off quickly. Linda would have to travel right next to Velvet in case she developed breathing problems.

I was also concerned about keeping Velvet quiet enough to allow her abdomen to heal after the surgery. Due to their normal body position, much of the weight of her abdominal organs would be pressing on the incision, just as it was pressing on the hernia. Also, little elk like to run and jump and play, all of which could stress sutures. It would be necessary to keep her in the chain link pen until she completely healed; she would be unhappy about that, possibly even fighting the wire to the point of injury. Linda and I both lost some sleep over the whole situation until someone emailed her with the suggestion of using a belly band to press a flat disc against the bulge. With omentum forced into her abdomen, we believed the hole might seal naturally, even though she was a couple weeks old by then.

I gave Velvet a tranquilizer to keep her calm enough to tolerate being handled by strangers before Linda and her husband Dan came over, bringing a plastic disc and tape that would adhere to her hair. The process went better than I expected. Other than bucking and kicking a few times when we let her go, Velvet seemed to tolerate the band and the unusual handling quite well. I could slide my finger under the disc and feel the hole so we knew there was no longer a pocket containing omentum. We were hopeful this less invasive treatment would work and Velvet could eventually be released with wild elk.

For the moment, the three babies were stable so all I had to do was feed them five times a day. I was no longer feeding any of them in the middle of the night, because they were eating and growing well. Feeding times were 6:00 a.m., 10:00 a.m., 2:00 p.m., 6:00 p.m., and 10:00 p.m. Velvet was eating more than the two deer combined, so my other major project was keeping enough goat milk and whipping cream on hand. Fortunately we have enough freezer space to hold many gallons of milk, allowing me to purchase it (40 miles round trip at that time) only once a week.

37

Little Joe's feet remained in a normal position when I removed his splints after about five days. His rostrum was healing well and Solo's nose continued to improve. Little Joe and Solo had to be upgraded from baby bottles to larger ones with lamb nipples, always a chore. They dislike changes like that, but the baby nipples soon become too short for long deer mouths and eight ounces of milk per feeding is no longer enough. Fortunately Velvet started with a nipple that would fit the much bigger bottles she would soon require.

Because she was growing so fast, it was necessary to change Velvet's belly band each week. Elk are like mule deer in that they easily become calm and tame (if they're going to be tame at all). She allowed me to change the band myself without resorting to tranquilizers or someone to hold her. Velvet was much larger than the little deer so I'd have been unable to do it without her cooperation. The hole in her abdomen was shrinking and the bulge was gone, even when the band was off temporarily, but I wanted to be sure the opening didn't expand again.

It was interesting that I was raising three different kinds of animal – an elk, a white-tailed deer, and a mule deer. Shortly after I jokingly said all we needed were a moose, a bighorn sheep, and a mountain goat to have the full range of native hoofed animals that live in our immediate area, a game warden called about a sick baby moose.

CHAPTER 8

A kind couple named Tori and Don have a beautiful home in the woods about 10 miles south of us, with a deck overlooking a pond. They had been watching a cow moose and her twin babies for a couple weeks when they noticed one of the calves was acting strangely. She appeared somewhat unsteady, no longer moving as well as her twin. She would lie down rather than follow her mom, sometimes crying as though in pain. Finally, unable to stand, she lay on her side, occasionally thrashing her legs and crying. Her mother went to her a number of times but was unable to help.

Cow moose can be extremely dangerous, especially when they have babies to protect. People have been kicked and stomped to death by them, so approaching a baby moose, let alone picking one up, is not something we wanted to do. However, we couldn't just leave her there; she clearly needed help. My husband Don drove us to Tori's home in his pickup, which has a canopy on the back. He backed as close to the baby as he could, and I climbed into the truck bed to steady her once she was loaded.

The baby was near a dense stand of willows where her mother could easily have been hiding just out of our sight. This was a precarious situation as an adult moose certainly could outrun my husband, even with the pickup that close. Tori and her husband stood at a safe distance to watch for the mom while Don hurried to the calf, scooped her up, and slid her into the truck with me. He quickly shut the tailgate, jumped in the cab, and drove home. The baby kicked a few times, but was fortunately too uncoordinated to get up or move around.

The young moose was four to six weeks old and weighed 90 to 100 pounds. If she hadn't been so sick we would have been unable to handle her at all, or even get close to her. When we arrived home, Don carried her into the house, laying her on the floor in our front room. I found no sign of injury, but her stomach was bloated (expanded with gas) and she was somewhat dehydrated.

I picked two large ticks from behind her ears, allowing me to hope she had tick paralysis. This is caused by a toxin in the tick's saliva, with symptoms involving progressive paralysis, eventually leading to death. I've known of dogs and even humans who died because a tick wasn't found till after death. If the tick is removed soon enough, the condition immediately begins to improve, with the animal quickly returning to normal. This illness would have been great, because we could probably return the baby to her mom within a few days. Sadly, my hopeful diagnosis was wrong.

The calf was able to swallow some electrolytes squirted through a tube into the back of her throat. Because of the bloating, I didn't want to put much into her stomach, though. I called Dr. Linda for recommendations before driving to her place for injectable electrolytes, oral antibiotics, and medication to help with gas.

I slowly dripped electrolytes into the little moose through a small needle placed under the loose skin between her shoulder blades. This is similar to administering IV electrolytes, but easier because it's unnecessary to insert a needle into a vein or regulate the speed of the drip. Because the skin is loose in that area, fluids form a pool and are slowly absorbed into the blood stream. When she had received about 200 cc, I removed the needle. After that dose of electrolytes had been absorbed, I gave her more. I ground her antibiotic pills using a mortar and pestle, mixed the powder with water, and used a syringe and soft rubber tube to squirt it slowly into the back of her mouth. She seemed unable to lift her head and her leg movements weren't purposeful.

The baby moose eventually began urinating, but I could see no evidence her intestines were moving at all. This is dangerous for ruminant animals (those with a multi-chambered stomach such as cows, sheep, deer, and moose) because, when the stomach quits contracting and emptying, it fills with gas, inflating so much it can actually suffocate the animal. The lungs are unable to expand adequately because the swollen rumen (stomach) presses on the diaphragm. Lying down on the side reduces the movement of gas out of the stomach so bloating worsens. We slid a stomach tube down her esophagus, releasing some gas, but the bloating still gradually increased. Over a period of time I gave her aloe vera juice, which can help heal the gastrointestinal tract, and a mild laxative to hopefully start her bowels moving.

I propped the little moose on her chest in a more normal resting position, hoping it would help gas escape her stomach. She would stay in that position for a short time, but then slip down, again lying on her side. We even tried to stand her up using a sling under her chest and abdomen. She was unable to support any weight on her legs and was too heavy for us to hold for more than a few minutes; still her stomach remained bloated.

I called some large animal veterinarians to ask for advice, but their responses were unhelpful. One said we had to take her to their clinic and leave her; another said it was illegal for them or me to do anything for her, even though a game warden had asked me to help. Because of limited funds in the non-profit donation account Judy maintains, full veterinary care is out of reach for seriously ill or injured wildlife in our area. The fund usually doesn't fully cover food and medication expenses for normal or only slightly ill or injured animals, which of course have the best chance for successful release. It is unfair to ask veterinarians to donate too much time or supplies, but fortunately some generously allow us to buy drugs at cost. A veterinarian does help at the state wildlife center in Helena, but it's 160 miles from here and we seldom make that trip.

By the next day, the calf was in more distress and we had run out of options. With further Internet research, Linda believed she might have West Nile virus, but she was unable to find any information about moose having been infected. Tori (who came several times to help me with the baby) and I finally decided the only humane solution was to euthanize her. The little moose was obviously uncomfortable, and her condition continued to deteriorate no matter what we did. We drew blood to be tested for the virus before ending her suffering. Linda sent the blood to a state wildlife lab where it was forwarded to a lab in Wisconsin.

Several days later the lab confirmed she had West Nile virus antibodies in her blood. They were unable to say definitively that she was sick from it, but due to her age (she hadn't had much time to develop antibodies for that and then become this ill with something else) and symptoms, we believe she was suffering from the encephalitis form of the disease. Because West Nile virus can infect humans, the lab reported the incident to our local health department, which put an article in the newspaper about the baby moose.

A research paper Linda found on the Internet said mammals (as opposed to birds) with the disease do not have a high enough concentration of the virus in their blood or other tissues to infect any other animals or humans. Apparently they are even unable to transfer enough viruses to a biting mosquito to spread the disease in that manner. Most mammals, including humans, who have the disease do not become debilitated and in fact may not even know they have it. Those who do become seriously ill usually have the encephalitis form. Treatment consists of supportive therapy, such as what we were doing for the calf, to keep them alive until the disease runs its course. Fatalities occur when there is no supportive therapy or the condition is too serious, as in this case.

After the moose died, I was back to caring just for Solo, Little Joe, Velvet, and the occasional bird who needed short-term help. When the fawns were big enough (four or five weeks old), I let all three out into the larger back yard. They ran and jumped and played where I could enjoy watching them from the deck. Solo would run as fast as he could before executing a few stiff-legged mule deer hops. Little Joe performed long, graceful, white-tailed deer leaps. Velvet ran with her head held high, nose pointed straight forward, in the position characteristic of elk. They seemed so full of life and joy; watching them interact and play always made me smile.

During the summer, Aten and Ara (our emu pair whose stories are coming up) normally live in the back yard as well. If another animal runs, the emus love to chase it. This is not intentionally aggressive unless they are driving off a predator, such as a dog; they are just playing when they run with deer, chickens, and wild turkeys. Unfortunately, when the fawns are tiny, some become frightened of the giant birds, so I have to lock the emus in their winter pen for a while or leave the fawns in the deer pen till they're somewhat bigger.

Solo, Little Joe, and Velvet, though, accepted Aten and Ara immediately, never appearing afraid of them. While they were in

42

the deer pen, the youngsters apparently became accustomed to the emus from seeing them through the fence frequently. After I let them out in the back yard, they would often all run together. Sometimes it appeared the emus were chasing Velvet and the fawns; other times the fawns and Velvet ran behind the emus. The birds run with their necks stretched straight out in front, reaching speeds of up to 35 miles per hour. It is amazing and uplifting to watch several completely different kinds of creatures playing together.

CHAPTER 9

Making the decision to euthanize an animal is always difficult for me. I usually wonder whether I could have done something else or if I gave up too soon. However, allowing unnecessary or unproductive suffering is harder and most of the time I'm able to feel the animal giving up. Once they are gone, I focus on the fact they are no longer terrified or in pain, doing my best to let go of any guilt or other negative feelings. Instead, I remind myself we release 60 to 70 percent of the birds and animals who come to us for help, most of them unlikely to survive without at least temporary assistance.

The year before the little moose came to us, I decided to euthanize a white-tailed fawn I initially thought would be fine. He had a badly fractured front leg with the break too close to the joint between the cannon bone (fused metacarpals) and the toes for my peace of mind. Mid-shaft breaks in that bone normally heal quite well, though, and an imperfect front leg is usually a fairly minor impairment for deer. Hind legs, on the other hand, need to be strong and highly functional for them to escape predators and jump over fences in populated areas or downed trees in the woods.

This fawn, found in a horse pasture, was under two weeks old. The person who brought him to me thought he may have been stepped on by one of the horses. At that age they usually adjust to the bottle within a day or two, but I was unable to convince this little guy to eat voluntarily at all, even though his leg was splinted, greatly reducing his discomfort. He should have been hungry, used to being handled, and feeling less pain within a few days. Several times a day I squirted milk into the back of his mouth using a syringe and soft tube, without giving him as much as he should have taken voluntarily. The stress of being handled can outweigh possible benefits, including a full belly. Worse, he somehow managed to remove his splint a few times, even after a neighbor helped me apply it. After struggling with him for more than a week without improvement, I felt I was torturing him by keeping him alive against his will. I again made the decision to euthanize an animal.

Euthanasia isn't always directly related to the severity of an animal's injuries. Several years earlier, I cared for a white-tailed fawn who had been much more badly injured by horses. He was panting, foaming at the mouth, and rolling his eyes when he arrived here, looking as though he was going to die before I could do much of anything. He was clearly in a lot of pain, overheated from riding in a dog carrier in the back of a pickup, unable to stand, and obviously terrified. I'm sure he was also in shock. We laid him on the cool tile floor and I immediately started squirting cold electrolytes into his mouth. I also dampened his head, hoping to cool him more quickly through evaporation. He was able to swallow, so I continued giving him electrolytes every 15 or 20 minutes until his breathing became more normal and his eyes were stable.

I examined him then and found fractured ribs and pelvis; his legs initially seemed fine. I could actually feel bones grating in both his chest and his pelvis. They didn't appear to be significantly displaced, though I couldn't be sure about the pelvis. He quite readily took offered goat milk, indicating he was feeling better and hadn't given up.

I placed him in a more normal position on his chest, propped up on folded front legs. Unlike the little moose, he stayed in the position that allowed him to hold up and move his head. I was afraid he would try to stand on the slippery floor, so we took him outside to the chain link pen, putting him on a soft bed of clean hay. He probably felt safer there as well, because he was unused to people and older than most fawns who come to me for care. He seemed to become stronger and more stable as I continued giving him electrolytes and goat milk.

Because of the pelvic fracture, I didn't have much hope for releasing this little guy. Without x-rays, I was unable to tell how seriously injured he was and knew he wouldn't be releasable unless both hind legs worked well. We are legally required to euthanize unreleasable wild animals, generally a kinder outcome for them than being kept in captivity. However, he seemed relatively comfortable when at rest and I wasn't ready to give up on him.

With a strong will to live, animals (and people) are frequently able to overcome seemingly insurmountable obstacles.

For several days I let him continue lying down, most of the time in a normal, upright resting position, turning him from side to side several times daily to decrease the threat of pressure sores. When I finally helped him stand, he was fairly stable on three legs. He didn't put any weight on one hind leg nor did he try to walk at first, not surprising because of the pelvic injury. One front foot remained bent so he stood on the top of it with his toes pointing backward, but I was unable to feel any fractures in the foot. I splinted it in the correct position, giving him more stability.

He was quite strong and readily taking milk from the bottle, though obviously still in pain when I moved him. I cut small willow branches for him which he ate enthusiastically. Willows contain a compound like aspirin which helps with pain, inflammation, and fever. This compound can also reduce clotting, so I make sure bleeding isn't an issue before I offer it to injured animals. Because deer love to eat them, I also give willows to healthy fawns when they're ready to start eating solid food.

When I removed the splint in a week, his front leg appeared to be completely normal. He continued to improve, though experienced pain for quite some time. When he began to walk around and was able to stand and lie down on his own, I let him out of the chain link pen into the bigger deer pen and later into the back yard. Eventually he walked with only a slight limp and was even able to run.

That winter, at seven or eight months of age, he hopped over the fence to follow the wild deer who regularly come into our yard. He came back fairly often and, when he walked slowly, I could still detect a slight limp. Later, I occasionally saw a beautiful white-tailed buck I thought was him, but I couldn't be sure because he no longer limped at all. Now, of course, I have no idea whether he is still alive, but I'm glad I didn't have to euthanize him.

Sadly, the moose calf wasn't the last euthanasia during the summer I raised Solo, Little Joe, and Velvet. After they were stable, a woman brought me a young mule deer with head and leg injuries. The fawn was four to five weeks old, so she had been

47

following her mother for two or three weeks. If she hadn't been so badly injured, no one would have been able to catch her. She had a lump on her head and seemed dazed. The fawn was able to stand and walk, but was somewhat uncoordinated, moved slowly, and was unable to put weight on one back leg. She was found at the base of a rocky hill; the woman thought she may have fallen, possibly after catching her leg in a hole between rocks.

The injured leg had apparently been hyper-extended and/or severely twisted at the hock (actually the ankle joint), damaging the Achilles tendon and/or joint ligaments, so that joint would fold too far forward and even slightly backward as well. Normally it is bent forward, never straightening completely, like a dog's hind leg. I hoped the ligaments or tendon were simply badly stretched and, if I was able to tape it in the correct position, they might return to normal length and elasticity. I used a figure-eight bandage, which held as long as the fawn moved slowly. She would only swallow milk and electrolytes when I used a syringe and tube. Because of her age, fear, and injuries, she would not suck from a bottle.

Within a couple days, the fawn was much less dazed, far more mobile, and terrified, making her difficult to handle. I put her in the emus' shed because it is enclosed on all four sides, thinking she might feel safer there. However, she panicked every time I opened the door to feed or work with her. When she did that, she put extra stress on her leg which continued to hyper-extend. They can literally break a leg by kicking so hard against the ground in their struggle to get away from someone they think means to harm them; the bandages were definitely not strong enough to hold her leg in a normal position.

I tightened the bandage and kept giving her milk from a syringe, all using force which increased her fear. By the third day I gave up. The poor little thing was so panic-stricken she was further injuring her leg and I believed the tendon was torn rather than stretched. It would not heal without major surgery and she would not be releasable in her condition. She probably would never become tame enough for me to feed and handle her properly, either, so I decided to end her suffering. Necropsy (medical examination after death) validated my decision because the tendon and all of the ligaments in that joint were irreparably torn.

We were asked to pick up another elk calf the summer Velvet, Solo, and Little Joe were with us. He was seen lying next to the road near our place, after being hit by a car when the herd crossed the road the night before. I was unable to find any external injuries but his color was bad, with dark membranes in his mouth indicating insufficient oxygen in his blood, and he was breathing hard. I thought this could be due partly to shock, so we put him in the chain link pen. I gave him electrolytes and a tranquilizer to help him relax, then left him alone hoping to decrease his fear. Sadly, he died within a few hours due to internal bleeding; I wish we had euthanized him immediately to save him from the fear and discomfort he must have experienced in those few hours.

When animals die, either like this little elk or by euthanasia, I remind myself, and people who are saddened by the loss of one they attempted to rescue, that death is natural. Living in the wild away from people is certainly no guarantee of a full life span. If all wild fawns, for example, grew to reproductive maturity, we would be walking on deer. Of course we wouldn't, because many would die of starvation and illnesses long before that.

Mother Nature maintains a balance, with more babies being born than are needed for the survival of the species. Population densities vary in cycles; when food supplies increase, animals who depend on that food produce or raise more babies till the food source decreases again. The same is true with predator and prey species. When prey numbers increase, more predators are born and survive to reproduce. Then numbers of prey species decrease, thus providing less food for predators whose population again declines.

These cycles continued successfully for millions of years before we appeared. Now we try to control them in ways we consider of value to us, usually with poor results for animals, plants, humans, and our planet. There are too many variables for us to be able to do this well. I hope one day we will understand and truly begin living within the normal balance, thus causing

49

far less damage and allowing Mother Earth to heal herself, to our advantage as well as that of other species.

CHAPTER 10

Toward the end of July 2007, Solo's first summer, my friend Deanna came to visit from Portland, Oregon. I had met her years before in Portland, when I moved into the opposite side of the duplex where she lived. It turned out we had quite a lot in common, including having taken some of the same classes at Portland State University, an interest in biology and psychology, and an affinity for snakes. She kept a pair of rainbow boas, Lucifer and Curley. In addition to many hours of drinking wine and talking, Deanna and I started cleaning animal skulls together. This led to our cleaning and articulating whole skeletons, projects we did separately because she had moved to another town by then.

Deanna and I decided to go to Yellowstone National Park while she was here. Since I started taking care of fawns several years before, I had not left home for more than a few hours during the summer. However, our neighbors, Tom and Brian, said they would feed the babies, which were then about seven weeks old. Velvet's belly band was off and, though I could still feel a tiny hole with the tip of my finger, there was no pocket with omentum in it. Solo and Little Joe were doing great as well, so I was sure they would all be fine with different caretakers for a few days.

I was only feeding The Trio three times a day by then. Since it was about time to do so anyway, I decided to reduce bottles to twice daily so they would be hungrier when Brian and Tom came to feed them. The men had had occasional contact with the babies and Solo and Velvet were fairly comfortable with strangers. Actually, Solo didn't consider anyone a stranger and Velvet was only temporarily wary around new people. This is characteristic of human-raised mule deer and elk youngsters before they start living with wild ones. Little Joe was a typical white-tailed deer in that he was wary around everyone but me. I believed he would relax and eat for Brian when he was hungry, especially when he saw the others eating.

Having three or more to feed is quite a challenge because I can only hold two bottles at a time. They were all so pushy with me by then that I had to feed Solo and Little Joe first through a fence. Velvet refused to eat that way, insisting on standing right next to me to suckle. I couldn't feed the fawns while she was pushing me around nor could I feed Velvet while the fawns were head-butting me. She soon learned she would be given her bottle after Solo and Little Joe finished theirs so she began pushing them away from the nipples while I was on the other side of the fence, unable to keep her away from them. Fortunately, they were so persistent they were still able to eat enough.

Deanna and I were just going to be gone two nights so Brian only had to feed the babies four times – two mornings and two evenings. I fed them in the morning before we left and the night we returned home. They did well, but as expected, Joe was too nervous to eat as much as usual. They were all eating grain, hay, and whatever wild grasses and bushes they could find in the yard, so none was deprived as a result of my vacation.

Up to this point Solo acted much like other mule deer raised by people. He was a curious, loving little guy, full of life and energy. If I bent down to his level, he licked my chin, and he enjoyed being petted. Solo followed Don around as he fed and watered the other animals each morning. He ate well and grew normally. Small bumps that would be the pedicles, or bases for his antlers, were beginning to develop and he was even starting to act like a buck.

Male deer mount other fawns in breeding position when they are quite young. At that age they don't care whether the other one is male or female, or even if it is a deer. When they get bigger, young mule deer bucks I raise try to put their hooves on my shoulders from behind; I haven't had a white-tailed deer do so. They are quite gentle about it, but I discourage the behavior by pushing them away or by taking a few steps. I doubt they would be that gentle when mature and much heavier, so this can be a problem in captive-raised animals.

Solo would follow Don or me into the garage when we went to the freezer for goat milk, and would have been on our deck much of the time if we didn't have a fence around it. I'm sure he'd have come in the house if we allowed it. I have a small wildflower garden around our deck which wouldn't survive deer or emus without a fence. Even the deck has a fence above the rail to keep chickens and wild turkeys from roosting on it and making a mess. One time, not knowing Solo had followed him into the garage, Don shut the door without looking when he left. I soon heard Solo cry and let him out.

In caring for these animals, I'm somewhat torn between sharing them with others and keeping them away from people. Unless they are ill or injured, my contact with them is almost exclusively at feeding time. I sit on the deck to watch them, but don't talk to them or go in their yard. It is tempting to play with them because they are so cute, but I know that would be harmful to youngsters who need to become wild. Sometimes I allow other people to see them from the deck, especially children, but mostly they have contact only with each other, the emus, and wild animals and birds.

I have occasionally allowed other people in the yard for a short time, but tell them not to approach the fawns. If one comes to them, they can touch it briefly and carefully; playing with them is not acceptable. The less contact rehab babies have with other people, the more wild they are likely to be when it's time for them to leave. Solo, however, seemed to be an exception to that rule.

I am also careful about allowing loud or hyperactive children and aggressive adults near any of the animals. Not only are most of the fawns and wild birds nervous around strangers, loud noises, and sudden movements, but we had three parrots in the house, two of which were from difficult homes. They became disturbed when people were loud or moved quickly. I am quite protective, believing animals have the right to peace in their homes

When I see YouTube videos or movies of humans interacting with wild animals needing rescue, healthy ones at national parks, or whales and dolphins in the ocean, I am amazed to see people moving quickly and aggressively, and to hear them screaming, squealing, and talking loudly in their excitement over seeing beautiful wild beings. I always want to ask them to be quiet, still, and respectful. They seem to think these animals are the same as dogs who live with us instead of sensitive beings who have certainly had unpleasant experiences with humans.

We often have wild white-tailed deer around our house, including in the back yard with the fawns. This is great for them in that they are thus exposed to wild ones of different ages. When we put grain on the ground for the fawns and our chickens, many local deer and wild turkeys come in to eat, too. The fawns often try to play with wild deer, but most are usually adults who do not care to play with strange fawns. I've seen Solo put his head down in front of yearling bucks, inviting them to play the mock head-butting game. He would hop and bounce around, obviously trying to entice them. They tolerated him, but were too dignified to join a game with a baby. Little Joe tried this a few times, too, but was more comfortable playing with Solo and Velvet.

Solo also interacted with wild turkeys. Male turkeys often grab a piece of tissue above the beak of another one and hang on as they walk around in a circle, using this normal behavior to establish dominance. One time when three were doing that, creating a pinwheel of turkeys, Solo walked over and bumped them lightly with his head. They ignored him, continuing their battle, so he gently prodded them with a front foot. He appeared to be trying to either play with them or make them quit fighting. When they did stop, he chased them, but again it seemed more in play than aggressive and the turkeys weren't particularly upset. They fly into a tree or over the fence when they feel threatened or tire of the games.

Fawns I raise will sometimes try to nurse from adult does. A doe will occasionally get cranky and kick at pushy babies, but are relatively gentle. I've never seen one hit a fawn hard enough to injure it. It is their nature to just associate closely with their own young, allowing only their own to nurse. The adults kick at each other sometimes, much less gently. Does especially become annoyed by yearling bucks; they also seem to have a pecking order with each other around food. Sometimes two will stand on their hind legs, batting at each other with front legs.

Velvet tried to play with the wild ones as well, and not just deer. One time I saw her prancing around a pine tree in an odd manner. Then I noticed a red squirrel (native here, unlike fox squirrels that live mostly in town) on the tree. It seemed to be trying to reach grain on the ground, but Velvet was preventing it from doing so by blocking its path. Finally, when the squirrel ran up the tree, Velvet stood on her hind legs and jumped gracelessly toward it, touching the tree with her front hooves like she was trying to climb with the squirrel. Another time she approached a mourning dove who was on the ground eating grain, reaching her nose toward it. When it flew, Velvet jumped awkwardly into the air, looking as though she wanted to fly with the dove.

CHAPTER 11

Because of our location, we are able to provide fawns with what is called a soft release, meaning they go wild from here at their own pace. They are able to come back for small amounts of grain when they choose, though we never give them enough to depend on for survival after weaning. Most of their food must come from natural sources. I normally wean youngsters about the first of October, often a couple weeks after letting them out of the back yard. By then I've reduced them to only one bottle daily, so most of their food is already hay, grain, and wild plants.

White-tailed deer usually go wild quickly and easily. By the time they are weaned, they usually will not come close to anyone but me, and only approach me at feeding time. After weaning, Don is around them more because he puts out the grain. By following wild deer and orphans from previous years, fawns raised here learn what is threatening and where to find food and water in their territory. Because wild ones run when humans approach, rehab fawns learn to do so as well. They are less nervous with us than wild deer when in our yard; away from our yard, they run from us as well as strangers. White-tailed deer have relatively small territories so fawns come back frequently. Within a month or two of weaning them, I am usually unable to tell which ones I raised and which grew up with their mothers.

I was concerned about releasing Velvet here because she had had no contact with other elk and was too comfortable with people. We frequently see wild elk in large pastures near our place, but have never seen them in our yard. The longest I had previously cared for an elk calf was one month. Before, the game wardens just left them here until they could take them to the state rehab center in Helena, where there were usually several elk calves. They raised them with less human contact, probably feeding them with nippled buckets hung on a fence rather than hand-held bottles. After weaning, they took them into the mountains in horse trailers for release. I considered several options, including asking a game warden to take Velvet somewhere else or us taking her to a neighbor's place when a herd of elk was there. Sadly, that was a decision I did not need to make.

Shortly after my Yellowstone trip, the pocket on Velvet's belly returned, seeming even worse than before. Because of the stress of surgery, concerns about her healing when she was so much bigger and more active, fear of bad reactions to anesthesia, difficulty in transporting her to and from a clinic because of her size, and the expense, I had to rule out surgery. I could feel intestinal gurgling near the hole and believed it was only a matter of time before a piece of bowel became constricted. When enough material slips through the hole into the pocket, blood vessels are compressed, the trapped tissue dies, and infection develops. Also, the bowel becomes blocked so waste no longer passes through. Even if that didn't happen right away, it surely would in a couple of years due to increased abdominal pressure when she was pregnant. She would also be jumping more when she ran with the wild ones, putting more weight on her abdominal muscles.

The condition would have killed her and dying from a constricted bowel is long and agonizing. I couldn't in good conscience release Velvet to that, so again had to make the most difficult decision for a rehabber and Velvet was euthanized. Because she didn't seem to be ill or in pain at the time, and she had been here for a couple of months, it was even harder than usual. I had to console myself with the thought that she probably would have had a slow, painful death if she hadn't come here and at least she had two enjoyable months in this lifetime. Necropsy showed tissue death and infection were beginning in that area, so postponing euthanasia would have been unkind.

After all the animals that came in that year, we were down to just Solo and Little Joe. I hoped Solo would go with Little Joe after they were weaned, maybe finding his way to wild mule deer who live as close as half a mile from our place. Unfortunately, that plan also didn't materialize. Both of them stayed in the back yard for several months, with neither seeming inclined to leave. After I weaned them, I seldom went into their area. Don had some contact with them every day when he put out their grain and fed our outside animals. Solo was the only one who approached Don, always coming to be petted and making a nuisance of himself by getting in the way.

One day that winter I noticed Solo, but didn't see Little Joe. Don hadn't seen him earlier that morning when he was feeding, either. I hoped Little Joe had decided to hop over the fence with the wild deer. White-tailed deer jump fences and other obstacles easier than mule deer, perhaps because their bodies are more slender and their legs relatively longer. When I finally went out to explore, I found Little Joe's body in the deer pen. There was no evidence of illness or injury, but on necropsy he was found to have a chest full of blood, probably from a ruptured aneurism. I was glad he hadn't been ill, that it wasn't something I should have noticed or could have fixed. I was certainly sad to have lost him and Solo clearly missed him, too.

I kept expecting Solo to jump over the fence, but he still showed no inclination to do so. The only other mule deer I had released from here was Skipper, an orphan I raised three years before (mule deer were then usually taken to Helena like orphaned elk). When he was about six months old, Skipper started jumping the fence, behaving as I hoped Solo would before he was a year old.

Skipper would frequently come back into the yard for a few hours or a day or two before leaving again for up to four days. When he came home, I occasionally went out to visit with him. He always came up to me, resting his jaw against my chest with his nose under my chin to give me a deer hug. He visited some of the neighbors and I was told later he had appeared to be aggressive toward someone's grandson. I suspect he wanted to play with the child, but he was growing small antlers by then and weighed nearly a hundred pounds.

Skipper left for the last time about the first of June, when he was a year old, and we didn't see him again in our yard. A neighbor saw him a few months later but Skipper didn't approach him; Don spotted him with white-tailed deer in another neighbor's pasture a couple times when he drove to town. The last time Don was sure he saw Skipper was less than a year after he left us. Not long after that I was thinking about Skipper, as I still occasionally do, when I

59

suddenly felt slightly dizzy and experienced a shocked sensation. I hadn't felt like that before nor have I since. The sensation lasted only for a few seconds before I again felt completely normal. The sad thought came to me that Skipper had just died and was letting me know he was moving on. It was during hunting season, so he was probably shot.

Not long after Little Joe died, Solo developed bumps on the joints of his hind feet which seemed to be painful. While eating grain, he would pick up one foot and then the other as though it hurt to stand on them. I gave him homeopathic calcarea/phosphorus tablets, cell salts (called bioplasma), and MSM (methyl sulfonyl-methane) several times daily for a while. We also trimmed a couple of his hooves which had become too long. Like cutting fingernails, this is not painful for them. Normally their hooves, which grow continually, wear off because deer walk and run a lot, sometimes over rough ground. When their hooves are too long, deer are unable to stand up on their toes properly. I thought that may have caused the swelling. Within a couple of weeks, Solo was again moving around normally. The bumps seemed to be shrinking and he no longer acted like his feet hurt. We still don't know for sure what caused the problem, but it didn't recur during the time he was with us.

For several years after the summer with Solo, when so many of the babies I cared for died for one reason or another, I tried to stop doing wildlife rehabilitation. I told Judy I was tired of being around dead animals and having to decide to euthanize them. Our usual release rate of 60 to 70 percent is really quite good considering at least most of them would die without our help. (These statistics come from a record Judy keeps of everything that comes in, so she can complete reports for her permits.) Unfortunately, it had become too easy for me to focus on those who died, especially the ones like Velvet and Little Joe who stayed longer, instead of feeling good about all those I helped and released in a short time without becoming so attached.

However, I kept receiving phone calls about animals in need, including from Judy, and didn't have the heart to refuse. Judy usually came for them on her next trip to Hamilton or I took them to her, so I was mainly picking them up or acting as a drop-off point for short-term emergency care. I didn't even want to do that at the time, though. I also wanted more freedom, especially during the summer, to travel and visit friends. My whole belief system had begun changing in 2002, five years before Solo was born in 2007. Though I didn't know it then, I'm sure this difficult period of time was part of my learning and growth, and also because of energy and magnetic changes on our planet, something of which I was totally unaware at the time.

CHAPTER 12

In the years before (and for a number of years after) I became wildlife rehabilitator, I was an angry atheist. I told a friend, sometime in the year 2000, there was nothing that could make me believe in a god or any religion. I thought my only two spiritual options were science and atheism, the absence of spirituality, or belief in a god defined by some religious organization. I've studied many religions through the years and would still choose atheism and science without hesitation if organized religion was the only other spiritual option.

I was raised by Protestant parents, often attending Sunday school as a young child. My parents usually took us to church, but we sometimes did fun things (camping, fishing, vacations) on Sunday mornings instead. When I was in eighth and ninth grades, Dad taught high school classes and coached in Klickitat, a small town in Washington. Another teacher was a Southern Baptist minister who, with my parents, opened a church there. Before I underwent the ritual of total-immersion baptism (my parents' decision, not mine), the minister asked me if I believed in God. I told him I did because I was afraid to tell the truth, but I already knew I didn't.

According to Webster an atheist is "one who believes there is no god." That was certainly my belief, though I didn't know to call myself an atheist until I was 17 years old and met a scientist who was one. He suggested I study as much as I could about different religions and philosophies, think for myself, and then decide what works for me. He never suggested I believe as he did, nor did he even really explain his beliefs to me. He simply let me know there were many options and suggested I study them. I will always appreciate and respect him for this advice and for avoiding pushing his beliefs on me, a refreshingly different approach from that of so many religious people.

I believed science could explain our world without the need of any kind of god. This certainly did not give me license to harm others in any way, nor have I ever wanted to do so. I was told by a couple of horrified people that I must be a Satanist, since I didn't believe in a god. They did not understand when I explained a devil is the same as a god. I never believed a devil existed, either, and certainly would not have worshiped such a being. I still believe both gods and devils, as defined by organized religions, are created by humans with more human characteristics than godly ones.

A major reason I became an atheist is because the god of my parents and the teachings of religions I studied later seemed unkind to me. Even as a child, I didn't think a god who could create the wonders of this world and the life in it would be judging, punishing, jealous, or even rewarding, as they taught. They kept talking about love, forgiveness, and free will, but they also said we're born in sin and must believe in the right god or be banished to some form of hell after death. That never seemed logical, reasonable, or godlike to me. A god would certainly know threats of punishment seldom if ever work as well as understanding, respect, and gentle guidance.

I fail to understand how free will can be given us by a god who then threatens to torture us eternally if we don't make the supposedly right choices, which vary somewhat from one religion to another. I also am unable to imagine a god who would create a devil to provide temptations and then torture those who succumb to them. That's like telling a child not to eat candy, offering him a piece of candy sometime later, and then beating him if he takes it. Where do unconditional love, free will, non-judgment, and positive guidance fit in here?

I remember my father telling me when I was quite young that it is most important to be a decent person, which I understood to mean being kind to others, and fulfilling my responsibilities. This message made sense to me. A god who would eternally punish someone who was decent, but didn't worship in a specified way, didn't deserve to be called a god or to be worshipped. I also didn't believe a godly being would require worship in order to feel fulfilled. That is a human concept and emotion, as is jealousy. Neither is godly.

My favorite subject from early childhood was biology and the more I learned the more fascinated I became. By the time I was in my early 20s, I firmly believed a god or creator was unnecessary in order to understand the universe and life on this planet. Evolution could be scientifically explained and demonstrated with no evidence of divine intervention. All living beings on our planet, including plants, fill a niche and wouldn't exist otherwise. The main concept scientists have yet to demonstrate in a laboratory is the actual beginning of life, when the first living forms appeared on Earth around four billion years ago. However, a number of theories about this have been proposed. I believed those questions would eventually be answered scientifically.

I was comfortable thinking I was here only for this lifetime and would simply cease to exist when I died. Dying can be difficult and unpleasant, but to me death was the absence of any thought, feeling, or existence, therefore nothing to fear. Living a lifetime in fear of the possibility of eternal damnation or even non-existence seems counterproductive to me. It is much better to enjoy and appreciate what is here and to live with joy and the morality of treating others with kindness and respect.

I have never attended a funeral. To me they are for those left behind; since I dislike them, partly because of the usual religious ceremony involved, I see no reason to go to them. Also, I was a senior in high school when President John F. Kennedy was assassinated. Forcing his young wife and tiny children to go through some of their shock and grief in front of the whole world horrified me; I avoided TV during that time as much as possible, even though my parents thought I should watch because of the historical significance.

I decided even if I was wrong and people do have eternal spirits, my loved ones who passed would know how I felt about them, no matter what I did or didn't do. If I was right, they certainly wouldn't care whether I attended their funeral, because they would no longer know anything. I chose to grieve in private. I didn't (and still don't) believe funerals, or any rituals after death, have anything to do with what happens to a soul. When I made those decisions and for many years after, I didn't think we had one.

I believed people create gods to fill their needs. I had science, common sense, and a belief in compassion and respect for other living beings to fill mine. I didn't need gods or religious leaders or books to tell me what is morally right; I could figure that out for myself. "Do unto others as you would have them do unto you" is one of the positive quotes from the Bible that simply makes sense. It includes people from different religions, nationalities, races, lifestyles, and societies, and it certainly includes animals. A form of that belief is a basis for most religions, one of many concepts they have in common, though a lot of people focus on minor differences instead.

My anger as an atheist was directed toward those who harm others in the name of religion, such as: missionaries who wipe out cultures and promise to help people only if they change their religious beliefs; religious leaders who instigate wars and persecute their concept of heretics in the name of religion; people who frighten children and adults with threats of divine punishment; con artists who take money from believers with the promise of heaven or other divine rewards.

Fortunately, I have since learned it is possible to move completely past judgment, even against those who cause apparent damage to others. It was several years and many lessons after first changing my beliefs before I realized my judgment was the same as that of those whose opinions and behaviors I considered wrong. They feel their opinions and beliefs are justified, too. However, from the level of Eternity and Spirit, all paths are needed and equally important. Just learning that is a huge step toward enlightenment, no matter where each individual starts.

In his book *The Future of God*, Deepak Chopra defines atheism as the "adolescence of spiritual seeking." That certainly describes my experience with it! My rejection as a child of beliefs that seemed unkind was a major step toward my current spiritual beliefs, even though it took many years to progress from there. I now gladly believe there are no bad people, souls are perfect, and the universe is unfolding as it should. I am so excited to be one of many people raising their consciousness now, giving me hope for humans, the other animals who share our planet, and Mother Earth herself.

CHAPTER 13

When I was in my early 40s, I subscribed to the monthly newspaper published by the Freedom From Religion Foundation (FFRF) based in Madison, Wisconsin. The organization still exists, but I no longer maintain contact with them. They are active in separation of church and state legal cases, among other current issues. There was some philosophy in the newspaper and they sold books written by freethinkers, many of which I bought. I was mostly interested in the philosophy and books; I have never wanted to be involved in politics or activism. I bought and enjoyed wearing T-shirts and sweatshirts from them with the following sayings: "Blasphemy Is A Victimless Crime," "I'm Your Friendly Neighborhood Atheist," "Just Say No To Religion," "I'm A Freethinker."

Through FFRF I met my friend Ruth Van Beber in 1989. She was also a member who lived in Portland, Oregon, where I was at the time. Ruth wrote FFRF asking them to help her contact other members in or around Portland. They sent me a copy of her letter (hard copy – there was no email then, at least not for most people) and calling her was one of the best decisions I've ever made. I was hesitant at first, partly because she was 87 years old. I wondered whether it would be difficult to talk with her because she might have hearing loss and/or some degree of senility. I also thought she might need more help or companionship than I was prepared to offer. I was quite busy working full time and taking care of a houseful of snakes. I didn't want anyone to depend on me for anything more.

All my concerns were groundless. Ruth was a fascinating, independent woman who, although she had attended formal schools only through seventh grade, was knowledgeable, well-read, and highly intelligent. She considered reading fiction a waste of time. Instead, Ruth read books on history, philosophy, anthropology, sociology, homosexuality, religion, psychology, mythology, and even began reading some of my biology books. She became an atheist fairly late in life, but quit going to church in childhood, after she was old enough to rebel against her parents.

We had such wonderful discussions! Ruth would often hand me a book, asking me to read a passage she had marked. Her eyes would sparkle and her face showed a child-like sense of wonder at the ideas conveyed.

When Ruth was 90 years old, a friend gave her a tape recorder and some blank audio tapes, suggesting she record the stories she told us. Everyone close to her appreciated them; Ruth was a wonderful storyteller. During the next year she dictated 26 ninety-minute tapes about her amazing life. I collected a few stories she'd left out from people who knew her, transcribing and editing them all into a book for her friends and family. It wasn't quite finished when she died in November 1994, at the age of 92. By then she was ready to go. Her eyesight was deteriorating so badly she was no longer able to read for more than a few minutes at a time, intolerable for her. Also she was still living independently in her small apartment but would soon be unable to do so.

Even though Ruth experienced some major traumas in her life, she always saw beauty in everything around her. She treated people with kindness, respect, and understanding. One woman told Ruth she couldn't be an atheist because she was so kind. I still miss her and would love to be able to tell her about the animals I care for and what I've learned since she died. It would be fascinating to hear Ruth's thoughts again!

Humanitarianism, the doctrine that humankind may become perfect without divine aid (dictionary.com), has been a consistent theme among atheists I have known or whose books and essays I've read. I've never met one who wanted to kill, torture, segregate, exclude, or enslave anyone, finding them to be far more compassionate, trustworthy, and responsible than many religious people. I've often wondered how the concepts of "Christian charity" and "judge not" and "forgive others" were lost by those who profess to be better than people who do not believe in their god or who live a different lifestyle from theirs. It amazes me that some people appear to think humans are unable to live morally or ethically unless they believe in and follow a god or some religious dogma.

I still hold many of these beliefs to some degree, but most have since become modified due to my experiences with animals, some teachers, and information from many new books and the Internet. All of my changes began during the year 2002, when I was 56 years old, and are still continuing. I find it fascinating how sure we can be of our beliefs and for how long – until we become exposed to new ideas and concepts from trusted sources. Even then, we must be ready and open enough to analyze and possibly accept other ideas.

Several changes in my life, including learning about telepathic animal communication and some other new areas of study, created my awakening interest in spirituality. I still believe there is no jealous, judgmental, punishing god and have no desire to be involved in any organized religion, but now I know religion and atheism are not the only two choices. Since I came to that understanding and became a spiritualist, the Universe opened and amazing knowledge, awareness, and experiences became a part of my life. What a wonderful and exciting journey!

CHAPTER 14

Late in 2000, my sister-in-law and dear friend Diana was diagnosed with lymphoma. She underwent a lumpectomy then and a couple rounds of treatment in 2001 which put her into remission. Early the next year Diana's son-in-law Scott suggested she take a self-hypnosis class being offered through the adult education program in Hamilton, thinking she might learn helpful skills for her experiences with cancer. I decided to go with her, initially intending to support and encourage her. Diana has benefitted from the classes and is enjoying her grandchildren and even great grandchildren years longer than predicted. Totally unexpected for me is how profoundly something so seemingly simple would change my life!

The three-term class was taught at the local high school by Clinical Hypnotherapist, Certified Hypnotherapy Instructor, and author Roberta Swartz. Diana and I started in the second or winter term, the section about using self-hypnosis for improving health. We spent two and a half hours in class one evening a week for eight weeks. The first term focuses more on behavior modification and is also eight weeks long; the third term (six weeks) is about spirituality and psychic phenomena. From the first class I was hooked. I had expected something superficial and was amazed at the depth and quality of information we received. I took as many notes as in complex college classes.

I began to learn about the power of the human mind to create both what we consciously want in this life and what we consciously prefer to avoid. The subconscious mind holds all our memories and underlying belief systems and sometimes it and the conscious mind are at odds. When this is the case, the subconscious mind prevails over time because it is stronger. This is the reason willpower alone usually works only for short periods of time, if at all.

However, it's actually quite easy to learn to work with both of them cooperatively; then it is amazing what an individual can create for him- or herself. The truth is our thoughts and belief systems create what we experience, but many times that is not what we consciously want. People often have difficulty with this concept because they know they didn't choose this illness or these emotional issues or problems. Of course, on a conscious level they didn't, nor did they do it with awareness.

When the subconscious mind is explored, especially with a well-trained hypnotherapist as a guide and teacher, people find subconscious decisions were made, usually in early childhood when they had limited knowledge and experience, leading to many of the problems they experience. The beauty of this is that, if the mind can create our problems, it can also un-create them. Part of what pleased me so much about this is we can learn to help ourselves through simple techniques for tapping into the power of our own mind. We are able to use conscious intent to create what we choose in this lifetime. I began to feel more empowered than ever before, a feeling I love!

A few weeks into the term, Roberta started talking about training some people to be hypnotherapists. I immediately expressed interest and hoped enough others would sign up to make the classes worthwhile for her to teach. Not only did I want to learn more about this fascinating subject, but I thought to myself, *I have a lot of family and friends I could help if I learn to do this.* I wasn't planning to do it professionally at the time. Again I didn't know I would benefit even more than others with whom I later worked.

That spring I took the metaphysics class, mainly because I enjoyed being in school again and Roberta is an excellent teacher. I had read about telepathy, other psychic phenomena, and reincarnation years before and found them interesting, though was unsure they were real. They seemed like pleasant beliefs, but I assumed special talents were required to participate in the paranormal skills; lots of other subjects were more fascinating to me at the time. I thought spirituality had to do only with religious beliefs and was uninterested in exploring those further. I was mildly interested in what Roberta might say about this, but certainly didn't think I would learn anything of much value to me. Once again my expectations were flawed.

74

The first metaphysics class, far from superficial, covered consciousness, universal awareness, the trinity of mind, body, and spirit, and expanding awareness, senses, and perceptions. Roberta described the life force as part of a vast sea of energy or consciousness in which we are all embedded and which gives us life. We are filled with it so it is within us as well as surrounding us; we are always directly connected to it, with access to all the information contained therein.

Roberta often used the word spirit rather than soul for this part of each individual, making it more palatable to me. Every being must have a life force or spirit to be alive. This is the part of us that scientists have been unable to create in a laboratory when trying to prove the beginning of life on our planet from interacting chemicals and environmental conditions present here when life began on Earth.

We learned about energy, which can neither be created nor destroyed and is the beginning or bottom level of all matter on our planet and in the cosmos. Even stones are made of and held together by energy, as are atoms, electrons, protons, and neutrons, the tiny particles of which we are all composed. So I am energy, the same as that which surrounds us and is in everything in the cosmos. That makes sense to me.

Mind, body, and spirit can't really be separated and, through Spirit (Creator, Source, Sea of Consciousness, Universe, God) and our five senses, we are connected to all that surrounds us. The mind gives us awareness, the ability to recognize what we sense and name, and to understand it. The body gives us the ability to feel (sense) and experience this life. The spirit gives life to the body and is directly connected to the sea of consciousness around us, what I call Spirit or Source and some call God. Maintaining awareness of and balance between the three, the trinity that is each of us, is the healthiest way to live.

I began to accept that explanation of a spirit, but still had more to learn before I started believing a spirit maintains its integrity as an individual after death. After all, energy can dissipate or change form, just as molecules and atoms dissipate and are recycled when a physical body decomposes.

75

During the five other classes in this series, we learned about telepathy (non-vocal communication between beings), cellular communication (between cells in a body using chemicals and electrical impulses), psychometry (picking up information from the past by handling an object), ghosts, out of body experiences (when the living physical body remains in one place and the spirit travels), automatic writing (allowing the hand and subconscious mind or Spirit to write messages without input from the conscious mind), and manifesting what we choose for this life. In workshops we practiced many of these skills.

We participated in exercises involving sending and receiving telepathic messages to and from others in the class; I was amazed how often verifiable information was received in this way. Automatic writing didn't work for me, but did for some students. I was able to pick up some accurate information from unknown objects enclosed in paper sacks (psychometry), which astounded and pleased me, thereby encouraging me to continue exploring these subjects.

One night Roberta suggested we practice increasing our awareness on the drive home from class by opening our minds and being aware of what we sensed. As I was driving about a mile from our place, I suddenly had the clear thought, elk in the road. When I rounded the next corner, they were there. We do have elk near our home and see them in pastures fairly frequently, but I rarely see them on the road. I'd been driving home late from class for weeks and this was the first time, though deer had often crossed in front of me.

When we think about it, I believe most of us can remember times when we somehow knew who was calling before answering the phone, even though we weren't consciously expecting to hear from that person. Or we suddenly start thinking about a friend or a distant family member with whom we've had no contact for a long time – and then receive a message or phone call from that person or hear something about him or her from someone else. Airline studies involving cancellations prior to flights that crashed show that a statistically significant higher number of people change their minds before boarding one of those planes. Many people have a sense of knowing about a loved one who has unexpectedly died or been injured – before they receive the phone call about it. These are all normal forms of telepathy most of us take for granted without exploring it further.

I began to believe psychic phenomena are not limited to especially-talented people, but actually are experienced by most, if not all, of us. Our ability to notice them can be enhanced by increasing our knowledge and awareness, an idea that was fun and exciting to me. Children who have not yet been told, "It's only your imagination," often have a greater awareness of psychic phenomena than older people who have been taught they aren't real or perhaps are something to fear.

CHAPTER 15

Another of the early steps in my spiritual transformation occurred in March 2002, when I asked Lyn J. Benedict, a telepathic animal communicator, to talk with some of my animals for the first time, beginning an association that greatly expanded my knowledge and awareness of Spirit over the next decade or so. Valerie, a friend I met through Don's business of selling air purifiers, gave me Lyn's phone number, saying she might be able to help our parrots. Val, who lived next to a wildlife refuge, successfully kept deer from grazing in her garden simply by asking them to avoid that area instead of building six-foot high fences around it. I had watched Pet Psychic on TV a few times by then as well, so was open enough to give it a try.

Tisha, a young female African grey parrot, came to us in July 2001, from a woman who loved her but was no longer able to fill her emotional needs. The bird's name was initially Morticia, but I always used her nickname. The woman was only 19 years old when she obtained Tisha. She had subsequently married, had three children, undergone a difficult divorce, and was working many hours, leaving Tisha alone most of the time. She chose to give Tisha to us because we could provide a more stable home for her.

African grey parrots are highly intelligent, social beings who normally live in flocks of a hundred or more. They have a long life span (up to 70 years) and mate for life when possible. These birds are picky about their life partners, with a large number to select from when they live in the wild. As with humans, individuals have different personalities and preferences.

Youngsters spend a few years learning, first from their parents and then also from other flock members, what they need to know to survive in their social group and environment. They usually don't mate until they are 10 or more years old. Living with humans can be extremely stressful for these magnificent beings; they are often kept in small cages without enough social contact or intellectual stimuli. When another bird of the opposite gender is introduced for breeding, they may not be compatible as mates, frustrating for people and birds.

When we brought Tisha here, she had plucked nearly all of her feathers, leaving mostly just those on her head which she couldn't reach with her beak. Short pieces of two or three of the large primary feathers remained on each wing after she had bitten off the ends – and that was all. Tisha had plucked them due to severe stress, literally pulling most of them out of her skin. This is at least as painful as pulling hair, probably more so because quills are much larger than hair shafts. She was extremely uncomfortable with any change in or near her cage, including new toys, and she panicked at sudden sounds and movements. For a while I left her in her cage most of the time, allowing her time to get used to us and our home. Because she had virtually no feathers, Tisha was unable to fly, but her instinctive reaction when frightened was to try; this resulted in a hard landing, not too dangerous when confined to her cage, though potentially serious otherwise.

At first Tisha continued pulling feathers as they grew; fortunately over time she began to let some grow on her back, wings, and tail. When she seemed more settled, I opened the cage during the day, only closing her in at night. She often sat on the back of my chair or even my shoulder while I crocheted and watched TV. She was a sweet bird, always somewhat shy, rarely allowing anyone to pet her but me and eventually Don.

I thought Tisha might be happier with a mate, or at least another African grey parrot, so we found Simon a couple months after she came here. Both of them hatched in 1994 so were only seven years old, too young for mating but certainly in need of companionship within their species. Simon had some behavior problems in that he would often bite viciously. He especially distrusted women, but could be quite friendly with some men.

Simon had been returned to the breeder by his first family because the woman disliked him. He had been purchased as a companion for a disabled child and the child's mother, who had to take care of him, was terrified of him. I was told Simon would chase her around the house if he got out of his cage, but he never behaved like that with us. He hated vacuum cleaners, even when they were turned off, and anything else that moved on wheels in the house (e.g., a hand truck or cart). Brooms and sticks also upset him at first; he gradually accepted them when he learned we didn't threaten him with them.

Simon was living in a small cage when we bought him, with barely room to turn around and certainly not enough to spread his wings. I immediately built him a big one, using woven fence wire (two- by three-inch openings with wire covered in green plastic) and one-inch PVC water pipe to create a roomy cage (four feet wide, eight feet long, six feet high) with wooden perches, branches, and hanging toys. I thought he would feel uncomfortable with so much space after being in such a small cage, but he immediately left his old one and never went back to it.

Tisha and Simon were uneasy with each other at first, so I was careful to keep Simon in his cage for fear they might hurt each other. Tisha's cage was right next to his, allowing them limited physical contact through the wire. Even then they had some squabbles, though neither was injured. Simon was a more aggressive bird; I wasn't surprised they chose not to become friends immediately. I was greatly relieved to find that Lyn was able to learn from the birds, and many other animals over the years, how I could better help them.

CHAPTER 16

When I first talked with her, Lyn had completed several seminars in animal communication but was still working on a donation basis. Later she began charging as she gained confidence in her skills and results. I paid her regular fees for animals who lived with us; she kindly and graciously worked at no charge with wild ones who came to me. This allowed me to ask for her help with them many times through the next 10 years or so. The following paragraph describes Lyn's general practice when working with animals for me. Her web address, which provides current information, is in the References section.

Prior to her formal conversations with animals at my request, Lyn talked with me to learn what was intended or needed and enough about the animal to connect with it. Then, sometime later when her schedule permitted (often the next morning), she sat quietly in an area of her home where she wouldn't be disturbed, focused on the animal till she felt a connection, and began the communication. Using a form of automatic writing, she wrote her questions and comments as well as what the animals told her. At an agreed-upon time, usually later that day, I called her, she read the communication to me, explained it, and answered my questions. I found copies to be helpful, allowing me to read them again later. Eventually I typed them for this book.

The following is a transcript of Lyn's Acknowledgment of Received Communication/Therapy for Animal Communication, which explains more about what she does.

> When I perform an animal communication, I am working with energies. What I receive during the communication is an energetic message from the animal, which I interpret for you.

> In performing an animal communication at your request, my intentions are always of a higher purpose. I am here to assist both you and your animal friend, with no judgment of the information. I offer the communication with the

intention that it may be helpful based on what I believe the animal has relayed to me, as animal communication is an art and not a science. This is not a replacement for veterinary advice or treatment for the animal. The animal's caretaker is responsible for making decisions regarding the use of the information in this communication.

In addition to talking with the animal, Lyn uses a book and cards set called *Medicine Cards,* by Jamie Sams and David Carson, at the beginning of every formal animal communication. It consists of a pack of 52 cards, each with a picture of a different animal, and a book with Native American beliefs about what the spirit of each animal teaches us. Lyn allows her subconscious mind or Spirit or animal spirit guides to direct her in picking a card. The animal on the selected card has volunteered as a guide for the communication, thus adding to the message for the animal and/or the person requesting the communication. When a card is drawn upside down, it is said to be in Contrary position, somewhat changing the message from that animal.

After Lyn told me about the book and cards, I bought a set and still find them interesting and helpful. When I have an unusual experience with an animal, I read its chapter in the book. Occasionally I'll pick a card when I have a question about something in my life. I spread the cards on a flat surface with the picture down, hold a question or intention in my mind, then slowly move one hand a couple inches above the cards. It still amazes me that I feel something different in my hand, usually tingling or heat, when it is over a card and then find the messages provide relevant insights and helpful suggestions. If I think about it too much, it doesn't work; when I simply remain open to whatever I feel, my attention is drawn to a particular card. Then life becomes even more wonderful and fascinating!

Lyn talked with Tisha and Simon for the first time on March 9, 2002. She had never physically met them or me and, as is her usual practice, talked with them from her home, then in Butte, Montana, across the Continental Divide to the east of our town. I gave Lyn some information about Tisha and Simon on the phone, including a description (feather and eye color, approximate size, gender, and age), how long they had been with us, and what I wanted her to ask them. My questions were: Why is Tisha still plucking feathers? How does she feel about Simon? Does she need to be farther away from him or closer? Why does she seldom talk? Why does Simon dislike women? What can be done to help him feel more comfortable?

The following is a transcript of Lyn's conversations with Tisha and Simon:

Lyn: (Tisha greeted me immediately. I asked her if Simon would want to talk with me or through an intermediary. She said I should ask him. I did. He said, "Harumph!" with his back to me and then lowered his head, turned around to face me, and said he thought he could talk with me since I asked so nicely and since I wasn't there "in his face.")

Lyn: Tisha, Adele would like to know what more she can do to help bring about a harmonious balance in your life, for she is aware that if you were balanced you would not need to be plucking your feathers.

Tisha: Oh, yes! Yes! Yes! I need more harmony – more balance – as Elk has said. I would like an hour during the day by myself with no one in the room and with some Mozart, Beethoven, or Bach playing softly in the background. I need high energy foods – nuts, grains, and sprouts would be wonderful – about 1/4 of my diet in these foods alone. I would like more female company such as you and Adele.

Lyn: Tisha, how do you feel about Simon?

Tisha: Only prefer the opposite sex when it is time to mate and that time hasn't come yet.

85

Lyn: Adele says you don't talk much. Is there a reason, since many parrots do say a lot?

Tisha: The trauma of my first person's pain and anguish still resides in my body. It is slowly healing and as it goes then I will feel more like talking. We are small in body and feel others' pain so intensely that finding ways to let go of that stress can be difficult for us.

Lyn: Would Rescue Remedy help you? [Bach Rescue Remedy ™, flower essences]

Tisha: Yes, Rescue Remedy – a drop daily in my water – would be a great help. Thank you for suggesting it. Continue it until the plucking stops and the voice comes back.

Lyn: Thank you, Tisha! Anything else you'd like to say?

Tisha: Tell Adele how grateful I am for what she has done for me. I wasn't sure I would live to a ripe old age with my previous person, but I have great hopes now! Thank you, Lyn, for being here today with us!

Simon

Lyn: Simon, do you care to tell me about how you feel about women?

Simon: They don't like me. They think I'm horrible!

Lyn: (I felt a lot of anger in Simon with these statements and, under that, fear.) Adele doesn't think you are horrible and neither do I.

Simon: I know you don't and you are the first women

who are not afraid of me. Adele still thinks I want to bite her and sometimes I do. The fear she has of me still makes me angry. Your lack of fear of me and total love, well – I have no desire to bite you or hurt you.

Lyn: I do understand, Simon. How can Adele help you like her better?

Simon: She could take some Rescue Remedy herself and give me some flower essences that will help me overcome my anger and fear of those who fear me. One drop of each per day in my water will be of great help.

Lyn: Thank you, Simon. I will pass this on to Adele. Anything else you have to say now?

Simon: Lyn, I don't hate women. They have never liked me until you. Thank you! And thank Adele. I am so happy to be here – and Don loves me and is not afraid of me.

Lyn: Would you bite Adele?

Simon: Yes, if I sense the fear of me in her.

Lyn: Thank you so much for talking with me and sharing with us how you really feel.

Simon: Lyn, I really think I could like a lot of women if they were like you and didn't fear me.

Lyn: Yes, Simon, I do indeed know that is true. Anything else?

Simon: No. Just thanks to you and Adele and Don. My

first life with the other people was difficult and I'm glad to be here.

Many parts of these communications were helpful for me, as well as for Tisha and Simon. Lyn's description of Simon's initial reaction (turning his back and then lowering his head and turning around) surprised me, mostly because I've seen him act exactly like that. Lyn had never met him physically and was seeing him through their telepathic connection. She also had few communication experiences with birds prior to this and is more familiar with dogs, cats, and horses. As with all her communications, the personality that comes across from her is what I have observed after living with the animals. Tisha also seemed true to form.

I immediately bought some Rescue Remedy, which helps relieve shock and stress, and other flower essences Lyn thought might help Simon and Tisha (and, yes, I took Rescue Remedy, as Simon suggested). A number of different companies and stores make and/or sell flower essences, with each type of flower having different energetic qualities. My superficial understanding is that these characteristics are distilled in some way, allowing them to be shared. The people who make them explain on their websites, as do those who make essential oils. All of these have to do with types of energy healing, a subject I was only beginning to know exists.

I also began giving Tisha and Simon foods other than simply the pellet diet for parrots and veggies that Linda (veterinarian) suggested. She had told me many captive parrots are given too much oil through nuts and seeds, causing them to develop a fatty liver which can kill them. I hoped Tisha and Simon would avoid this problem by being offered a wide variety of food and getting more exercise than parrots who live in small cages.

Some time before Lyn's first communication with them, I had cooked a mixture of different kinds of beans for Tisha and Simon, adding peas and some other vegetables. I made big batches, freezing it in small containers. For some reason I had quit doing this (probably because I don't like to cook even for Don and me), but after the first communication, I started giving it to them again, as well as their hard-boiled egg, fruit, and of course, treats. Tisha liked dried papaya with Simon preferring fresh fruit, so I offered some of each. They always had more food available than they ate, allowing them to regulate their intake according to their needs and preferences.

We had been giving Tisha nest boxes (plural because we made them from one-inch pine boards and she always chewed them up). It was difficult to give her alone-time because their cages were in the living room, so I took her nest box into a bedroom, providing her with something familiar to sit on while she listened to classical music in a private place. She went willingly and calmly which surprised me; Tisha otherwise didn't like being far from her cage, nor did she want anything near it moved. I also spent more time with her sitting on my shoulder in the evenings. Her comment about not expecting to live to a great old age brought tears to my eyes.

I was surprised to learn Simon bites women because he believes they don't like him, but it made sense when he explained. Lyn said that wouldn't have occurred to her as a reason, either. I don't blame him for being angry about it, but he does bite hard and drew blood by biting me a number of times. Bruising is perhaps the most painful result of a parrot bite; it is definitely not like being sliced with a sharp knife. It was difficult to avoid jerking my hand away from him when I thought he was going to bite. I worked on it and we soon got along much better. Simon even let me pet him occcasionally, but I remained somewhat wary of him. I was afraid to let other women reach for him because most of those who came here had limited experience with parrots. If he bit and they jerked away from outside the wire fencing, they could seriously hurt him as well as reinforce his anger, insecurity, and fears.

CHAPTER 17

Since that communication went so well, I decided to have Lyn ask some questions of Nicki, our Chattering Lory, a brush-tongued parrot native to Australia. He also hatched in 1994 so the three birds were the same age; I had purchased him from a breeder in Missoula (not where I found Simon) when he was less than two months old, not yet weaned, and almost ready to fly.

A short time before this, I had met a couple of Rainbow Lorikeets (somewhat smaller relatives of lories) when I visited my friend Ed in Tacoma, Washington. I thoroughly enjoyed Wally and Joey (the lorikeets), who ran around on the floor, climbed on Ed and me, and talked.

I had also recently met Arnie, a starling raised by Judy Hoy, the rehabilitator; he talked to her and clearly knew what he was saying. He asked for what he wanted, sometimes even giving information. Once when I was visiting, Arnie looked at me and said, "Come here." I moved closer to him and he proudly stated, "I love Judy!" To Judy he always said, "I love you, Judy." Even she was surprised when he so appropriately changed the phrase.

One day when she was in his room feeding an orphaned bird, Arnie asked, "What are you doing?"

Judy said, "I'm feeding a little bird."

Arnie thought about this for a minute and then said wistfully, "Arnie is a little bird."

I wanted a bird who could communicate with me (this was years before I learned about telepathic animal communication), so I went looking for one as soon as I returned home from visiting Ed in Tacoma. Nicki (a lory) was the closest species to lorikeets I could find in Missoula. I was immediately attracted to him and we quickly bonded deeply.

I had no idea what I was getting into or how much a part of my life this little guy would become. Lories live 25 to 30 years so Nicki is now a little past middle-aged. He knows he is the most important member of our household, reminding me of this frequently and punishing me by screaming and/or biting when I don't seem suitably impressed or do what he says quickly enough. He can also be gentle and sweet; his courtship behavior is adorable and loving. Don tells people I'm a bigamist because Nicki considers me his mate.

A phenomenon I have noticed in raising wild birds is they start becoming wild about the time they begin learning to fly. This makes sense because babies are helpless while in the nest, their only defense being to remain unnoticed. When they leave the nest and begin to fly, it becomes necessary for them to recognize and avoid danger. I intentionally handled Nicki a lot during that time, including gently wrapping my hands around his body, unnatural and frightening for birds. At the same time, I was doing something non-threatening and distracting with him, such as letting him lick my tongue or feeding him from a syringe before he was weaned. At first he was uncomfortable with the physical contact but soon became used to it; I am still able to handle him that way without upsetting him. He will sit on Don's shoulder, hand, or lap, considering Don part of his flock, but Nicki doesn't let Don or anyone else touch him like I do.

Lories and lorikeets are a whole different kind of parrot. African grey parrots walk slowly and deliberately unless they are frightened. Nicki is highly energetic, always busy and rushing around, comfortable on the floor as well as on high perches.

At first I locked Nicki in a cockatiel cage at night, leaving him free in the house all day. I didn't trim his wing feathers, so he learned to fly, making circles through the house and frequently squirting feces on floors, furniture, and walls as he flew by. Nicki also began destroying plants and books by chewing on them. I'd find a pile of chopped vegetation on the floor beneath my hanging plants and small pieces of paper next to books. He loved to throw things on the floor; it was most fun for him if they made a lot of noise when they landed. Water glasses and jars that broke were favorites.

Nicki began saying a few words when he was about three months old. I didn't try to teach him to talk, mostly just speaking to him as I would to a young child. His vocabulary rapidly increased and it became obvious he knew what he was saying, allowing us to carry on conversations with him. Years later, he still sometimes adds new words and phrases. When I look out a window near his cage he often says, "Solo! Where is he Solo?" He has heard me call Solo, of course, but he made up the sentence, modified from "Where is Solo?" and "Where is he?"

One day in December 1994, when Nicki was between three and four months old, I went to my sister-in-law Diana's home in town to help paint her living room. Nicki still doesn't like it when I leave the house. Shortly after I left that day, when Don opened the door to call Ginger, our yellow lab, Nicki flew out over Don's head, made three circles above the house, getting higher with each circle, and then took off toward town. The road goes north for a couple miles before it turns east toward town, but he headed straight northeast, the direction of Diana's house. Nicki had never been there; I didn't know whether that was coincidental or if he knew what direction to go to find me. With what I've learned since, I'm sure he knew I was in that direction.

When Don called to tell me of Nicki's escape, I rushed home to have one of the worst days of my life.

Winter in Montana is not a good time for a tropical bird to be outside. There was snow on the ground and we even had a small amount of freezing rain that day. None of Nicki's normal food would be available for months. Don called the sheriff's office, animal shelter, local radio station, and our close neighbors to report him missing. A number of us tramped around in the snow for hours, calling and looking for him. It seemed a bright red bird would be easy to spot, but he could have huddled high in a ponderosa pine tree. Of course I imagined all kinds of horrible things happening to him, from being attacked by dogs, cats, or hawks to sitting, wet and hypothermic, under a tree somewhere wondering why I didn't come save him.

By late that afternoon I was sure he must be dead and I vowed to never have another pet. It was entirely too painful to become so attached and then lose one. I curled up in bed in a state of major depression. About dusk I heard a screech outside the bedroom window that sounded like Nicki and then I heard a demanding voice shouting, "Nicki! Come here!" I ran outside with boot strings flapping, nearly falling as I climbed over the fence into a neighbor's pasture, and there he was, sitting on a branch in a pine tree. When I was under him, I spoke softly till he flew down onto my shoulder. I grabbed him, cuddling him under my chin to warm him as I carried him back in the house. Nicki was shivering and smelled like pine sap, which I think he had been eating, but seemed to suffer no ill effects from his adventure.

He still usually calls me Nicki; sometimes he uses Me or Adele. The "Me" confused me until I realized I call myself Me when I talk to him or others, never saying anything like, "Come to Adele" as a mother would say, "Come to Mommy." He also knows he is Nicki and will tell me, "Nicki want some!" when he sees me eating something. He calls Don by name, as in, "Go see Don" or "I wish Don was here." Of course he hears Don call me Adele so he does use that once in a while.

The day after Nicki's escape I trimmed his wing feathers so he could no longer fly freely, and we built his big cage. It is made out of the same kind of fence wire as Simon's but the frame is two-inch by two-inch pine lumber. Tisha and Simon would make short work of a wood frame; Nicki only chews up softer material like paper and plants. His cockatiel cage hangs in the corner of the big cage; we have a bedtime ritual during which I lock him in the little cage and cover it with a towel just before I go to bed. He sleeps under a hand towel on the floor of the cage rather than on perches. His food dishes are in the cockatiel cage with twist ties to keep them in place. Otherwise, he opens the little door to remove the dishes, joyfully flinging his powdered food and nectar all over the cage and surrounding area.

Nicki was frustrated and confused for a short time about being unable to fly, but he soon adjusted and seems quite happy running around. I left his wing feathers long enough to allow him to fly short distances up and down, so he lands safely when he flies off a perch. Only the feathers are cut in this procedure. Once fully grown, they are the same as hair and fingernails in that they have no nerves or blood vessels. The birds molt once a year, growing new feathers which also need to be trimmed. After a couple of years I quit cutting Nicki's feathers, but he still only flies short distances. He is unable to get much lift or fly around the house, a lot easier for me as well as safer for him. He could exercise his flight muscles and re-learn flying as youngsters do, but fortunately he doesn't know that.

I later learned, to my horror, that some bird breeders or dealers actually amputate part of the wing, including bone, muscle, and skin, so some flight feathers can't grow back. Presumably this is more convenient for humans, eliminating the need to trim a few feathers yearly, but is certainly cruel to the birds. No anesthesia is used.

Lories and lorikeets are called brush-tongued parrots. Little bristles (papillae) on their tongues are used to pick up nectar, pollen, and fruit juice in the wild. Nicki eats a powdered diet (Avico Lory Life™ or Blessings Gourmet™) made for these birds, and Kern's Papaya Nectar™ or organic apple juice. His feces are quite liquid and he ejects them some distance from his body. Lories are messy little fellows. Nicki also likes some fruits, vegetables, and cooked meat; he mostly shreds these treats, just swallowing the juice. He loves ice cream, yogurt, and chicken as well, sometimes sitting at the table with us picking at the food on our plates. Mostly he flings it around, laughing as he says, "What a mess!"

According to books on their care, lories and lorikeets should not be fed much protein because it can cause them to develop gout. At first I was quite careful about that, but some of Nicki's feathers began breaking, mostly on his tail. He was not doing it with his beak; they simply broke during his normal activities. It appeared his feathers were weaker than they should be. Nicki soon showed me a way to help, as animals will often do if we pay close attention to their behavior.

We bought crickets for several small tree frogs we kept in a big terrarium at that time. A few crickets always escaped and Nicki would sometimes catch one on the floor, pick off its back legs (I know – not a nice thing to do, though not malicious on his part), swallowing juice he squeezed out of the legs. One day he was on the floor in the kitchen when he saw a cricket zip under the stove. He ran over, peered under the stove, and said, in a quiet, coaxing voice, "Come here. Come here." When he gave up, he shrugged and said, "Lost ya."

For feeding wild birds, we also keep a meal worm colony in a kitty litter tub. One day I found Nicki perched on the edge of the tub picking up meal worms. He would squish them all along their length, swallow the contents, and drop the empty shell. So I started giving him a few meal worms every day. As long as I continue this, his feathers remain beautiful and unbroken. Nicki calls the meal worms and other insects "crickets." He reminds me to bring them by saying, "Nicki want some cricket!" if I don't provide them soon enough in the morning.

Nicki categorizes animals in his speech. Insects are crickets; dogs are mostly Ginger, the first dog he knew; lambs, goats, and fawns are goats. We have raised several baby lambs and goats, most of which stay in the house for a while. They get along better on tile floors than fawns, so I let them wander around. Right after we got one lamb, who was still unnamed, he went over by Nicki's cage and Nicki said, "Hi, Goat! How are ya?" So the lamb became Goat. Another time Goat was wandering around crying for food while I was warming his bottle. Nicki said, in a concerned and sweet little voice, "What's the matter, Goat? You want some juice?" Nicki calls his papaya nectar "juice."

One summer when Nicki was a year or two old, Don and I worked in the mountains doing timber stand exams for the Forest Service. We slept in a tent during the week; I came home on weekends to shower, do laundry, and pick up supplies. Nicki went with us and I essentially wore him for the summer. I didn't worry about losing him; he made sure I never got far away. Also he was unable to fly well because of trimmed wing feathers. A few times he climbed too high up a tree for me to reach him, but I was able to entice him down by offering jerky, which he loves, or threatening to leave him. He was aware of hawks overhead, noticing them well before I did, so I wasn't too concerned about that danger.

Nicki dislikes traveling in the car when he can see things whizzing past him, so I wear a loose, long-sleeved shirt over a t-shirt. He rides under the big shirt, either resting inside a sleeve or hanging from the neck of my t-shirt by his feet. He also hides under the outer shirt when I am in direct sun, which disturbs him for some reason. Nicki doesn't defecate where he sleeps, waiting till we let him out of his hanging cage in the morning, so my clothes were reasonably safe except when we were out of the car and he was on my shoulder or head. Then my back was at risk.

I took Nicki's cockatiel cage with us at first, expecting to put him in there at least at night. However, he was upset about being unable to get to me, screaming, pacing, and frantically rocking back and forth when I put him in his cage, even though it was right next to the bed. So he slept in the sleeping bag with me. Fortunately, he prefers to sleep in his cage when we're at home.

Nicki is not a good bed companion. He insists on sleeping clear down by my feet, whether we are in a bed or a sleeping bag. I have to be aware of him relative to my feet, because he bites my toes if they get too close to him. That is not a pleasant way to wake up! I make sure the bag is unzipped or the top sheet is loose so he gets enough air. He poops over the edge when he first wakes up in the morning, so feces in bed is not a problem. When it's time to go to sleep, Nicki dives under the covers from the top and runs clear down to my feet, giggling all the way. Then we have to play the game of biting toes for a few minutes before he settles. He enjoys that game a lot more than I do, but it's hard not to laugh with him when he plays it.

One of my favorite Nicki stories happened when I was sitting on the ground entering data about trees into a portable computer as Don gave it to me. Nicki, who was playing near me, climbed the flower stock of a beargrass plant. When he got nearly to the top, his weight was too much for the stalk and it began to bend slowly. Nicki ended up on his back on the ground with flowers in his face. I laughed because he looked so startled and I knew he was unhurt. He let go of the plant which sprang back to normal position, stood up as tall as he could, and shouted, "Quit it! QUIT IT!" Laughing *with* him is fun; like us, Nicki doesn't appreciate being laughed *at*. He definitely knows the difference.

During the evening, Nicki often played on big cushions I propped against the side of the tent as a backrest when I was reading. The top of my head was slightly lower than the top of the cushions; a couple of times Nicki aimed the wrong way and defecated on my head. Needless to say, it was an unpleasant shock to feel warm feces running through my hair down the sides of my head. My hair was long then and washing it in the woods was a major production. Water from the creek was so cold my feet went numb if I stood in it. I had wet-wipes which helped, but they created a problem as well.

As long as Nicki has been with us, he has become positively incensed by anything soft or floppy in my hand, especially if it's white. He immediately attacks and bites my hand, not the object, if he is anywhere close. He recognized the wet-wipes container, so getting it far enough away from him to safely pull one out was difficult, as was using one when I had it. Wiping my nose with tissue when he was around was also risky.

One evening when I could tell Nicki had to go, I tried to direct him to the end of the cushion where I had put newspapers on the tent floor for easier cleaning. Nicki knew I didn't want him to go, but didn't understand I just wanted him to go in the right place. Finally he couldn't stand it. He ran over to the other end of the cushion and squirted against the tent. As soon as he did, he said, in a loud, deep, and thoroughly disgusted tone of voice, "OH, *GOD!*" I'm sure I must have said that the same way when he pooped on my head.

I still laugh when I think about that experience, and at the time I laughed so hard my stomach hurt. This time, instead of being angry with me for laughing, he simply looked confused, as though he didn't understand my reaction. For a long time I was unable to tell the story because I couldn't quit laughing long enough.

CHAPTER 18

Lyn's communication with Nicki on March 11, 2002, follows. As usual, the personality of the animal comes through loud and clear, even though Lyn had yet to meet Nicki in person.

Nicki: Hello, Lyn! I'm a pretty bird! I'm a pretty bird!

Lyn: Yes, I can see that! It's great to get to talk with you! Have you things you would like to say?

Nicki: Yes, indeedy! I'm Mister Talk! Talk! Talk! I already know what Adele has asked and I'll just answer you right off. I'd like more TV please. I like the talk shows, I really do!

Lyn: Sure, Nicki. I'll tell her. About the biting...

Nicki: Yes, well, that is quite reflexive, particularly when she waves those white flags. I just can't tolerate that. I bite her hand to tell her to stop it. It drives me crazy. Flap! Flap! Flap! Flap! [Nicki flapping his wings while hanging onto a perch, which he does when he's agitated.] Makes me mad enough to bite! It is agitating to us birds. Flapping wings really incite us to fight and this seems much the same. Please ask her not to flap things.

Lyn: I will, Nicki. I'll be sure to let her know it is enough to incite you to riot.

Nicki: Oh, yes, it is! As far as biting Adele, quick movements bring out that reflexive action of biting, so maybe if she just makes a point to be deliberate all the time. Of course, stressful situations can cause me to bite, too. Adele can be slow and deliberate and I like that. It feels good!

Thanks for talking to me! That's why I hollered at you on the phone yesterday. I think it is so neat that there are people who understand what we say. The more the better! Thanks, Lyn! Thank Adele and tell her how much I love her and adore her! We are kindred spirits and have had some wonderful past lives together – as great or better than this one!

Lyn: I'll pass all of this on, Nicki. Thank you!

I had noticed Nicki is calmer when I move slowly and only move one hand near him at a time. He definitely gets upset if anyone close to him is expressing anger or other strong emotions. I make an effort to be slow and deliberate when I handle him, but sometimes it's a nuisance if I'm in a hurry. That, however, is my problem and shouldn't become his. So I take a deep breath, relax, just enjoy being with Nicki, and we get along fine most of the time. I was already careful about "waving flags" around him because I knew he would bite me. I do find it interesting that he wants me to be slow and deliberate when he is anything but. He is busy, rarely moving slowly. His "past lives" comment was interesting and helped stimulate me to learn more about reincarnation, a belief I now hold and greatly appreciate.

One afternoon when my sister-in-law Diana and her daughter Teresa were here, Nicki asked to get out of his cage ("Nicki want out!"), so I took him with me when I sat down to visit with them. Not paying enough attention to him as he was bouncing around on me and the chair, I moved my second hand too close. When he bit me, I grabbed him with my other hand. As soon as I stood up to take him back to his cage, Nicki said, sounding thoroughly disgusted, "Aw, shit!" He knew he'd blown it and didn't struggle or bite while I carried him. Diana and Teresa couldn't believe it and we all laughed. Once in a while when he's annoyed with me Nicki says, in a threatening tone of voice, "You want your cage?!"

The day she talked with Nicki, Lyn also did a follow-up communication with Simon.

Lyn: Simon, are you there?

Simon: Yes, Lyn! Good morning! So glad to talk to you again. Thank you so much for telling Adele all I said. She has another question for me, doesn't she?

Lyn: Yes, she does. She'd like to know why you are plucking feathers from the inside of your thighs.

Simon: It feels tight. The muscles are tight. Some energy work, such as stroking down my legs, would help – from a distance, without touching me. Twice a day. Until I move away. That is my signal that it is enough.

Lyn: Thanks, Simon! I'll tell Adele.

I did that with Simon for a while, but often my proximity seemed to disturb him. Sometimes when I moved close, he reached down and pulled out a feather, jumping as though it hurt, so I backed away. According to books about keeping African grey parrots, they sometimes learn plucking behavior from other parrots near them. I thought Simon might be jealous because Tisha was handled more, perhaps copying her behavior in an attempt to gain more attention. Both of them became much better about pulling feathers, but it took some time. Sadly, it also didn't last.

Tisha seemed to enjoy having alone time with her classical music. Then – all of a sudden – she didn't want to go into the bedroom anymore, appearing anxious when I forced her to go. I felt it had something to do with Simon, but didn't know why. I decided to call on Lyn again so on March 15, 2002, she talked with Simon, Tisha, and Nicki.

Simon: Lyn, I'm so glad to talk to you again. I am still biting because I wanted to talk with you. I really don't like my foot petted. I like my feathers stroked much better but before, a foot being petted was the best I could get from Adele.

Lyn: Is she pushing too much?

Simon: Well, only she knows that. It should be a natural reaction to a natural feeling – that she likes me – not that she has to do this. I'd say, do what comes naturally – relax more! Oh, yes, the energy touching is helping – four times a day would be plenty.

Oh, I'm glad she asked about the music. I am a country music lover from way back. This classical stuff is not for me. Tisha is miffed because I made a few rude remarks about her music, but I didn't mean to send her into a molt! Jeeeezz! That's why she didn't want to go to the bedroom on Tuesday and plucked more feathers that night. Tell her I'm sorry! If I can listen to country-western while she is listening to her prissy stuff, I won't make any more comments about her music.

Lyn: I'll tell Adele! Thanks, Simon.

Simon: No, I don't get angry when Adele pets Tisha and Nicki. I just think it's a lot overdone. Yes, well, I am a bit jealous. They get so much and I get so little. But that is changing. It's okay. Tell her not to worry about it. And be sure to tell her how happy I am she doesn't call me "the Grouch." That is so much nicer and more respectful. Golly, but I appreciate that.

Lyn: Thanks for talking with me Simon.

Simon: No problem! Anytime!

Often when I ask Lyn to talk with an animal, I learn he or she has been trying to get me to call her. I'm more aware now, more likely to recognize it as coming from them instead of being my brilliant idea. The difference is there, though sometimes subtle.

I had been calling Simon a grouch, being careful to use a pleasant, friendly tone of voice rather than a critical, annoyed, or belittling one. He even started saying "Simon is a good grouch" sometimes. Once I learned how much they truly understand, I stopped that and wanted to know how he felt about it. I also wanted to know why he would no longer let me pet his foot through the cage wire. I had been doing it as a safe way to touch him because his head was usually through the wire far enough above his foot to prevent his biting my hand. However, he was beginning to let me pet his head once in a while for a short period of time, one or two strokes.

My interpretation of his reaction to the energy touching was apparently wrong. This consisted of moving a finger past his leg (fairly close, but without actually touching him) from the top down with the intention of moving energy. I think I was trying to do it for too long at a time when a couple of passes was all he could stand. Now he wanted me to do it more often but for shorter periods of time, which I did.

We all have an energy field around and through us which can be measured by science; it intensifies and even expands when we experience strong emotions. Whether we are consciously aware of it or not, we feel this energy from others when we are near them, sometimes even taking on their emotions without knowing the feelings are not truly ours. This is what those who notice auras are seeing; it can even be photographed as well as measured.

Negative energy can be pulled or pushed away from someone with intent, something Lyn began teaching me about so I could better help animals. This is what I was doing with Simon's legs. There are professionals, both for animals and people, who are trained to do it well, and it can be extremely helpful. I had no idea then that I would be learning much more about energetics and energy healing, or that it can be just as effective from a distance, even much farther than I was from Simon.

Apparently Simon had said some extremely unkind things about Tisha's music and she, being so sensitive, responded quite strongly. Lyn thought they both minimized it in their communications; it must have been intensely emotional. After this communication, they seemed to forgive and forget, so all went back to normal.

Lyn: Hi, Lady Tisha!

Tisha: Hello, Lyn. I see Simon apologized for making fun of me and my music. So sorry to upset Adele with all of this, but it did hurt my feelings. I enjoy it so much! Tell Adele – Thanks! Thanks! Thanks so much for the room and the music! It is so wonderful and she sees that it helps. Tell Adele that the bean dish is doing the trick. I had forgotten about it or I would have asked for it. It is helping. I still enjoy some sprouts and grains and my nut [peanut]. They are a real treat!

I am ashamed to admit I eventually became lax about their music for some time. After I later re-read this communication of Tisha's, I turned on a classical music station, telling Simon we'd play Tisha's music for a while and then I'd find a country station for him. As soon as I turned the music on, Tisha moved to the far corner of the room on top of Simon's cage to listen. Nicki unfortunately chose this time to do some screaming, no doubt diminishing the soothing effect for Tisha.

My excuses: We got tired of building a new 18-inch nest box every two weeks because the old one was falling apart. I'm still amazed at how fast parrots can turn solid wood into toothpick-size pieces. My brother Dan, who is a welder, made a steel nest box for Tisha that is too heavy for me to move. When I put Tisha on my night stand in the bedroom, she started chewing on it and I didn't want to leave her on the bed or the floor. Instead, I bought the birds a CD player and a couple of CDs with whistled songs for parrots. They like them, so I played them frequently for a while. I was afraid to put Tisha's classical CDs on it because I didn't have any country music for Simon. Of course I could have purchased some. Tisha and Simon were getting along better by then and seemed more settled.

Anyway, I again faded off with providing their music for a while, but then found classical and country radio stations on their CD player. Don watches TV a lot; I seldom do since I quit crocheting several years ago. He considerately listens with headphones because I dislike hearing it if I'm not watching something. So the birds didn't even get to listen to the TV. Lyn said they could hear it through Don, if they chose to tap into that, but still I'm sure they would have been happier with more stimulus choices.

Lyn: Hello, Pretty Bird Nicki!

Nicki: Hello, hello, Lyn! And top of the morning to ye! Erin go braugh and all of that. Have a touch of fondness for the Irish, I do! What can I do ye?

Lyn: About the screaming.....

Nicki: Oh, that. Gets on their nerves, does it? Well, how about that! Goes with the territory! If I don't like what they are about, I tell them. Bosses can do that, you know!

Lyn: Yes, they can, Nicki, but the best bosses don't because it puts people off.

Nicki: You are right, of course. I will try to be more respectful, but they don't always jump when I say "Jump!"

Lyn: They are doing the best they can, Nicki.

Nicki: True! True! I'll try to be more patient.

Lyn: Thanks, Nicki.

Nicki: Hey, Lyn. Luck of the Irish to you! Come back when you can chat all day. Okay? Ha! Ha! Ha! Thanks!

These communications were a couple of days before St. Patrick's Day. Lyn said an Irish accent would never have occurred to her, but that's what she heard from Nicki. I still laugh when I read this. It is so like Nicki!

Incidentally, Nicki still screams when he isn't happy with the service around here. Delayed gratification doesn't work for him. He does warn me, though. He'll say, in a threatening tone of voice, "You want some screaming? I'll get you some screaming!" And then he screams a few times and says, "You need some screaming! Screaming and screaming!" And then he screams some more and says, "You hear me screaming?" The scream is insistent and demanding, definitely attention-getting! Unfortunately I usually get him what he wants, thus rewarding his behavior. Nicki has trained me well!

An interesting part of this is I've never said those phrases and sentences to him, so he is not copying me. He created them with his knowledge of English. He knows the word screaming, because I ask him why he is screaming and to quit screaming. He has also made up other phrases, as Arnie, the starling, did.

Lyn talked with Simon again on March 20, 2002, the last of her communications for me for a couple of months.

Simon: Squawk! Good morning, Lyn! I'm feeling better!

Lyn: Great, Simon! I'm so glad to hear that. Tell me how it's going.

Simon: Adele is not petting my feet anymore and I really like my music. I've quit saying nasty things to Tisha, too!

Lyn: I think that is wonderful! I am glad for you and proud of you!

Simon: Gee, thanks!

Lyn: Adele tells me you are still biting her.

106

Simon: Oh, that. Well, she is still somewhat afraid of me. When I sense that fear in her, I bite.

Lyn: I understand your response, Simon, but when you bite her, it hurts and that causes her to continue to be afraid of you. Is it possible for you to not bite her when you sense that fear? Not biting Adele will be what makes the fear you hate so much go away. It really is a vicious circle. Someone just has to stop. I could ask her to stop petting you if you would like. She wants to pet you and give you affection, but not if you are going to bite her. She and I both know it is a hard thing for you to stop that instinctive impulse.

Simon: Squawk! (Pacing back and forth on a perch, head down sometimes). Well, now, I will do my best not to bite her – but if I do, tell her not to pet me for two days. That may be what I need to help me remember, if I forget. If I bite after two days, tell her to wait three days before petting me. This is all on condition that she doesn't pet my feet anymore. I really like to be petted on my head. I think I will remember - No Bite - No Bite - No Bite. (Simon thinking out loud to himself)

Lyn: Thank you so much, Simon, for your willingness to not bite Adele anymore! You will certainly reap the benefits in added love and attention!

Simon: Oh, I know, I know! Things are already so much better! Thank you and many thanks to Adele for her love and patience with me. I am truly grateful!

Simon improved a lot and, as long as I was careful and paid attention, he rarely bit me anymore. I learned to be less afraid of him and to have more patience, which I'm sure helped. We even played some games. He often walked into the kitchen when I was eating, so I shared food with him. Kitchen cupboards suffered some from his beak, but they're not too bad. Sometimes he even gently took my finger in his beak; I was often able to pet his head and even his back for short periods of time. Simon and I developed a bedtime ritual similar to the one with Nicki, so he felt less left out. He really is a good guy. I've known lots of people who took much longer to get over a difficult early life.

CHAPTER 19

Early in May of that year (2002), Lyn came to Hamilton
to facilitate a two-day Beginning Animal Communication
Workshop. This was the first time I met her in person. Quite a few
people attended, including Valerie, the woman who had told me
about Lyn, and we all learned more about this skill. We practiced
telepathy with at least most of us finding we were able to send and
receive some information from each other and from some animals
after looking at photos of ones who weren't there. It was a lot of
fun and I began practicing with my animals.

We were given a copy of the following Code of Ethics for
Interspecies Telepathic Communicators as formulated by Penelope
Smith in 1990:

Our motivation is compassion for all beings and a desire to
help all species understand each other better, particularly
to help restore the lost human ability to freely and directly
communicate with other species.

We honor those that come to us for help, not judging,
condemning, or invalidating them for their mistakes or
misunderstanding but honoring their desire for change
and harmony.

We know that to keep this work as pure and harmonious as
possible requires that we continually grow spiritually. We
realize that telepathic communication can be clouded or
overlaid by our own unfulfilled emotions, critical
judgments, or lack of love for self and others. We walk
in humility, willing to recognize and clear up our own
errors in understanding others' communication (human
and non-human alike).

We cultivate knowledge and understanding of the
dynamics of human, non-human, and interspecies behavior
and relationships to increase the good results of our work.

We get whatever education and/or personal help we need to do our work effectively, with compassion, respect, joy, and harmony.

We seek to draw out the best in everyone and increase understanding toward mutual resolution of problems. We go only where we are asked to help, so that others are receptive and we truly can help. We respect the feelings and ideas of others and work for interspecies understanding, not pitting one side against another but walking with compassion for all. We acknowledge the things that we cannot change and continue where our work can be most effective.

We respect the privacy of people and animal companions we work with, and honor their desire for confidentiality.

While doing our best to help, we allow others their own dignity and help them to help their animal companions. We cultivate understanding and ability in others, rather than dependence on our ability. We offer people ways to be involved in understanding and growth with their fellow beings of other species.

We acknowledge our limitations, seeking help from other professionals as needed. It is not our job to name and treat diseases, and we refer people to veterinarians for diagnosis of physical illness. We may relay animals' ideas, feelings, pains, symptoms, as they describe them or as we feel or perceive them, and this may be helpful to veterinary health professionals. We may also assist through handling of stresses, counseling, and other gentle healing methods. We let clients decide for themselves how to work with healing their animal companions' distress, disease, or injury, given all the information available.

The goal of any consultation, lecture, workshop, or interspecies experience is more communication, balance, compassion, understanding, and communion among all beings. We follow our heart, honoring the spirit and life of all beings as One.

This Code appeals to me as a kind and compassionate philosophy for dealing with other people as well as different species. I am grateful it expresses the knowledge that telepathic communicators can easily inject their own fears, beliefs, assumptions, and judgments into communications, as we all do to some degree when interacting with other people or interpreting animal behavior. The more aware we are of this as a potential problem, the easier it is to avoid. When we keep the conscious, analytical, thinking mind out of the way, we are much more open to receiving what is actually being sent. This applies to other people, animals, spirit guides, archangels, our higher self, whomever we look to for information, support, and understanding.

In addition to my psychic phenomena classes with Roberta and the parrots' communications through Lyn, this workshop increased my awareness and understanding of spirituality, reincarnation, and telepathy as a natural ability. I began reading books by various animal communicators, strengthening my belief in it as valid by learning that a wide range of communicators receive similar messages from many different animals under varying circumstances. The whole field is becoming more accepted and available all the time, which is great. Animals, wild and domestic, have much knowledge to share with us, especially when we can hear them on this level!

At some point around this time, a friend told me about John Edward, the psychic who hosted the TV show Crossing Over. I thoroughly enjoyed watching a number of his programs and reading his books. I didn't hear him talking about reincarnation, but he convinced me, skeptic though I was, that he truly was in contact with spirits of people's deceased friends and relatives. What I like most about John Edward is the feeling of kindness, understanding, and lack of judgment he radiates. His messages are often funny, usually quite simple, sometimes deeply moving; his intention always appears to be helping people with grief, loss, and feelings of guilt or regret. John Edward has a membership group online in which he offers videos similar to his TV show, among other things.

A lot of people are now reporting near death experiences, too. Initially I believed these to be attributable to brain activity around some form of trauma, illness, medication, fears, and/or religious beliefs, the usual response by those still stuck in earlier, more traditionally measurable scientific beliefs. However, details of these reports are amazingly similar and yet come from children and adults all over the planet. These people certainly didn't know each other, listen to the same religious leaders, read the same books, or survive similar problems around their temporary death. One book I found totally believable and uplifting on this subject is *Dying To Be Me* by Anita Moorjani. Many others are now available and interviews with some of these people can be found on websites and YouTube videos.

So, okay, I give up. I have to believe death is not the end of existence and spirits are real. If they are real after death, they (the spirit or soul part of each individual) must be real in life. If we can actually communicate telepathically with living animals and people – without language barriers – we must be speaking to and from a spirit of some kind. If time and distance are irrelevant in these communications, we must truly be part of a sea of consciousness in which everything is connected.

The next step in this process is to consider reincarnation. After a great deal of thought and study, it seems to me quite wasteful for a spirit to experience only one lifetime and then maintain its integrity as an individual on the Other Side for eternity. Mother Nature is not wasteful of energy; recycling spirits through different lifetimes is much more reasonable. My earlier belief that the energy which is the life force of a living being simply dissipates, as chemicals do when a body decomposes, is also a form of recycling. However, this negates what I have learned from animals and various teachers, classes, and books. Furthermore, one lifetime is the blink of an eye relative to eternity, such a terribly limited amount of time for learning all the possible lessons of life in a physical body on Earth.

Reincarnation seems more reasonable, logical, and compassionate than any religious beliefs I've studied. It also intuitively feels right to me, as no other spiritual beliefs have. My concept of reincarnation, beginning in 2002-2003, was that each individual spirit chooses its next lifetime and even whether to experience other lifetimes in physical bodies. The intention is to learn, experience, and grow spiritually while here, taking that information back to the whole, the sea of consciousness (or universal pool of energy, unconditional love, cosmos, God), after the death of the body. I feel so much more at peace as my understanding and integration of this philosophy expands and deepens.

My expanding beliefs didn't mean I had to believe in a god, though. I still associate gods with demands, rewards, punishment, and judgment. What I like most about my developing thoughts and beliefs is the lack of those elements and the depth of kindness, respect, understanding, and compassion involved. Unconditional love and free will actually mean unconditional love and free will. I love this stuff!

CHAPTER 20

I next asked Lyn to talk with Tisha, Simon, and Nicki on May 21, 2002.

Lyn: Good morning, Tisha!

Tisha: Good morning, Lyn! So nice to chat with you again!

Lyn: How are you feeling, Tisha?

Tisha: I'm feeling restless! Like birds of a feather should flock together!

Lyn: Is that why you are plucking feathers again?

Tisha: Oh, my! Yes! Itchy! Twitchy! That's how I feel! You may describe it as spring fever. It's not due to hormones alone. It is stimulated by the electromagnetic charges in the earth that drive migrating birds and such. Even though we don't migrate, we are sensitive to it.

Lyn: Adele knows this is not a healthy behavior for you and wants to know if she can do something to help alleviate your need to pluck feathers.

Tisha: If only she could! Maybe a new change in routine for a while. Not a lot, but I feel so restless, like I just have to get out and do something!

Lyn: Would you like to sit outdoors in your cage?

Tisha: Yes, that might be nice – smell the air and listen to the earth! I'd really like that!

Lyn: I'll tell Adele. Do you have any other concerns or things you'd like to say?

Tisha: As a domestic bird with spring fever, I do feel pulled in opposite directions – the goal to fly and move as opposed to being a companion for Adele and Don. The seasonal pull will soon be over and I'll be more balanced then. Tell Adele how excited we are that she is communicating with us with awareness now.
We will help her all we can.

Lyn: Thanks, Tisha! I will tell her!

Tisha had been doing much better about letting her feathers grow, with almost all of them grown in before she started plucking again, so I was concerned. After this communication I began taking her onto the deck with me sometimes, and made sure I left windows open as much as possible depending on weather. She seemed to enjoy it, but didn't want to be left out there without me. Earlier in her time with us she would not have wanted to be that far away from the safety zone around her cage. It is too big to take outside without taking it apart, so I didn't try that. As she said, this behavior didn't last long and she again allowed her feathers to grow.

Lyn: Good morning, Simon! How are you doing?

Simon: Very well, Lyn! I am getting more and more relaxed around Adele! I know she told you! I'm pleased with myself! It has been a struggle. Tell Adele Thank you! Thank you! Thank you! This is the happiest I have ever been! I am so delighted that Adele is talking to us and listening. She always could and we knew, but it is so great that she now knows, too! We are all much closer!

Lyn: I'll do that, Simon! If you are so happy, why are you plucking feathers and in new places?

116

Simon: Oh, I feel jittery, jumpy, itchy, twitchy! Spring fever really can be felt quite strongly by birds, you know.

Lyn: Can't you move around more rather than resorting to plucking feathers?

Simon: Now, that's an idea! I know I can't fly through the air from tree to tree, but I could move more in my cage and in the house.

Lyn: Adele is really concerned about the plucking because she knows it is unhealthy behavior.

Simon: Yes – oh, she's right. Just didn't occur to me to move more when I feel itchy-twitchy! I'll try that instead of plucking feathers.

Lyn: Does plucking feathers make you feel better?

Simon: No, it is just a type of displacement behavior, but one that caged birds do a lot because they feel so much and internalize things more than other species!

Lyn: Okay. I didn't know that. Do you have anything else you'd like to say, Simon?

Simon: No, but Nicki does!

Lyn: Okay. I'll talk to him next. Thanks, Simon. Keep up the good work!

Simon: You bet, Lyn. Thanks!

Simon hadn't been plucking feathers before, except a few on his legs, so I was concerned that I was doing something wrong or not doing something right for him. As usual, I was blaming myself for not filling his needs rather than respecting him as a separate individual with his own concerns. I didn't think about their growing closer to reproductive age, but I now suspect that was becoming a issue for them, too. Anyway, Simon got better and then worse again and then much better. For a while he didn't act at all nervous or disturbed.

Lyn: Good morning, Nicki!

Nicki: Hello! Hello! Hello! Thought you'd never get here! Got lots to say!

Lyn: Okay! Let's hear it!

Nicki: Adele is doing just great! Tell her to keep on responding to what she imagines we are saying! She is not just making it up! We all wanted her to contact you because we wanted to give her some extra validation. Now that we finally have her awareness, we don't want her to lose it. Suggest to her that she try talking with Val's animal friends to get some more validation before she leaves, or through pictures while Val is gone. [Val was getting ready to go back East for surgery.] Tell her to do ones for other people that she knows will provide validation. She is doing well with us – better than most people do – but going outside for more validation will help all of us even more.

And one more thing – I feel itchy-twitchy, too, but I move a lot and talk a lot, so I am acting out and it does help and keeps me from plucking. Just wanted Simon and Tisha to know!

We appreciate all Adele has done and is doing for us! We love her dearly – and we all want to tell her so. Don't we, guys?

118

Tisha and Simon: Yes, Nicki!

Nicki: Time to go, Lyn!

Lyn: Bye, Nicki. Thanks!

Nicki has never plucked his feathers and he certainly does move around a lot. It was validating to find I had once again decided to call Lyn only to learn the animals had been telling me they wanted to talk with her, thereby passing on messages to me. I appreciate their showing me I'm hearing them!

I did begin talking with animal companions for other people, receiving the validation Nicki said I would. I still do it once in a while with some good results. I don't go into as much depth as Lyn does and still question myself sometimes: Am I thinking this up on my own or am I really getting it from the animals? Ego interference is one of the main blocks to telepathic communication. I so look forward to moving past this issue!

CHAPTER 21

Another communication with Tisha, Simon, and Nicki on July 23, 2002, follows.

Lyn: Hello, Simon! How are you?

Simon: I am great, truly great!

Lyn: That is so good to hear! Adele would like to know why you are pulling feathers from your chest and under your wings.

Simon: There is an imbalance. That is why I am plucking. Adele is uptight about me and that makes me nervous. When I feel Adele being uptight, it unbalances me more and I get frustrated and my reaction is to attack. It is like having a bad day at work and coming home and yelling at the kids and the dog. It is not an "I don't like Adele" bite at all! Please tell her I am sorry she feels I don't like her. That is not the case!

Lyn: Do you get upset when Adele puts Tisha in her cage at night?

Simon: Yes. Tisha doesn't want to go, but she doesn't feel she should make a fuss.

Lyn: Is that right, Tisha?

Tisha: Yes, it is. I'd like to be with Simon, but as Adele says, there are some problems with that. I would like to try my cage in his, though, for the nighttime.

Lyn: Okay. I will pass that on. Simon, would you like more physical contact from Adele when Don starts traveling more? [Don traveled occasionally for his business at that time.]

Simon: Oh, yes! But it would help if she could be more relaxed at those times.

Lyn: Why do you find it easier to be petted by Linda [veterinarian]?

Simon: She just projects love. She doesn't think - worry - fear that I will react negatively. She is relaxed around me – same as you are. [Lyn did not try to touch or even approach the birds when she visited our home a few times. Her primary contact has always been telepathic.]

Lyn: Tisha, Simon, do you feel that Nicki gets more attention than you do when people come to visit and does that bother you?

Tisha and Simon: Yes, Nicki does get more attention, but he is not so overwhelmed by visitors. We both feel that sometimes people can just be overwhelming. Too much! Some are so excited that they come on too strong. Some are fearful and try not to show it.

Lyn: How do you feel about children?

Tisha and Simon: The quiet ones are great. They hear us and see us. The excited ones have their own agendas and never see us for who we are.

Lyn: Nicki? How about you?

Nicki: They don't bother me much! Most of them are cute and really think I'm great! I don't want to be held tightly, though. Some would literally squeeze me to death!

Lyn: Simon, do you feel slighted because Tisha gets out of her cage more than you do?

Simon: Yes, some. But I also get overly excited and do things Adele doesn't like. I think if I were balanced, I could handle being out better and not be so destructive.

Lyn: What do both of you think of the parrot seed mix?

Tisha and Simon: We like it!

Lyn: Is your diet giving you all that you need?

Simon: Yes, but could we have more melon?

Lyn: I'll pass that on to Adele. Tisha, why are you still picking feathers?

Tisha: Has to do with going with the program and not being able to speak up about my needs. Simon is helpful to me that way.

Lyn: You mean about not wanting to go into your cage at night?

Tisha: Yes.

Lyn: What else would you like, Tisha?

Tisha: (Bashfully) I'd like people to pet me more and notice me more – like Nicki. But I don't want to be overwhelmed by the excited ones or fearful ones.

Lyn: I think Adele can help you with that.

Tisha: That would be so wonderful! I hate to ask for more. She does so much for us, but I think I would like some more attention when people come.

Lyn: I'll tell her! Simon, do you have anything more you'd like to say?

Simon: Just the same as Tisha. We are grateful, Adele! Thanks so much! Love you!

    I distrust a lot of people around the birds (and other animals who live here). As I said earlier, people (children or adults) who are noisy or aggressive or move too quickly disturb me as they do the animals, so I become protective. I have refused to allow some children in the house because of their loud or hyperactive behavior. This is the animals' home as well as ours; they have the right to feel peaceful and safe here. Some children insist I make Nicki say something. I tell them he talks when he wants to and says what he decides to say. I don't try to make him do anything.
    Everybody wants to touch the parrots, which is understandable, but I rarely allow it. The parrots can step up on the hand of a few people, if one of the birds so chooses. Simon liked Linda and a few men I trusted to treat him kindly and carefully. He actually allowed our neighbor Tom to lift him off the floor and Simon walked up and down Tom's arm and across his shoulders. I was so happy for Simon when Tom visited him. Simon liked to get on the floor and walk around when people were here; I sometimes let him do so, depending on how many people there were and how they behaved. We were used to watching out for him, as were our dogs; I was afraid others might bump or even step on him.
    Tisha seemed to like it when some people spoke to her, but she would rarely put her head down inviting a pet from anyone but me. She probably would have if they had taken more time to visit with her first. I watched carefully for signs of nervousness to appear and, when they did, I moved the focus away from her. Nicki, on the other hand, loves being the center of attention, always ready to provide the entertainment. He will sometimes scream obnoxiously when people quit paying attention to him, whether they are trying to talk with Don and me or with Tisha and Simon. Nicki doesn't

want anyone but Don and me to touch him, though, and won't even sit on Tom's shoulder for more than a few seconds. He loves it when I pet him and hold him upside down with his back in my hand.

Linda has kept several rescue parrots including two cockatoos. One of them, Veronica, is aggressive toward people other than Linda, including Linda's husband Dan. So Linda is used to birds who have been abused and Simon's beak is small compared to Veronica's. Consequently, she is more comfortable with aggressive birds than I was, but I improved and Simon's behavior reflected that.

My intention in locking Tisha in her cage at night was to keep her more safe and comfortable. After this communication, however, I decided to let her sleep wherever she chose and also opened Simon's cage. From then on neither of them spent much time in either cage; both were usually on top of their cages or on the back of my recliner (which suffered some from parrot beaks) or, especially Tisha, in the nest box. Both got down on the floor to walk around sometimes during the day, and usually slept in a corner on top of Simon's cage at night. Safety didn't prove to be a problem; I was happy to notice both seemed more relaxed.

We eventually had to fix the walls around their cages by putting up solid plastic paneling and metal molding because Tisha and Simon were chewing up wood molding and panels. I suspect this is due to nest-building behavior and boredom. I thought the ceiling was high enough so we didn't cover it. However, they tore all the outside paper off the ceiling panels above Simon's cage.

I decided to take apart Simon's cage and build them a play structure out of two-inch plastic water pipe, giving us more room and keeping them lower. I did not want them to chew a hole in a ceiling panel to gain access to that space!

CHAPTER 22

In August of 2002, someone brought me an injured adult raven. Judy suggested he may have been a raven/crow cross. He was small for a raven, which are normally bigger than crows, yet had some raven characteristics. His left wing had been injured at the wrist, with an open wound and bone damage. I was afraid he would never be able to fly, therefore requiring euthanasia. This bird greatly appealed to me, more than just because I like ravens and crows. He seemed somehow special; I felt unusually drawn to him.

I took him to Judy because she knows more about dealing with difficult injuries, thinking she could give him the best chance to survive. Back home, thoughts of him kept popping into my mind, so I told Judy I wanted to keep this bird when he healed, whether or not he was able to fly. She agreed to return him to me when she had done all she could for him.

I contacted the raven telepathically to tell him he would be coming back here when his wing healed. Suddenly, my left wrist began to hurt, though nothing was wrong with it and I wasn't even using it at the time. This sensation is difficult to describe; it somehow didn't feel like my pain in that it was more distant and not really uncomfortable, but it was definitely noticeable.

Finally I remembered the raven's left wrist was injured. I had heard of animals being able to show their pain to people in this way and was sure that's what had happened. When I asked him about it, he gave me the pain again. I asked him to take it away and my wrist quit hurting. For some time after this, whenever I contacted him telepathically, the same thing happened. I believe he was using that method to show me I was connected with him. I planned to call him Magic, the key word for Raven in the Medicine Cards book. However, he later informed Lyn of the name he wanted us to use.

When Judy brought the raven back, I put him in a large cage in the house, where we had housed a rescue iguana for a while. He was unable to fly, but the wound had healed and the wing stayed in near-normal position, only drooping slightly. I didn't want to put him in a cage outside, thinking it would be unsafe for him, but he was clearly uncomfortable in the house. I began to think he might be happier, and relatively safe, in the wallaby pen. He would be unable to walk through the six-foot fences and there are fruit trees he could climb. I had some concerns about it so decided to ask Lyn to find out what he would prefer, as she did on August 19, 2002.

Lyn: Are you there, Raven?

Raven: Yes, Lyn, I've heard about you from the others. Thank you for talking with me. I'm a male and I'm still a young bird [other questions I had thought about]. Call me Ross. I am Ross. Ross! Ross! Ross!

Lyn: How did you injure your wing?

Ross: Playing around.

Lyn: Can you elaborate?

Ross: Swooping, diving around with others and I didn't see the tree branch coming. But I wanted to find a way to hook up with Adele and this did it. We have had many lives together. One was as eagles – mates. Adele wanted to be a human so she could help birds. Having been a bird many times before, she could see how much birds could use help from people.

Lyn: Would you rather live in the wallaby pen or the cage?

Ross: Wallaby pen.

Lyn: Do you realize that if you get into the fruit trees and flutter down, you may end up outside the pen and be vulnerable to cats, dogs, or whatever?

Ross: Yes, I understand. Tell Adele if I do that it is my choice and I am ready to go. She is not to worry or feel guilty.

Lyn: Adele wants to know if you understand this is the only place you can live. Without being able to fly, you will be quickly eaten.

Ross: Yes, I do realize that. In fact, that is why I asked Adele to keep me. I am not ready to go yet, even if I can't fly. Thank her for listening and asking to have me back. I owe her! I won't forget!

Lyn: Anything else you'd like to say, Ross?

Ross: Just many, many thanks to Adele and Don for what they do for us. I am here to bring magic to Adele. Things are happening and I am her newest guide!

Lyn: Thank you, Ross!

I put Ross in the wallaby pen after creating a ramp so he could climb to the lowest branch in the apple tree. We placed a platform for food and water dishes in a fork of the tree, offering him soggy dog food (dry pellets soaked in water) and occasionally scrambled emu eggs. Ross spent some time in his tree and some on the ground. He was clearly much happier there than in a cage in the house. He didn't want me to get close to him, so I respected his need for personal space. In his body as a wild raven, direct human contact was unpleasant for him, even though we clearly had a strong spiritual connection.

No matter what they know on a spirit level, animals (and humans, for that matter) must follow the patterns of the body they inhabit and the experiences they have in this life, at least to some degree. Ross eventually surprised us all and definitely improved my confidence with communicating telepathically.

I don't know why I am still amazed at how kind, forgiving, grateful, and understanding these beings are. They've reminded me many times to let go of any guilt, saying I did what I needed to do at the time, even if it wasn't enough to save them or keep them comfortable. They say they are following their own path, expressing an acceptance of the way things are; it's not my place to interfere with that. We can learn tremendously positive skills and attitudes for living rewarding, joyful, and peaceful lives from them.

Past life as an eagle, huh? With Ross for a mate? Sounds great to me! There are differences of opinion about this concept, even among people who believe in reincarnation. Some think we are never animals, with others believing animals don't reincarnate, but maintain their individuality as spirits on the Other Side. I definitely disagree with those who believe animals have no soul at all.

The explanation that works best for me is that we can choose to experience life in an animal body, either with the whole soul or a piece of it. Some people may never decide to experience animal lives, but I'm inclined to think we can place a part of our soul in an animal or even an insect or a rock, reintegrating it and its experiences into the whole after passing. The book *Star Origins, Talks With Animal Souls* by Jacquelin Smith contains information from different animals about this.

Too many animals have mentioned past lives with me for me to discredit it. Also, as with Ross, Nicki, some other animals, as well as some people, I immediately felt more of a bond when I met them than I can explain otherwise. Furthermore, they talk of lives in different kinds of bodies, leading me to believe souls are not limited in their choice of physical bodies.

CHAPTER 23

The next communication Lyn did for me was with an animal I had known and loved years earlier. When I was in my 30s and 40s, I lived in Portland, Oregon, where a friend (Deanna, the woman with whom I went to Yellowstone National Park) had a couple of rainbow boas (non-venomous snakes from South America) I enjoyed handling. I'd loved snakes as a child but hadn't kept any as an adult. Since I lived alone in a rented, two-bedroom duplex, I decided I could care for one of the big snakes. I found a breeder and bought Ara, a baby reticulated python (often shortened to retic). Her name came from a girl I had known who was killed at the age of 16 in a hit and run accident when she was jogging with a friend. I used the name Ara again years later for our female emu.

Ara (python) and I learned a lot together, becoming close friends after a period of adjustment for both of us. She was around three months old when I bought her and we were initially terrified of each other. She was only about three feet long and slender, as baby reticulated pythons are. However, Ara was quite aggressive, sometimes striking at me even when I walked past her cage, as well as when I reached toward her. Ara was going to become huge (females grow up to 30 feet long and can weigh 300 pounds). We were going to have to get along or I would be unable to keep her because she would be too dangerous.

Hitting solid objects when striking is a harmful and frequent problem for captive snakes, often causing injuries. They often develop a serious mouth infection involving the jawbone; tissue on the snout can also be damaged from rubbing against rough surfaces while trying to escape a cage. Healing these wounds is difficult, possibly requiring surgical scraping of bone under anesthesia. I never used wire for snake cages because of this danger and later used Plexiglas instead of glass. Because it is slightly more flexible than glass, injury is less likely to occur. Glass and wire are not strong enough to hold big snakes anyway; they are extremely powerful. Sand or gravel (or anything else hard or rough) as a substrate can also be a problem in reptile cages.

131

It sticks to food animals, scratching the mouth as they swallow. Snakes sometimes inadvertently hit rocks when they strike at prey, too.

Decorative cages can be quite attractive, but I've found them to be unsafe for animals and difficult to clean effectively, especially with large snakes. They urinate and defecate copious amounts; washing sand, gravel, or rocks is such a chore most people do it rarely. The animals can develop skin problems from prolonged contact with unclean material. Initially I used indoor/ outdoor carpet (the kind that looks like grass) on an easily-washed glass bottom. It gave them a padded surface to crawl on and I could take it out for cleaning. I kept extra pieces, changing them frequently. Later, when I built large wooden cages for big snakes, I put linoleum on cage floors with towels (removed during feeding times) for bedding and to absorb moisture.

Cloth bedding can be dangerous to snakes, especially during feeding time. If a tooth gets caught on a piece when they are swallowing a food animal, they may swallow the cloth as well, which must then be surgically removed from the stomach. They can even suffocate if the cloth is too big to swallow and they're unable to regurgitate it. Feeding two snakes in the same enclosure can cause a similar problem. If both grab the same prey animal, one snake may ingest the other, even if snakes are not their normal prey, because it is perceived as a continuation of the food animal.

Retics are notoriously aggressive, whereas Burmese pythons are known to be relatively easy to tame and keep in captivity. As I raised more snakes, I found they follow their own patterns as individuals, not necessarily exhibiting the expected behavior for the species. I later had other peaceful retics and a couple of unmanageable ones. And I had a Burmese python (Dawn) I got along with because I was careful, but she scared other people (with reason), especially when she weighed over a hundred pounds.

At first I fed Ara one juvenile rat per week, as suggested by the person who sold her to me. When I later asked a different reptile person about her striking at me, he suggested I feed her more. Duh! The poor little snake was simply hungry. Baby pythons

132

strike at nearly anything that moves because it is likely either a threat or food. Ara had both problems – I was scary and she needed more food. When I later raised two other retics from about 10 days of age, they were over 10 feet long and weighed more than 30 pounds when they were one year old. Ara was three months old, three feet long and probably didn't weigh more than half a pound. She didn't seem emaciated; she simply wasn't getting enough to eat for normal growth. No wonder she was striking at me! I never made the mistake of under-feeding snakes again.

After I began feeding Ara more frequently, I started slowly touching her before she finished digesting a meal, waiting till it was partially digested a few days after feeding. Through experience, I learned pythons have a period of time around feeding when they are more aggressive, sometimes seeming to experience a feeding frenzy similar to that described in sharks. They will swallow one food item and immediately strike again at something else, just in case it is more food. It takes a variable amount of time for them to feel full and stop feeding. Dawn's aggressive time could be up to a day; most are shorter than that. Ara's was only a few hours when she was little (much shorter when she was older), but I didn't want to handle her when she was still bloated from her meal. That can cause them to regurgitate; they are in a vulnerable state, unable to escape from danger as quickly, so unloading food when disturbed may save their life.

When Ara's swollen belly began to decrease in size after a meal, I would slowly and carefully pet her back (not her head) without picking her up. Later I would slip my hand under a coil, letting her crawl across it. I moved slowly, being careful to never make her feel threatened or trapped. When that kind of handling had worked well for a while, I began lifting a coil, still without picking her up or gripping any part of her body. Reaching for the head can be perceived as aggression, triggering a strike reflex, so I was always careful to avoid doing so.

Eventually I was able to pick Ara up completely. She would even coil around my body or drape around my neck without squeezing me. As long as I was careful to move slowly, let her know I was there before touching her, and remained calm and unafraid, she no longer struck at me. This was long before I was aware of our personal energy field, which they – and we – are able to feel. I now know I was projecting non-threatening energy to which Ara was responding calmly and without fear.

I also learned to make sure no part of my body, especially my hands, smelled like their food animals when I was handling snakes. That is one of the most unfailing ways to invite bites by a captive snake. When pythons are older, after they have gained some experience, they are better able to judge what is truly a threat or the right size and odor to be a meal for them, so their strike reflex is triggered less frequently and more appropriately. They have to swallow meals whole because their teeth and jaws are not built for chewing or tearing. Babies will try to eat food that is too large until they learn to judge more accurately. When I changed from one type of food to another (e.g.,from mice to rats, baby chicks, or rabbits), I usually had to rub a familiar item on the new one to transfer some scent. Otherwise the snakes did not recognize the new animal as food, and many wouldn't eat it. [Baby chicks were culls euthanized on a chicken farm.]

A hand is often perceived as a suitable size for food; big snakes may recognize it as small, warm, and living, without seeing it as part of a much larger human. If it smells like a rat, mouse, rabbit, or anything else they're used to eating and it moves past their head, it will be bitten if the snake is hungry. Pythons don't see details well, responding primarily to movement, scent, and temperature; striking is reflexive when conditions are right. When they are extremely hungry or in feeding mode, they may strike at any moving object, regardless of its appearance.

Another way to reduce the risk of accidental bites is to feed snakes only in one location. This can be a particular corner of the cage or in a special cage; handling the snake should not occur in that place. Snakes can learn food is only found there, so are less likely to bite somewhere else. They learn many other things as well, as I found out during the years I lived with them.

When I first began keeping snakes in Portland, I believed them to be so primitive they would only exhibit a narrow range of instinctive behaviors. Their brain is quite small and, anatomically, mostly limited to those areas associated with controlling bodily functions and instinct. However, I found they definitely learn from experience and also exhibit what I can only call emotions. They recognize individuals, both human and animal, respond in specific ways to different emotions in humans, experience a form of grieving, demonstrate curiosity, and even ask for help.

After Ara and I became friends, I bought Atlas, a male reticulated python. He was younger than Ara had been when she came to live with me, and more mellow from the beginning. I fed him more appropriately so he rarely struck at me after he passed the baby stage, and then only when I did something foolish. When Atlas was big enough to avoid being squashed by Ara, who was much bigger by then, I put them in the same large cage, separating them only at feeding time. Later, when they were both a lot bigger, I snake-proofed my rented duplex and left them out of cages. They usually coiled up together between feedings, even with access to several comfortable places in the house, clearly aware of each other and liking each other's company. Both were still too young for breeding and I observed no courtship behavior between them.

Snake-proofing a house for large, free-ranging pythons is a challenge. I nailed half-inch hardware cloth (galvanized wire mesh) over the windows, intending to avoid escapes if someone threw a rock through one while I was at work. I removed ceiling lights, replacing them with drum fixtures so snakes couldn't crawl on them, sending themselves and glass crashing to the floor. It is amazing what a 10-foot snake can reach when it is in climbing mode. From the floor they could slide over doorknobs, brace themselves on them and climb to the top of door frames. They easily pulled themselves to the highest level of brick and board bookshelves. From there they could reach light fixtures and would have tried to use them for the next purchase point. I also tacked heavy curtains over the windows so nobody could see inside. Curtain rods had to go because they were not strong enough to hold a climbing python. Anything electrical (e.g., heating pad or electric blanket controls, stereo system) had to be well-covered with plastic so snakes wouldn't be electrocuted if their urine touched it.

135

The bathroom was off-limits to snakes except when I was with them. I didn't trust them around the cabinets, shower rod, or toilet, even though the seat was always closed. They could have easily pushed it up, possibly even going down into the sewer system which was too cold for them to survive. The snakes loved soaking in a tub of warm water so they often took baths. It was especially important when they were getting ready to shed their skins. Portland has fairly high humidity, but the house was dry compared to a jungle. Shedding is a problem for snakes if the old skin becomes too dry. Then, rather than peeling off in one piece like pulling off a sock inside out, it begins to flake and peel in patches. They have eye caps, a scale of clear skin covering each eye, and can develop eye infections if those are not shed with the skin.

For a while I raised rats and mice for snake food in the utility room off the kitchen. Taking care of rodents and avoiding smelling like them was a challenge; frequent showers and clothing changes were necessary. I made a hardware cloth and burlap door to cover the large archway between the living room and kitchen to keep snakes out of the kitchen, farther from rodent cages. I also reduced heating bills by turning the thermostat much lower in the kitchen than in rooms where snakes lived.

The living room contained snake feeding cages, bookshelves, and two vinyl-covered beanbag chairs, but no cloth furniture for them to get into, tip over, or eliminate on. In one of the two bedrooms, I covered the hardwood floor with loose indoor/outdoor carpet, putting an electric blanket under it. I found a large wooden box that had been used to hold firewood, covered it with several layers of enamel paint, and placed it on the electric blanket in their bedroom. Ara and Atlas often slept in the woodbox together. I could lock them in that room when it was important to do so.

At first I was a bit nervous about sleeping in a room to which they had access, but I worked at it until it seemed perfectly normal. My first bed then was a sheet sewn into a tube and stuffed with washable pillows. Later I put a double mattress on the floor, covering it with plastic to protect it from snake urine. I kept the house at about 85 degrees, with some warmer areas for the snakes (e.g., their wood box on the electric blanket and feeding cages with heating pads under them). Pythons are tropical, refusing to eat and/or developing pneumonia if they're too cold. If they do eat when they're not warm enough, the food rots in the stomach rather than being digested and the snake will probably die. I mostly just wore a long T-shirt when I was home because the house was too hot for more clothes.

Ara was able to tell me what she wanted, even letting me know when something was wrong in the house. I'd be sitting on a beanbag reading and she would crawl into her feeding cage, which was open at the top. She'd stay there for a while and, if I didn't get the hint, she'd crawl out, slide across my lap, and go back to the feeding cage again. I tried to feed them at regular times and, when she was that big, I only fed her once a week. However, Ara knew better than I did when she was ready for food. I'd finally give up and feed her off-schedule.

Ara was a non-aggressive feeder by that time, with her feeding mode lasting only a couple of hours. I was offering them only pre-killed animals then. I had been told by the woman from whom I bought Ara that they need to kill live food as a way to release aggression. After I lived with them for a time, I learned snakes can be injured by prey animals and that it was actually fairly simple to teach them to accept dead food. That made life much easier for me (I no longer had to raise rodents), as well as safer for them. I kept their food in a freezer, simply thawing and warming it before feeding them. I also came to believe eating pre-killed animals makes them less likely to be aggressive, because they no longer need to strike at warm, moving objects, or kill their prey.

Some snakes (Dawn, for example) strike and encircle even dead animals, but Ara just moved toward them, poked around until she found a head and then peacefully swallowed her food. After one animal moved down to her stomach, she calmly found another and so forth. As babies they learn it is much more pleasant to swallow something head first because the legs fold back easier than they fold forward; swallowing fur with the grain instead of against it works better as well. I've seen little ones begin swallowing a mouse from the middle, which means the whole thing has to fold to go down, requiring much more stretching of mouth, jaws, and esophagus. Sometimes they have to give up, spit it out, and start over.

In order to switch Atlas and Ara from live to dead food, I held mice or rats by the tail with forceps or tongs to keep my hand out of the way, slowly moving the food past them. At first they struck and coiled around it as though they were killing it, engulfing and swallowing it when they realized it was dead. I only needed to do that for a short time before I could just dump an appropriate number of dead animals in their feeding spot. I always had to be careful about feeding Dawn (and a few others over the years); she was triggered to expect food by my approaching her cage. I couldn't allow any part of me to be inside her cage because Dawn would strike extremely fast and bite whatever she happened to hit first. She also coiled around it immediately; having her miss a rabbit and get my hand or arm could have been disastrous when she weighed more than I did. Snakes are so fast, by the time you know they're going to strike and coil, they already have.

I also had to be careful when cleaning Dawn's cage. Usually I just opened her door and stepped back, allowing her to crawl out onto the floor. Handling her there was relatively easy because she didn't expect food. I was still careful about moving around her, making sure a foot or hand didn't swing past her head and that she always knew I was there. From that location, I was even able to pick up part of her by interlacing my hands under her body, two or three feet below her head. She would curve partly around my hands, letting me drag her across the smooth wood floor without making her feel confined (she could easily slide over my hands). I did this both when she was in my way and to take her to the bathtub when she needed to soak after eliminating in her cage or when preparing to shed her skin.

Ara was so calm about feeding and so friendly toward me that I eventually fed her on the floor rather than in a cage. I'd sit near her and drop a dead rat close to her head without fear of her striking. She would pick it up calmly and deliberately, swallow it, and wait for the next one. It was an inefficient way to feed her because she was big enough to eat a lot of rats by then, but I enjoyed the contact with her.

When Ara and Atlas were living with me, I was struggling financially. I worked full time, but was still paying off student loans and using public transportation because I couldn't afford a car. Carrying live mice, rats, rabbits, and snakes on buses was somewhat nerve wracking, which is why I started raising their food animals. I don't think the bus company – or most of the passengers – would have approved if they knew what was in the boxes I carried. Some of the bus drivers suspected, but they looked the other way because I made sure nothing got loose. I also carried 50-pound bags of dog food home on the bus to feed the rats and mice. That was a chore!

I remember being especially careful with money for a month so I could save the $20 I needed to buy a bottle of powdered reptile vitamins. I filled gelatin capsules with the powder, then stuffed capsules into dead prey animals. I kept a record of all feedings for each animal (type, size, and number of food animals, and number of vitamin capsules), noting any medication given or problems observed. Sometimes one of the snakes would refuse food for a fairly long period of time without other symptoms. Snakes past the baby stage can go without eating for amazing lengths of time with no apparent damage, but it always bothered me a lot when one started fasting; I watched carefully for signs of weight loss or illness.

CHAPTER 24

One night when I was sleeping, Ara came to my bedroom, slid across me, and then, when I didn't get up, began pushing the mattress away from the wall by crawling between the two and flexing. She had done that before when she was trying to shed her skin (I got up, drew a warm bath, and helped her complete the process), but this was between sheds. It didn't take long for me to know something was bothering her, so I got up to investigate. Part of the door between the kitchen and living room was open and I was unable to find Atlas. In the kitchen I noticed a couple of cactus plants in the sink, having been pushed from the window ledge. It took a while to find Atlas because he was curled up under the stove. I had to move it to get him out and he was dangerously cold.

As soon as I picked Atlas up, he wrapped around me and hung on. I took him to bed with me and turned the electric blanket on; he stayed plastered to me the rest of the night. I was nearly hypothermic from trying to warm him, even with the blanket. In the morning when it was time to get ready for work, I had to pry his tail from around my neck. I put him into a cage with a heating pad under it and he was fine by the time I returned home.

Another time when Ara woke me up, Atlas, who was nine or ten feet long at the time, was crawling along the top of a bookshelf. The books were pushed against the wall and the snakes usually just crawled on the board in front, but he started moving behind them, pushing books onto the floor, causing vibrations that disturbed him and Ara. I wasn't careful to make sure Atlas knew I was there before I touched him, so he swung around and bit my hand. He immediately let go without coiling around my arm and then let me lift him off the shelf.

Blood was running down my hand, dripping onto the floor, but when I washed it off and the bleeding stopped, I only found a number of tiny holes. It healed quickly with no sign of infection, little bruising, and no soreness. I don't know if their bite wounds bleed more than expected from the tiny size of the holes because they have an anticoagulant in their saliva or because their teeth are so sharp. It is possible the teeth cut all blood vessels they contact rather than pushing most of them out of way, as hypodermic needles do. In any case, I've found python bites bleed freely for a while. Unless a person jerks away so teeth slash the skin, their bites seem to be no problem. I've never been bitten by one bigger than Atlas was, though. I heard of one man whose finger was amputated when a large python bit him. I suspect that was due to slashing rather than a clamping bite as from a dog. In any case, avoiding bites is preferable.

When Atlas was two years old, 11 feet long, and about 25 pounds (normal size for a male retic because they are shorter and slimmer than females), I noticed a bump on the back of his neck about a foot and a half from his head. I kept watching it, sometimes unable to see a lump. When I was sure it was there, I took him to a veterinary clinic a couple blocks from my home, the one in which I had worked for two years.

I still didn't have a car so I put Atlas on a sheet, tying it to form a bag around him. He was far too large to fit into a pillow case which I used to safely carry smaller snakes (they are escape artists, so boxes or crates don't work well). Then I put him in a cardboard box so no one could tell what I had and carried him to the clinic. We x-rayed Atlas, finding definite bone changes indicating deterioration of a few vertebrae. This veterinarian didn't take care of snakes; he found another one for me who did work with them and arranged an appointment for me. I took Atlas and the x-ray across Portland on buses to the other clinic, hoping they could help him. Twenty-five pounds doesn't seem like a lot to lift, but I only weighed about a hundred pounds. Carrying him to and from bus stops was definitely a chore for me!

The veterinarian thought the mass was consistent with osteomyelitis (bone infection) and suggested surgery to scrape away the infected bone. There was no guarantee it would help, but that was Atlas's only chance so I used a credit card to pay for it. I stayed with Atlas during the surgery, carrying him home on buses afterward.

At home I put Atlas in a warm cage, remaining with him till nearly dawn to make sure he had no breathing difficulties while recovering from the anesthetic. He was such a good patient! I had to give him antibiotic injections daily for two weeks and he never tried to bite me. Sometimes when I would reach in to give Atlas his injection, he would lift his head and rest it against my hand. I felt he was asking me for help and it was horrible to be unable to do more for him. Ara didn't like having him in a cage and would crawl in on top of him if I left the lid off. I was concerned she would hurt him, so had to push her away while I was caring for him.

I had Atlas x-rayed again after finishing the antibiotics and found the problem was worse. He essentially had a broken back, though the bones were not out of place yet and his spinal cord appeared to be unaffected at the time. I knew that could not last and it had to be painful. Spinal injuries in snakes are critically serious. Their skeletal system consists of skull, vertebrae, and ribs – and that's about all. I was sure he'd soon be paralyzed and decided the only fair response was to euthanize him.

Snakes grow lethargic and unaware when cold, so freezing them is a relatively humane way to kill them. I put Atlas on the kitchen floor in his sheet for several hours to cool him. When he was cold, nearly in a hibernating state, I put him in the freezer, one of the hardest things I've ever done.

Ara kept looking for Atlas. She would pace around the house, crawling in and out of the cage he had used while he was sick. This went on for quite some time before she finally gave up. If I had known about animal communication then, I'd have explained to her what had happened. She probably would have been less stressed.

After the experience with Atlas, I couldn't get past being concerned that Ara would become ill or injured. I knew I'd never be able to carry her to a clinic because she weighed at least 50 pounds by then. However, she was in great health and I loved living with her.

I had been collecting biology specimens for years, occasionally cleaning and articulating skeletons of different animals. It is amazing how many dead animals can be found without killing them. I had purchased a used freezer (the one I used to euthanize Atlas) to store snake food and specimens until I was ready to work on them. Six or eight months after Atlas died, I decided I wanted his skeleton and skin. To me, a dead body is like an old car or clothing we no longer want; the being who made the body important is not there and certainly no longer needs it.

I took Atlas's body out of the freezer to thaw. When it was ready, Deanna, the friend with whom I had worked on skeletons before, came over to help. We carefully skinned and eviscerated the body, putting some of his fascinating organs into formalin (diluted formaldehyde used as a preservative) in specimen jars. Some of the paired organs in snakes (e.g., lungs, kidneys, testes) are not side by side as ours are; instead, one is in front of the other, closer to the head. Also, these organs are long and slender rather than rounded. They have most of the same organs we have, but testes and penises (snakes have two) are internal. Dissection and skinning took several hours; Deanna left the rest to me.

I washed the skin, put it on towels in the attic, and covered the flesh side with borax and salt. The amount of fluid that soaked into the towels was astonishing! I knew the skin would be stiff and brittle, but didn't know any tanning procedures or have appropriate chemicals. After it dried somewhat, I tacked the edges to boards to prevent shrinking and curling. It took a long time to completely dry. Then I made a backboard for it out of half-inch hardware cloth covered with burlap, sewing the skin to the frame with strong fishing line. I still have it, all these years later. It's not nearly as pretty as when he was alive; the colors fade with death and time.

I had a large kettle for boiling bodies to clean bones, but it wasn't big enough to hold all of this body. Snake vertebrae fit together so well it would have been difficult, if not impossible, to cut it apart without damaging bones. By keeping the bulk of the body in an unheated container nearby, I was able to cook as much of one end as fit in the water-filled pot. After the flesh had cooked enough to allow me to remove a piece without losing ribs or vertebrae, I moved and cooked the next foot or so, continuing the process until all 11 feet had been separated into manageable chunks.

I put the partially cleaned sections on paper towels laid out on kitchen counters and shelves. Then, when it was all in manageable chunks of about 12 vertebrae and rib pairs, I began re-boiling and completely cleaning each section. Clean bones were laid out on numbered paper towels, keeping matching ribs and vertebrae in order. Neck and tail vertebrae are smaller, as are corresponding ribs, but the middle ones are so similar in size and shape, it would have been nearly impossible for me to put them in the right order otherwise.

When cleaning skeletons, I put ammonia and borax, which help soften and loosen cartilage, in the first cooking water. After the body has cooked long enough, I remove most of the soft tissue. Then I reheat bones in water containing dishwashing detergent to finalize cooking and remove grease from the bones. Using a small, dull knife, I scrape the last of the soft tissue off before putting bones in hydrogen peroxide to bleach. They come out beautifully white without being damaged. Chlorine causes bones to deteriorate to a chalky consistency, so is not good for bleaching them. Once bones are all cleaned, bleached, and dry, I begin gluing them back together.

I mounted Atlas's skeleton on a piece of wood paneling, making a frame out of 2" x 2" lumber to keep it from bending. I glued a section of 12 vertebrae and the corresponding ribs together and, when they were solid, added them to what I had done before on the wood paneling. It was shaped in a series of s-curves to shorten it from his 11-foot length, thus keeping the size of the paneling more manageable. The skeleton was held in place with wire threaded through holes drilled in the board.

Cleaning the skull was difficult and tedious because bones in snake skulls are loosely articulated, necessary for their method of feeding. The lower jaws are connected to the skull and to each other with elastic ligaments. They use these bones individually to walk food into the mouth, with one side at a time moving forward, hooking the prey with recurved teeth, and pulling it into the mouth. When part of it reaches the esophagus, muscles there constrict around the food, using a form of peristalsis (rhythmic movements of the digestive tract) to move it down to the stomach.

145

The bones of the skull also spread during feeding, allowing the snake to swallow prey larger than its head. They have a lot of teeth which easily fall out during cooking and cleaning. The objective is to remove as much soft tissue as possible without the whole thing falling apart and then having to figure out how to put it back together. Lots of time and patience are required.

I used to keep track of the hours spent cleaning and articulating skeletons, but I don't remember the end result with Atlas. I do remember he had more than 400 vertebrae and 400 pairs of ribs. Some neck and tail vertebrae do not have ribs. I kept his skeleton on my wall for quite a few years, giving it to a friend when I moved to Montana in 1992.

After it dried, I hung Atlas's skin on the wall above my bookshelves. I didn't think Ara would recognize it because their vision is limited, and I was sure it couldn't still smell like Atlas after all the borax, salt, and time. I had also washed the skin with detergent before drying it. However, shortly after I put it up, Ara climbed to the top of the bookshelves and reached up to touch the skin with her tongue. She had never shown any interest in that wall before. I immediately took the skin down and put it back in the attic, feeling sad that she was still looking for Atlas a year or more after his death.

CHAPTER 25

When Ara was 16 feet long and weighed over 70 pounds, I decided I could no longer care for her well. She needed much bigger food animals (rabbits rather than rats) and I still didn't have a car. I continued to be concerned she would develop physical problems with which I'd be unable to help her physically or financially. I couldn't give her injections because she was too strong nor could I carry her at all, even to get her out to a car if I had one. So I gave her to the person from whom I'd purchased her. This woman had many large reptiles and was set up to care for them well. She also had help when she needed it and a lot of knowledge about reptiles.

I sent Ara's wood box with her so she would have something familiar and hoped for the best. I was afraid to go see her, because I knew if she wrapped herself around me I'd be unable to leave her. Sadly, about a year later Ara contracted a parasitic infection. The protozoan, *Entamoeba histolitica*, causes severe diarrhea and frequently death. Ara did not survive the illness. I was deeply saddened when I heard about her death sometime after the fact, but have since learned to believe she chose to leave her body at that time.

Around 20 years later, I found myself thinking about Ara a lot, sometimes even feeling her presence over my right shoulder. I had no specific questions, but felt Ara was trying to tell me something so again I asked Lyn for help. The communication of September 4, 2002, is as follows:

Lyn: Ara, are you there?

Ara: Oh, yes, Lyn. I am here.

Lyn: Adele has been aware of your presence, especially lately, and she thinks of you often. She wonders what you have on your mind to tell her.

Ara: Oh, many things! Many things! We need her. We

need her to be able to hear us! We all want to help her with her animal communication skills. We (all animal species) are so excited to have people awake and know that we speak! Adele has always spoken with her heart and listened, too. But now we need her to do it on a conscious level. Soon we will need as many communicators as we can have for the changes that are to come.

This is not to scare anyone, but to say that now is the time for people to awaken and be aware of all of us. This mass awareness will be what saves us and our planet.

Adele, I am always with you. I have never stopped loving you. I have no regret or remorse in my heart about our parting. It was the right thing for you to do at the right time. The other woman took good care of me. I decided to leave my body because I wanted to be of more help to you. By being in spirit form, I could be in many places at once and one of them was to be where you were.

My only sorrow has been that you were not always aware of my presence and my love. But that time is gone now. Ross [raven] has heralded the coming of magic from the unseen world into your life. The magic is awareness of the unseen – such as me and many others. Just the fact that you wanted to hear from me speaks volumes about your new awareness. How thrilled I am! Lyn will tell you! I wanted to speak last night, even before Lyn could listen. I am sorry if my presence is so overwhelming as to disturb either of you. It is my joy and enthusiasm that you both are feeling, which I can't always restrain.

It is my hope that whatever fears you have, Adele, (or guilt feelings) that you will put them aside – forever – and just let us enjoy being together. Still! Always! For that is my joy – to know that you now know what has been in my heart. Never did I blame you or feel you should have, or could have, done differently. Leaving was my choice and not caused by you. I am still with you. My love has always been there, guiding you and supporting you. This is true of all those you have loved who have gone on. They are still with you!

Yes, many of us have come back in other forms to lead other lives, but understand – we can be in many places at once. Time is not as you know it or see it. Part of me is elsewhere on earth continuing to support the new consciousness on this planet. Part of me always stays with you to support you and watch over you. No, I'm not always a snake. I have been an osprey, a giraffe, an elephant, a skunk, a gazelle, a sea creature or two or three.

I have not wanted to be a human and live without my awareness. Those of you who have chosen to be human, meaning living in the dark, have my utmost love and respect. It is a great path to be able to find your way out of the darkness into the light and to lead others. All of you who are listening to other species now are leaders and therefore being supported by us who wish the love changes to occur on this planet now.

If you could see the bigger picture, you would know my thrill and feel the lump in my throat as I watch the light slowly come to each of you. That is the wellspring of my joy and enthusiasm.

Dear Adele, ask me any and all things and I will answer! As will we all! Just ask! We are here for you and you are doing great things for all of us!

Lovingly, Ara

Well, that brought tears to my eyes, both when Lyn read it to me and again as I typed it. These wonderful beings seem to have a much higher opinion of me than I have of myself. I am ashamed to admit I had forgotten much of what Ara said until I typed it several years later, and feel I've wasted a lot of time being too involved in superficial daily activities. I am so humbled by the greatness of these beings and so blessed to have had contact with them.

It was a while before I started learning much about raising consciousness on our planet, which Ara mentioned, and other changes that are happening. The Kryon books, by Lee Carroll, tell a lot about it, as do some other people and books listed in the References section. My superficial understanding is that energy frequencies on our planet are changing, resulting in less support for the duality of third dimension. This means it is becoming much easier for us to raise our consciousness to the level of greater awareness, compassion, and the spiritual knowledge of unconditional love.

Changes in the magnetic grid of the planet, which are being observed by scientists, are involved. According to Kryon, this is at least partly due to the Harmonic Convergence in August 1987. My understanding of this is that many humans worldwide meditated at the same time, sending thoughts of love and peace around the planet. Because of their actions, we avoided some form of the predicted imminent destruction, giving ourselves and our planet another chance to continue and improve.

I'm sure my change from atheism to my current form of spiritualism occurred because it became easier for me to raise my consciousness and awareness, or perhaps more difficult to avoid doing so, beginning in the 1990s and strengthening after 2000. The changes are still occurring, seemingly faster all the time. Even the apparent chaos and upheavals are part of it. Those who are still unaware do feel and react to the energy changes, but often still with fear and anger rather than awe, compassion, and love.

However, I believe conditions on the planet are improving. More and more people every day become aware of the power of love and gratitude over fear and anger. Negatives, duality, ideas of good and bad, are less and less supported so maintaining them becomes more difficult. We are approaching a time when this understanding will be nearly universal, as we reach a tipping point. I love being part of it! What an amazing time to live!

Lyn talked with Ara again on October 25, 2002.

Lyn: Hi, Ara! How are you doing?

Ara: Just fine, Lyn. I'm keeping Adele company.

Lyn: That's what she says. She wanted to know if you had anything on your mind to say to her.

Ara: Well, you might tell her that she doesn't have to work as hard as she thinks to listen to us. She can listen as she works, which is what she does anyway, but it's scary for her to have to think about trying. She really doesn't have to think or meditate. She just needs to take what comes to her mind as she goes through the day. She already does this, but she needs to do it with greater awareness now. Tell her it is not about finding quiet time to meditate. It is simply listening to us as she goes through her day – and I hope she believes me when I say she already does this. More awareness is all she needs! We so want to help her step into her new awareness! She is so close!

Much Love, Adele! Trust us! Ara

Their patience with me is humbling. I had forgotten this communication as well. And I notice Ara is hanging over my shoulder again. Bless her for her love and kindness!

CHAPTER 26

On the same day as Ara's second communication, Lyn talked with Ross, my raven friend, again.

Lyn: Good morning, Ross!

Ross: Good morning, Lyn! I'm a happy bird! - happy bird! - happy bird! (Singing)

Lyn: How is it in the wallaby pen?

Ross: Just great! Love those little dears! Tails look like big worms!

Lyn: I see! Adele wanted me to tell you that this winter when it gets cold, you can go in the wallaby shed to stay warm. There are heat lamps in there. She knows you might not be as warm with your injured wing.

Ross: Thank you, darlin,' and thank her, too. She's a love – pure LOVE! I will enjoy some heat this winter, I am sure. So kind of her to pass that on.

Lyn: Adele says the magpies come and visit a lot.

Ross: Some visit! They help themselves to my food!

Lyn: Do they bother you, Ross?

Ross: Naw, they are good sorts, for the most part. I can handle them, I can!

Lyn: Do you like the food?

Ross: Yes, it is decent, but I dream of a good juicy worm, I do. Those wallaby tails set my mouth to watering.

Lyn: I'll tell Adele. Maybe she can find you a few worms.

Ross: What a dear! What a dear!

Lyn: Anything else you need or would like to say?

Ross: Life is grand! Life is grand! With a worm or two. (Singing) Maybe some ripe tree fruit or a berry. Always loved a berry or two in the fall. Miss those! Balanced is fine, but fruit is so divine! (Singing) Thank the dear sweet lady and lad that take care of me. Life is a whole lot easier now than when I was wild. I miss the swoopin' and soarin.' But this is a sweet life, my gal! Take care! And thanks!

I had found it funny to watch Ross with the wallabies. He would sneak up on them and peck at their fully-furred tails. He didn't hurt them at all, but it did startle them. They'd turn to look at him, sometimes bouncing off a few steps. I bought some bait nightcrawlers for him and made sure he had fruit in addition to his dog food and scrambled eggs.

Not long after this communication, Ross began climbing to the top of the apple tree. There were no longer any leaves on the branches so he was able to perch where his wings were unobstructed. He would hold them out away from his body, sometimes flapping them slowly while grasping the branch with his feet. I was concerned he might let go and glide over the fence. His wing still drooped a bit because that joint was unable to fold completely. Though he was probably able to keep himself from falling, I doubted he would be able to fly up once he was on the ground, or have sufficient control to stay safely airborne and avoid obstacles.

Then one morning Ross was gone. I can't see the whole wallaby pen from the kitchen window, but with vegetation quite low because it was nearly winter, I could tell he wasn't in any of his usual places. A magpie suddenly flew over and landed in a lilac bush right next to the kitchen windows, a place I hadn't seen them before. When I asked the magpie if he knew where Ross was, he flew around the house and to the north. He passed another window, so I knew he wasn't flying above the house, also unusual. I followed him to the other end of the house and looked out the bedroom window. The magpie was calling and hopping around in one of the pine trees. I kept looking up as far up into the tree as I could from inside until finally I spotted black tail feathers. Sure enough, Ross was sitting on a limb high in the tree.

I thanked the magpie and then ran to fix Ross some food, quickly putting it under the tree for him. I told Ross he could come down to eat and, if he stayed around where I could see him, I would continue to provide food. If he let me catch him, I would put him back in the wallaby pen where he would be safer. I assumed he had used wind to lift him over the house to the pine tree; there were no limbs near the ground he could have climbed to get that high.

Later I went out to try to catch him when I saw him on the ground. I could tell it was Ross because of his droopy wing. He squirted through the fence into the neighbor's pasture to avoid me, but was apparently unable to take off from the ground and fly. I decided he knew what he was doing and gave up on catching him. I kept watching for him and, every time I tried to contact him telepathically, my wrist would hurt for a moment. I felt he was fine, doing what he chose to do.

Then one morning a few days later Ross was back in the apple tree inside the wallaby pen. I believe he was showing me he could now get around well enough so I should quit worrying. He was gone again later and I only saw him once more, sitting on a brush pile in a neighbor's pasture. Once in a while for a couple months my wrist would hurt for a moment; each time I sent thanks to Ross for checking in. I still feel him occasionally, but wrist pain no longer accompanies the contact. He apparently decided I was aware enough to no longer need that reminder. I have no idea whether he is still in the raven body or has moved on but, like Ara (python), he is still around.

CHAPTER 27

By this time I was taking the Hypnotherapy as a Career classes, becoming more enthusiastic the more I learned. I was surprised and thrilled to find, during the first class, that we were to start hypnotizing anyone who would agree to it. In the beginning, of course, my classmates and I just taught people some relaxation techniques without any therapy.

I also took the first term of the Adult Education self-hypnosis classes, one of the requirements for Hypnotherapist certification. There were four terms in the advanced classes, each involving 50 hours of lectures plus several books, videotapes, and lots of practice time. Clinical Hypnotherapist certification required an additional 100 hours of internship during which we worked with clients. We only went to class one evening per week until we reached internship, so it took a couple years to finish the training. It was time well spent!

We learned in the self-hypnosis classes, and in more depth in the advanced classes, that we are unable to hurt anyone with these techniques and this form of therapy. The worst we could do was leave clients as they were before we worked with them. People will follow their own morals and values, no matter how hypnotized they are. They also will accept only those suggestions that make sense and seem beneficial to them. Brainwashing, which can alter behavior in harmful ways, requires much more forceful techniques and the intention to overcome barriers without consideration for the health and well-being of the individual. Fortunately most hypnotherapists, like most psychologists, choose to help, not abuse, those with whom they work.

A hypnotherapist acts as a guide to help clients uncover old, outdated, unhelpful ideas and beliefs, and also as a teacher to help them better understand their own mind and learn helpful ways of using the power they have. This type of therapy gets to the root of problems because it involves direct contact with the subconscious mind, which holds all our memories and is where our emotions come from. When primarily dealing with the conscious mind, it takes much longer to find and correct misperceptions and harmful beliefs we acquired in the past, if it can be done at all.

Because the subconscious mind directs the Autonomic Nervous System which controls our bodily functions, people can also learn through hypnosis to improve their health and physical comfort. This is not a replacement for professional medical care by any means, but it can be used to greatly enhance the beneficial effects of it and the comfort of those who require surgery or are injured, ill, or experiencing childbirth.

I have seen so many amazing transformations in people from this therapy. The books *Me, Myself and Mind* by Roberta Swartz and *Medical Hypnotherapy* by Tim Simmerman describe these therapy methods and results in much greater depth. I underwent six or seven private therapy sessions with Roberta, accomplishing my own improvements and making me even more enthusiastic about becoming a Clinical Hypnotherapist. I still intended to mainly use the information for family and friends who were interested, and would have been happy just gaining the knowledge myself without directly using it for others.

With my new and deeper understanding of psychology, I began to develop some major changes in perspective. It helped me feel far more empowered and positive. I learned I could improve my emotional and physical life with some short-term therapy followed by using self-hypnosis techniques. It also gave me a better understanding of people's feelings and behavior, making it easier to let go of anger toward those I felt were wrong, especially when I thought they were harming others. It would be great if children were taught some of what I learned about the subconscious mind and how to use their own subconscious and conscious mind in beneficial ways. I'm sure parts of my life would have been better if I'd known about it earlier.

I had thought I was fairly non-judgmental, with a bottom-line belief that each person should be treated according to his/her behavior rather than based on any group or association, such as race, nationality, sexual orientation, gender, religious affiliation, education, social status. Through these classes, I became more understanding even of those who do cause what I perceived to be harm. This doesn't mean anyone should be allowed to continue hurting others without consequences; I definitely think those people need to be stopped. However, they wouldn't be violent or unkind unless they had been damaged in some way first. Hating them or treating them with anger and disrespect is behaving much the same as they do.

Child abusers were abused children, a generalization of a much broader concept, but a kind and more accurate way of thinking of those who cause harm. Hatred or anger toward another person damages the hater more than the hated, without improving anything. Later I learned an even better and more accurate way of thinking about those who hurt others. As with much of what we learn, my growth happened in steps and is still continuing, for which I am most grateful!

CHAPTER 28

In May 2003, Jeri Ryan, Ph.D., an internationally renowned animal communicator, facilitated an Intermediate Animal Communication seminar near Butte, Montana. Valerie and I both attended, as did Lyn, who graciously let Val and me stay in her Butte home that weekend. The seminar was great for all of us. It further increased my knowledge and confidence, although I still have no plans for using it professionally. I'm happy to refer people to Lyn or other practitioners for animal communication.

The students (14 of us from Montana and Idaho) were asked to bring pictures of some of our companion animals to the seminar. In the exercises, of which there were quite a few, we would look at a photo of someone else's pet and ask it for specific information. We were told only the age, name, and gender of the animal, with most of them remaining at home rather than being there with us. We were to write what we received from the animal and then read it to the group. The person who knew the animal would provide feedback which frequently became validation for each of us.

During the exercises, I was mainly aware of mental pictures (usually snapshots instead of videos) and feelings to which I assigned words. I don't recognize as much information as Lyn does, nor do I usually hear a voice, but with all my animal guides' (and Lyn's) help and encouragement, I began receiving a lot more. The most important factor in this is learning to keep the conscious mind out of the way, thus remaining open to what comes in without judgment or expectation. Practice improves skills and confidence.

The results from a couple exercises greatly surprised me. I picked the photo of a cat in Idaho for an assignment of asking the animal to show or tell us something about its environment. Respect toward the animal is important, so I explained to the cat that I was a student and asked for her help first. I looked at the photo, then closed my eyes and relaxed as I asked the cat to tell me something about her surroundings.

Suddenly I became aware of a strong smell of plastic.

161

Nothing had changed in the room nor had I smelled it there before. When I asked the cat to take the smell away, helping me know I had received it from her, it disappeared. The smell reappeared and again disappeared at my request. I felt the cat would like to smell more fresh air.

Then I felt a sudden sharp pain next to a fingernail, as though a splinter had just poked it. I hadn't moved my hand and it was nowhere near anything sharp. Again I asked the cat to take the pain away, bring it back, and take it away again – and the same thing happened as with the plastic smell.

When we reported information we had received, the woman with whom the cat lived said she was a stray the woman had picked up in an effort to help her. The cat was living in her basement because there was nowhere else she could safely stay. To my amazement, the cat's bed was on top of a plastic tarp. No one else in the room had smelled plastic. The woman knew nothing about a sore paw, but said she would check the cat's toes when she got home. I didn't hear back about that, but believe the cat either had a problem or was sending me pain as a teaching aid.

I asked the same question of a dog I believed was in another room inside the house where we were, and received a strong scent of damp earth. The dog also took it away and re-created it at my request. I found out later the dog was outside at the time and it had been raining. Again, no windows or doors had been opened; no one else in the room had smelled damp earth.

I have never been able to intentionally create odors with my imagination, even though I have tried to recall the scent of lilacs (my favorite flower) when I was in hypnosis, just as a fun exercise. It would never have occurred to me that I might receive a scent from an animal telepathically. Of course, after reflection, the sense of smell is important to cats and dogs and would be a logical way for them to describe a place. I am convinced the odors came from them telepathically.

In an exercise with another dog, I received a mental image of him wearing a red collar running in a field near a man who had a large beard. I found out during the validation part of the exercise that the dog always wears a red collar, not visible in the photo I saw, and his favorite human is a man with a large beard (he did not attend the workshop nor was he in the photo I saw).

After all this, I had to believe I can send and receive telepathic messages from animals; they had proven it to my satisfaction. I just needed to be more consciously aware of receiving their messages, incorporating that awareness into my daily life, as Ara and Ross said.

Before learning about telepathic communication, I had thought I could tell what animals wanted or felt because I cared, studied the nature of their kind, and paid attention to their body language. I learned what I could about the natural behaviors of the species involved so I could determine how to handle them in ways appropriate for that type of animal or that individual.

Snakes are a good example of this. The more I lived with them and thought about their normal environment and what it would take for them to live there, the more aware I was of their needs, capabilities, and limits. I read and thought about their social behavior (e.g., did that type of animal live alone or in a group; were babies cared for by parents or on their own from birth; what type of predators did they have; what behavior was necessary for them to obtain food?) Now I believe they were telling me about their needs and personalities as well and I was interpreting this information as my own thoughts.

Not long after the seminar, Judy, the main wildlife rehabilitator in our valley, asked me to find out from Jenny, her Welsh Corgi, what her favorite new toy was. Judy only told me it was an unusual animal. This is what Lyn calls going out on a limb, something that doesn't always work well. I didn't really want to do it, thinking I might make a fool of myself or prove to Judy that telepathic communication wasn't possible. But when I asked Jenny about her toy, I saw what looked like a hedgehog. I didn't want to tell Judy because I thought it had to be wrong, so I didn't call her back. She called me a couple of days later, pinning me down. Of course Jenny's new toy was a plastic hedgehog.

I've also talked with some of the horses, mules, and dogs who live with a neighbor. She calls if one seems to be having a problem, asking me to talk with the animal. Usually I can tell her where it hurts (e.g., left side of the neck up by the head) or what it is experiencing (e.g., upset stomach, sore mouth, disturbed by something in the environment). I always suggest a veterinarian or horse chiropractor if it seems serious or doesn't start improving quickly. The animal doesn't necessarily know what it needs or how to fix it, nor do I.

CHAPTER 29

By the end of 2003, I was beginning to work with a few hypnotherapy clients, even though I hadn't yet received even Master Hypnotist certification (that happened in February 2004). I didn't charge, of course, and clients knew I was still a student. I asked Roberta for suggestions and people experienced good results. I became a Hypnotherapist in June of 2004, and a Clinical Hypnotherapist that October, after 100 hours of internship. My initial plan of working only with family and friends had changed so I worked with others, too. I was seldom busy, which was fine with me. Most of my clients came through word of mouth, important in a rural area like ours. After certification, I worked on a sliding fee scale, sometimes seeing clients who were unable to pay me at all. I enjoyed the work, feeling especially rewarded when people were successful in achieving their goals.

I find it interesting that I even taught a few classes, including one term of Adult Education self-hypnosis classes. When I first attended self-hypnosis classes, I was anxious about being asked a question in class or to be a demonstration subject. I sat at the back of the room, hoping to remain invisible. At the first advanced class, we were asked to stand in front of the other students (12 women at that time with nine of us completing the course) to state our names and the reason we wanted to become hypnotherapists. I was shaky and extremely uncomfortable, even though it only took about a minute.

Roberta later said I should think about teaching and I thought, *Yeah, right! I don't think so.* I had always been uncomfortable in groups and never wanted to be the center of attention. Talking with people one-on-one was fine; I did not want to talk around more people than that, even when they were friends or family, let alone stand in front of a group and lecture.

Toward the end of 2003, a neighbor asked if I would talk about hypnosis to a group of students in a psychology class in Missoula. I said it sounded like fun. When I told Roberta, she laughed and said, "Did I just hear that come out of your mouth?" It didn't surprise her, but it certainly surprised me when I stopped to think about it.

I hadn't worked specifically to eliminate my fear of public speaking, but hypnotherapy often has a snowball effect. Relieving some issues seems to transfer to others. I'm sure my self-confidence was improving, giving me much less fear of being judged. I also love the subject and believe self-hypnosis can greatly help many people. I did fine with the psychology class after the first few seconds, talking for nearly an hour and a half. The instructor even asked me to come back a couple more times. I also gave a self-hypnosis behavior modification seminar in Portland once. I still prefer working with individuals and mostly avoid groups, but am glad I can present information I'm enthusiastic about to groups if the occasion arises.

Around this time an aunt loaned me two of Sylvia Browne's books. I was instantly fascinated. I bought more of them and have enjoyed each one, though I don't have all the many books she wrote. Ms. Browne was a hypnotist and psychic who died in 2013. She was often on the Montel Williams TV show, giving participants messages from the Other Side and answering questions using her psychic abilities. As a hypnotist, she worked with clients to help them heal trauma left over from past lives, among other things. She researched all the past life regressions she shared in her books, not using them unless she was able to find some corroboration.

Sylvia believed we go to the Other Side after death, analyze what we learned from that lifetime, and then create a blueprint for the next lifetime if we choose to experience one. Browne's descriptions of the Other Side make sense to me and, though I don't know whether she is right in all details, thinking about her beliefs is much more peaceful, compassionate, and empowering than any others I'd heard or read about at that time. It sounds like a great place in which spirits reconnect, learn, and live as they choose. Animals are there as well, a belief that also appeals to me.

Michael Newton's books *Destiny of Souls* and *Journey of Souls* are similar, with more depth and science. He, too, is a hypnotherapist who has systematically studied life on the Other

Side through hypnosis with hundreds of people. His book *Life Between Lives: Hypnotherapy for Spiritual Regression* describes his techniques in detail.

The *Conversations With God* books by Neale Donald Walsch contain much information along these lines, too, and greatly help many people. I completed a webinar (online seminar) with the author sometime later, which was well worthwhile. These three authors (as well as Rosemary Altea) present a much different picture of a god than any I had been exposed to before. Their books are always uplifting and empowering, radiating love, peace, kindness, and hope. All of the beliefs expressed fit well with what animals say to Lyn and other animal communicators, further validating the information for me.

CHAPTER 30

Now we come to stories about our wallabies, the next recipients of Lyn's communications for me. Sometime in the late 1990s, an acquaintance of ours (I'll call him John) told us about some wallabies he had seen when he went on a trip. I'd always been fascinated by kangaroos and other marsupials so I kept thinking about living with a few of them, eventually doing Internet research on breeders and care. I learned they have no problem living in climates like ours as long as they have access to a dry, heated shed in winter and shade in summer. I also learned they require fences at least 6 feet tall, woven wire with small holes because babies are quite small, and plenty of room to run. We could provide all that. Don called appropriate state officials to determine whether permits were required for keeping wallabies and was told there were no Montana laws regulating them at all. This has since changed so permits are now required, a policy I think is good.

When I called a wallaby breeder in Bend, Oregon, the woman told me she was bottle-feeding a baby who was ready to go to another home. Joeys are often removed from the mother's pouch before they are weaned or begin climbing out and hopping around. This seems the easiest way to tame them enough to be pets. I arranged to meet the people in Lewiston, Idaho, in the spring of 2001 to pick up our first little wallaby.

While I was preparing to go get him, an all-day round trip from here, Nicki became quite upset because he could tell I was leaving for more than a short time. He kept trying to talk me into staying home.

He said, (vocally, not telepathically), "You gonna take a shower?"

"No, Nicki. I already took a shower."

"Nicki wanna take a shower."

"I don't have time right now. You can have a shower later."

"You wanna take a nap?"

"No, Nicki. I have to go get a little wallaby. I'll be home later."

When I was making the last trip out to the truck, Nicki said, in a quiet, wistful voice, "I wish she's tired!" He would much rather I take a nap than leave the house.

The trip was a peaceful, beautiful drive over Lolo pass which winds through mountains next to a river. I easily found the people at a truck stop near Lewiston. I had taken a cat carrier for the baby, not wanting a wallaby hopping around in the cab of my pickup while I was driving.

The baby had been born in late 2000, so was not yet weaned. After taking him from his mom, the breeders kept him in a pouch made of quilted cloth, with a strap to go over a shoulder so he could be carried in safety and comfort. He was fully-furred and able to get out of the pouch to hop around, though he only weighed about four pounds. The woman gave me a couple of pouches she had made, some powdered macropod (kangaroo) milk replacer, and pelleted feed made for captive kangaroos and related species.

The little guy did fine, seeming quite calm about the carrier and a new person. I named him Casey on the way home as we began to get to know each other. I had purchased a playpen (the one I now use for baby deer) and more kangaroo milk replacer before going to pick him up. Casey had been away from his mom for a while, so was quite acclimated to people, and he ate well for me from his bottle. I was surprised at the shape of the nipple. It is long, slender, and soft, less than half as big around as a pencil, much different from those I use for other animals. Wallaby mouths and tongues are relatively long and narrow; the nipple went clear to the back of Casey's tongue. This is apparently similar to their mother's anatomy when they are in her pouch. The milk slowly ran out of the nipple and down his throat with little sucking.

At first Casey did well in the house. I covered the playpen so he couldn't jump out and hurt himself. He easily hopped in and out of the pouch which I hung in a corner of the playpen. He would literally do a somersault into the pouch – diving in headfirst and flipping over with his head out one side of the opening, his tail out the other, and his belly facing up. Casey pulled his head and tail all the way inside to sleep. I was able to carry the pouch around with the strap slung over my shoulder. He weaned himself in a couple weeks, just eating the pelleted feed and some fruits and vegetables.

We began letting Casey loose in the house, which worked okay for a while. Then he started hopping on chairs (and urinating and defecating on them, incidentally). One day I caught him on the counter in the bathroom. He would also hop onto the seat of Don's recliner and then onto the back of the chair. I was concerned about his jumping down onto hard, smooth tile floors from those heights. When he began chewing on paper and, much worse, electrical cords, we put him in the big outside pen. I felt he would be safer there, probably much happier as well with more room to move and better footing.

Casey loved playing in his yard! It was easy to build up speed on the ground with such good traction. He'd tear around the whole area, seeming to gain speed and length of leap as he went, apparently just for the joy of moving. He quickly located his shed where we put dishes for water and food pellets, and the vegetation in the enclosure was safe for him to eat. We buy their pellets from a nice family in Missouri, at first delivered by UPS, later having a pallet of it shipped to us by truck about once a year.

I kept two baby elk for short periods of time that year, putting them in with Casey because we hadn't yet prepared the deer pen. They got along fine and provided him with some company. I also raised two fawns who lived in the wallaby pen until they were big enough for the back yard.

Wallabies grow quite fast so Casey was a lot bigger by fall. His coat was thick and I noticed he was much more active during cool mornings and evenings than hot summer days. We put a heat lamp and a heated water bucket in his shed, covering the floor with clean hay for bedding. Casey seemed comfortable hopping around in snow, even when the temperature was as low as 0 degrees Fahrenheit. Sometimes he lifted one of his feet as though it was cold enough to hurt, but he went back in the shed to get warm when it bothered him too much.

I dislike keeping animals without others of their kind, so the next spring (2002) I found another breeder who had a baby wallaby to sell. Don brought her home from Salem, Oregon, and

I named her Cricket. She had been away from her mother for a much shorter period of time than Casey and was a few weeks older than he was when we bought him. Consequently Cricket was never comfortable being handled, not letting us close to her until near her death many years later. She weaned herself soon after she came here so we put her outside with Casey.

Casey and Cricket were Bennett's or red-necked wallabies. Wallabies are closely related to kangaroos and similar anatomically, socially, and behaviorally, though quite a bit smaller. They are marsupials, meaning their young are born as embryos after a short gestation period, finishing their development in a pouch containing mammary glands on the mother's belly. Because they are so tiny, it is difficult to know whether a baby is in the pouch until it is big enough to make a visible bulge.

When we put Cricket outside with Casey, they immediately bonded, hopping around the pen together, one in front of the other, as fast as they could go. We could see them easily from kitchen windows, and always enjoyed watching them. That winter I saw them mating; by early the next spring (2003) I could tell they had a baby. I had known it was possible before that but, without catching Cricket and examining her pouch (upsetting to her and dangerous for her and the baby), I had to wait until the pouch bulged and wiggled enough to see it before I knew for sure.

The babies are born after slightly more than 20 days' gestation. They are about the size of a jellybean, looking embryonic with blurred features, blunted extremities, eyes closed, and thin, pink skin with no fur. They appear far less mature than newborn mice, also hairless and with eyes closed. The front legs are more developed than back ones, completely opposite of more mature wallabies, because newborns need the front ones for climbing from the birth opening to the pouch. They attach themselves to a teat for several months, mostly just eating, sleeping, and growing. The mother opens the pouch with her front feet, licking the baby and her pouch to keep them clean. The oil from her skin inside the pouch protects the delicate baby skin.

When baby red-necked wallabies are about 154 days old (around five months), their eyes open. Not long after that fur begins to grow, first on the head and later on the body. By six months of age they start popping their little heads out of the pouch, initially for short periods of time. They act like it's a bit scary out in the big world, but later appear more curious, leaving their head out longer to look around. From 230 to 275 days of age, they hop in and out of the pouch, developing coordination and learning to get around by jumping.

I was able to watch this baby one of the first times he was out on the ground. He fell over a couple times because his legs didn't work together in a coordinated way; he was only able to manage a couple of hops before diving back into the safety of Cricket's pouch. Later he would hop in circles around Cricket, staying close to her. He became more adventurous as his motor skills improved, and he spent more time out of the pouch. After a while, when I was able to see him clearly enough to identify him as a male, we named him Toby.

When Toby was bigger than Casey had been when we got him, Don and I caught him and brought him into the house. I didn't feel good about it, but we had told John, the man who had first talked to us about keeping wallabies, he could have Toby. We didn't want a mob of wallabies nor were we planning to sell them, and we didn't want to have to worry about inbreeding or fighting. I believed Toby needed to have some human contact before we transferred him to John. He did okay in the playpen and artificial pouch, but was never tame like Casey was. In fact, with good reason, he acted more like Cricket had.

John had a lot of different kinds of animals; we had transferred some that needed a home to him in the past. We knew he loved them because we had seen him interact with our animals, but we hadn't been to his home, 60 to 70 miles from us. He had seen our wallaby enclosure and facilities and said he could easily create something similar for Toby at his place. John also had plans to find a companion wallaby for him.

Sonny (not his real name), a young friend of John's, came with him to pick Toby up. I put him in a pillowcase so he couldn't escape in the car. Sonny held Toby on his lap all the way home – and ended up with wallaby urine in his lap as well.

Jordan was born that winter and, as with Toby, we didn't know of her existence till spring (2004). She was less adventuresome than Toby, so was older before she began exploring farther away from Cricket. That could be due to different genders, or Jordan may simply have a more wary personality, or Cricket may have been more nervous because we had kidnapped her first baby. We planned to let John take Jordan and perhaps trade her to a wallaby breeder for a female baby unrelated to Toby. Fortunately that didn't happen and we never touched Jordan till we evacuated wallabies and emus due to forest fire proximity in the summer of 2012.

CHAPTER 31

In June of 2004, Don and I went to John's place to attend Sonny's high school graduation. It was the first time we had seen Toby since he left our place a year before. We found him in a dark basement pen only about twice as big as Nicki's and Simon's cages. The floor was linoleum and cement, with no hay in the enclosure for bedding. Toby had a few toys, but no sunlight, fresh air, or anything interesting to see. Don and I were horrified! We both knew we couldn't allow that to continue, but didn't say anything to John at the time.

On the way home we talked about the steps we would need to take before bringing Toby home. Another pen and shed would have to be built because he and Casey were both adult males who could seriously hurt each other due to male rivalry. In the wild they can get away from each other more easily than in pens, so their battles establish dominance usually without major injuries. When fighting, they face each other, use their small front legs to reach for the other's face and kick at bellies with their powerful hind legs. Their middle toe is quite large with a thick, strong nail, so they can cause damage, especially in the unnatural conditions of captivity.

I wanted Toby's pen to share a fence with Cricket and Casey's so they could interact through the wire and see each other during the adjustment period. The new pen could be relatively small (though it is bigger than his basement cage), because I didn't intend to leave Toby in it long. We decided to have Toby and Casey neutered, both to eliminate or decrease aggression by lowering testosterone levels, and to prevent more babies. We had planned to keep only two wallabies and now we had four to care for until they finished their life span. Neither of us wanted to let any more of them go somewhere else. By this time I was seriously questioning the morality of keeping any exotics in captivity.

Don started building Toby's fence and shed the next day. We called John to tell him what we were planning. He knew he'd made a mistake and that we were not happy about it, but he really didn't want to give Toby back. No money or paperwork had been involved when he took Toby. We were prepared to take a deputy sheriff and a veterinarian (Linda) there to get him if it became necessary. I bought an injectable tranquilizer from Linda because I thought the trip home might be stressful for Toby. I planned to transport him in a dog carrier in the back seat of Don's extended-cab pickup, where I could watch him.

I called Lyn about Toby before we brought him home, asking her to talk with him, Cricket, and Casey, which she did on June 5, 2003.

Lyn: Toby? Cricket, Casey, I'm having trouble connecting to Toby.

Toby: Hi, Lyn.

Lyn: Hi, Toby. Are you hiding?

Toby: Yes! I'm so afraid!

Lyn: Of what?

Toby: That the man will give me to some other people before Adele comes. He brought some to see me last week and I went ballistic! Didn't want them to think I was a nice little pet.

Lyn: My animal guides and I will send you lots of love to keep you safe until she comes. The important thing to do is visualize Adele coming to get you and forget the rest.

Toby: Okay. Thanks, Lyn! She's really coming?

Lyn: Yes, she is. She's set her mind to it

Toby: Oh, I've been calling to her or anyone who might hear me. I just didn't think I could stay on Earth if I have to remain here. I didn't have any purpose – nothing to do. I knew I'd have to leave my body soon if things didn't change.

Lyn: (I talked to Cricket and Casey. They were glad Toby was coming back. Casey was fine with the neutering as I outlined it, as Adele told it to me. He said he'd be willing to do that to keep the family together. Cricket was excited to have Toby coming back. She seemed full of motherly concern and was happy to hear that her new little baby would be staying permanently.

I then explained to Toby that Adele planned to come on Sunday and that he would be given a tranquilizer so he could sleep on the two-hour ride home. He would be in a dog crate on the back seat of the pickup. He was fine with that and also the shed with a door to go outside when he got home. I explained the neutering procedure and he felt like Casey – small price to pay to keep the family together.

All three wondered if Adele was feeling guilty and hoped she wouldn't. They were just overjoyed that Toby was coming home, so thankful that Adele and Don would do this for Toby. They wanted Adele to know that they knew she thought she was doing the right thing when she gave Toby away.

Toby was really hungry for a banana. I got the feeling that was because his potassium levels were low. When asked what he wanted to do most, he replied:)

Toby: Look at the sky and the stars. I really have missed seeing stars.

Lyn: (When I asked if there was anything else, they all said to tell Adele they call themselves "witch doctors," in the good sense. They are the reason she can give the birds she cares for so much help. They are constantly helping her care for the birds. They have a lot of magic!

Then they all wanted me to be sure to tell Adele how much they appreciate what she has done and is doing for them. They are thrilled that they can all live together. Cricket said to tell Adele that the adjustment would be easy, but not necessarily fast. All were excited to think Toby would be coming home soon.)

Here's another communication that brings tears to my eyes, especially the part about Toby wanting to see the stars. When I read this communication to John on the phone, he quit arguing about letting us take Toby. He said Toby had hopped frantically around his cage when someone went to see him, even hitting the wire and cement walls. I had thought John might try to hide Toby so we couldn't take him; Toby's fears indicated he had been considering that course of action. (Lyn did not know this till after the communication.)

I felt sorry Toby had been trying to reach me for so long and I hadn't noticed. I normally don't go to graduations or other group events, even for relatives who live in Hamilton. Somehow I felt we really should go to this one; I'm now sure it was because I did finally hear and respond to Toby. Usually when an animal leaves me for whatever reason, I think of it once in a while and do my best to assume it is fine. Apparently that attitude covered up Toby's messages to me that he was far from fine.

A week after we first saw Toby at John's place, Don and I went back to get him. John caught him so I could quickly inject the tranquilizer, then put him in the dog crate, and carried him out of the pen. We left him in the dark basement for a short time, allowing the tranquilizer to take effect before moving him. I expected Toby to lie down and sleep due to the medication, but he stood in the carrier, riding peacefully all the way home. Every time I looked over my shoulder to see how he was, Toby was looking out through the small bars toward the windshield, as though he wanted to see everything he had been missing for so long. He was less than a foot from me, a distance I had thought would be too close for his comfort, but Toby never showed any anxiety after we put him in the truck.

When we arrived home, Don and I carried the crate to the new shed and opened it. I thought Toby would be nervous about being in the open because of all the different stimuli he'd been unable to experience for a year. However, he spent most of his time outside the shed and I frequently saw him standing tall with his nose pointed toward the sky. I had the feeling he was taking in all the fresh smells he could. He and Casey had a few confrontations through the wire so we put a piece of plywood between them to prevent injuries. Toby could still poke his nose through to see and smell the others, but they were no longer able to kick each other.

CHAPTER 32

We had Casey neutered first. The procedure went okay, though it was quite stressful for Linda and me, and especially for Casey, of course. Linda had never taken care of wallabies. Ours are the only ones in the area, as far as I know, and they hadn't needed medical care before. She researched the castration surgery, and appropriate anesthesthetics and dosages for them. We got more of the injectable tranquilizer, Don was able to catch Casey, I gave him an injection, we put him in the dog carrier and then, half an hour later, drove to the veterinary clinic.

Don grabbed Casey by the base of his tail (a safe way to pick up a wallaby for the animal and the handler), pulling him partly out of the carrier so Linda could inject him with a drug that would put him nearly to sleep. I sat with him in a quiet, dark room until the medication took effect. We then lifted him onto the surgery table, placing a mask over his face to deliver gas anesthesia. I have a difficult time doing anything to animals and birds that scares them. The thought of being cornered, trapped, or forced bothers me a lot, so to do that to animals even for what I believe to be good reason disturbs me. Once Casey was asleep, I felt much better. He was no longer scared and I trusted Linda to do the surgical procedure safely.

Because the drug we used can cause hallucinations when awakening from anesthesia, we gave Casey another injection of the tranquilizer after the surgery to reduce those effects. At home, Don and I carried the crate into their shed, opening the door for Casey to get out when he chose. He was still groggy, but awake enough to leave the carrier. He was clumsy for a while so I sat in the hay, watching to make sure he remained safe. Eventually the anesthesia and tranquilizer wore off enough so I felt comfortable leaving him alone.

I asked Lyn to talk with Casey the next day because I felt he was still quite distressed and I was concerned he might remove his sutures.

Lyn: Casey, how are you feeling?

Casey: I feel horrible! Gosh, what hit me? I can't think, I'm dizzy, hurts to walk, I've lost my appetite, just feel terrible!

Lyn: Some of that is from the medicine they gave you to put you to sleep and the pain is from the incision.

Casey: Am I dying?

Lyn: No, Adele says you are fine. Some of these side effects are worse on some than on others. I am sorry I didn't tell you about them. I probably should have so you would have been prepared, but I honestly didn't think of it. Adele says if you can eat willows they will help reduce the pain.

Casey: I tried. Made me sick to my stomach.

Lyn: Adele also needs to check you to make sure there is no infection and that it keeps on healing well. She says she can't touch you anymore.

Casey: I don't want it to happen again.

Lyn: Well, it won't unless you chew on the stitches and pull them out. Then you would be put to sleep again to have the stitches put back in.

Casey: You mean if I pull out the stitches, I'll have to go through it all again?

Lyn: Yes, except for removal of the testicles.

Casey: Man, oh, man! I am not going to touch those stitches. No way!

Lyn: Good. Adele and the vet did everything to make it as easy as possible. Without all they did it would be much worse.

Casey: Guess I know that. Just didn't think I'd feel so bad.

Lyn: I will do 15 minutes of healing for you with gemstones to help bring your body back into balance and unblock the pain so it can be released.

Casey: Thanks, Lyn. I'll be grateful for that.

Lyn: Adele asked if there was anything you wanted?

Casey: There is. No pain, a clear head, and a good appetite.

Lyn: Hopefully the gemstones will help those things.

Casey: Thanks, Lyn!

Lyn then did 15 minutes of healing with gemstones. She had been studying the energy of stones for some time, using them for herself and her animal companions as well as those with whom she communicates professionally. She has found them to be helpful and, though I knew nothing about them, I trust her judgment and the reactions of the animals. Lyn wrote, "Casey was going 'Wow!' a lot at the end. Said he felt much better."

Later that day Lyn wrote in an email, "Adele said Casey was nibbling on grass and willows, looking more perky. She wants me to use the stones Saturday and Monday mornings. She will call me Monday evening to let me know how Casey is doing. They sewed him up with cat gut so by the fifth day (Monday) he may experience itching from the suture material. I am to tell him about that and that Adele is only giving him what he needs to bring his body back into balance now. I will find stones to help with trust and forgiveness, too. He still won't let Adele get close to him."

Casey healed fine so two weeks later we went through the same procedure with Toby. He responded well and recovered more quickly than Casey had. On July 11, Lyn talked with Toby and Casey to find out whether they were ready to have direct access to each other.

Casey: Hi, Lyn. We are doing fine.

Toby: It was not as bad as Casey said. I'm sure glad he talked with me, but it sounded so bad I was scared.

Casey: Didn't mean to scare him. Just didn't want him to be surprised and shocked like I was.

Lyn: Glad it went so well! How are you two feeling about coming together in the big pen?

Toby: Fine.

Casey: Give me a couple more weeks. The hormones are lessening and would probably be all right now, but a couple more weeks would be safer. Takes a while for the testosterone to leave the body.

About a week after this communication, I removed the plywood from the fence so Toby and Casey could interact more. They showed less aggression and were completely healed so a week later we cut a hole in the fence between the pens. Toby went into the bigger enclosure where everyone got along fine. He and Casey did exhibit some of the male aggressive behavior, but appeared more to be playing than seriously fighting. They never did hurt each other. All of them learned to go through the opening in the fence and Toby especially liked to spend time in his shed.

Some marsupials practice delayed implantation or development, which means females can have a fertilized egg in the uterus for months before it actually begins to grow. In this way, they can have a baby in the pouch and a fertilized egg in the uterus at the same time. The egg begins to develop some time after the older baby is weaned. Because of this I thought it was possible Cricket could have another baby after Jordan was on her own. I observed mating behavior between Casey and Cricket at times even after the surgery, but thankfully no new baby developed from earlier matings.

Sometime later, I bought the book *The Crystal Bible* by Judy Hall and began the fun practice of collecting gemstones. Because different materials vibrate at different frequencies, I was able to believe these stones could actually have specific and varied energetic effects on us and animals. I decided if the only benefit of them is to focus intentions and thus create a placebo effect, they are of value. Most of those I have are small enough to carry in a pocket, something I often enjoy doing.

With what I've learned since that time about energy and varying frequencies, I now believe rocks do have individual characteristics that create more than a placebo effect. I am often able to feel their energy, further reinforcing my beliefs. Though I didn't think it would happen, I can now even see auras around many living things, primarily trees and insects, so I'm more aware of energy as the basis for everything.

CHAPTER 33

The next animal communications with Lyn involved our emus, who had been with us for several years. We bought Aten, the male, in 1998 when he was only two or three days old, and another slightly older baby from a different breeder. Aten (pronounced AH-ten) is named after an ancient Egyptian sun god. I named the bigger one Zebanessa after a huge Burmese python (275 pounds) I had known a number of years before.

We kept the little emus in the house for a while, which was both entertaining and challenging. They managed fairly well on tile, but I also put down large pieces of outdoor carpeting (the kind that looks like grass) on the floors so they could run without slipping. They, like all birds I have known, defecate frequently, so I made an extra set of carpet pieces. I'd hang some over the fence to wash them with the hose, using others in the house while the first set dried. Fortunately that type of carpet dries quickly.

Baby emus are so cute and silly! Aten and Zeb would flop down on their bellies, looking like they'd collapsed, then jump into the air and land running. One would go one way and the other went the other way. Then they'd run toward each other, screech to a halt, stand up tall, and fluff up their downy feathers. They'd dodge around each other, continuing the routine till both were panting. Sometimes when they flopped down they'd kick only one leg, rolling completely over before jumping up to run. They often sat by our feet to nap during the day, though they had a bed with a heat lamp in a corner where they slept at night.

Linda came over to sex them when they were two or three weeks old (it has to be done with a superficial internal exam, slightly opening the cloaca to determine whether a phallus is present). She found they were male and female, with names connected to the right gender. By the time Aten and Zeb were two months old, they were tall enough to pull things off the kitchen counters so we put them outside. They no longer had enough room to run in the house anyway, because they were too big. We put them into what is now their winter pen, after building a small shed for them to sleep in with heat lamps for cold weather.

We had three free-ranging peacocks at that time, one male and two females. They were beautiful and interesting, but caused some problems with neighbors, who justifiably resented their habit of sitting on cars, scratching paint and defecating there as well as in carports or on decks. The male peacock seemed to be confused about appropriate mates, even with two peahens available to him. He killed two of a neighbor's ducks by trying to mate with them. They were unable to escape from him when he stood on their backs in mating position. Because of his weight and/or differences in anatomy and behavior, their backs were broken.

Shortly after we put Aten and Zeb outside, the peacock apparently decided young emus looked like big, beautiful peahens. No matter what I did to drive him away, he kept flying into their pen, chasing the terrified babies. I don't think he intended to harm them, any more than he wanted to kill the ducks, but they interpreted his following them as a threat. Their only defense was to panic and run. Unfortunately the pen was too small for them to get far enough away from the peacock. Older emus will kick or stomp on animals that seem threatening, especially if they have a nest or babies, or feel they can't escape by running.

The situation was frustrating for me because I couldn't protect the babies by keeping the peacock out of their pen. I'd chase him out and check later, only to find him terrorizing them again. The babies became seriously stressed, panting and frantic every time I went out. I kept hoping he'd give up and quit. Then I noticed Zebanessa was bleeding from the mouth. I was unable to find any wounds on her neck and thought she may have ruptured some blood vessels in her trachea from high blood pressure or breathing so hard. Later I saw blood on Aten's mouth, too. Don was expecting a group of people for a business meeting at our house, not one of my favorite things (major understatement). I was trying to get ready for them, but seriously distracted by my concern for the baby emus.

If we could have caught the peacock, I'd have found a different home for him. However he flew well, even sleeping high in huge cottonwood trees. Now I would request Lyn's assistance in asking him to stop, and/or ask him myself, but this happened before I knew about animal communication. The only two choices I could think of at the time were to let him kill the little emus or have Don shoot the peacock. I chose the latter action.

Sadly, it wasn't soon enough because Zeb bled to death from a damaged trachea. Apparently she had repeatedly hit her neck against something when trying to escape from the peacock. I held her as she died, feeling sorry I hadn't protected her. Aten and I both missed her a lot. She was such a sweet bird, even friendlier than Aten was at the time.

When Aten was a year old, we saw an ad for an emu in the free section of the classifieds in our local newspaper so we brought Ara home. (Recycled names can be confusing; however, I certainly didn't expect python Ara to reappear in my life). She was about Aten's age, but had been raised outside as livestock so was less friendly. He still comes up to us for hugs, even letting most other people pet him if they wait quietly for him to approach them. We are able to handle both of them easily when necessary, even herding them into their enclosure when it is important to keep them out of the back yard.

Aten and Ara bonded almost immediately and have remained friends and mates for years. They love to run in the early morning or late evening when the temperature is cool, and we enjoy watching them. Even now, when they're a lot older, they still occasionally run, making me laugh as they kick and play like goofy kids.

CHAPTER 34

We usually find eggs not long after Ara lays them, even though she covers them with grass and pine needles, or hay when she lays in their shed. They are a deep green color and quite large, containing about two cups of liquid. I usually drain them, giving the egg shells as gifts because they are so beautiful and unusual. However, in July 2004, the summer we brought Toby (wallaby) home from John's place, the birds were successful at keeping their nest hidden until they had a clutch of 11 eggs. We found them when Aten began sitting on the nest. I didn't have the heart to take them away from him, so decided to let him hatch their eggs.

In emu families, the father handles parenting duties, incubating eggs and even caring for babies. The female lays an egg about every three days during the breeding time, covering them with grasses and, in our yard, ponderosa pine needles. When the nest contains at least 10 eggs, the father takes over all responsibilities for eggs and babies.

Aten was such a good dad! He did not leave his nest the whole seven weeks, even to eat or drink. He would stand up once in a while, turn his eggs, change position, and carefully sit on them again. I was worried because he was in the sun part of each day, with temperatures often in the 90s. Their feathers are quite dark, so I could imagine the heat he was absorbing. I took food and water out to him, trying to talk him into eating and drinking. I even squirted water in his mouth with a syringe, but he didn't want it. Lyn talked with him on July 11, 2004.

Lyn: Hi, Aten! How is the egg sitting going?

Aten: Very well, Lyn! I know Adele is concerned about me and just reassure her that I am fine. I will not jeopardize my health for the eggs. If I did that, the eggs wouldn't survive. They need me on them most of the time. If I were to drink then I would be getting us too much. Actually, I'm in a hibernation-like state. My whole body has changed and is suspended fromnormal operation.

Everything is on hold and outside conditions are not that threatening. You see, I know how to think so as to make this possible. It is how we procreate and survive, so it doesn't seem strange or difficult to us. Please tell Adele that I am fine and that she could do the same thing, if the need ever arose. What you think you can do is what you can do!

I finally believed Aten knew what he was doing so just checked on him several times daily. Because their eggs are such a dark color, they would quickly absorb heat from the sun. I suspect if they were exposed to it for more than a few minutes they would become hot enough to kill the babies. As usual, animal behavior makes sense when I learn enough about the circumstances and their requirements.

A concept I learned in hypnotherapy classes is: What the mind can imagine, the mind can create. Aten knows this without going to school, as I suppose most non-human beings do. He simply put it in a different way. And of course some enlightened and highly motivated humans have meditated for long periods of time with little or no food or liquids. Once again, I am unable to argue with what the animals say.

After about seven weeks incubation, the babies started hatching on August 10, with the last two appearing on the 11th. Nine of the 11 eggs hatched and all babies were fine. Then I had to decide what to do with them. We did not want a whole flock of emus, having no intention of selling them or using them for breeding. Kris, one of my hypnotherapy classmates and her friend Cindy have a few acres of land in this valley, and a number of different animals. They had met Aten and Ara and thought they would like to raise a few baby emus. Two weeks later we found a couple who wanted two of them for pets; they also seemed to be kind and knowledgeable people who asked a lot of questions about their care.

I wanted to be sure this was okay with Aten and Ara before I agreed to anything, so I asked Lyn to talk with them. She connected with Aten on August 12, 2004. Aten was protective around his babies, showing more aggression for a while. He always let me approach him and the little ones, though.

Lyn: Good morning, Aten. Are you free to talk?

Aten: Yes, Lyn, I am! Have you seen our babies?

Lyn: Adele told me about them. Your ability to just sit on those eggs for seven weeks truly amazes me!

Aten: Me, too. I leave my body, you know. I hover around above and just keep enough contact to stay in touch. I can quickly jump back in if danger threatens or if I need to move around on the eggs. Being out of body really makes it easier; I can move and focus on other things. Being unable to move around would be the worst part, if I couldn't do that. People can do this, too, and even do it when they sleep. The difference between sleep and what I did was intention and awareness.

Lyn: I believe you, Aten. It was quite impressive. It will remain with us, now that we have seen it done. Thank you!

Adele would like to know if you will be okay if Kris and Cindy take two or three of your chicks in a few days. Adele says they must go soon, if they are to go, so they can adjust well to their new home. Kris and Cindy live north of you and have other animals – horses, sheep, pigs, dogs, a cockatiel. Adele feels they have the land and knowledge to take good care of emus. She intends that you should raise and keep the rest. How do you feel about this?

Aten: Sure. The other people can have some, too. They are welcome to them. Raising the rest I can do, but it will be a big job.

Lyn: Adele plans to help and will start feeding them chick food in a day or two, when they are old enough to eat it.

Aten: That will be great! She is a big help. We need her. Can't think there is much more to do. She keeps us clean and well watered. All will be fine.

Lyn: Are you going to start eating again soon?

Aten: Yes, I already have. My appetite is slowly coming back. The more I move around in my body, the more energy it will require. Food intake is regulated a lot by body movement. No movement – no requirement. Tell her not to worry. I will be careful with the chicks. I have heard her concerns about my weakness hurting them. I am being careful. Eating too much too soon would cause more problems. The digestive system starts slowly. Too much food and my system would rebel.

Lyn, tell Adele that keeping two of the babies is all I really care to do. If she finds homes for the rest, that would be fine. If she can't, that is fine, too. Just so she knows how we feel!

Lyn: I'll tell her! Thanks, Aten. Blessings on you and your new chicks!

Aten did appear to be out of his body much of the time when he was sitting on eggs, though I hadn't thought about it before. Even when I pushed my hand under him to try to count eggs, he mostly ignored me. When someone else approached him with me, he would stretch his neck out against the ground, trying to hide himself in the long grass. If they were too close, he seemed anxious, so I told people to stay away from him, rarely letting anyone in the pasture. Aten did start eating well again, with no apparent ill effects from his long fast.

The babies were so cute! Aten stayed with them on the nest for a couple days while they finished absorbing their yolk sac and learned to walk. When they are nearly ready to hatch, the remainder of the egg yolk moves into the abdomen and the opening closes, similar to closing the umbilical opening in mammal babies. Their bellies are quite distended at this time and they are too weak and uncoordinated to stand long or walk well. They don't start eating and drinking till they are several days old, at which time, because they are precocial birds, they are even able to run and play.

Ara seemed interested in the babies, but on August 12 I found one with a wound on its face. I think Ara must have pecked at the baby. I brought it and another one (for company) into the house for a few days till the wound healed, then gave them back to Aten. I was concerned that Ara might hurt more of them, so I moved Aten and the babies into their winter pen, leaving Ara in the big enclosure. It was easier to give the babies access to emu starter pellets there anyway. Also, like tiny fawns, they could slip through fences around the bigger area and I was afraid some might get away from Aten.

None of the babies Aten incubated had any physical problems, often a concern with artificially hatched emus. I've been told by breeders that hatching nine out of 11 eggs is a good percentage, especially when there are no deformities. Again I was shown how Mother Nature does it best. All our research and equipment couldn't compete with Aten's innate knowledge and abilities. I now believe his telepathic connection to his babies, before and after hatching, was a factor in his success.

Kris and Cindy took three chicks and the other people took two, leaving Aten with four to raise. He was attentive and protective, doing a great job as a dad. The babies would crawl under him to keep warm and, when they were too big to fit, would still stick their heads into his soft, thick feathers. They were too small to survive the cold without him. In Australia they would have hatched at the beginning of the warm season instead of shortly before our winter.

CHAPTER 35

In October 2004, when Ara began to limp, I noticed the big middle toe on one foot was swollen. She let me examine it, but I was unable to find any kind of wound or other injury. The toe felt hot to me, so I thought she might have an infected puncture wound. Linda was also unable to see any reason for the swelling when she came to check Ara. She suggested we give her antibiotics for a possible abscess. The toe could have been fractured, but the bone did not appear to be out of place, and splinting it would be nearly impossible. We put Ara in Toby's pen (with the hole in the fence blocked to keep wallabies out), giving me easier access to her than the big yard.

Ara was good about squatting down, resting on her chest and folded legs in normal sleeping position, to allow me to handle her, even though she usually prefers I don't get close enough to touch her. She knew I was trying to help, so she even let me put pills in her mouth, swallowing them without complaint. If she hadn't cooperated, I'd have been unable to medicate her. She weighs more than I do and is much stronger, not to mention faster. Both she and Aten allowed Linda to vaccinate them a few times for various Clostridium organisms, but otherwise Ara seldom lets anyone touch her at all.

When it was time for vaccinations, I put Ara and Aten in their winter pen. Linda and I went in, with Linda staying back until I had calmed and stopped one of the birds. Linda then walked up behind them and injected the vaccine. Ara usually squatted down for the procedure, so I'd kneel beside her, petting her to distract her from the prick of the needle.

Don could probably control them with strength, but I'm so glad we didn't have to fight with them! I probably would have avoided the vaccinations if that was the case, because I so dislike forcing and upsetting them. After they had annual vaccinations for several years, I stopped giving them boosters, thinking they probably had developed enough immunity to last longer.

The first antibiotic for Ara's toe didn't seem to help. She appeared to feel more pain after receiving it for a few days, so

I got a different antibiotic and called Lyn to talk with Ara. The communication was on October 26, 2004, when the babies were about two months old and still in the winter pen with Aten.

> Ara: Lyn, I'm here. No, we haven't talked before but I know you. You have spoken to Aten. He suggested I have Adele call you. My foot is painful. I stepped on something sharp. It could use some soaking in hot water. The antibiotics will help, but soaking may help things to open and drain. Tell Adele I'll be good – 20 minutes, four times a day – until the swelling and heat subside. It's not getting better. I told Aten I was concerned.

> Lyn: How do you feel about your baby emus?

> Ara: They aren't mine. They belong to Aten – the big fool! He should have let them go and paid more attention to me. Kids are such a nuisance. He actually likes them! Harumph! I know they will grow up, but if they weren't here, he could pay me more attention. I need his attention and he's too busy! Yes, I do feel rejected! Certainly not cherished or loved!

> Lyn: Is there anything Adele can do for you? She wants you to feel happy.

> Ara: She's a dear! I know! No. There's nothing like an old fool – and that's Aten right now. Serves him right! Hope he is happy! I'm not speaking to him! (much) Adele is great and thank her for thinking of me and for having you talk with me. It's a help. It really is!

Ara and Aten were normally mating at that time of year; I'm sure she was missing his companionship. They are usually near each other even in the bigger area, sleeping close together regardless of the time of year. I knew she wasn't happy, but didn't know what to do other than keep her away from the youngsters till they were big enough to move out of her way if she became aggressive with them.

I tried soaking Ara's foot, but it didn't work well and she soon quit allowing me to do it. I think it hurt worse to be handled or maybe even to have it in warm water. Linda told me I could give Ara acetaminophen for the pain, which I did. The caplets stuck in her mouth, so I slipped them into gelatin capsules which were easier for her to swallow. Her foot began to improve and, several days before I was supposed to quit giving her the antibiotics, she refused to take any more pills. I'm sure she knew she'd had enough, choosing to finish healing on her own. A few days later I let her out of Toby's pen and she completely recovered.

Ara had let me help her with another health issue a couple years before this, when she developed a swelling in the soft area between the two halves of her lower jaw. There was no redness or apparent pain and it had appeared within a couple of days. Of course I called Linda, who suggested I massage the area, saying the golf-ball-sized lump was probably due to a plugged saliva duct. Ara let me do that until the swelling suddenly began to decrease. When she opened her mouth and shook her head, I saw flecks of pellet feed on her tongue. I believe it had somehow gotten into the duct, preventing saliva from being released into her mouth. Fortunately, there was no infection and Ara was fine.

When the emu babies were big enough, I let them out into the main enclosure. They and Aten and Ara would run around, appearing to be chasing each other. They behaved the same as Aten and Zeb had in the house – flopping down, jumping up, confronting each other with head high and feathers flared, swerving around, and running again. Ara seemed to tolerate them better when Aten wasn't required to watch them so closely. She didn't lay eggs again until well after the babies were a year old, though.

Aten and Ara absolutely love to be showered with a hose during the summer. They lie down in a puddle, letting me spray their backs as they roll back and forth in the water. Resting on their lower legs, they stand half-way up to shake. This is worse than being too close to a dog when it comes out of a creek, so I quickly learned to stand behind or in front rather than beside them, keeping away from the majority of the flying droplets and mud. They frequently get into a large wading pool when we fill it with water, though they barely fit in it together. The babies liked being sprayed by the hose, too. It was great fun to have all six birds lying in a row, loving their shower!

By the time the four babies were nearly a year old, they were almost as big as Aten and Ara. The became quite unmanageable, the equivalent of rowdy teenagers. We hadn't handled them since they were tiny so they weren't tame like Aten and Ara are. I knew we would be unable to treat them medically and was even concerned they might bump me if I was in their way when they were running. They didn't herd well at all and the winter pen would have been far too small for that many emus, both because of their need for exercise and because they were becoming aggressive toward each other. This isn't a problem when they have enough room to escape an aggressor. The babies would also have been impossible around fawns; they were even beginning to annoy Aten and Ara.

We gave them to our friends Joe and Clover Quinn, who own and operate the Wild Rose Emu Ranch a few miles from here. They are kind people who take excellent care of their birds. Because Ara lays so many eggs and lays for a while during two different times each year (most only have one laying season per year), they thought our babies would be good to add to their breeding stock.

Ours were three females and a male. We were able to identify gender by then because they were beginning to vocalize. The females create a wonderful drumming sound using a large air sack at the base of the neck. Males make more of a growling or burping noise. I love listening to Ara and, though the sound doesn't seem loud, it can be heard in the house even when doors and windows are closed. I often thank Ara for drumming, and a badly injured fawn told Lyn her drumming was soothing for him while he was healing.

Moving the birds was a challenge, but Clover and Joe are adept at it, with a trailer modified for transporting emus safely. We locked Aten and Ara in their winter pen and somehow managed to herd the young ones into the deer pen. Unfortunately three of them began picking on the fourth while we were in the house. He finally jumped over the short gate into the back yard, but not before he had cut a foot and scraped his neck trying to escape over the six-foot fence. We were finally able to separate the youngsters by using the chain link pen and Toby's pen after blocking the wallabies' entrance hole, preventing further aggression.

Joe quickly caught all of them in their small enclosures, directing each to a separate space in the trailer. Emus have small wings they are barely able to move. People who raise the birds as livestock stand behind them, holding the wings to force them to walk where they need to go. Clover said the scared one, the little male, didn't settle down for a couple of weeks, but he was fine after that. Life became much more peaceful here for us and for Aten and Ara.

CHAPTER 36

In March 2005, Toby, the first wallaby born here, developed a condition called, unimaginatively, Lumpy Jaw. It is a frequent problem in captive wallabies; I don't know whether wild ones commonly have it. It apparently starts with an abscessed tooth in the upper or lower jaw, with the surrounding bone also becoming infected. One method of helping it is to remove the tooth, scrape the bone, and administer antibiotics, but completely eliminating the bone infection can be difficult. When the mandible (lower jaw) is affected, it can deteriorate enough to break because the bone is so slender. I am sure the condition is painful, as is an abscessed tooth in humans.

The problem can improve, then reappear later; many affected animals die from it eventually. Wallabies' jaws are extremely narrow, and their mouth does not open wide at all. It is difficult to get instruments, let alone human fingers, inside to extract molars. Their two lower incisors point forward rather than up toward the top teeth, with long roots embedded lengthwise inside the jaw bones. Removing them would be difficult without breaking or weakening the jaw.

I noticed Toby's lump one day while I was watching the wallabies from our kitchen window. As with Ara's swollen toe, sometimes I could see it, other times I was unsure it was there. I telepathically asked Toby to lift his chin for better viewing and he did so, keeping his nose in the air for a couple minutes while facing the kitchen window where I was standing. There was definitely a lump on the left side and underneath, between his mandibles.

When I called Linda, she groaned before beginning to research the problem. Fortunately we had already successfully used anesthesia with wallabies when Toby and Casey were neutered so she had that information. Surgery is the only good option she could find, so we agreed on a day and time for the procedure.

I locked Toby in his shed alone by closing the door when he was in there. This was partly to provide him with a cleaner environment away from the others while he was healing. Also, we needed to make sure the others didn't ingest his antibiotics which were in a cherry-flavored syrup I put on his fruit. Linda thought it would be good to have antibiotics in his system before the surgery. Catching him for transport to the clinic was much easier on him in the smaller area, and for us as well.

I asked Lyn to talk with Toby about this new issue. The communication of March 21, 2005, follows:

Toby: Hi, Lyn! I'm right here, waiting to talk with you! So glad to hear from you any time!

Lyn: Likewise, Toby. What do you know of what's happening and how do you feel?

Toby: I feel mostly good. My mouth is sore but not dreadfully painful, by any means! Adele has told me I am to be alone so I can get well faster. I need a clean environment, was what I heard. She says I'm a good wallaby and that I'm important, so I'm getting extra special care and attention! She makes me feel so good!

Lyn: All of that is correct! Do you know of the upcoming surgery to remove the bump that is causing the pain in your jaw?

Toby: Only that it is soon. What will they do to me?

Lyn: First you will be given something that will make you quite relaxed and calm. Then Adele will take you to the vet's. There you will be put to sleep so you will feel no pain. Adele will be with you the entire time, sending you thoughts of love and wellness. The vet will remove the abscess and infection and then sew up your jaw. Then you will slowly come back to normal consciousness and probably feel quite a bit of pain in your jaw and mouth. Adele will take you back home that same day to recover in the place you are staying now. That is when it will be important to eat as much and as often as you can and to eat the food with the antibiotic in it to help fight any infection that might come along. As your jaw heals, you should start to feel better and better until you are well and then you can be back with the other wallabies.

Toby: Okay. I can do that. I did it once before, didn't I? When I was neutered?

Lyn: Correct!

Toby: They were all nice to me and I thought I recovered well. This will go well, too!

Lyn: Yes, I think it will. Adele has seen it early and you are strong.

Toby: Yes, I am still strong. I showed my lump to Adele. Casey told me to. He said she would want to know.

Lyn: Why aren't you taking the antibiotics twice a day? Do they taste bad?

Toby: No, it is not a bad taste, but I don't feel I need that much medicine right now. I am strong. Ara is wise and she says it is best to go with my own judgment. Sometimes good things can be too much, so I am to do what I feel is best for me. I just don't need that much right now. I will eat as best I can after surgery and take what medicine I feel I need to get well. Thank them for offering more than enough!

Lyn: Would you like some different foods or care?

Toby: Bananas would be good and cherries – they are red, right?

Lyn: Yes. Anything else?

Toby: I'd like a voice – company – like when I was small. My mom was always humming to me. It's soothing and stress-reducing. It's a low sound – lower than you could maybe hear.

Lyn: If we can't hear it, we probably won't be able to reproduce it for you.

Toby: Yes, you can. Just think a song in your head and sing it in your head. That's what I would like!

Lyn: I'll tell Adele. Toby, what about having me send some colors from gem stones?

Toby: Oh, yes! Ara said I was to ask. That's why I wanted Adele to call you. So you could send me some. She said they helped her a lot. I'd like yellow (amber), pink (rose quartz), light blue (aquamarine), gold (citrine), green and white (nephrite), orange (carnelian), blue (lapis lazuli), milky white (moonstone), purple (amethyst), clear white (hiddenite). Thank you! That's quite enough. Can you send them for three days after the surgery? I'm fine now.

Lyn: Yes, I'll send them each morning with loving, well thoughts to go with!

Toby: Thank you very much!

Lyn: Is there anything else that would help you keep your stress levels down?

Toby: Ara is doing this already. She is having everyone send me beautiful thoughts. Just let Adele know, so it will help keep her stress levels down.

Toby responded well during and after the surgery. He had a large abscess that did involve the bone (we were able to see bone changes on x-ray). Linda opened and cleaned it from the bottom rather than trying to go through his mouth, risking breaking bones or dislocating his jaw. The infection seemed to come from the root of one of his lower incisors, which was cracked, but we didn't extract the tooth. I believe he damaged that tooth by hitting it on the cement wall when he panicked at John's place due to fear of being hidden from me. Linda inserted small plastic beads impregnated with an antibiotic into the cleaned abscess pocket, which were to stay there for the rest of his life. His soft tissue would fill in around them and they wouldn't bother him, but they would slowly release the drug directly into the infected area.

I put antibiotics and pain medication in cherry juice for Toby. He took what he decided he wanted, though not as much as Linda thought he should have. Unlike Ara, I was unable to give him medication directly because he was too uncomfortable about being handled; I was unwilling to stress him by grabbing him every day. He was fine with my going into his shed to feed him as long as I respected his personal space.

After the incision healed, I released Toby back into the big pen, where he seemed fine until the summer of 2007, over two years after the surgery. One day in July I looked out the kitchen window to see him lying on the ground in an unusual position. He was flat on his side which is common when they're resting, but his head was also flat on the ground. I watched for a minute without seeing twitching ears or signs of breathing. Opening the window and speaking to him elicited no response. I went out and found Toby was dead. Both Don and I had watched him that morning without noticing anything wrong. There was no sign of injury and he was in good flesh. The ground was undisturbed, indicating he hadn't struggled during the dying process.

Lyn's comment on learning of his death was, "I wonder what he'll decide to be next!" I think of Toby often and send him good thoughts. I thank him for the time he spent with us, and for his love and his bubbly personality. He was a joy to watch as he hopped at top speed around their enclosure. He looked like he was loving life and what his body could do, a good example for us all.

I decided I wanted Toby's skeleton because they are so unusual and fascinating, so I did a necropsy. His chest was full of blood, as though an aneurism had ruptured. I was sorry he hadn't stayed with us longer, but relieved to think he didn't suffer long. It was also good to learn there was no way I could have known he had a problem. I found a lot of abdominal fat which is normal for them, but almost none in his chest. All of his organs looked healthy to me.

When Toby's skeleton was clean, I saw no sign of current infection in the place where his jaw had healed. Extra bone had grown there to form a solid, smooth lump. He also had a swelling that showed no sign of current infection on the left maxilla (upper jaw), which was smaller but similar to the one on the mandible. It was so small I had been unable to see it when he was alive. The root of the molar under the maxillary bump was dark, indicating it was probably where that infection started. It's possible the second infection was active at the same time as the other, thus healing at the same time due to the antibiotics we gave him.

CHAPTER 37

In March 2005, Don was introduced at a local fair to a dog he thought we should bring home. We only had Eden, a young female black lab, at the time. Don intended this dog, Clover, to be mine, though he is the dog person in our home. I just rolled my eyes, because we'd had a couple of difficult experiences before when bringing a new dog home.

Ginger, the yellow lab who lived with Don when we married, got along quite well with Eden at first. Eden was only three months old when we brought her home late in 2001, so Ginger was still top dog. They played together, seeming to add fun to Ginger's senior years. Then we got Indy, an adult chocolate lab we had taken because she needed more room to run than was available where she was living. Two female dogs in a family are often friends, but three can become a pack with two picking on the weakest one. Ginger was older by then (2003), beginning to have health issues, and both Eden and Indy were larger, younger, and stronger than she was.

One day I came home in time to see Eden and Indy attacking Ginger in the front yard. No one else was there when the fight occurred so I had to break it up. Indy backed off when I yelled, but Eden was too far gone to respond to me. I had to grab her and drag her off. As soon as I had control of Eden, Ginger stood up and staggered over to the front door of the house, panting and quivering almost too much to walk. She had punctures in her belly and other places, and was covered in mud, terrified, shocked, and devastated. The poor old dog had never experienced anything like that before. I called Linda, who soon came over to care for her.

Linda gave Ginger a heavy sedative and we laid her on the dining table to clean and examine her wounds. She healed well from those relatively minor injuries (none even required sutures), but I don't think she ever recovered from the emotional trauma.

We gave Indy back to her former owner, closely watching Eden and Ginger after that in case Eden again became aggressive. This was one of many times I so appreciated Linda's practice of caring for animals in their homes. Going to a clinic would have added even more trauma for Ginger.

Then Don brought Teddy home, also because the dog was in a situation that was not the best for him. He was a cute little guy, a yellow border collie mix less than a year old. The only problem was that birds weren't safe around him. We had him neutered, hoping that would help, and Don worked with him a lot, but he wouldn't quit chasing chickens in the yard. I was concerned about allowing him in the house with the parrots. After he killed the second chicken, we took Teddy to the local animal shelter for adoption, telling them he needed a home without birds. We learned he was soon adopted, hopefully into a great family for him.

When Ginger was nine years old she developed Cushing's Disease. We treated her for a while, but she grew more ill over time. One day I looked at her and knew Ginger was done. I called Linda, who agreed to euthanize her. She initially gave her a tranquilizer to reduce the anxiety phase of the strong anesthetic used for euthanasia. Ginger passed quietly while resting on her own bed in front of the TV. For quite a long time after that I felt she was still there, lying in her place, keeping watch over her family and especially Don, her favorite person.

After difficult experiences with two other new dogs and then Ginger's illness and death, I wasn't optimistic about taking in Clover, another adult dog, even though we only had Eden at the time. Clover was about two years old and had been rescued from a puppy mill by people from the animal shelter. She had already had two or three litters of puppies, so her mammary glands were greatly stretched, though no longer lactating. She was a yellow lab/shar pei mix, a big and beautiful dog with a soft coat and some extra wrinkles.

For a couple of days after Don told me about her, I frequently thought about Clover, for some reason. I didn't want to have to worry about another dog around the birds and wild animals, nor did I want to have to get rid of any more dogs, but I knew something was going on. As usual, I called Lyn for help, resulting in the following March 29, 2005, communication.

Lyn: Clover!

Clover: Good Day, Madame! Thank Adele for honoring me with your kindly ear tuned to me. I'm impressed and hope to find a home with her and Don.

Lyn: You're most welcome! Do you know why Adele keeps thinking about you when she's really not interested in dogs much?

Clover: We go way back! I have been her mentor many times – which is proven by the fact that she heard me calling, even though she doesn't find much worthwhile in a dog's body. Adele has come a long way in a short time and is now ready for me once again. The proof is in her openness to bring me home. Nothing will be gained by either her or me if I chase birds. Tell her if I ever chase animals on her place, then it is I who is choosing to leave. I am fully aware, as I should be if I am to mentor one as advanced as Adele. She will need to continue to listen to me with her heart for now she needs advanced counseling from the invisible world to keep her balance. For those of you working with awareness at this time, learning to balance equally – one foot in the earth plane and one out – is extremely important. I will be listened to better than the birds she so reveres or snakes, because I am not so much to her liking. I have been sent to aid her. Not to say her other animals have not, but she needs more balance – that is the law – so the work can be done.

I will harmonize well with the entire place. It must be so if I am to be there for Adele. She needs to take some time daily to listen to me. Five minutes – no more – otherwise things may become difficult for her. My past in this lifetime was arranged so I might have the perfect opening into Adele's life at the right time. The puppy mill, my puppies, my foster home (who didn't want me)

211

were all part of my creation so I could reach Adele at this time. (She and I set this up long ago!)

Lyn: (This was a secret she whispered in my ear).

Clover: I like my name! I am Adele's four-leaf clover. Even by my name she knew me! We set that up too! It's important that you both recognize that chance plays no role in your lives. All is set forth and perfect from long ago, from your own choices. All is according to plan! We are all One!

Time to go! Ta! Ta! Much appreciation!

Clover did fit into our home well. She killed a guinea fowl in the yard one day, but it was probably accidental. I think Clover got too close to the guinea hen's babies, thinking nothing of it because she had no harmful intentions, and the mom flew into her face, triggering her reaction. She ignored chickens as they walked all around her when she was lying in the yard. Clover just moved away from Tisha, Simon, and Nicki, even when they occasionally bit one of her toes. She seemed to want to mother the fawns when they were in the house, but never acted like she would hurt anything. I can't allow fawns to be mothered by a dog, of course, but Clover and Solo interacted comfortably when he was in the front yard with her, even though there wasn't much common ground in their favorite games.

Until I typed this communication much later, I'd forgotten what she said about our being together before and planning this, but I'm not surprised. Don intended Clover to be my dog, which didn't happen, but she did tell me things now and then. I liked to gently poke her cheek with my finger to see her shar-pei wrinkles appear and she played with me whenever I allowed it. She was gentle, grabbing my arm without leaving marks, though her mouth was large and strong enough to break my bones. She got along fine with strangers, both children and adults. Don said she would be aggressive with anyone who acted like he might harm me.

Eden and Clover usually went with Don when he left the house. A neighbor called a few times to tell me she saw Don go by – again – with his blond girlfriend in the pickup. Clover sat up tall in the passenger seat, with Eden sprawled in the back seat. If another human went along, both dogs rode in the back seat. Neither of them was happy when Don left them here. Eden cried a lot till he came home, sometimes even howling if he went somewhere without her. Clover was more stoic, but became visibly happier when he returned.

Clover was right that it is easier to listen to animals with whom I don't have a close relationship. Ego interference kicks in more when my emotions are involved. I wonder now how much Clover told me or suggested to me that I accepted as coming from my mind rather than hers. Probably quite a lot. In any case, I greatly appreciated her help, gladly accepting further enlightenment and awareness even if I'm unaware of where it originates.

She was also right about my not being a dog person. It isn't that I dislike them, but they don't appeal to me as much as some other animals. I loved a couple of dogs when I was a child and am the one here who watches their health, taking care of them when they have medical problems. However, I dislike dog hair all over the house and don't allow dogs in my car for that reason. I also dislike being licked or jumped on by them, especially those who are so big. Scales, feathers, and bird or snake urine and feces are less bothersome to me. And parrot screaming is usually easier to tolerate than barking. (I know – it doesn't make sense to me, either.)

Dogs do demonstrate unconditional love and tremendous loyalty, often even in cases when it appears undeserved. They seem able to quickly forgive a lot of injustices, responding to what is happening in the moment. However, I am more attracted to exotics and wild ones, perhaps because earning their trust is a challenge. They are more foreign and therefore more interesting to me.

I also prefer creatures who don't require (or respond well to) training; I live with them without expecting them to change their behavior for me. If I don't want them to do something (like

213

tear holes in the walls in the case of the parrots), I simply modify the house or their cages to prevent it. I expect dogs to learn not to chew up the furniture, but I don't have the patience or knowledge to train them. Fortunately Don does and his dogs always love and usually obey him.

So it was good that Clover chose Don as her person instead of me, yet she and I interacted daily during the years she lived with us. She would often sit in front of me looking at my face. If I ignored her, she gently put one foot on my leg to get my attention. Sometimes she simply wanted to go outside; other times she was trying to tell me something more significant. I didn't always get it, but I appreciated her efforts.

CHAPTER 38

In 2006, the summer before Solo (the special mule deer) was born, I raised four fawns, all of whom had difficult and unusual experiences. Sunny (my little sunshine deer) was a mule deer like Solo; Hope, Bucky, and Missy were white-tailed deer. Sunny and Bucky's moms were hit by cars. I wasn't able to learn Hope and Missy's stories, but they may have been kidnap victims.

Sunny's growth and development were normal until sometime after she was weaned when I noticed a number of painful, swollen joints in her legs. This started with one joint on the lower part of each back leg and spread to others there, eventually including joints in her front legs, too. I finally took her to Judy, hoping she could help her. Judy gave her cell salts and other homeopathic compounds and Sunny did recover. However, her legs didn't grow as long as those of most mule deer so she seemed quite short. She lived with Judy for several years, disappearing one hunting season, along with Bunny, her hybrid fawn (white-tailed deer father).

Hope was brought to me a week after she had been picked up. The woman (I'll call her Donna) was concerned about her because she had severe, watery diarrhea. She named her Hope because she so wanted the little deer to survive. Donna had been hospitalized with a serious illness for a few days after she acquired Hope. Someone else had cared for the fawn and, as soon as Donna had time and strength to learn where to take Hope, she brought her to me.

Hope had been fed cow milk, the people making a common mistake of adding water to it when Hope became ill with diarrhea. Little deer do not digest cow milk well and diluting it with water makes the problem much worse. She was so sick and weak I was concerned she might not survive. I gave Hope a pectin anti-diarrhea liquid and electrolytes when she was settled in the playpen. Soon I started her on goat milk with a small amount of whipping cream added. Her diarrhea quickly stopped and she grew to adulthood without further problems.

Hope continued coming into our yard occasionally for more than five years, bringing twin fawns every year from when she was two years old. In 2013, one of her babies was killed by a car, the first one she had lost prior to weaning (I didn't recognize them when they no longer stayed with their mother and they never became tame). She was a great mom! Hope didn't allow us to touch her from shortly after she was weaned, but she seemed more relaxed than wild ones when we went outside. We often recognized her especially long face.

Bucky was brought to me a month after he had been picked up by a well-meaning couple. From the description, he was a week or less old when the rescuers found him beside a road next to his dead mother. The people were from California but had purchased land here and were building a house. Because they needed to go back to California for the winter, they were concerned about abandoning a dependent little deer in the fall. They called me to ask questions about my care and facilities, seeming quite reluctant to give Bucky up. They finally brought him here a couple days after I talked with them. I hoped, if I didn't push or threaten, they would decide bringing him to me was in the fawn's best interest. If they had hesitated much longer, I would have asked a game warden to go get the baby.

When they brought him, I honored their request to see the deer pen and the other fawns, mistakenly thinking they would soon leave. They had Bucky follow them, which he did too slowly to suit me. When I picked him up to carry him the rest of the way, the woman became angry with me because, she said, "He hates that!" They had been taking him for daily walks and, though he was outside on his own part of the day, he slept in their basement at night. Bucky was within a few days of being the same age as Sunny and Hope, but was much smaller. The bigger fawns picked on Bucky a bit by kicking him and pushing him around, which is normal fawn behavior. The woman was unhappy about that, too, becoming angry with Sunny and Hope even though they didn't hurt him.

She fed Bucky as she had been at their home, using a baby bottle with the same size holes as for newborn humans.

Fortunately, they did give him goat milk (pasteurized rather than fresh and without whipping cream), but they only fed him three times daily. It took so long to get milk through those tiny holes that he gave up before he'd swallowed enough. His tongue and jaw must have hurt from the amount of effort it took to suck milk through that nipple. I was still feeding the others five times daily; they ate a lot more at a time and much more quickly. No doubt that is why they were so much bigger than Bucky; fortunately he did appear healthy.

The people stayed more than two hours. I was afraid they'd never leave or that they might hesitate to let Bucky stay. Finally they did go, but called the next day to tell me they'd changed their minds. I had to tell them coming to get him wasn't an option, that I would call a game warden if necessary because it was illegal for them to keep the deer. I reminded them they had turned the little guy into a pet, making it more difficult for him to become wild. It was going to take some effort on my part to undo the damage they had done. When they asked about visiting, I said they might be able to come once at the end of the summer for a short time, but that was all.

Bucky eventually caught up with the others in size after he began getting enough to eat, seeming to have no ill effects from his delayed growth. When the people came back much later, Bucky wouldn't go to them at all at first, though he came to me. I let them offer him willows so they were eventually able to touch him briefly. I was pleased he showed that hesitation, because he was still more tame than the other white-tailed fawns I'd raised. Don and I believe he continued coming in our yard for at least a couple of years, thinking he was a beautiful two-year-old buck who came for grain every day, seeming much less nervous with us than other bucks that age. He wouldn't let us get close enough to touch him, so I'm sure he was more wary around other people, especially away from the safety of our place. Later we were unable to tell whether he was one of the bucks who come here.

Missy's story is much more sad. She was also picked up about the time Bucky was, but she was kept by other people for seven weeks. They put her in a bathroom, feeding her cow milk and cat food. They couldn't have fed her much because she was about half the size of others her age. Some neighbors saw the fawn and were horrified about the way she was being treated. A teenage girl finally talked them into giving her the deer so she and her mom could bring Missy to me.

This fawn was severely constipated, her tail had been broken, and her head looked malformed in that the proportions were somewhat wrong. She refused to eat well from a bottle, but would occasionally swallow some goat milk and cream when I fed the others. I tried putting milk in a bowl, but that didn't work, either. We offered her everything we could think of (other than dog or cat food, of course), but, unlike Bucky, she made no significant progress. I was able relieve the constipation with a few enemas. Her fractured tail had already healed in the wrong position so I was unable to do anything about it. I suspect someone grabbed it or closed a door on it; I doubt she was born that way.

Missy learned to run around the back yard with the others and seemed normally active, but I never felt she was thriving. She didn't interact comfortably with me, only coming close when the others were there at feeding time. Many times she would refuse the bottle one or more feedings each day. One day in late August I saw that Missy had a badly broken front leg. Because it was bleeding, I knew it was a compound fracture, with bones poking through her skin. I could see the leg was shattered, even without getting close enough to touch her. I thought her bones must have been brittle to allow that kind of break; I couldn't imagine it healing properly, given her poor condition. I also didn't believe she would ever be releasable, and knew she would be severely traumatized by the contact required for prolonged treatment. I again made the decision for euthanasia which was done quickly to release her from pain.

Later that year (2006), a game warden brought me a bald eagle who was extremely sick. He didn't appear to be injured, but had a full crop and was unable to fly. Thinking perhaps he had eaten too much without being sufficiently hydrated, I gave him electrolytes before putting him in a large dog carrier on our deck. Unfortunately, the eagle continued to decline and died within a couple days. We put his body in a freezer for the game warden to pick up later for testing. I never heard lab results, but now believe he had severe lead poisoning from eating carcasses and offal (internal organs removed by hunters) from dead game animals which contained pieces of lead ammunition.

CHAPTER 39

When they were about 12 years old, Tisha and Simon, our
African grey parrots, began to exhibit courtship behavior. I had
started to think they were unacceptable to each other as mates,
which was fine with me. I mainly wanted them to have parrot
companionship in some form to help fill some of their social needs
without putting more parrots into the pet trade. I used to believe
keeping captive- born rather than wild-caught birds as pets is less
unkind, but I now know they have some problems due to being
taken from their parents too young, in addition to those of being
unable to live in ways normal for their kind. Instincts are powerful,
no matter where they are born. I was also concerned about trying
to find good homes for youngsters. Keeping a flock of parrots was
unacceptable, too, simply compounding the listed drawbacks. I
believed even Tisha and Simon would have to eventually go to
someone else, an unpleasant thought, because they should outlive
Don and me.

I considered possible ways to prevent fertilized eggs from
developing. Letting Tisha sit on them seemed potentially less
traumatic for her than just removing her eggs in the beginning
as I usually do with emus Ara and Aten. However, birds will
often continue laying until they have enough eggs in the nest, a
behavior that could deplete Tisha's calcium levels and those of
other nutrients used to create an egg if I kept taking them. One
possibility was to cool the eggs for a while, though I knew freezing
would break shells. Simon took this decision away from me by
breaking their eggs in the nest box.

I asked Lyn to find out what they were thinking, resulting
in the following communication on June 17, 2006:

Tisha and Simon: We are here, Lyn! It's us – Tisha and
Simon. We have come to talk with you as Adele has
asked. Thank her so much for caring enough to ask us
how we feel. We feel honored to be considered in this
decision she is making.

Lyn: Do you understand her viewpoint or do I need to clarify it more clearly to you?

Tisha: No, we know how she feels and her position.

Simon: So let us tell you ours. We have appreciated that Adele has thought we might court and become lovers. Until now we have been immature. Now we are of an age to want to court and be together. We also feel we have a stable home life and that having young ones in our surroundings is definitely possible. Some wild animals cannot procreate in captivity because the needs for such behaviors are not met.

Tisha: But ours have been and we are ready. There are souls out there waiting to join us here. We feel it will be beneficial not only for us but for our offspring as well. We know that we out-live our people. Captive parrots know this when they choose their bodies. We also know that we can call to us those with whom we choose to live.

Simon: Which means we don't have the fears of multiple homes that people have for us. Yes, there is a new experience every time that happens, but even if it is traumatic, that doesn't mean it is bad or not our choice. So those who choose to be our babies will already be able to deal with those situations.

Tisha and Simon: We are asking Adele to put aside her fears for us and our children, as well as her own cares and concerns, and allow us to have our babies.

Tisha: When we know Adele is agreeable, then Simon will stop breaking the eggs. It is better for him to do that, though, than to have them taken away and brought back cold. [My intention was to re-warm them before putting them back, and to take them one at a time. Adele]

222

I would know there was no life in that cold egg and, therefore, no point to sit on it. Sitting on the eggs does not fulfill my need to have babies. It is the heart connection when they hatch and I care for them that is fulfilling. I respect Adele's care and concern for me and my needs. Tell her I could and would rather not lay eggs than to let her think we would be fooled by that ruse. We do have free choice, just as you people do, and we can choose not to have offspring. That is the best choice if Adele really does not want us to have babies.

As for the nest box, it is in a good place. The female builds the nest and therefore picks the spot. If I should decide that Simon's presence is not helpful to me, then I can more easily drive him out. Better to have the nest box where it is. It gives me better control that way.

Lyn: Other than needing to have the eggs hatch, do you have any needs that Adele can help you with? (Tisha and Simon looked at each other.)

Simon: No, our diet is excellent and we are loved and allowed every freedom possible. We are quite happy and we hope Adele will allow us to build a family in her home and do the honor of finding homes for our children. We trust her and them to work together to find their new homes. This will be a step in trust for Adele, a big one. We, as parents, know we must raise our young ones to be the best parrots possible, and then we must allow the Universe to carry on from there.

Tisha and Simon: Much love, Adele, and we will honor your decision either way, but let us know and then we will act in accordance with your wishes.

I decided to honor their wishes. After all, I need to follow my budding beliefs that everything works out as it should, and they have free will just as I do. They are intelligent, eternal, beings who know far more than I do about things spiritual and certainly about their own paths. My beliefs about reincarnation follow what Tisha and Simon said in that each soul picks its own path before coming here, including unpleasant and challenging experiences. Animals seem to better grasp the concept of eternity vs. one lifetime, knowing this lifetime looks much different from the level of Spirit/eternity than when immersed in it.

Lyn talked with Tisha and Simon again on June 19.

Simon: Hi, Lyn!

Lyn: Hi, Simon. How are things going?

Simon: Just great! Couldn't be better! Adele is such a sweetie! We are thrilled that she is okay with us raising a family now with her. Tell her many thanks!!

Tisha: As far as when the babies should leave, it is a while after they are weaned. We teach them to fly and then we go with them to help them adjust to that really big world out there. Our job doesn't stop at weaning. It just really starts. (Looking at Simon) We would like to keep our babies through six months and then have Adele look for homes for them between six months and one year. It would be best if they all had homes by that time. This is a long period for Adele, but it will help her see that what people think and do may not really be in our best interest. It will help her when she writes her book about us. It will be about living compatibly with birds, especially parrots, and will include all of these conversations.

Birds, Lyn, are leaders in this Earth Plane on relationships. Humans can and do learn a lot from us. That is one reason we are so popular. We care and we work at building good relationships with our families – parrots and non-parrots. When ego steps in, many hearts can get broken. Respect, care, and humility help relationships grow. Ego can quickly kill relationships. We are teaching more than just you, Lyn, as you can see!

Simon: Enough sermonizing, Tisha! Now, about the stopping being friendly. That may happen. There's a time for concentrated bonding and teaching. Mostly humans don't understand this and they can make things quite difficult – even mess things up greatly – so for the babies' sake, we become less friendly. Adele may see some of that, but I seriously doubt it. She is so respectful that she may not be a problem. At any rate, she'll understand to back off if we get stand-offish and she won't collapse over it as some people do. Tah-Tah! Thanks so much!

I had not read this communication since shortly after Lyn talked with them and didn't remember a lot of it. The part about my writing a book amazed me. I didn't start thinking about it at all until Solo's communication (in a later chapter) two years after this one with Tisha and Simon. To find they had said I would use these communications in it astounded me further. I wasn't planning to include Lyn's work when I started the book, which initially was going to be a short story about Solo. Apparently, Tisha, Simon, and who knows who else (no doubt along with my soul on the Other Side as we planned learning experiences for this lifetime) had the whole thing in mind and were directing me toward it all along. I now wonder what other plans they have for me and this book. I'm sure they will let me know when the time comes. I thank them all for their patience with me, and remind myself – again – that Earth-Plane time and concerns are significantly different from those of Spirit and eternity.

Many parrot breeders and books suggest baby parrots be taken from their parents at two weeks of age, or at least before weaning, to be hand-raised by humans. Linda told me she has read studies showing that is unnecessary for successfully taming the birds. I had already decided I wasn't going to take babies away from Tisha and Simon, because it seems disrespectful, unkind, and unnecessary. We had participated in that behavior with the wallabies and in a way with Nicki, who was taken from his parents at two weeks of age and wasn't quite weaned when I bought him. I choose not to do so again, with wallabies, birds, or any other babies if I can help it. I did want to know how long Tisha and Simon felt they should keep their babies and appreciated their thorough answer.

Simon quit breaking eggs so Tisha began incubating for the first time. I gave them each half of a hard boiled chicken egg when I fed them in the morning, putting Tisha's egg ration and some of their pellet feed on the ledge of her nest box for easy access close to her eggs. Also I didn't want Simon to eat her cooked egg as well as his, both because I wanted her to have it and because I didn't think that much egg yolk would be good for Simon. He was being cranky with me, though, acting like he didn't want me to put food on the nest box.

I decided to try letting Simon feed Tisha (normal behavior in the wild) after explaining to them I quit putting food on the nest box for that reason. He was less aggressive part of the time, but didn't seem to be feeding Tisha enough. She had to climb on top of her cage to reach the food dishes and Simon was eating her hard-boiled egg. I went back to putting it on her nest box, using a flannel baby blanket to distract Simon when I removed food and water dishes for cleaning and feeding. I flipped part of the blanket onto the top of the cage where Simon was waiting for me. He attacked it so we played tug-of war while I picked up dishes with my other hand. We continued doing that, creating a game enjoyable for both of us.

Simon began trusting me enough to let go of the cage, hanging from the blanket by his feet while I gently swung him back and forth. We played the game at bedtime, too, just because it was fun. He even let me pet his back and stretched out a wing for me to touch while he was biting the blanket. We destroyed a number of blankets because he tore lots of holes in them, but better the blanket than my hand, and the light-hearted contact was good for Simon and me. At last I'd found a way to directly interact with Simon with only positive results.

All seemed to be going well until Simon broke their eggs again after Tisha had been incubating them for a while. He seemed anxious and frustrated, mostly with himself, which certainly fit with my perception of his personality. After that Simon gradually seemed to feel better. They produced more eggs (three different times over the next year), none of which Simon broke, and Tisha conscientiously incubated them for at least 30 days each time. However, there was no sign of development in any of the eggs. I didn't know whether they had a fertility problem, were just inexperienced, or if Simon was practicing a form of birth control because he was still feeling insecure. I had decided to accept whatever they chose to do and both birds seemed mostly comfortable for some time.

Simon was still plucking feathers, though. His whole chest and belly were bare, as were spots on the underside of his wings and around his neck. Lyn had recently taken online classes in shamanism and suggested using her new knowledge to help him.

On November 2, 2007, Lyn did a shamanic journey for Simon. As I understand it, during these journeys Lyn is working with kind and compassionate spirits, including some of her spirit guides and ancestors of the recipient, to heal the spirit of an individual. She holds the agreed-upon intention for the journey in her mind, mostly observing what happens and only participating when spirits request it. Lyn "travels" to places in non-ordinary reality with the guidance of spirits, who actually do the work.

The following is part of Lyn's Shamanic Journey Statement of Disclosure:

> I am a compassionate and caring Shamanic Practitioner, providing a service to you and/or your animal friend(s). My services are the creation of a Sacred Space into which I invite only compassionate, loving spirits to participate in a journey into Non-Ordinary Reality for my clients. Before I start the journey, I talk with my client (human

or animal) or an animal's human; we decide together on the purpose of the journey. I hold that intention throughout the journey.

Lyn said the spirits did a soul retrieval for Simon, reconnecting him with a small part of his soul which had separated due to some traumatic experience. He continued plucking so she did a second journey for him on November 24, which was an extraction (pulling some harmful energy, or intrusions, away from him). Lyn said he sat on her shoulder and didn't bite her (in non-ordinary reality, of course. She was physically in Butte and Simon was here at home). Lyn didn't know why the spirits chose not to heal everything during the first journey, but apparently they decided this way was best for Simon.

A second part in this journey was to learn what caused Simon's intrusions. She found that in a past life Simon was a human who caught and sold wild parrots. Now, in this lifetime, his role was reversed. Lyn's power animal said Simon's biting is his resisting this life and the painful act of plucking feathers is his way of trying to relieve his karmic debt. She was told the only way Simon could completely heal would be to forgive himself for this life and his past life. She asked Spirit how we could bring that about and was told that every path is different, but most helpful in this change would be for Simon to see how much others really do love him and care. Because his spirit participated in the journeys, Simon learned all this at the same time Lyn did.

I wondered if their fertility problems might not be related to his past life experience. When I mentioned this to Lyn, she replied by email (December 26, 2007), "I think you are probably right there. He wants to please Tisha and she wants babies, but in his heart he can't think that having more baby birds in captivity is a good thing. He is kind of caught between a rock and a hard place, poor guy! I hope he can get to a place where he feels good about himself, sooner rather than later. It is good you are relaxed about him. That will be, and probably has been, most helpful to him."

Lyn decided to do a third journey for him that day. She said this time the spirits did a complete, multi-layer healing for

Simon. After that Simon seemed calmer and even began letting some feathers grow, only missing a few by fall of 2008. He continued to seem more at peace with himself and his world. I was willing to wait and see whether they decided to actually have babies sometime, thinking it was okay either way, and hoping they thought so, too.

At that time Tisha was only picking her feathers when she was nest-building, and just those on her chest and belly. These feathers are used to line the nest, providing a soft surface for babies. It also creates a brood patch, an area of bare skin which rests against eggs and babies, creating the perfect temperature for them. In between those times, Tisha let all her feathers grow back. I was so glad she finally felt that comfortable!

Karma and karmic debt are concepts with different meanings depending on people's belief systems. Some understand it as a form of punishment for so-called bad behavior, often in previous lives. I don't believe in any form of divine punishment because it seems inconsistent with unconditional love. Instead, I think all living beings (plant and animal, including humans) choose what to experience in our lives. This means we plan both pleasant and unpleasant lives and circumstances for ourselves, with the intention of providing many different experiences in physical bodies. For example, we have probably been both wealthy and poor, male and female, victims and victimizers, healthy and ill, different races and nationalities, and so forth. Those with the widest range of experiences (old souls) may have the greatest amount of knowledge.

From this philosophy, Simon's karmic debt was based on his perception, not something inflicted on him by a divine entity. He had simply chosen to experience the concept of parrots in captivity from a different perspective – perpetrating the condition in one life and living it in another. This doesn't make it any easier to live the lives we set for ourselves – at least until we come to that understanding. When we can see our experiences as those we set for ourselves with the intention of learning – and when we really grasp the concept we are eternal beings (souls or spirits) having a physical experience – our lives take on a whole new meaning. I now find life fascinating and amazing on an entirely different level, filled with miracles and joy. I still need to remind myself once in a while, especially when I'm exposed to painful experiences in others (animal and human), but remembering becomes easier all the time.

CHAPTER 40

Solo, the mule deer who came to me as a starving baby in 2007, remained in our back yard through his first winter, unlike other fawns who left with wild deer by six months of age. In early spring, 2008, when he was nearly a year old, I gave up on his jumping over the fence and encouraged him to follow me through the gate into the front yard. He seemed quite comfortable in the new area, immediately walking to the willow trees to eat new leaves and small branches. He stayed close most of the first day and I let him into the back yard that night. From then on he would pace next to the gate when he wanted in or out, usually coming home to be let in at night.

Occasionally Solo stayed out overnight, not returning home in the evening. He often slept under my bedroom window when he wasn't in the back yard, both at night and when he napped during the day. At first he was always home in the morning. I'm sure he traveled some during the nights he stayed out of the yard; deer normally wander and feed at night. Neighbors reported his visiting them during the day, which some thoroughly enjoyed as Solo allowed petting. I saw him following joggers a few times, concerning me both because he was on the road and his behavior might frighten people who didn't know him. This was when I really began to understand that he was an unusual deer. Even Skipper, the mule deer I had raised earlier, didn't follow strangers.

Lyn suggested a shamanic journey for Solo when I called her about my concerns. The intentions and key issues we set for Solo's journey were to: 1) help Solo break his bonds with his current home and follow his instincts to become a wild deer; and 2) help him find deer who would guide him and teach him what he needed to know to survive in the wild; 3) increase his confidence and reduce his dependence on people; 4) assist in healing any left-over trauma from losing his mom and nearly starving to death as a newborn. In some ways it worked, but it turned out Solo had different ideas about his purpose in this lifetime.

Lyn's short description of the journey follows:

An elk volunteered to participate in Solo's journey. He took Solo's spirit into a circle of deer who, along with other spirits, worked to help him. Solo's mom told him she had tried hard to get back to him but was prevented from doing so by an encounter with a mountain lion. Lyn and I assume she was killed by the cougar.

This journey was done on Tuesday, April 22, 2008. About 10 days later, on the morning of Saturday, May 3, Solo left without returning home that night or the next day. I told neighbors he was missing, asking them to tell me if they saw him. Of course I looked for him outside whenever I was near a window. Don, some neighbors, and I watched along the road every time we drove anywhere, hoping not to see a dead mule deer.

Monday evening, May 5, a woman named Tracy called me. She had had an unusual encounter with a deer that afternoon and was told I might be able to explain his behavior. Tracy had gotten my number through her grandmother who is a friend of my parents. This is a small valley; I'm related to many people who live here and a lot of others know of my work with wildlife.

Tracy said a young buck who was starting to grow antlers had confidently walked up to her and her children, letting them pet and hug him; she hadn't noticed whether he was a mule deer or a white-tailed deer. He had several injuries, though none she thought were serious. Tracy gave him some water in a Tupperware container, which he drank. She thought he would stay where he was because he seemed quite tired, so she left the water dish for him. The deer was lying next to a fence when she went home. It almost had to be Solo, though the location made that seem unlikely.

When she saw the deer, Tracy was working in the organic garden at Teller Wildlife Refuge, about 12 miles northeast of our home by road (a bit shorter as the crow flies). Solo would have had to cross the Bitterroot River which was approaching high-water stage, the town of Hamilton, and the town of Corvallis, not to mention roads, farms, and subdivisions, to get there. I thought he must have been picked up by someone and dumped off at the refuge. Don, our neighbor Tom, and I took Don's truck to the refuge as soon as Tracy's call ended. After finding her Tupperware container, we walked and drove around calling Solo until dark, but were unable to find him.

That night Lee (a neighbor) and I told Solo telepathically that I would go back to the refuge in the morning (Tuesday). If he wanted to see me he was to be near the plastic container. I drove my car and looked all over for him, but again he stayed away. I was sure he received our messages because Lee and I are good at sending them.

Later that morning Tom called to tell me a story about Solo. Tom had just overheard someone in the restaurant where he worked say something about an unusual encounter with a deer. He interrupted the woman, asking her to start the story at the beginning. While she and her husband were at the Hamilton Kmart store Saturday, the day Solo left home, a deer was wandering around visiting people in the parking lot there and at the neighboring Super One grocery store. Everyone who saw him was amazed. The woman's husband even said he might have to change his attitude about hunting after his experience with the tame deer. When the deer was ready to leave, he stepped to the curb next to Highway 93, looked both ways, waited until traffic had stopped in all four lanes, then slowly walked across the street.

When I heard the story, I knew Solo must have traveled all the way on his own. Those stores are about halfway between our home and the refuge where Tracy met him. I told Lyn about Solo's travels and she was amazed and awed by his display of confidence. It appeared the shamanic journey accomplished that, though Solo hadn't accepted the message to avoid humans and find wild deer. When Lyn talked with him briefly, he told her he had received Lee's and my messages, but hadn't decided what he was going to do next. Apparently his decision so far was to avoid me.

Tuesday evening of that week Tracy's sister called to tell me Solo was at her neighbor's place about two miles north of the refuge (even farther from our home). The people had tried to make him go into a pen so they could hold him for me and I asked her to tell them not to do that. Wild mule deer live in that area. Since Solo went there voluntarily and didn't meet me at the refuge, I was ready to let him stay. Lyn's visit with him helped me to be comfortable with that decision, knowing he was doing what he chose.

Then the woman told me the neighbors had put a collar on Solo. I asked her to have them take it off, but he wouldn't hold still. They had tried to attach a chain to the collar, again to hold him for me, so he no longer trusted them. Deer do not tolerate being held by the neck, or restrained in any way, for that matter. Solo would have fought till he seriously hurt himself if they had been able to attach the chain. The collar was definitely cause for concern. They can easily become caught in fences and even brush, potentially dangerous for him. Also, Solo still had a lot of growing to do and the necks of bucks swell during mating season in the fall. I was afraid the collar would become too small for him, cutting into his neck or restricting his breathing and/or swallowing.

So I drove there to look for Solo – again. My intention was simply to remove the collar and check his wounds. One of these people said there was a gash in his back and a flap of torn skin on his flank. His right antler was also bleeding. I took a bottle of emu oil to put on the wounds, intending to leave him there. I may have been able to talk him into getting in my car, but thought it would be unsafe to drive with him as a passenger.

However, I was again unable to find Solo. I talked with a nice man and his young daughter who said Solo had spent much of the day with them while they worked in their yard. He followed the lawnmower, climbed the steps to their porch, ate some flowers, and lay down to rest in the shade. He even trotted down the road behind their car when they left to run errands. They offered to take their four-wheeler out in the pasture to look for him. I gave them my card and the bottle of emu oil, asking them to try to take the

234

collar off and drip oil on his wounds if they found him. I didn't hear from them so assumed they were unsuccessful.

CHAPTER 41

When I got home, I called a game warden to tell him of Solo's journey and that he was wearing a collar. I thought someone was likely to report the strange deer to the police or the Montana Fish, Wildlife, and Parks office in Missoula. The game warden also was concerned about the collar. He wouldn't have imagined this was one I had raised because of the location and he knew I wouldn't have collared a deer. He said they might have to anesthetize him with a dart gun in order to remove the collar. I told him Solo would allow me to take it off if I could find him, so the warden agreed to call us if he received a report about Solo.

The next morning (Wednesday) Tracy's sister again called to tell me Solo was sleeping under a tree at one of the places I had looked for him during my Tuesday night search. Don and I took his truck this time in case Solo acted like he wanted to go with us. We thought we had a good chance of finding him, but again he avoided us.

That Thursday afternoon I had scheduled a hypnotherapy session with a client. After I finished, Don called me from his cell phone to tell me he was with Solo, but was unable to remove the collar. The game warden had called Don after receiving a report about a collared deer. About that time a friend named Ken came to the house to see Don so he and I jumped in my car, hurrying to where Don was. Solo was back in Hamilton just east of Highway 93 and slightly north of where he had been in the parking lots of stores.

I went through the gate into a back yard and there stood Solo. I spoke to him and he walked up to me, lifted his nose to my chin, and leaned his face against my chest. I heard the woman say, "You can sure tell she raised him!" My first concern was to get rid of that collar. When I moved it around to open the catch, Solo backed away. I let go, spoke to him again, and waited till he came back to me. I stroked his face with one hand while carefully unhooking the clasp with my other hand and the collar was off. What a relief!

I hadn't even spoken to Don or the people yet. I was too focused on Solo. He had lost weight and did have some relatively minor-looking injuries. I said, "You've had some amazing adventures, haven't you?" He just stood there, rubbing his head against me. When I finally thanked the kind people for calling about him, they told me Solo had been in their yard Saturday, the day he left home and was seen in the parking lots. I knew then he was retracing his path, traveling toward home. I didn't want him to have to make his way through town again, so decided to see whether he would allow us to load him into the back of Don's truck and give him a ride home.

Don had a bunch of paraphernalia under the canopy on his pickup so he and Ken transferred some of it to my car. Solo followed me to the pickup, watching as I climbed into the back. He just stood by the tailgate looking at me so Don boosted him up and in, quickly closing the tailgate and the canopy window. The only time Solo had ever been in a vehicle was when he was tiny and starving. Even though he was thin, as a yearling he weighed nearly a hundred pounds. Solo was way too strong for me to control and being stepped on would hurt, to say the least; deer hooves are hard and sharp. I thought I might be in trouble riding with him, but wanted to stay there to help him remain calm. He did move around the whole time, but was controlled and careful not to bump or step on me.

Ken drove my car and Don, bless his heart, tried to drive us home as quickly as he could. He spent a lot of time looking in the mirror to make sure we were okay. I kept touching and talking to Solo, who seemed fine until Don started driving faster. He turned a few corners too quickly, accelerating fast enough to unbalance Solo which made him a bit nervous. We arrived home safely, the only casualty being Solo's right antler. He had scraped off some of the velvet in his travels and he bumped the sore spot on the way home so it was oozing blood again. When Don opened the back of the pickup, Solo hopped right out and began eating willow leaves, acting as though he'd never been gone.

Solo followed me into the back yard, where I filled his grain bucket and examined his wounds. He had apparently been doing more traveling than eating, though his antlers were noticeably bigger. Quite a bit of the velvet was scraped off the front of his right antler. It didn't appear infected, but I didn't know how the damage would affect its growth. All of the injury seemed to be above the pedicle, so I believed he'd be able to shed that antler the next spring and future antlers would grow normally.

Pedicles are the bony projections on top of the skull from which antlers grow. The same skin and hair as is on the skull covers the pedicles. Growing antlers have what is commonly called velvet on them, a type of soft skin (covered with fine, velvety hair) which contains the cells that build antlers. When antlers have grown as much as they will for the year, velvet begins to dry as blood vessels in it shrink. The deer then rubs them against bushes and tree trunks to remove the dried skin. The brown color of antlers is mainly due to sap, which stays on them after bark is damaged by scraping.

Late the next winter or early spring, antlers fall off after being released from the pedicles; in a few weeks new ones begin to develop. Each year they are bigger and have more points until they reach a maximum size and number. Usually a one-year-old buck (females of the species that live here do not have antlers) will simply have unbranched spikes and two-year-olds will have two or three points on each antler. This is not an accurate way of telling the age of a buck, though, because antler size varies depending on diet, condition, and possibly genetics.

Solo also had a cut on his back that was several inches long. He had come home with cuts there before this journey and I've seen them on other deer. I believe they were caused by his going through barbed wire fences. He had managed to get the front part of his body safely under the wire, but stood up too quickly so was gouged by a sharp barb over his pelvis just above his tail. I had dripped emu oil on a couple of these cuts before, but Solo was able to reach them with his tongue and quickly licked it off. I could see scars from older cuts; they had healed well and I assumed this one would, too. There was a small, three-cornered tear in the loose skin of his flank just in front of a hind leg. This wound looked worse than the others in that it appeared infected. I managed to put some emu oil in it, but again Solo licked it off. He had a couple of scrapes on his neck and the front of one shoulder, which were superficial. There were also a couple of spots on a hind leg that looked like shallow punctures, possibly from a dog bite. They weren't swollen or inflamed so I was confident they would heal.

Solo looked scruffy as he was still shedding his winter hair. He had started earlier in the spring and it seemed the process was going more slowly than normal. I used a dog brush to remove a lot of loose hair, which appeared to feel good to him. His new reddish, summer hair was beginning to grow underneath; some patches of red showed where the gray winter hair had all been shed, making him look spotted.

That evening I left Solo to his grain in the back yard where he seemed to feel comfortable and content. Aten, our male emu, had been behaving more aggressively toward him, pecking and sometimes even kicking at him before he left. Solo was quite stoic about it, simply moving away. He refused to run, which was probably frustrating to Aten. Ara was getting ready to lay eggs again so Solo may have been considered a threat to them.

It was a relief for me to know Solo was safe, but I didn't know what, if anything, I should do about him on a long-term basis. I was torn between wanting to protect him and believing he had the right to decide for himself how to live. Part of the problem is my sense of responsibility as a wildlife rehabilitator. I am supposed to raise these animals in a way that avoids their becoming so habituated to people that they are a nuisance or, much worse, a threat.

Some deer raised as pets have become aggressive toward people when they grew up. I've only heard of this happening with white-tailed deer, but it may happen with mule deer as well. I also haven't heard of does harming humans, but they certainly do kick each other, sometimes standing on their hind legs and boxing with hard, sharp front hooves. Tame deer may treat people as they would other deer by kicking at them to establish or demonstrate dominance, considering them rivals and fighting with them, or even trying to play head-butting deer games. Any of these actions from an adult or near-adult deer can result in serious injuries to a person. We simply are not built to receive such treatment safely. I would feel at least partially responsible if one I raised hurt someone through no fault of the person.

I could have asked a game warden to take Solo into the mountains where he would be unable to find his way home, but people live in and close to the mountains everywhere except deep in wilderness areas which are not accessible to trailers. I believe Solo would have simply approached people (including hunters) wherever he was, continuing to behave as he had been. One of our game wardens lives out of town on the east side of the valley not far from where Solo had traveled. Wild mule deer live there and it would be a good area to release orphans. However, all of the same concerns apply and Solo knows how to return home from that part of the county. I could have kept him in our yard since he hadn't tried to go over our fences, but that would have been unfair to Solo as well as illegal. Asking the game wardens to euthanize him was also an option, though certainly not one I wanted to consider. I procrastinated, simply continuing to let him go where he chose, waiting to see what would happen next, hoping he would decide to go with wild deer during the fall mating season, becoming more comfortable with them and less habituated to people.

Aten's aggression toward Solo began to concern me so I locked him and Ara in their winter enclosure. That is unfair to them because the yard was their home first and they do like having more space when the ground isn't covered with snow or ice. Solo stayed in the back yard for about a week, resting, eating, and healing. When he started standing next to the gate, we let him out again. We would then lock the emus up only at night, letting Solo into the back yard when he came home in the evenings, and reversing the process in the morning.

CHAPTER 42

On Friday, May 23 of that year (2008), a woman named Julie called me about a mule deer fawn someone had picked up and taken to her. Fawns here are usually born at the end of May or the first two or three weeks in June. This baby was found lying near a bike path after her twin had been attacked by a dog. The people took the injured fawn to a veterinarian, who had to euthanize it because it was so badly damaged. This one seemed fine so they left her there, thinking her mother would come back to care for her.

The next day she was still lying in the same area, so the people thought her mother hadn't returned. I'm sure she had because a fawn that young would have been distressed after more than 24 hours without food. I agreed to raise her rather than have them take her back for several reasons. That area didn't seem to be a safe or private place for her to spend a couple weeks growing big and strong enough to leave with her mom. Feeding would probably be frequently interrupted due to human activity. In fact, the mother may not feel safe enough to care for her at all during the day if there was much traffic on the bike path. Also, many people take dogs with them and one fawn had already been killed. Furthermore, the people who called me about the fawn were not the ones who picked her up, so they didn't know exactly where she had been found.

We went through the routine of setting up the playpen, thawing goat milk, and driving to the store for whipping cream. Fortunately I had purchased a gallon of milk a short time before just to be prepared. When the people arrived, Solo, who was in the front yard, came over to visit. I introduced him to the fawn (he didn't seem particularly interested) before taking her into the house.

The baby, who appeared healthy, was at most a week old. I started feeding her with a human baby bottle, which she accepted better than most do at first. She had been away from her mother for nearly a day by then so was quite hungry. Our friend Tom named her Lily and she was, of course, adorable. I kept her in the house for a couple days before putting her in the chain link pen during the day. We brought her in at night for a while because it was still chilly (high 30s and low 40s).

I received a call about another fawn on Wednesday, May 28. The people had called Judy, the main rehabber in our valley. She no longer takes care of the larger mammals (deer, elk, etc.) but is still busy with small mammals and birds of all kinds. Judy talked with the man and told him it sounded like they should put the baby back where they found it. She explained deer behavior and he reluctantly agreed. Judy gave him my number after telling him to use it *only* in the case of an emergency, such as the fawn running around crying.

The man's wife called me about five minutes later, insisting the fawn was hypothermic from rain and the mother was not taking care of it. After the first few minutes, I knew she was not going to listen to anyone, so I told her to bring the fawn to me. They arrived late that evening with a tiny mule deer who seemed fine, though probably only a day or two old. I was concerned he may not have had time to receive a sufficient amount of colostrum from his mother.

Colostrum is the first milk the mother produces after giving birth. It contains many antibodies the baby needs to fight infections and diseases; they usually don't survive long without this protection. It is necessary for a newborn mammal to receive the substance within the first 24 to 48 hours after birth because that is the only time antibodies are absorbed directly into its blood stream from the intestine. After that, colostrum is digested normally, meaning antibodies are broken down into their component parts, no longer effective for anything other than providing nutrients.

I put the new baby, Michael, in the playpen where he and Lily spent the night. I was glad for Lily that she would have a companion, but believed Michael should have stayed with his mother. When I fed him, he ate fairly well, though he didn't appear to have been starving. His face had an unusual shape in that his forehead was more rounded and his rostrum (the part of the face between eyes and nose) was shorter than normal. This birth defect seems to appear more frequently now, a problem Judy attributes to pesticide exposure during pregnancy. [see Judy Hoy in References for more information]

Deer hugs from Solo when
he was nearly a year old.

Baby Solo enjoying
his bottle.

Solo making himself at home at the Stock Farm.

Velvet and Solo (elk and mule deer) about three weeks old.

Sunny with Adele in the deer pen.

Sophia, baby white tailed deer born when her mom was killed by a car.

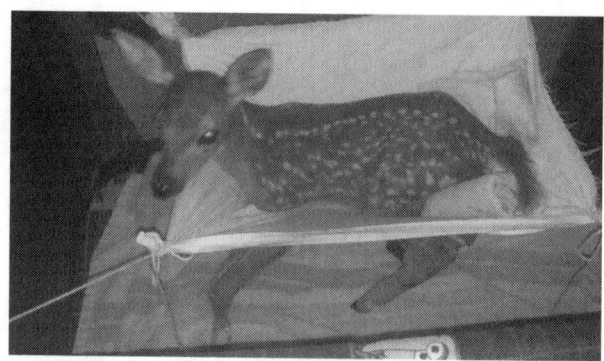

Adele's brother, David, with a moose calf.

Wendy (baby cougar) with Adele.

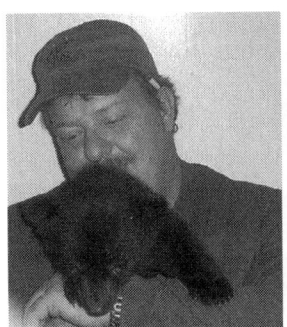  

Bo with Tom.

Baby Bo being
fed by Adele.

Bo with Don.

Bo playing with a pine cone on the kitchen floor.

Baby raccoon, held by friend Valerie, who introduced Adele to Lyn.

Baby fox squirrel in Adele's hand.

Cinco in Judy's flight room, determined to go home!

Female bald eagle with a non-repairable wing injury, due to electrocution.

Spirit just after leaving the carrier, on his way up the hill to reunite with his parents and sibling.

Spirit sitting on his "ankles." Photo by Sarah Monson.

Adult female golden eagle who was hit by a car. Photo by Sarah Monson.

Adult female osprey with Judy Hoy. This osprey was healed and released.

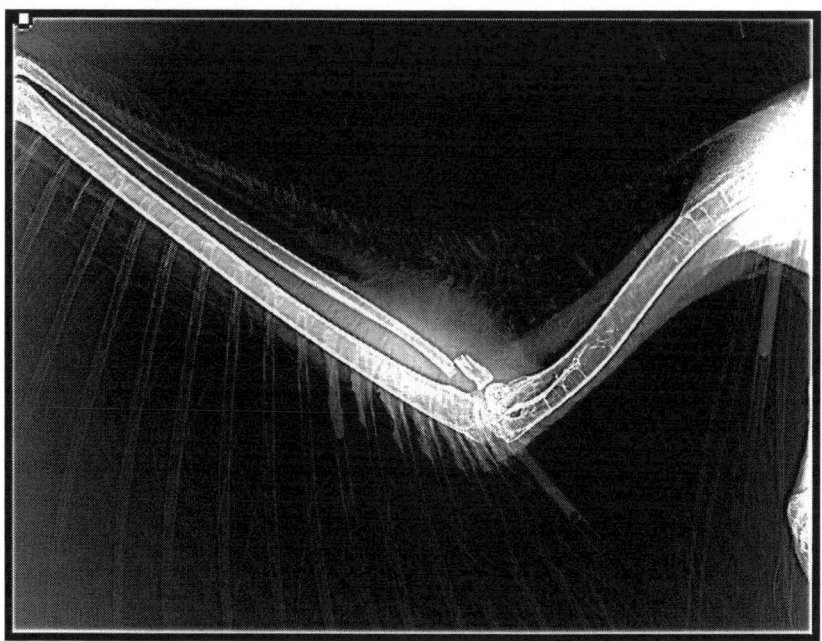

X-ray of osprey's wing fracture.

Adult great horned owl.
Photo by Sarah Monson.

Great grey owl with
Adele just before release.

"Oscar's Wildest Dreams" photo by Sarah Monson, 2nd place winner of the Ernst Peterson Photo contest, 2012 (Ravalli County Museum).

Oscar eating his mice. (Saw whet owl) Photo by Sarah Monson.

Star Owl when he was nearly dead from being fed poisoned rodents by his well-meaning parents.

Tube feeding a baby bird. Photo by Sarah Monson.

Screech owl babies whose nest tree was cut down one spring.

Ginger tolerating emus, Aten and Zebanessa.

Aten and Zeb about two months old.

Aten and Zeb about two weeks old.

Handsome Aten.

Pretty bird Nicki and Don.

Simon at the World Parrot Refuge, identifying himself to Adele.

Tisha, when she had most of her feathers.

Baby Casey.

Cricket and baby Toby.

Toby's skeleton.

Ara (reticulated python) at about 50 pounds. This was the last time Adele was able to hold her because she was too big.

Ara, about 16 feet long and 70 pounds, with Adele.

CHAPTER 43

On Friday evening, May 30, I noticed a pickup stopped on the road toward the south end of our property. Our wallabies can be seen from the road so stopped cars are common, but this was too far south to be wallaby watchers. I immediately thought about Solo, a vision of him being hit by a car flashing through my mind. When I walked out to the road, I saw Solo standing next to the truck visiting with people. He ignored me when I called to him. Then another car stopped and Solo immediately went to visit the new people. I wanted to go down there – being protective of Solo – but I was wearing slippers and my car keys were in the house. Finally the pickup driver pulled up to me and stopped. The people told me they had been going to take pictures of the beautiful deer by the road, but were unable to do so because he was too close to the camera when he poked his head in the window.

I asked the pickup driver to return to the corner and tell the second group they should leave, in the best interest of the deer. Their car was parked in the road and a woman was standing beside it petting Solo. I explained to those in the pickup that Solo needed to go wild and it was better for him if people didn't interact with him. They drove back and explained, but the second group still didn't leave and I became angry. I rushed back in the house for my keys, driving quickly to the corner where Solo's head was in the window of a third car. I jumped out of my car and yelled, "Hey!" I was planning to tell the people they had been asked to move on and I would greatly appreciate it if they would do so. When Solo stepped back, I saw my neighbor Tom in the car. He, too, had seen the vehicles and driven there out of concern for Solo. I said, "Oh, Tom, I'm so glad it's you!"

Solo walked up to me and began rubbing against me hard enough to push me backward. Then he went behind me, rearing up in an attempt to put his feet on my shoulders. I pushed him away, backing up against Tom's car to prevent that behavior.

Tom said the people had been thrilled to actually touch a deer. They were from another state and never thought they would have such a wonderful experience. Tom, too, had told them it would be best if they didn't interact with Solo.

I finally began to think, and realized I was over-reacting. There is no way I could keep people away from Solo while allowing him to be free. I couldn't follow him all the time to monitor every situation he experienced. He had made an amazing journey entirely without me, surviving many new encounters about which I would never know. I decided to lighten up and begin trusting Solo to make his own decisions and take care of himself. Easier said than done!

I walked back to my car and drove slowly home, with Solo trotting along behind. Tom came into the yard with us, saying Solo had cried pathetically when I got in the car. We put him in the back yard where he could rest and eat and I relaxed, knowing he was safe at least for that night.

The next morning, Saturday, May 31, Solo left again and didn't come home. I'm sure his leaving was due to my reaction to his visitors the night before. We didn't hear anything until the following Thursday when Don's bridge partner, Judy (not the rehabber), told Don Solo was at a place called the Stock Farm. She heard about his visit when she was there playing bridge and had even seen him. I found out later Solo had been at a flower shop, eating outside flowers, between leaving here and arriving at the Stock Farm. Five years later a photo of him crossing the highway near the flower shop appeared on Facebook, posted by someone I don't know. I recognized him and knew the photo had been taken in 2008 because of the shape of his antlers; due to the injury one had received on his first journey, it was growing in a recognizably individual shape. In subsequent years, new antlers would have another configuration.

Solo must have taken a different path on this journey because the flower shop is at the south end of Hamilton, with the parking lots he had visited before on the north end. A neighbor about a mile south of us stopped one day to tell us Solo often followed her while she was jogging and had visited their place. Three bridges cross the Bitterroot River in and around Hamilton, one a few miles south of us on the main highway, another three miles (by road) north and east of our place, and the third at the north end of Hamilton, also on the main highway. Solo may have used the two closest to us, one for each trip. I doubt he would have been able to cross the river with the water so high, but I may still be underestimating Solo.

The Stock Farm is also on the east side of the valley, a bit farther east and a few miles south of the refuge where Solo had been before. It is an exclusive gated community with huge homes, a clubhouse, and a golf course. I haven't been there and it isn't visible from the road. The place used to be a large ranch, called the Stock Farm, where cattle and horses were raised, as they still are on parts of the property. At least some of the people who have homes there are only in residence part of the year. I believe cabins are available for rent or lease as well.

Tori, the woman who had reported the baby moose who died of West Nile virus the summer before, works at the Stock Farm. She had met Solo as a baby when she was helping care for the little moose. I emailed Tori, telling her about his travels, so was able to learn of some of his exploits and adventures from an insider. I chose to leave him there without trying to visit. The only complaint I had heard about Solo so far was his habit of eating flowers; this continued at the Stock Farm. He began hanging out on the golf course where people occasionally had to move him out of the way so they could play. He was a bit of a nuisance, but Tori thought nearly everyone wanted him there. He posed for pictures with many of their employees, residents, and visitors, hung out with the golf caddies, and followed golf carts.

Solo often slept by one of the cabins, traveling several miles each day from a cabin on one side of the compound to the maintenance barns at the other. Tori was concerned that he was becoming too comfortable with humans, but he was way past that already. Some people there drive too fast and some have dogs that could be a threat to Solo, which also worried Tori. I reminded her that Solo had already crossed busy highways, dealt with traffic here and in town, and had no doubt come across unfriendly dogs and people. Tori thought about bringing him here or taking him to her place, which is farther away from people and closer to the mountains. I suggested to her that we continue to let him do what he chose unless he became too much of a nuisance. She said she would try to trust that Solo knew what was right for him. I could certainly relate to her difficulty with that concept!

One day toward the beginning of Solo's visit to the Stock Farm, some people left the door to the men's locker room open while they were working there and Solo wandered in to visit. Then he developed the habit of standing in front of the clubhouse door until someone let him in. We have a photo of him in the employees' break room, seemingly watching TV. Tori said he had also learned how to walk up and down a staircase of more than 20 steps in one area, a difficult feat for many four-legged, hooved animals.

Then one day a homeowner got tired of losing flowers to a deer and he shot (or shot at) Solo with buckshot. When Solo left the Stock Farm as a result, many people there were angry with the man for driving him away. It is illegal to shoot at native wildlife except during hunting season (in designated areas with appropriate permits), or under special circumstances if the wild animal is physically threatening people or livestock.

Wild deer are found nearly everywhere in our valley, including in towns. Everyone who lives here deals with them in yards and gardens. Don puts six-foot high fences around anything we want to protect from them. People who run plant nurseries can suggest decorative plants that do not appeal to deer. Solo was more bold in that he raided yards during the day when people are around, even walking onto decks and porches where flowers are in pots and planters. However, he is far from the only deer here who has frustrated people's efforts to grow many different plants.

A few years before this, Lyn had a big problem with wild moose entering her yard and eating the bushes she had planted as a hedge. She had spent a lot of time and money on the plants and, though she appreciated being able to see the moose, she was becoming frustrated. She explained to them that they were causing damage and she would rather they eat somewhere else. Also, they could be dangerous to her, her husband, and her dogs. The moose apologized, saying they hadn't realized it was a problem. For the rest of that year, they stayed farther away, allowing her hedge to grow as she wished.

After I explained telepathic animal communication to my friend Sandy, she began asking deer in her area to avoid the plants, flowers, and fruit trees in her yard. She renews her request each year, offering them fallen fruit in the fall which they gladly eat, but they cause no further problem with plants and flowers she wants to save. Most people, however, are unaware they can ask this of animals, or that they will often (not always) comply when they understand.

The next Thursday, June 12, not long after Solo left the Stock Farm, I received a call from a woman named Barb, telling me Solo was eating flowers at a car wash near the highway at the north end of Hamilton. Barb is a rehabber who takes care of some orphaned baby birds in our valley. She had met yearling Solo at our home when she was picking up a baby bird, so was aware of his behavior and travels. After eating what he wanted, Solo lay down in the flower bed to rest. I assumed he was again on his way home so Don and I jumped in the truck and rushed downtown. On the way, Don's cell phone rang; a woman he knew who worked at a title company near the car wash was also reporting a Solo sighting. He had tried to follow someone into the building and was creating quite a stir in their parking lot. Everybody there was thrilled about being able to meet him.

When we arrived, a number of people were photographing Solo as he calmly ate grass by the parking lot, with Barb keeping an eye on him for us. When I walked over and spoke to him, Solo came up to give me deer hugs as he had before. He was in much better condition than the last time he came home from a journey. I could see no sign of new injuries and the old ones were completely healed. The velvet had grown back on his right antler and looked healthy. That antler was shorter than the other one, but both were bigger than when I had last seen him. A knob at the base of the injured antler looked as though it would become an extra point where one normally doesn't grow. I assume the velvet injury had changed the normal growth pattern. The tops of both antlers had divided so he was a two-point buck rather than a spike, as is more common for yearlings.

I climbed into the back of the pickup, with Solo again following me. He stood at the tailgate waiting for Don to boost him inside, a more difficult chore than before. Solo was noticeably bigger this time so didn't fit quite as well inside the canopy, but he didn't seem to mind. Don drove more slowly so the trip was uneventful except that a police car followed behind us when we were nearly home. I expected him to pull into our driveway to ask why a deer was in our truck, illegal under most circumstances, but he went on by. He may have known us or called dispatch and been told what we do. Dispatch often calls us about wildlife, either because a game warden requests it or because we are on their list for helping wild birds and mammals, including problem bats.

CHAPTER 44

Don and I have been vaccinated against rabies which infects a few bats here. Most of those we're called about are simply in the wrong place, just needing to be moved elsewhere. Occasionally one is injured, ill, or dehydrated due to summer heat. As with other wildlife, our objective is to care for them until they can be released. The majority of the bat calls I receive occur during their migration times in spring and fall, when those unfamiliar with this area stop to rest where people are more likely to see them.

A small percentage of the sick bats do have rabies, as confirmed by laboratory tests. One of these was a youngster I thought had simply crawled or fallen out of the roost in someone's attic before it was old enough to fly. The bat bit my finger right next to the nail while I was showing it to the people who had found it in their yard. There was no blood because their teeth are so tiny, but I did feel a slight prick. The little guy would have been unable to break the thicker skin on other parts of my finger. I was unconcerned about the bite at the time.

At home, I noticed the bat was behaving strangely, moving in an uncoordinated manner and reacting too strongly to any stimulus, leading me to think it might have rabies. Because it was found in a yard after falling from a roost in an occupied house, I euthanized it and sent it to a lab for testing.

A lab person called the same week with a positive report; the bat had rabies. The lab technician asked whether anyone had handled it or if pets had been exposed to it. I always ask those questions when I pick up a bat and felt comfortable this one hadn't been touched by anyone but me. However, I called the homeowners to warn them because other bats in the colony may have been infected.

During a phone conversation I mentioned the incident to Linda, our veterinarian. She asked if I'd been re-vaccinated for rabies since the bite. I had had a titre (blood test to determine immunity to a disease) run the month before which showed my rabies immunity was good. Linda said it is still necessary to receive booster vaccinations when exposed to the disease, and the sooner after exposure they are given the better. Great! It had already been five or six days since I was bitten and it was Friday night. Of course medical offices were closed until Monday.

I called the emergency room, but no one would answer questions about the availability of vaccine unless I went in. I did so, taking the report showing my antibody levels. I tried to be patient as a couple students went through the routine of recording vital signs. My blood pressure was high, though it is usually normal or even low, so the students said I may have to stay there until they could figure out why it was high. I knew why it was high, was completely unconcerned about it, and was not going to stay in the hospital. I simply wanted to tell a doctor what was going on so he or she could find out how to get the vaccine if there wasn't any in town. I could have accomplished that on the phone, with much lower blood pressure!

The doctor was quite concerned that I had waited so many days after the bite to come in. He hadn't seen the lab report of my titre and was extremely relieved when I told him about it. Then everything calmed down so I could explain the situation. I knew more about what needed to be done than he did and told him my source of information was a veterinarian. The doctor called a state authority who recommended the same procedure as Linda, of course. There was no vaccine in Hamilton so he was going to make phone calls to find some. I said, "Great! Then I can go home and you can call me when you have the information." He agreed.

A short time later the doctor called to tell me one of the hospitals in Missoula had the required two doses of rabies vaccine. He asked the pharmacist to take it to the Now Care office in the complex, where I would pick it up. Missoula is 50 miles from our place and it was about 10:00 p.m. by then, but I drove up to retrieve the vaccine. I took it to the Hamilton ER where a nurse gave me the first injection and put the other vial of vaccine in their refrigerator. I was to return in a few days for the second dose. My rabies titre is probably now off the charts, but that is fine. It was a good lesson for me, though an expensive one. Total cost was $500.

Another rabid bat was brought to me by a family who lives in the mountains south of here. One of the children had found it in an area that had burned recently in a forest fire. Because the bat was slightly singed, we thought it had suffered from heat and/or smoke and would probably be releasable. They had taken care of it for a couple days so the parents and two children had touched it, though they didn't think anyone had been bitten.

Bats lick themselves when grooming so touching an infected one can cause exposure to rabies without being bitten. The virus is carried in bodily fluids, especially saliva, and can be transmitted to another mammal through mucus membranes around the eyes and mouth, or breaks in the skin. People can also be bitten without realizing it because the teeth are so tiny. Not long after I received the bat, I noticed its behavior was abnormal. Because of its close association with the family, I euthanized it immediately and sent it for testing. I called the family about my concerns, suggesting they talk with their doctor or the local health department. I wanted them to have a plan in case the bat was rabid. They agreed and we waited for the lab report.

After the lab called the next day with a positive report, I again contacted the family. Their doctor thought it would be safest for the whole family to receive post-exposure treatment. This was done and everyone was fine. Fortunately the treatment now is much easier and safer for people than it used to be. It consists of a few vaccine injections in the arm instead of an earlier regimen of many in the abdomen.

Rabies is fatal. I'm unaware of anyone who has survived after exhibiting symptoms of the disease. I know of one man in Montana who died of rabies a few years ago, some time after he found a bat in his bed. He had not been aware of being bitten, though a bite while he was sleeping could easily have been missed. Unlike vampire bats, the small bats living here are unable to create a noticeable wound with their tiny mouths and teeth.

The vast majority of bats are rabies-free and of great value to us. Those that are insectivorous consume huge numbers of mosquitoes and other flying insects. When I asked Dr. Linda about protecting our emus from West Nile virus, which is transmitted by mosquitoes and often infects birds, she suggested we put bat houses on our property. Nectar-eating bats pollinate flowers and fruit-eating bats transfer seeds. Contrary to popular opinion, bats do not try to get into people's hair nor do they bite unless we handle them incorrectly. Even rabid bats do not purposely attack people or other animals, though all bats I have handled, whether healthy or sick, did try to bite when I picked them up. This is normal defensive behavior exhibited by most wild animals, so people should avoid handling them. Vampire bats, which feed on blood, do bite without provocation, but they don't live here.

Infected bats and other mammals become sick and die from the disease. I was told by a research scientist that if captive bats remain healthy for 30 days, they do not have rabies. To my knowledge there are no carrier animals that survive infection, though the course of the disease and amount of time between exposure and death vary greatly depending on virulence of the virus, method and location of introducing it into the body, and quantity of virus transferred.

CHAPTER 45

When we arrived home after Solo's second journey, he again hopped out of the truck, seeming pleased to be back. I was certainly happy to have him here! He followed me into the back yard, drank some water, and then waited for me to fill his grain bucket. I locked up Aten and Ara because Ara was still in egg-laying mode and Aten was still aggressive toward Solo. After a few days we started letting Solo out of the yard again, often only seeing him in the morning and evening. He still followed joggers and visited neighbors.

One evening Tom heard a noise at his back door. He thought it was Megan, his cat, until the door knob wiggled. Tom opened the door to see how she had reached up that far. He was looking down at cat level so was startled to find Solo asking to come in. He had never been in Tom's house before, but apparently assumed he would be welcome – as of course he was. Tom let him into the utility room which he explored for a short time. He found and ate a piece of Megan's cat food, nuzzled Tom, then turned around and left.

On Thursday, June 19, I received a call from a woman who lives outside of our valley. She and her husband had found a pair of fawns, presumably twins, who were starving. One was much smaller than the other and terribly weak. They had watched the babies run around crying for a couple days before taking them in. Because they lived so far away, they would be unable to bring them to me until the weekend, so I explained what to do for the babies. They said they would call to let me know when they would be here.

The smaller fawn died, not surprising given their description of its condition. The people put the stronger one outside again to see if her mother would show up, but the baby kept running around crying. I believe the mother must have died, because I have never known of one voluntarily abandoning a normal baby. The couple fed her pasteurized goat milk purchased from a grocery store, limiting her intake to about four ounces every few hours to avoid over-feeding after the long starvation.

They arrived on Sunday with Rosie, a white-tailed deer a week to 10 days old. She was in fairly good shape due to their care. I put her in the playpen and warmed goat milk with whipping cream. She took about eight ounces from a baby bottle with no hesitation. I kept her in the house till the next day to make sure she was digesting the milk normally before putting her in the deer pen with Lily(the baby found near a bike path after her sibling had been killed by a dog) and Michael. They accepted her and she was unafraid of them, as is usual when I bring in a new fawn. Rosie was already tame enough to accept me without having to spend adjustment time in the smaller chain link pen.

Michael, the mule deer fawn I thought was a kidnap victim who perhaps hadn't received enough colostrum, kept having intermittent bouts of diarrhea. He would stop eating before Lily, hunching his back and straining as though he had abdominal cramps. I tried everything I could think of to stop the diarrhea. He was still active, running and playing with the others, but sometimes he would pass mucus, indicating inflamed or irritated intestines. I even saw a spot of blood in it a couple times. Everything would seem normal for a day or two and then the diarrhea and cramps returned.

He also sometimes produced foul-smelling gas, though that stopped after I gave him some beneficial intestinal bacteria intended for calves. I had given him dried intestinal bacteria made for animals in general and some for humans, in addition to over-the-counter anti-diarrhea products, aloe vera juice, electrolytes, and cell salts at various times, all of which have helped other fawns. Diarrhea is common in fostered fawns as they adjust to new and unnatural food, but is usually easy to stop. Each treatment seemed to help Michael but only for a while. Lyn did a shamanic journey for him on June 24; he was better for a few days, but then became worse again.

Finally, after Michael started refusing some of his bottles early in July, I decided to try antibiotics. I called Linda and drove to her place for oral Amoxicillin. By then Michael sometimes refused as many three of the four daily bottles, and he never ate as much at a time as Lily. After a day and a half of the new treatments, he accepted the other two bottles one day and all those I offered him the next. I later saw him running with Lily so he apparently felt better. Michael still ate less than he should, but I was hopeful he was moving past his health issues.

CHAPTER 46

One evening after Solo's second return, when I glanced out my bedroom window, I noticed a car stopped and people standing in the road with a camera. I looked around and of course found Solo near the road in the neighbor's pasture. Still wanting to discourage this behavior, I walked out to the road, hoping to help Solo through the barbed wire fence and back to our place. He walked over to the fence and let me pet him as I spread the wires apart, giving him room to step through. Solo put his head under the wire but refused to continue. He still stayed on his side of the fence when I moved to a different place where I could spread the wires farther apart.

I gave up in frustration, going back through the gate into our front yard toward the house. Solo walked over to the woven wire fence between our place and the neighbor's, hopped over it as though he'd done it a hundred times before (he probably had), gently rubbed his head against me, and then followed me into the back yard. The people watched this whole incident, still standing in the road with a camera. I hadn't said anything to them nor did they speak to me. Needless to say, I was a bit embarrassed. Solo kept working patiently to train me, but at times I learn slowly.

About 10:00 the next evening, after I had fed the fawns, a neighbor called because he had seen a small fawn in his yard that worried him. His dog had chased it earlier in the day; then he found it lying in some tall grass and watched from a distance for quite a while without seeing the mother. The man thought she might be unable to find her baby because it was in a different place from where she had left it. I drove over and walked to the fawn, who was in hiding mode. I put a towel over it to avoid touching it with bare hands, guiding it to stand so I could check for injuries. There was no blood and, as soon as I let go of it, the fawn ran off, looking perfectly normal and healthy. The man shined his flashlight around, spotlighting the mother where she stood in the trees watching. As we were walking back to my car, I asked about his encounters with Solo.

He said Solo was a nuisance in that he ate flowers on their

porch; he was quite persistent even when they became annoyed with him. I told the man my two options were to put up with him, hoping he would go wild as Skipper had, or have him euthanized. Of course the neighbor didn't want him killed. He was to let me know if Solo became a serious problem.

The next morning (Wednesday, June 25, 2008) Solo left, again probably due to my interference in his life. No one called us about him for quite some time. I had looked up petting zoos and wildlife safaris after Solo returned from the Stock Farm, thinking I might find a place where he could be safe, live in a large area, and yet interact with a lot of people.

I wasn't happy with what I found until I saw an article in a local paper about a large animal sanctuary about three hours north of here. They had a lot of rescued domestic animals (horses, cows, llamas, pigs, sheep, etc.) on about 400 acres and they allowed visitors. What excited me was they had a mule deer named Wendy who was too tame to be released. An elk with an injured leg joint (from an arrow), making it unable to survive in the wild, also lived there. I thought it would be a good place to keep in mind if Solo got into serious trouble. Several years later this place was featured in local newspapers due to animal neglect and financial difficulties. I don't know what happened to all the animals, but am glad Solo wasn't there.

On July 6, 2008, I asked Lyn to talk with Solo, which she did the next morning. She was to make sure he was okay, and give him information about bow hunting season (which starts in September here) and about the animal sanctuary.

> Solo: Lyn, I'm so glad you came to talk with me. I've been wanting to talk with Adele. She's worried about me, isn't she?

> Lyn: Yes, Solo. She's concerned about you.

> Solo: Well, tell her I'm fine and I'm big enough now to take care of myself. I'm not going to tell her or you where I am. Good or bad (and who determines that?), I am

living as I choose. I've been able to find my way back most of the way, and if I want to come back again, I will. Even if I'm penned, I'm ministering to others and even if Adele doesn't hear about me, tell her it's okay. She's got to let go! There isn't a real easy way to do that. I thought this coming and going and hearing where I was would be helpful, but I'm not sure that is the case. Tell her to send me love and light whenever she thinks about me. That is what I need most. Our connection is strong and will never go away, but she needs to let go and trust that whoever looks after the other deer will look after me.

Lyn: Are you interested in living in a sanctuary? That's where they keep animals safe and give them more room to roam than most people have [on their property], but it is nothing like what wild deer have. However, you don't have to worry about hunters killing you and they do allow people to come to see you some. I don't know how much or to what extent.

Solo: Lyn, tell Adele Thank you so much! I do appreciate her care and concern, but Lyn – tell her I'm a Master [Being]. I'm here on a mission. I came to minister to those who might never understand otherwise. I am not alone. You know that. There are so many Masters reincarnating now in unusual bodies that you would be totally shocked if you knew how many there are. There are enough so that every human soul will encounter at least one and some have met many more than that already. Tell Adele I need to be free to do what I came here for. When I am done, I will take leave of this body and not before. She cannot keep me safe or protect me. I now need to live my life.

Lyn: Adele also wanted you to know that bow hunting season starts on Labor Day, two moons or seven and a half weeks from now. She wanted you to know there are people who will kill you for the fun of it, or some for meat.

Solo: Tell her thanks for her thoughtfulness to warn me of dangers. I'm deeply touched! Lyn, tell her I have already seen unkind people that she knows naught about and I am still doing what I need to do. I was even a bow hunter myself once. There is always a strong relationship between predator and prey animals, and each takes a turn at each so as to better understand the different bodies and perspectives. I do not wish to belittle Adele in any way. I am here to help her grow just as I will help all who meet me. Remind Adele that Altea's [Rosemary Altea, psychic and author] repeated message was love and gentleness to all. That is my message to all I meet, too, and particularly to her. We would not have been so long together if we were not already close, but she must see that now it is time to let go – in love and gentleness – unless I come back to her of my own free will. That is how it must be.

I love her deerly (pun intended) and I want her to write her book – but make the theme "Letting Go" – not a story of an unusual deer. It should be more about her awakening than mine, like *The Parrots of Telegraph Hill*.

Love! Blessings

Some of this communication brought tears to Lyn's eyes and to mine when she read it to me over the phone. My first comment when she finished was, "Wow!" I couldn't even think of anything else to say. Solo is so kind and understanding and such an amazing being! Lyn suddenly knew he was a Master Being just before he told her. She felt he was reluctant to say it, but did so because he believed I needed to know. I feel so fortunate to have had contact with him for slightly more than a year. Though I hope I'll get to see him again and give him another hug, I'm able to accept his decision to go his own way.

Part of my problem in letting go is a feeling of responsibility as the rehabilitator who raised Solo. Though I've had no other released animals behave as Solo has, I still felt I must have done something wrong with him. It is also difficult after raising one from a helpless state to realize and accept that it no longer is helpless. Further, I thought he would be better off living in the wild with other deer. That is not my decision to make, of course, because Solo does not belong to me; he belongs only to himself.

It is easy to think animals are unaware of what is best for them, extending my feeling of responsibility to include deciding how they should live. The more I know of them, however, the more I realize that belief is inaccurate. Just as parents need to allow their children to make age-appropriate decisions, even when they are different from what the parents would prefer, so I'm learning to better respect the awareness and knowledge of animals. They are not babies except for the short time when they actually are. In some ways they know a lot more than we do.

I now think Solo would have lived as he is regardless of what I did. I was simply one of the people who helped him survive as a baby so he could live the life he chose for himself before he even came here. From what I have learned, beginning a few years before I met Solo, I believe he planned to be raised by humans in this life so he would be better able to complete the objectives he set for himself. Who am I to interfere with that? All I can do is feel blessed to be one of those who took care of him when he was truly helpless.

I had been concerned that someone might put Solo in a pen from which he would be unable to escape and that he might get hurt trying. Even after Solo's lessons about letting go, I told Tori all bets are off if I hear he is injured or penned. After further thought I decided if I heard something like that I'd ask Lyn to check with Solo and then work on respecting and honoring what he said, even if his answer was to stay away.

I had read my friend Anna's copy of Rosemary Altea's first book, *The Eagle and the Rose*, when I was visiting her and her husband Ed's home. Anna was given the book by another friend who thought it would be of value to her, but she hadn't gotten around to reading it. I read parts of it to her and it did help her with some problems and questions she had. I have since read more of Altea's books and certainly benefitted from reading them. Perhaps my favorite is *Proud Spirit*, part of which is a series of questions answered by Grey Eagle, a spirit who talks to Altea. As Solo said, the message is love and gentleness, certainly stressing non-judgment of others, no matter how different their beliefs and lifestyles are.

A couple of years before this communication with Solo, Lyn loaned me her copy of the book *The Wild Parrots of Telegraph Hill* by Mark Bittner. I enjoyed it so much I bought my own copy and then watched the documentary of the same title. It started out being about the wild parrots (mostly cherry-headed conures) in San Francisco, but the birds and his book unexpectedly changed the life of the author in some amazing ways.

More publications that had a profound effect on me came out (or came into my awareness) within a couple of years of this period. *The Secret* by Rhonda Byrne is a wonderful movie (and book) that describes the Law of Attraction in ways that are easily understood, with many examples from a simple one of manifesting good parking spaces to overcoming amazing adversity. Ms. Byrne and many others explain how and why we attract from the Universe that which occupies our attention. We can use their information to improve, one way or another, all of life's situations. I've watched the movie several times and have recommended it to countless people. I am always energized and more enthusiastic after watching it and would love to see a world in which everyone used the methods of living described therein.

What the Bleep Do We Know!?, a movie about quantum physics, also had a great impact on me. It is significant because it begins to meld my trust in the scientific method with my developing understanding of Spirit, without resorting to religious teachings. A statement on the front of the DVD case is: "Science and spirituality come together in this mind-bending trip down the rabbit hole." I certainly can't briefly describe it better than that and I highly recommend it to anyone looking for layman's knowledge about quantum physics. The book *The Dancing Wu Li Masters* by Gary

Zukav, also written for non-physicists, teaches quantum physics in much greater depth. Both provide examples of experiments which demonstrate the amazing and seemingly magical complexity of our world, including the concept of parallel universes.

CHAPTER 47

In one of our conversations Lyn told me many animals in the world now are interacting in unusual ways with humans. One example she gave was about a pack of wolves who made their den in an area that is readily visible to Yellowstone National Park visitors. The wolves are far enough away so binoculars and spotting scopes, set up at a viewpoint, are helpful for watching them. Normally wolves are shy, especially about their den and babies, often moving to a different area if people come close enough to see it a few times. These wolves, however, choose to stay in that spot. They have told Lyn knowing people are watching is somewhat uncomfortable for them, but their purpose is to help educate us to be more sensitive, aware, and appreciative of animals, the planet, and each other.

When I asked for her definition of Master Beings and more information about the animals behaving in unusual ways, Lyn emailed the following and graciously gave permission to include it here:

> As for my definition of a Master Being, I asked my guides how to put it into simple words. This is what I got and it is exactly how I feel about Masters. "A Master Being is a highly evolved soul who understands him/herself well and understands equally well his/her connection to the Creator."

> As for behavior changes I have seen in animals in the past 10 to15 years, I have found it remarkable how many of them are acting in a more highly-evolved manner than in earlier years. They know Earth works as we see it because of the interdependency of all life forms with one another. Humans have seen it to some extent and in some text books they call it the "food chain." In the wolf study program in Yellowstone National Park, they are seeing that culling of elk herds by wolves is allowing aspen trees in the park to take a new lease on life and grow better and

more abundantly. In this instance, humans can see that our interdependence goes further than just the food chain.

Many of the whale beachings that have occurred in the last decade have come about, not because the whales didn't know better, but because whales want humans to focus more attention on their species and their needs. Whales know if they are eliminated from the oceans (by sonar, contamination, and hunting) it will so greatly cause imbalances in the oceans that many changes will be set into action, which we will be unable to stop or reverse. The bottom line is that it will affect us and our world, perhaps to the point of extinction of humans. Other species are aware of this, too. The dolphins are doing their part by becoming more visible in many ways to help people see that we can live together on this planet in harmony, and more importantly, we need to if we humans want to survive as a species.

Anyplace where animals are becoming a problem in which humans must deal with them as they have never had to deal with them before is a place for human evolution, so that we, as a species, may understand how important all life forms on earth are to our "happy" living. The wolf reintroduction program in Yellowstone National Park has become so successful that now many states are having to decide how to deal with wolves in relation to ranchers and their livestock, environmentalists, and people in general. The wolves are willingly doing this to help us have the opportunity to evolve to a higher level now.

I was a professional dog trainer for about 25 years. I noticed in the last 10 years that the dogs were becoming more difficult for their owners to deal with than any dog they ever had in the past. In every case, the dogs were behaving in a way to show their owners that they needed to change their thoughts and attitudes in order to have peace and harmony with the family dog.

Canada geese became highly visible a few years ago in some parts of the country. They landed and stayed in areas inhabited by humans, where they had never done that before. These people had to figure out how to get the geese to move on without just killing all of them, for this has been our past pattern. Now more and more humans are starting to say this cannot be the best solution to the problem. People are also starting to become aware of the inhumane treatment of elephants in circuses and zoos. Some people who believe it is wrong to treat elephants this way are creating sanctuaries for them in order to change some of the problems they see on this planet.

Insects are doing a lot to let people know that exterminating them, first of all, does not work (they become resistant to pesticides), and they are willing to go elsewhere if we recognize they need a place to live in a manner normal for their species. There are still many humans who do not see that others (both human and other species) have as much right to be here as they do. They want their new housing regardless of whom it disrupts, or they want their cars and trucks, even if they foul the air and increase noise levels.

Plants are involved, too, and we will see this more and more if the greenhouse effect continues and plant life changes or just is unable to live on this planet. We are also seeing that inappropriate farming techniques, more rural development, and business practices which wipe out entire ecosystems are going to negatively affect plants, insects, and eventually us!

It has been documented that many species control their reproduction based on territory and food supply. Humans can do this as well, but have not yet realized they have the responsibility to control their reproduction. I am saying it doesn't take a law or a pill or surgery. All it takes is for humans, each one, to use their intention not to overpopulate the globe. This, of course, is what animals know and we have yet to learn. I feel strongly that the overpopulation of animal shelters is due to the fact that we have not evolved far enough, as a species, to ask our cats and dogs not to reproduce. It is clear to me that spaying and neutering are not being effective.

I feel Solo is just one of many, many animals who have chosen to lead an unusual life in order to help bring humans greater understanding of our connectedness and our responsibility to ourselves and to our planet. I believe he truly is a great Master!
Lyn J. Benedict

Lyn is far from the only animal communicator who is being told these truths by animals. A few books and other sources are listed in the References section and many more are available online and in bookstores. Articles about other communicators and books can also be found in the journal *Species Link*, published by Penelope Smith. More information about the journal, Penelope Smith, and telepathic animal communication can be found through her Internet web page.

Native Americans and many other hunter/gatherer people believe their prey animals give their bodies to provide food for them by allowing themselves to be killed. The people thank the animals for doing so and greatly respect and honor these beings. Even many animals in our zoos have allowed themselves to be captured in order to help people notice how special they are in the hope that we will be more protective of them, each other, and our planet.

When I was visiting a zoo with friends a few years ago, I saw an elephant who was clearly extremely disturbed. She was standing in one place swinging her head and trunk back and forth. This kind of repetitive movement is a response many animals exhibit when confined, though modern, more natural housing has perhaps reduced the problem. When I connected telepathically with the elephant, I felt anger and confusion without verbal communication. I called Lyn to see if she could help. She also received mainly strong negative emotions so she facilitated a connection between a captive orca she had met before and the elephant, then essentially listened to their communication.

The elephant said she had hoped to help people become more aware of the needs of animals and the planet, and therefore humans, but was discouraged due to the number of zoo visitors (and probably some employees) who are insensitive, unkind, and disrespectful. She no longer felt she was helping, which caused her to be extremely unhappy in her situation. The whale said he understood because he sees unkind people, too. However, he focuses on those who do respond positively to him and accepts the fact that he can't touch everyone. The elephant agreed to try that philosophy and to again contact the orca when she needed more encouragement. My friends learned the elephant soon seemed to be more comfortable, though I haven't heard anything about her since.

I am in awe of these beings who are working so hard to help us raise our consciousness and thus immeasurably improve life on our planet. They seem more aware of their connection to Spirit than most of us, intuitively knowing we truly are all eternal and interconnected with all that is. We are One!

CHAPTER 48

Everything everywhere in the Universe is connected through energy, the basic building block in the cosmos. In the same way that each piece of a hologram projects the entire image, so each of us is a piece of the vast pool of energy that is the whole; each of us reflects and affects all others.

Because thoughts are also energy and we are all connected within the pool, each of us influences the ratio of positive to negative by how we perceive the world and through our expectations of it. Thinking positively, focusing on gratitude, seeing other people and animals as perfect spirits rather than good or bad, not only benefits the individual but adds to the pool of positive energy. This affects our own lives and those of countless others in ways we may never know. Each individual is not an isolated unit. Our thoughts (followed by our emotions) affect others, even those with whom we will never have direct physical contact.

Lyn told me a few stories that powerfully demonstrate this and I will pass them on here. Two of them can be examined in more detail on the Internet and the other is an experience Lyn had when communicating with some animals.

The first story is called The Hundredth Monkey and my understanding of it is as follows: A colony of Macaque monkeys living on an island off the coast of Japan were fed raw sweet potatoes by people who lived on the mainland. The food was dropped onto a beach where it picked up sand, unpleasant for the monkeys to chew. One young female began washing her potatoes in a stream to remove the sand. Perhaps it was initially an accident, with a potato being cleaned of sand after falling into the stream. However, she continued the practice and other monkeys began learning from her. Eventually nearly all the younger monkeys were washing their potatoes. Some adults learned from their children, while others maintained the old habit.

Suddenly, after a large number (maybe 100) of the monkeys were regularly washing their potatoes, nearly all the monkeys began washing their food. What is even more astounding is that monkeys on the mainland and other islands also began washing their potatoes at the same time, even though they had no physical contact with the first group.

The theory developed from this experience is that when a high enough percentage of a population knows something or learns a new way, the knowledge becomes sufficiently powerful to be subconsciously and/or spiritually absorbed by most individuals of that species. And this includes humans, as demonstrated by the next story.

In June and July 1993, a study by the Institute of Science, Technology, and Public Policy was done on the effects of group Transcendental Meditation on the rate of violent crime in Washington, D.C. According to the article I read (see References), about 4000 participants stayed in Washington, D.C., for nearly two months, meditating daily with the intention of increasing coherence and reducing stress in the District.

[The Institute of HeartMath is studying coherence which they define as: "an optimal state in which heart, mind, and emotions are operating in sync and balanced physiologically. Coherence helps keep our immune, hormonal, and nervous systems functioning in a state of energetic coordination." See References]

FBI statistics for violent crimes (homicide, rape, aggravated assault, and robbery) examined before, during, and after the study were used to determine conclusions. Variables such as temperature and daylight hours were taken into consideration and results could not be attributed to changes in police staffing. Also, statistics showed there had been no significant decrease in these crimes during the five years prior to the study.

The end result was a 48% reduction of targeted crimes in that period of time. After the study the ISTPP recommended this approach "on a large scale for the benefit of society." The movie and the book *The Secret* talk about the benefits of being *for* what is wanted instead of *against* what we would like to prevent. Fighting against something only gives it more energy and strength. Mother Theresa said she would never attend an anti-war rally, but she'd be glad to participate in a pro-peace demonstration. Not only does it work better, but it also feels much better to focus on peace and education instead of the horrors of war, crime, hunger, child and animal abuse, pollution, and all the other problems on our planet.

The third story is something Lyn experienced shortly after the tsunami of 2004. Lyn is highly sensitive to negativity, so chooses to avoid the news as much as possible. Her belief, and I agree, is if there is nothing she can do to help, she may as well not know about it. Feeling sad, angry, or depressed about that over which we have no control is not only pointless, but it adds to the negative energy surrounding us. However, when the tsunami occurred, Lyn was visiting friends who watched the news. Lyn was saddened by the thousands of tragedies, of course. While sitting in a waiting room before an appointment later that week, she decided to ask some tropical fish in an aquarium what they thought about the tsunami, since they are water creatures.

What Lyn was told astounded her as it did me when she repeated their message to me. The fish said, "Consider it a blessing." Due to the massive size of the tragedy, people all over the world focused thoughts and actions of compassion and kindness toward those directly affected. There was an outpouring of donations of time, material, and money, and great numbers of people felt empathy for those who had lost so much. Before that, they were just a bunch of people from a different country and culture; most others gave them little if any thought. After that they were humans, just like us, who had suffered terrible losses.

The same thing happened after the terrorist attacks of 9/11/01. A tremendous wave of kindness and giving flooded that area from our entire country and from others around the world. What the fish meant is that these tragedies increased awareness of the feelings of others and strong thoughts of kindness, compassion, and empathy added to the positive energy in the world.

Thinking of it this way means even tragedies can have some beneficial results. Of course most people everywhere would have stopped the tsunami and the terrorists if at all possible, and that is as it should be. People in the airplane that crashed early on 9/11 sacrificed the ultimate in order to prevent even more tragedies. There are so many acts of heroism in this world, from small kindnesses to great sacrifices, when people help strangers as well as loved ones.

Both of those occurrences, one from the natural world and one due to terribly disturbed people, are filled with acts of heroism and outpourings of love and generosity. It not only feels better to focus on those and be in awe of and honor the heros than to dwell on the losses, it also increases the positive in the universal energy pool. The tragedies are in the past and can't be fixed. The example of the heros is still with us as proof of what people are willing to do for others.

Unfortunately, some people after 9/11 focused on hatred, anger, and blame. Many innocent people from mid-eastern countries have been treated unfairly since then, causing even more prejudices to surface. These frightened, angry people increase the negative energy in the world and are actually similar to those whose hatred and prejudice caused their violent behavior in the first place. Hating mid-eastern people is the same as hating Americans. The truth is that most people in the world, wherever they live and whatever their culture or religion, want to live in peace. Some leaders, whether religious, political, or both, work to create feelings of fear, hatred, and/or prejudice in an attempt to gain power. Sadly, some people in all cultures follow them.

This whole process is a vicious circle, with people on both sides of any conflict adding to the hatred and misunderstandings, thus perpetuating the problem. If more of us focused instead on love, compassion, and understanding, I believe conflicts and tragedies would decrease in number and frequency, eventually dying out due to lack of negative energy.

One of us is going to be the Hundredth Monkey who tips the balance. One more person is going to create the right number so we begin to see worldwide the positive changes experienced in Washington, D.C., when 4000 people meditated on peace for only two months. We are steadily moving closer to that state. What an exciting time to be alive!

CHAPTER 49

On Tuesday, July 8, 2008, (when I was raising fawns Lily, Michael, and Rosie) a nice woman named Judy (not my friend, the other rehabber) called me about a newborn white-tailed deer. She had seen the baby being born in her yard on July 1 and carefully watched mom and baby for a week. Then she noticed the fawn running around in circles crying. She knew it was abnormal behavior so she went exploring and found a dead doe. Judy was unable to determine what had killed the deer because predators had been there. The predators may have killed her, or she could have been hit by a car or shot for some reason. Judy continued to watch the baby for a while in case that doe wasn't her mother, but the fawn continued crying frantically.

The first part of July is late for fawns to be born here. Sometimes females who do not become pregnant during the first estrus cycle of the breeding season will cycle again a month or so later. I assume that's what happened with this little deer's mom. Being born late decreases their chance to survive the winter because their body mass is smaller, making them less able to withstand the cold. Also their mothers may wean them earlier as their bodies prepare for a new baby, meaning they receive less milk than those born in the spring.

Judy lives out of our area and was unable to bring the fawn the day she called me, but agreed to feed it goat milk and care for it until she could come. We decided on a place to meet the next day to transfer the baby she named Fancy. Judy also kindly gave me a generous donation for the rehab fund. She had done well with Fancy, who was in good condition and already accepting the new nipple. I was concerned that I would be unable to wean her with the others, but she ate so much she grew quickly and was nearly as big as Rosie by October.

I put Fancy in the chain link pen so she could have a small space in which to get used to the new home and another mom. She responded so well that I soon moved Rosie, the other white-tailed fawn, back to the deer pen to provide company for Fancy and opened the chain link pen. If at all possible, I avoid keeping baby animals alone. I'm sure Rosie would have preferred to stay in the larger area, but Fancy was so small she could slip through fences in the big back yard. She also needed to become used to Rosie and me first. When she had been here at least two weeks, I let Fancy and Rosie out in the back yard with Michael and Lily, after giving them their early morning bottles. Although Fancy was more nervous than the other fawns around people (including me, unless I had a bottle in my hand), she came with the others when I called them at feeding times.

Fancy and Rosie were so excited to be able to run more than they could in the deer pen! I sat on the deck after I released them to watch as they ran and leaped and played. Lily and Michael, the mule deer, got into the act, taking turns chasing and being chased. Michael tried to get the new girls to play his head-butting game but, being girls, they weren't interested. He and Lily executed lots of four-legged mule deer hops and everyone had a great time during the cool early morning, including me. After about an hour they all disappeared. They could have been lying in tall grass or in one of the sheds, where they spent much of the day until the next feeding time. When I called them for meals, they exploded out of whatever shelter they had chosen, running, leaping, and hopping to me to fight over who got to eat first.

Toward the end of July, Michael's front feet began to bend to the inside with his toes pointing outward. The left one was worse than the right, but both were clearly in trouble. Because the joints that look like knees in the front legs were curved inward (knock-kneed would be a description in humans), his toes were receiving uneven pressure, causing the distortion. They were clearly painful and he began moving around less. I even saw him lying down near their grain to eat, rather than standing like the others.

I gave Michael a tranquilizer and put a splint on his left foot to hold it in proper position. Because I had to do it myself and he was uncooperative even with medication to calm him, it didn't go on well and he was limping even more by the next morning. I removed the splint and asked Judy to come over to help. A couple of days later, after giving him the tranquilizer again and putting a blanket over his head, we were able to splint both feet without stressing Michael too much. I have used splints for similar problems in many fawns, but they were always younger; Michael was about two months old by then, much less comfortable about being handled and perhaps less likely to recover from this type of condition. Something had to be done, though, and that was all we knew to try.

By this time Michael was losing patches of hair, possibly due to a thyroid imbalance, and he was still eating poorly. Even with splints, he walked as though he was in pain and the joints in his back legs appeared to be uncomfortable as well. He no longer had problems with diarrhea, but was clearly not thriving like the others.

The day after we applied the new splints Michael managed to take the tape off the bottom of the left one so it was forcing his toes farther in the wrong position. I moved and re-taped the splint, but he had done the same thing with the right one by the next day. I had seen him licking at his feet as though they hurt; I'm sure he was peeling the tape off, though we thought we had used plenty.

Michael was miserable and I didn't think he was going to get better. He certainly would be unreleasable unless there was a lot of improvement and I no longer thought that was going to happen. I finally decided to give up on him and he was euthanized late in July. I'm unsure whether his difficulties were caused by receiving insufficient colostrum right after birth, pesticide exposure before birth, or perhaps both, but little Michael had always had health problems.

CHAPTER 50

Late in the afternoon of July 10, 2008, my nephew Harold again called to ask for advice. He and his co-workers (loggers) had been watching and listening for two or three days to a baby cougar as it ran around crying. As with Bo, the bear cub they rescued a couple years before, they were concerned about legalities but couldn't stand thinking about that poor baby whose cries were becoming weaker. I told him to pick up the cub and bring it to me.

Harold thought the game wardens might begin to wonder about him because he brought a bear before and then a cougar. I reminded him that he was more likely to find these babies than the rest of us because he worked in the woods. He is also observant and caring. He said all the men were worried about this baby, as they had been about the little bear, and they hated leaving them at the end of their work day. People think of loggers and hunters as being unconcerned about the environment and the animals, and some are. Many, however, do care and are especially soft-hearted when it comes to wild babies.

The guys gave the little cougar water, which she drank readily, and named her Wendy. Harold took her home where his wife Stacey gave her more water, a small amount of milk, and two tiny balls of hamburger. She had been quite lethargic as they drove down the mountain, but perked up at their home.

When she arrived here, I found Wendy to be dehydrated and emaciated, though I was unable to find any injuries. Because of her development and coordination, I believe she was four or five weeks old; she only weighed about 2 pounds. As with Solo, Bo, and other starving animals and birds, I gave her electrolytes frequently for a while. Then I made a mixture of goat milk, whipping cream, and strained chicken (baby food), which I put in a bowl. That was a mistake! Wendy knew she wanted to eat it, but had no idea how to go about it. She kept getting food in her nose and often bit the edge of the bowl. She was able to lap up some, but it was a struggle. I had to hold her front feet to keep them out of the bowl. In frustration she would grab the towel under the bowl with her teeth, nearly tipping it over.

Feeding became much easier when I put the mixture in a baby bottle with an enlarged hole in the nipple. Wendy definitely knew what to do with that! She had incisors and canine teeth, though her molars hadn't erupted yet. She wasn't interested in pieces of skinned mice, but she sure liked her milk mixture. I had to be careful to hold only the end of the bottle, keeping my fingers away from Wendy's sharp little claws. She attacked the nipple and shook it first before she settled down to suck. I didn't expect the nipple to survive long and sympathized with her mother.

I let Wendy sleep with me that night and part of the next because she cried when I put her in a dog carrier in the kitchen. I decided she had had enough of being alone and scared and, as with Bo, I wanted her to be able to wake me easily when she was hungry. Wendy curled up next to me and slept peacefully, only waking twice the first night for a bottle and once the next night. She was a much easier bed companion than Bo; I didn't wake up soaked in goat milk and urine. The second night I put Wendy into her dog carrier den after the first feeding and she slept peacefully there the rest of the time she was with us.

During the day I let Wendy roam around the house, but had to constantly watch her. Tisha and Simon, the parrots, were out of their cages most of the time and Simon would often climb down and walk around on the floor. A couple of times he and Wendy nearly had a confrontation. Wendy was stalking the bird and Simon was stalking the cat. I thought Simon would win a battle at that point, but didn't want either of them injured.

Living with Wendy was a lot of work because she was so busy. She did take naps, going into her carrier when she was tired. Wendy stayed with me from Thursday evening till the following Tuesday morning when a game warden picked her up and transferred her to the state rehab center in Helena. He asked me if I was sorry to see her go and I said no, it was time. I am not equipped to raise cougars or bears. It's unfair for them to be kept in backyard cages and they are not domestic animals, no matter how they are raised. I feel good about my small part in their rescue and fortunate and honored to have spent time with them.

Montana Department of Fish, Wildlife and Parks does not allow native wild cats (cougar, bobcat, lynx) raised by humans to be released into the wild, both because they may be a threat to people or livestock and because it is difficult for them (especially cougars) to survive in the wild. Cougars normally live with their mothers for up to two years while learning to hunt. They have the instincts to stalk and kill prey, but it's hard work, requiring a lot of practice to become proficient. Without help, captive-raised youngsters would become progressively weaker, therefore less effective as predators, before starving to death. If someone lives with them in the woods or somehow helps them for six or more months, their chance for survival is better, but few people are able or willing to do so.

CHAPTER 51

The Saturday Wendy was here, my parents, youngest brother Dan, and nephew D.J. came to visit. While they were here, Dan told us his friend Pat had seen a beautiful, friendly mule deer buck on a golf course at the south side of Missoula.

Of course I was interested, so Dan called Pat, telling him I wanted to hear about the deer. Pat is a construction worker who also does home remodeling. He had been working for a neighbor of ours a few weeks before, apparently between Solo's second and third trips. Solo had gone over to visit and Pat had seen him clearly. When Pat went to a job in Missoula, he saw what he described as "the same deer two or three weeks older, or his clone." He thought we must have taken Solo up there and released him on the golf course.

Pat had stopped and gotten out of his truck to photograph the deer, who walked over to him and began pulling papers out of the pockets on the truck door. That certainly sounds like Solo! The southern edge of Missoula is about 45 miles from here. I believe Solo walked there, spreading his message of gentleness to people in several small towns, many subdivisions, and lots of farms along the way.

Studies on white-tailed deer have shown they usually have a home range of a square mile to a mile and a half. Bucks may go somewhat farther during the rut (mating season), working to establish a temporary territory and harem of their own. Unless they are gradually pushed out due to human development or lack of food, they usually don't leave their area. Even when our population increases, they often adjust to it and stay. Wild white-tailed deer frequently enter towns and subdivisions to feed at night.

Mule deer, however, have annual migrations that could involve traveling quite a few miles. In the fall, as weather begins to change into winter, they move down the mountains to spend harsher months in foothills or valleys. In the spring, as snow melts and new vegetation is available, they move back up into the mountains. A game warden told me mule deer bucks travel quite far in search of mates, but this was not Solo's reason and I haven't heard or read about any who traveled as much as he did.

A month or so after Pat told us about his experience with Solo, I made a trip to Missoula. I watched for him, of course, but didn't drive into the area where Pat had seen him. I kept thinking about him, though, in a different way from my usual thoughts. I finally asked Lyn to contact Solo again to ask if he was trying to tell me something. She didn't have time to do a formal communication then, so just contacted him briefly while she was driving somewhere.

Solo told her he was fine, but he wanted me to contact him and listen to him, using an intermediary (one of the other animals to interpret and pass his messages to me) if necessary. As a good teacher, he was leaving the responsibility where it belongs, gently pushing me to take the next step. I can't believe how patient and persistent these animals are in teaching.

I did connect with Solo, filling nearly a page of ideas about this book, but still questioned whether the information was coming from him or from me. The problem is not emotional interference because of my feelings about Solo, as can happen when communicators talk with their companion animals, but continuing self-doubts about my abilities to hear and interpret what the animals say. An intermediary would make no difference with this problem, though time and practice have definitely reduced it.

A couple days later I was lying in bed reading when Ara (emu) started drumming. I love that sound and get to hear it often, but this time was different in that she kept on for quite some time. I began to think something might be wrong. It was shortly after dark so Don and I went out with flashlights to check on the animals. We have had wild bears and cougars on our property, as well as coyotes and wandering dogs. Aten and Ara acted fine, however, and nothing seemed out of order. Ara was still drumming when I went back into the bedroom, so I decided to ask her if something was wrong. Duh! Why wasn't that my first reaction? And these animals think I'm enlightened! It turned out she was volunteering to help me listen to Solo. She gave me one sentence which answered a question that had been bothering me.

The next day a young man named Adam called me about a red-tailed hawk who was in trouble. When I told him where to bring it, he asked if I was the woman who had raised Solo and, when I said yes, he said he really looked forward to meeting me. Apparently Adam was one of the people Solo approached when he stopped near here to admire the beautiful young deer. I'd love to hear from others whose lives he touched!

The only thing I could find wrong with the hawk was that she was dehydrated and emaciated. People had seen her on the ground in a field the day before, but she was standing so they thought she was simply feeding on something. However, the next day she was lying on the ground, abnormal behavior indicating a serious problem. Youngsters fairly frequently become thin during the time they're learning to hunt on their own, especially if they've gotten too far away from their parents, but this bird seemed older to me.

I gave her the usual electrolytes and small amounts of food (skinned mice at first because they're easier to digest without all the hair) and then took her to Judy so she could be put in a flight room when she was ready. The hawk ate well for Judy, including in the flight room, and seemed to be better, but she never gained weight. When she died unexpectedly, Judy found her body to be full of tumors.

CHAPTER 52

Living in wildlife areas can be challenging as well as fascinating. One night toward the end of May 2009, a black bear recently out of hibernation found part of our supply of wallaby food, a pelleted diet Don keeps in a large rubber garbage bin. During the winter when bears are hibernating, Don leaves it in a breeze-way between his shop and the wallaby shed. This year he had forgotten to put it back in his workshop where bears are less likely to smell it and would have more difficulty accessing it. The bags of feed are stored in an above-ground root cellar with two thick doors, 18-inch walls, and no windows.

Don found the food bin lying on its side about 20 feet from where it had been, missing at least 20 pounds of dry pellets. There were no drag marks across the dirt driveway and, from the four tooth marks at the top of the bin, we could tell the bear had carried it to the place where he fed. I have no idea how he managed that because the container is as tall as a regular garbage can and was nearly filled with 50 to 60 pounds of feed. The bear was polite about his theft. Nothing else was disturbed nor had any pellets been spilled on the ground. He simply ate his fill, then left to digest his huge meal, no doubt after drinking from the nearby creek.

Don put the remainder of the feed in his workshop before calling a couple of neighbors in case they needed to make some changes (e.g., moving feed or garbage cans) for a few days. He found the bear had also raided bird feeders on one neighbor's deck, probably before he found our stash of wallaby feed. I was somewhat concerned for him because I knew those pellets would swell when he drank water. I hoped he would be able to digest them without harming his stomach.

I called one of the game wardens, not to ask him to do anything about the bear, but to let him know it was around. Later that day someone called 911 to report a sick bear sleeping under a tree in a pasture across the road from our place. It was causing a bear jam in that several vehicles were stopped, with people milling around outside cars and taking photos. Some thought the bear was sick or injured because he didn't leave even though he wasn't far from the road. The game warden told them the bear was fine, simply recovering from eating the equivalent of two Thanksgiving dinners in one sitting. Don agreed to haze the bear when he came back to our place for more food, though nobody expected him to want to eat again for a day or two.

Later that day a neighbor and I saw the bear walking across the pasture toward the creek. Another car stopped on the road so, feeling threatened, the bear climbed a tree. Around midnight that night, our dogs smelled the bear and woke Don, who went into the back yard and fired a shotgun into the air a couple of times. I sent telepathic messages to the bear, explaining he was unsafe around humans and was better off going into the woods to live. We didn't see or hear about the bear again, nor did he return that fall or the next spring, as far as we know.

We – and our neighbors – were relieved he didn't have to be trapped and relocated or killed. After all, he was only trying to make up for months of hibernation and he didn't harm anyone. We would never have known he was here if he hadn't found the wallaby feed, which was our fault, not his. I find that to be the case most of the time when people have problems with wildlife. The animals are doing what is to be expected, following their nature, and we are in their space without respecting and adjusting to them.

CHAPTER 53

Tisha and Simon, the African grey parrots who were trying to have babies, did not create the outcome they wanted. Tisha laid eggs again in June 2009, conscientiously incubating them into July. They seemed more calm than they had before, but again their eggs didn't hatch and showed no evidence of fertilization when I took them from Tisha after a normal incubation period of 30 days. Both of them appeared to be grieving, with Simon plucking more of his feathers and Tisha not letting hers grow back after using them for her nest.

Lyn has a St. Francis of Assisi fountain in a special area of her yard. She has found that, when she presents problems or requests for animals to St. Francis, amazing things frequently occur. In mid-August I asked her to request help for Simon, with the intention of healing his emotional issues.

I wasn't home when Lyn presented Simon to St. Francis, but he seemed calmer to me when I returned a day later. He began following me around the house and I no longer saw him plucking feathers. Simon also allowed me to briefly pet him without biting, especially when he was walking on the floor. That location automatically put me in a dominant position relative to him, unlike when he was on top of cages, eye level with me or higher. Many animals are likely to be more aggressive when they are in positions of dominance. Simon, however, occasionally even let me pet him when he was on top of Tisha's cage level with my face. He was also then inside his territory which he naturally defends. I was so happy for him that he felt less threatened.

This began an extremely difficult period of time for Tisha, and for me as well. I had already been avoiding wildlife rehab as much as possible because I was no longer coping well with what seemed like too many dead animals. I also wanted to be able to visit distant friends, but felt unable to leave home during summer months, the best time to travel, when I was raising babies. Judy still sent emergencies when they were closer to me, but attempted to reduce my stress by taking the rehab animals (mostly birds) as soon as she could. Even that felt like an imposition, requiring too

307

much effort while I was in a state of depression. I wanted to curl up in bed and read novels (my favorite escape) most of the time, without having to deal with people or animals.

Then, in late August 2009, the situation became worse, as they often do when we try to ignore problems. Tisha began to exhibit behaviors indicating she was seriously disturbed. She acted afraid of me in that she would scream if I moved near her, sometimes even if I just looked at her. Nothing had changed from my perspective; I was unable to think of any explanation for her anxiety. I connected with her telepathically, asking if she had any pain or felt ill.

Suddenly it occurred to me she wanted to be presented to St. Francis, a great relief to me. Tisha's extreme behavior was apparently the only way she could get her need into my distracted head. I immediately emailed Lyn, suggesting she ask Tisha about her intentions because I was unsure what they were. Tisha told her she wanted to be healed of whatever was keeping her from having babies.

Lyn was getting ready to go on a trip, but took time to present Tisha to St. Francis on the morning of September 3. A short time later Tisha became even more agitated, flapping her wings as though she needed to escape danger, screaming even when I was several feet away and not walking toward her. She no longer ate her special treats, even when Don offered them, seeming to panic when he approached her, too. I asked Lyn whether she had time to do a shamanic journey or a communication. She was to leave in a couple of days and would be gone about a week; I didn't want Tisha to be so stressed for that long. Lyn graciously made time the next day for the following communication:

Tisha: Good Morning, Lyn! I'm sitting on your shoulder so you can hear me clearly!

Lyn: Thank you! What have you to say to me today?

Tisha: I'm extremely stressed. I want a family and Simon isn't helping. I thought maybe it was me, but St. Francis said he didn't think so. He suggested I see about getting a new mate. That's why he couldn't do much at this point. He didn't think I needed a shamanic journey, either. He said I'm well balanced, but that my instincts to be a mother grow stronger and stronger and, if something can't be done to help that, then maybe I will become out of balance and need healing.

I so hope Adele is open to helping me find a mate. I don't want a new home, but I do want a mate who would like to be a father. All of my squawking and nervousness was to let Adele know I need attention. If she will find me a mate, I'll settle down again. But my eggs will not hatch when Simon is my only option as a mate.

Lyn: I do understand, Tisha. I think Adele will do her best to find you another mate. I have no idea how long it will take or what will be involved. You can help it along by visualizing whom you would like as a father for your babies. We could give a different intention to St. Francis. We could ask for the perfect mate for you ASAP.

Tisha: That would be so great! Please do that. And thank Adele for this and tell her I'm sorry for stressing her out, too.

Lyn: Yes, I will, Tisha

Tisha: Oh, I feel so much better!

I began looking for another mate for Tisha and she did act like she felt better for a time. However, all of the possibilities, details, and concerns kept running through my head, causing stress Tisha heard and felt. Because both Tisha and Simon would need other homes at some point, I thought it might be best for Tisha to go to a different place where there was an appropriate male, hoping access to a new mate would decrease the stress of living in a new home. Living with another person who was less disturbed about it might also be a positive change for her. I still was torn about creating more captive-bred parrots, definitely not looking forward to taming and finding homes for them, either. I wondered if my concerns were part of their infertility problem, in which case a new mate here may not be the solution for Tisha.

I had always been concerned that Tisha and Simon had insufficient dark time. In the tropics, day and night are about the same length. In our home they had only six or seven hours without artificial lighting. Photoperiod can affect breeding success in many animals; if that was a problem, it would continue to be one with a different male. I explained all this to Tisha, hoping she would feel confident I was working to fill her needs in the best possible way, including asking her opinion about any decision.

By the time Lyn returned the next week, Tisha was acting even more stressed. She was trying to hide, but avoided her nest box, the best place for seclusion. She started wanting to be closer to Don, including hiding under his recliner, an unsafe place to say the least, with springs and hinges that could easily amputate toes or worse. She walked into his office to hide under a shelf next to his chair or under his computer desk, where one of the dogs often rested when Don was using the computer. She screamed when anyone came near her or even looked at her, including the dogs who had never disturbed her before.

Both Tisha and Simon had said in earlier years that fall is a time when they feel anxious, like birds that migrate (these don't). I thought the combination of everything (the need to be a mother, hormone levels, fall energies, my anxiety about it all) might simply be too much for Tisha. I have been told behavior of captive parrots often changes drastically when breeding urges become strong. My bottom-line conclusion is: It is extremely unfair and unkind to keep these birds in captivity! Being unable to envision or devise an acceptable solution for them deepened my depression.

When Lyn returned, she talked with Tisha again on 9/14/09.

Tisha: Lyn, oh, thank you for coming! I know you have been gone, but I'm so glad you're back! I do want a mate, one that touches my heart, but I don't want a permanent new home right now! I want to be with Adele until she can no longer care for me. She has told me that maybe it is time for me to move on permanently, but it isn't. I'd rather stay here as things are now than to have a new owner with the right mate. Please tell Adele! She's not listening to me! She's just got this idea in her head and is running with it. Squawk! Squawk!

Lyn: It's okay, Tisha. I'll tell Adele. She wants whatever you want! She has communicated that to me over and over. I'm sure she'll listen and be fine with keeping you and finding you a mate.

Tisha: Thanks, Lyn. I feel so much better!

I talked with Tisha several times, telling her she could stay here and that we would work things out as she chose. I visualized her with a mate, the two of them sitting together taking turns grooming each other. Simon had fed Tisha once in a while, typical courtship behavior, but I never saw any grooming between them. I think they were taken away from their parents so early they missed the opportunity to learn that or other normal behaviors between flock members.

CHAPTER 54

I called the breeder from whom I bought Simon years before, finding she had an adult male named Big Jim I could buy. I asked Lyn to talk with Tisha, Simon, and Big Jim to learn how they felt about this, which she did on 9/23/09.

Lyn: Tisha, have you heard about Big Jim from Adele as a possible mate for you?

Tisha: Yes, I have. I think he would be good. What does Simon think, and Big Jim?

Lyn: I'll ask them. Big Jim, are you there?

Big Jim: Yes, indeedy, Lyn, yes, indeedy! I'd love to come. I like all that I hear from the birds about Adele.

Lyn: All right. Simon, this is Lyn. Are you listening in?

Simon: Yes, I am. I thought it might concern me. I appreciate being included. Adele is right. I'm doing much better. I'm glad not to be Tisha's mate so Big Jim is welcome, as far as I'm concerned. But I don't care to return to the place where I was before. I am choosing to stay with Adele until she tells me I must go or when she takes leave of her body. So I'll be fine with Big Jim here, as long as we don't have to share a cage.

Lyn: Okay. Tisha, what is it you would really like to do?

Tisha: Have babies and Big Jim!

Lyn: All right. I'll pass this info on to Adele.

Whenever she was out of her cage during this time, Tisha was mostly hiding in Don's office or the bathroom until it was time to go to bed. I found feather parts wherever she was, because she was plucking them far worse than at any time since she came to live with us. She was missing many on her back and even her wings. The day after the communication I asked Tisha to stay in her cage while we cleaned the house, which she did. I was pleased to note no feathers on the floor of her cage for the first time in several weeks. She even took a couple peanuts from my fingers. When I asked if she was ready for Big Jim to come she made a soft cooing sound I interpreted as agreement.

The structure we had made for the birds when we removed Simon's cage was only partly enclosed, so we put fencing around the rest of it and made a door, in case Simon needed to stay inside when Big Jim was here. He had been spending most of his time on top of it and Tisha's cage (before she found that unacceptable) or on the floor. We also used the fencing to make a temporary cage for Big Jim which fit on top of a card table. The plan was to put it next to Tisha's cage and let her behavior determine when she was ready to have direct contact with him. A few days after the last communication, I brought Big Jim home. He was nervous at first, pacing quite a lot in the cage, but he didn't scream or seem to panic.

I asked Nicki and Simon to help Big Jim adjust. I had purchased two parrot toys in Missoula which Simon spent the afternoon picking to pieces. He seemed completely calm, not approaching Jim even though they were only a few feet apart. Nicki seemed unconcerned, as I had expected.

I was told Big Jim is quite aggressive, but he made no attempt to bite me, even when I reached in his cage to remove and add food dishes or hand him treats. I was quite sure he would bite if I tried to touch him, though. Within a couple of days, Jim no longer seemed particularly nervous. His beak and toenails needed to be trimmed, but I didn't want to stress him that much until he was more settled. Having a new personality in the house definitely made a difference; keeping everything as peaceful as possible seemed the best plan.

Then I saw what appeared to be a rash on the left side of Tisha's chest and probably under her wing. I'd noticed it a bit before, but thought it might just be where she had pulled feathers; she wouldn't hold still long enough to let me see it clearly. In fact, she became upset when I looked at her closely. I definitely did not want to catch and forcefully examine her. However, the spots should have healed by then and some looked swollen.

Again I asked Lyn to check with them, wondering if I could do anything more for them.

Tisha: Hello, Lyn. It's me, Tisha. Tell Adele thanks so much! Big Jim is wonderful! I'm so grateful to her for bringing him to us! Things are working out well! We are becoming better acquainted. Tell Adele I got her message about letting her know when I was ready to have Big Jim in my cage. I'll be sure she sees us touch when I am ready. Big Jim is ready now. I want to be sure this is right and not just get together too soon. After all, we mate for life. Most things are checking out A-OK on my check list, but tell Adele I appreciate her patience.

Lyn: All right, Tisha. Adele is also concerned about the red spots on your chest and under your wing. Do they itch or are they painful?

Tisha: No, I didn't know they were there. I'm not worried about them.

Lyn: Big Jim, how do you like Adele's?

Big Jim: Oh, love it – simply love it. Yes, indeedy! Good company, great food, respectful treatment, and windows to see outside. I've been telling Tisha how good she has it and about my old home. We have lots to talk about. She's a good listener, Lyn, just like you!

Lyn: It's good to hear that you are liking your new home, Big Jim. Simon, how are you doing?

315

Simon: I'm fine. I enjoy watching movies with Don. Tisha and Big Jim just ignore me and that is fine. They aren't expecting anything of me and I like that.

Lyn said she would never have thought of the phrase, "Yes, indeedy!" but it fit Big Jim's personality. The more he settled in, the more cheerful and easy-going he became. He was a good addition to our household. I still believed he would bite if I tried to touch him, but had no problem respecting his personal space and he made no attempt to attack.

Tisha continued doing quite well for a while. She began sitting close to the side of her cage nearest Big Jim's, not right next to the bars, but closer than her first preference of sitting on the opposite side of her cage. She definitely didn't seem disturbed by him.

Lyn found it interesting that Tisha was determined to get to know him better before wanting to be with him. As she said, that seems to reflect a high level of consciousness. With a life span and reproductive age similar to ours, plus amazing intelligence and obvious differences in personality between individuals, it would be odd if they mated with any bird offered by breeders. It would be much the same with us if someone locked us up with a member of the opposite sex they picked based on their preferences rather than ours. (Actually, slave owners used to do exactly that.)

Simon was frequently locked in his cage at this time because he unintentionally tormented Tisha by climbing on top of hers (the tallest suitable place in the room, therefore most appealing to him) when he was out. She screamed at him for invading her space, even though he wasn't trying to bother her. It was stressful for her, Simon, and me. I felt he was trying to reinstate the friendship they had developed, but she was not in the mood for contact with anyone.

I gave Simon toys to chew up and treats, often stopping to talk with him when I walked past. He had more room than the other two, but I'm sure he missed his former freedom. I missed having him wandering around on the floor, too. He was letting his feathers grow, looking better all the time. Once in a while I played a John Wayne movie for him and Big Jim, who also liked country and western themes, and various music CDs to accommodate their differing tastes.

One afternoon Simon paced in front of his door, asking to be allowed out of his cage after being locked up for more than a day. Instead of going to Tisha and Jim's area, he wandered around on the floor, visiting with our neighbor Tom. I left Simon's cage door open overnight and, after finding him in it in the morning, I again left the door open. He always seemed subdued and sad when I locked him in, as though he thought he was being punished, so I was happy he could be out.

CHAPTER 55

Tisha had a setback about a week into October, beginning an even more stressful few months for everyone in the household. She became extremely nervous again and created little bruises and abrasions on her chest apparently by biting her skin. Some parrots become so stressed in captivity they go further than plucking feathers and other unnatural behaviors, actually biting off pieces of their skin and even muscle. Imagine the emotional distress required to generate such unnatural and painful behavior!

Hoping to find something that would help, I made the following changes over a period of time: 1) bought a bigger cage for Big Jim since it appeared he was going to stay out of Tisha's space longer than I had expected; 2) moved Tisha and Big Jim into a less-frequented room; 3) covered part of Tisha's cage with a blanket so she could see him or not, as she chose; 4) hung a fluorescent fixture (with a broad-spectrum bulb to imitate sunlight) in their area; 5) added a timer to simulate tropical day/ night cycles; 6) changed their diet by including cooked grains and removing peanuts at the suggestion of a website about parrots.

None of the changes seemed to help. Tisha still screamed when someone approached or even looked at her (including Simon); she still followed Don around, sometimes chewing on the bottom of the bathroom door when he went in there without her. She still hid in places that were not safe, either for her or from her beak.

Her screams were extremely difficult for me. I'd be lying in bed reading or taking a nap when a blood-curdling scream caused me to jump up and run to make sure nobody was trapped or bleeding. It was also disturbing when I needed to use the bathroom, causing Tisha, who was hiding there in the dark, to scream as she sidled past me out the door. Lyn reminded me she had no other way to make her wishes known, and I do understand, but all the drama was seriously impacting me.

I frequently played CDs, mostly the classical music Tisha preferred. I was constantly thinking of possible ways to fix everything, thus causing more tension for all of us, but I was unable to just let go and allow Tisha to work it out for herself. After all, her options were limited by being in captivity, so to a great extent depended on what I provided for her.

I again asked Lyn to talk with her (10/11/09) and was surprised by the anger and frustration Tisha expressed. After I heard her, I understood more, though we still had problems.

Tisha: Hi, Lyn. Thanks for coming! Adele wants to know why I'm so stressed. Well, I feel pressured – by her, by Big Jim. It's like I'm on stage and everyone is watching my every move. It is stressing me out. I want to hide. I need to get away from all of those who expect me to do something!

I still like Big Jim but ask Adele what is it to her if it takes me a year to want to have Jim join me in my cage? (I call him Mikey. He likes that and it brings back great memories! We've been sharing.) I feel Adele wants me laying eggs right now. Tell her to just relax and watch and learn. I've squawked at her when she insists I go in my cage and I don't want to. Why do I have to do that if I am not causing trouble? Why is she afraid to let us be parrots together? We used to live in colonies and when we disagreed we would squawk and maybe fly off. It doesn't necessarily mean we have a problem that she has to fix.

Well, maybe the fix is for her to just back off and give us time and space. She's quite good at that most of the time, but lately she seems more stressed than the rest of us. Tell her to try Young Living Peace and Calming™ [essential oil] and Bach Rescue Remedy™ [flower essence]. That's from her Teacher! She wants to learn, but she needs to relax and not worry about every feather and see it as her own personal problem.

I'm sorry, Lyn, to let off steam like this, but it has just

been building. I needed some space from Jim – Mikey
– so I went to see Simon. We are like brother and sister
so I could talk things over with him. Then Adele decided
I couldn't do that anymore. What is she afraid of, Lyn?
Then Jim was pushing me to get off the top of his cage
and cozy with him so he could come in my cage. Well, I
don't like being pushed, so I told him! And then he kept
pushing and I really told him to back off and Adele gets
all upset. What does she think? That I'm just going to
let him push me around? In the wild, I would just fly to
another branch and sit by myself.

Ask Adele to please change her attitude toward us from
being our Mother Protector to being our friend. Ask her to
think like a bird when she hears me squawk instead of a
parent. I'm sorry! I'm just frustrated and feeling pushed. I
shouldn't tell her what to do, but it's hard enough trying to
build a relationship, and having someone watch my every
move is nerve-wracking. Tell her to trust me, that I will be
sure she is watching when I want Mikey to visit me and I
touch him.

Lyn: I'll pass this on. Anything else?

Tisha: Well, when I'm angry with her for telling me to go
back in my cage, I'm certainly not open to affection from
her. Timing is important. Ask Adele why she needs to pet
me when she's just made me angry. Is she trying to make
up? Tell her to find a win-win solution instead of force.
And Lyn, tell her thanks for calling you and listening.
There. I'm done and thanks!

Lyn: Big Jim, have you got any insights to share with
Adele?

Big Jim: Yes, I do – yes, indeedy! Tisha loves to call me
Mikey and I like that much better than Big Jim. Sounds

321

cuter and more cuddly and I'm for it if Tisha is! At times I've wanted Adele to touch me. She seems a bit afraid of me. Why?

Lyn: Your last person told her you were aggressive and Adele is used to Simon, who is aggressive toward her at times, so she is just being cautious.

Mikey: Got it! Makes sense! Yes, indeedy! Well, that WOMAN was not respectful and she and I did not get along. I like Adele. As long as I'm treated with respect, I'll treat her with respect, but bossing us around is not respectful. Asking us what we want is respectful and I really like that.

Lyn: Simon, do you have anything to say to Adele?

Simon: Hi, Lyn! No, I'm doing well. It was good of Tisha to come see me and talk with me. She's doing a good job of sizing up her new mate slowly. Tell Adele that I agree with Tisha. I think Adele should take Rescue Remedy and Peace and Calming about six times a day. Bye, Lyn!

Lyn: Tisha, I forgot to ask you if you are eating more because you are stressed. Adele was concerned!

Tisha: Oh, I'm fine. Again, she should watch and observe and learn and not assume we are sick every moment. If she keeps this up, we'll call some injured animals in for her to focus on instead of us!

Lyn: Is that a threat?

Tisha: No, it's a promise! If she has to find problems with those of us who are doing well, then maybe she needs to consider coming out of retirement so she can help those who truly do need fixing!

Lyn: How are you feeling now, Tisha?

Tisha: Much better, Lyn. Thanks for listening and thank Adele! I know we've stressed her out! I'm sorry for that, but she's too much with us right now. She should focus more on others for a while and just observe us. Okay. I'm done. And thanks!

When I hung up the phone after Lyn read me this communication, Don told me 911 dispatch had called about a goose with a broken wing. Don contacted the reporting person who said he was no longer able to see the goose, which had apparently wandered off. He was to call if he saw it again. I thought Tisha was letting me know she could back up her promise to bring me animals who needed my help, unlike her.

Lyn gifted me a bottle of Peace and Calming essential oil, which arrived early the following week. I rubbed a drop on my inner wrist and both the scent and my response to it were wonderful. When I put a drop on Tisha's cage or wherever I thought appropriate for the birds, it seemed to help them as well. I still use it and Rescue Remedy for myself and some animals.

CHAPTER 56

Late that evening, someone brought me a flammulated owl who had been carried into their yard by a half-bobcat pet. I was unable to find any wounds or fractures, but the tiny owl was clearly injured. I did what I could to treat it for shock, hoping it would be better the next day. Sometime early that morning an unusual noise woke me. I got up to find a friendly young cat rubbing against our front door and climbing on the screen, apparently wanting in. I didn't recognize her, but thought she must belong to a neighbor. She seemed afraid, so I didn't want to leave her outside to fend for herself, not only because of whatever had frightened her, but also because our dogs would chase her out of the yard when Don let them out a bit later in the morning. I put her in a cat carrier on our deck with the intention of calling neighbors at an acceptable time of day. When I checked the little owl, I found it had died. Examination showed it had a fractured skull. I did locate the owner of the little cat, with several neighbors saying they had heard some kind of a ruckus early in the morning, though nobody reported any livestock, pet, or wildlife injuries.

After dark the next evening, our neighbor Tom called to tell me he was stopped behind another car just north of us because a mountain lion was crossing the road, walking south toward our place. We know cougars live around here, but rarely get to see them. Years ago, when we had two young goats, Don heard their distressed crying in the middle of the night; he stepped out the back door in time to scare one away from their shed. Cougars seldom cause any problems here, though some people are apparently disturbed about them. I like having them here, as I enjoy and appreciate all the other wild animals. I thought this one may have been what scared the neighbor's cat the night before.

A few days later, the owner of the cat that killed the flammulated owl called to tell me a much larger owl was dead in his yard in downtown Hamilton. I don't remember ever going to get a dead animal as a rehabber (I did retrieve those I wanted for skeletons and biology specimens years earlier), but for some reason I decided to pick up this body. I wanted to know what kind of owl it was, for one thing, but decided later something more was going on.

When I arrived at the person's home, I found the bird was actually a grouse, not an owl at all. Both flammulated owls and grouse normally don't live in town. Also, flammulated owls migrate and we thought this one should have been gone by then. A game warden who came here for both bodies found this was the latest date any flammulated owl was found in our area. Its body was given to the biology department at the University of Montana in Missoula to be used as a study skin.

An hour or two after I got home with the dead grouse, I saw two cars stopped on our road in the wrong place to be wallaby or emu watchers. As I looked in an attempt to determine what was going on, I noticed two birds running away from the road. Don went out to see them well enough to identify them as ruffed grouse. When I looked out the bedroom window a few minutes later, I saw one in our yard. They have been at our place before, but we hadn't seen one for several years. That evening I heard, through my bedroom window, a bull elk bugling in a neighboring pasture.

So within a few days, right after Tisha said she could bring me some animals as a distraction from my obsession with her problems, I received a flammulated owl, a cat showed up mysteriously and insistently at our door, two unusual experiences with grouse occurred, and I was honored to hear elk bugling. Lyn suggested I look up Owl, Mountain Lion, Grouse, and Elk in the *Medicine Cards* book, and, as always, I found information in all of them that resonated with me at the time.

I was certainly not in harmony with anything at that point, nor was I reacting well to the stresses in my life, particularly those associated with Tisha. I was unsure whether she was responding to my emotions or I to hers, but there was definitely a connection which was unhelpful for both of us. Even with distractions and messages from animals, several days after the last communication were difficult for Tisha and me. I was in tears off and on and Tisha was as well, in her way. Every time I walked past her she screamed and I cried.

326

Tisha was then following Don around more all the time, even wanting to go into his bedroom with him at night. That is a cold place where the dogs also sleep – definitely not acceptable for a tropical parrot during a Montana winter. She had stopped screaming at Don, allowing him to pet her though she still wouldn't step up on his hand. He was patient with her, even making the dogs stay out of the bathroom so she could be in there safely while he took a shower. Eden and Clover (dogs) were careful with Tisha, not at all aggressive toward her, but they were so large that one misstep could seriously injure her. As long as they knew she was there and were paying attention, she was safe, though she might not be if they became excited about something and forgot her. I could not bring myself to allow her to make the decision about where to sleep, though I felt guilty every time I made her go to her cage at night.

I would speak to Tisha whenever I was near her, but mostly stayed away from her. As I felt less emotional, she also seemed less upset. I wondered about the skin on her chest and under her wing, but was unwilling to distress her enough to even look closely at her, let alone pick her up to examine her. She was eating well and walking around the house, so I assumed she was physically okay. I began asking her to sleep in or on her cage at night, but didn't close the door. She seemed to accept that compromise and remained in the cage until Don got up in the morning, when she followed him into his office.

During this time, I was reading newspapers and even Opinion pages and online comments, certainly not a soothing habit given the nature of most news. I was astounded at the anger, meanness, dishonesty, distortion, and other negativity expressed by so many people, both as opinions and in what is called news. I hoped the angry ones, whatever the subject, are a minority and simply loud and aggressive due to their apparent fear of change.

I had written a couple letters to the editor of local newspapers (one about the normal behavior of wolves, another about gay people, both subjects being distorted and misinterpreted by angry, frightened people). I also responded to some of the online comments. However, it appeared no amount of logic, scientific

327

evidence, or reminders of human kindness would change their opinions. In fact, I suspected responding to them simply made them more determined in their beliefs, though it's possible some good seeds are planted by kinder, more rational articles and letters, making them worthwhile.

One non-fiction book I read that fall (*The Instruction* by Ainsley MacCloud) suggests many angry, negative people are simply young souls who have had too few lifetimes to get past their fears and bigotry. That explanation pleases me for several reasons. One is it does seem to confirm my thought that they are a minority. Also, it is easier to feel empathy for them because they have lots of lessons to learn, some of which may be quite unpleasant. Feeling frustrated or angered by them is as pointless as being upset with a young child because he or she is unable to understand calculus. I chose to again mostly avoid newspapers, TV news, and opinions of others. I feel much better when I'm not dumping all that negative energy into myself so I continue that practice now.

I had started taking an adult education writing class held weekly in Darby, a small town about 15 miles south of us, about the first of October. The teacher is wonderfully creative and positive, designing a class that was both stimulating and fun. The only rule was that no criticism of any sort was allowed, including or especially of our own writing. The class format was simply to write anything in response to amazing prompts such as: "If I was a color, I would choose to be..."; or "I got off the train and..." We wrote and then read what we had written, if we chose to do so. There were no grades, no tests, no expectations, no criticism.

The other students were pleasant and I always felt good there, but after each class I often became critical of what I had written, sometimes to the point of not wanting to go to the next class. So I was in a downward spiral, using everything I did to prove to myself I wasn't good enough. I've helped hypnotherapy clients with similar problems (though not during that period of time), apparently easier than helping myself. Fixing this sort of habit of thought does not necessarily follow from intellectually understanding the problem or even possible solutions, especially when one is depressed enough to have a low energy level, as I was.

Perhaps the best long-term benefit of the writing class was that Mary Wolf, a retired wildlife rehabber, also attended. Both of us were on Judy's permits and had been taught by her. We had met in passing before, but never spent much time together. I found she had rescued parrots in the past so was knowledgeable and empathetic relative to my experiences with Tisha. The class was our primary contact for quite some time, but now we communicate frequently. Mary is a close and highly valued friend.

CHAPTER 57

Sadly, on November 1, 2009, disaster struck. As I walked past Tisha, who was on the living room floor, she screamed and raised her wings in flight mode, allowing me a glimpse of the area under her wings. I saw fresh blood there and a few small drops splattered on the floor. I had to catch and examine her, with her screaming the whole time. What I saw caused an emergency trip to Linda's home, even though it was a Sunday. Tisha had open wounds beneath both wings from biting her skin. I could no longer ignore my concerns about her self-mutilation, hoping it was minor and respecting her wishes to care for herself without being handled by me.

Tisha was calm in the carrier on the way to Linda's, but became upset when we took her out. Our intention was to put a collar around her neck to prevent her from reaching the injured areas of her body, giving the wounds time to heal. An Elizabethan collar, the large, round one that stands out from the neck, is disturbing to most animals and especially to birds, so we didn't want to use one on Tisha. Linda has a set of hard plastic collars in the shape of a ball about the same width as the bird's head. They are long enough to prevent bending the neck to reach a wound, hopefully causing less discomfort than the bigger collars. Anything different is stressful, though, and these collars are difficult to put on. I had to hold Tisha in a towel while Linda pulled on her head with one hand to straighten her neck. At the same time, she tried to hook the two pieces of the collar together with her other hand.

Tisha was screaming in anger and then terror at the top of her lungs the whole time, even becoming hoarse before I finally told Linda to quit without finishing the task. Of course our intentions were to help Tisha and most animals have to be restrained in some way while receiving veterinary care, but Tisha and I couldn't stand this.

I immediately held Tisha close under my chin where she seemed to feel safe, though she continued panting for some time. I kept apologizing to her, nearly in tears, feeling as though I had participated in the equivalent of a rape. I was so horrified by what we had put Tisha through that I was unable to let Linda examine her closely, so we still did not know the extent of her injuries. Linda gave us antibiotics and we left. Tisha again seemed calm in her carrier, but I sobbed all the way home.

The antibiotics were oral, in the form of drops, so I had to catch her every day to administer them. I also wanted to put something directly on the wounds. Rather than more drugs, I used emu oil and aloe vera juice at different times, knowing Tisha would ingest some of it and believing neither would harm her. I had so wanted to avoid the stress of handling her, thinking it would only make her emotional problems worse. However, I felt I had no choice at that point.

Something changed between us after the traumatic trip to Linda's in that Tisha was mostly calm with me, acting more like she had long before the difficult times. She squawked when I approached her with a towel, but as soon as I held her securely she quieted, appearing to be okay with the handling. I put a drop of Peace and Calming on my wrist before I caught her and on Tisha's back, where there were no feathers or wounds. She accepted the antibiotic drops, especially when I mixed them in a teaspoon with grape juice, which she liked. When I used aloe juice on her wounds, I mixed it with warm water in a small spray bottle and quickly spritzed her chest and the underside of her wings. Emu oil is thick and had to be dripped onto the wounds, but applying it became easier after I started warming the oil above room temperature to thin it.

Around this time I ordered a subscription to *Species Link*, a journal written by and for animal communicators. I also started reading their wonderful web page, which is full of positive information from animals about what is happening on our planet, as they try to help us develop greater kindness, understanding, cooperation, and compassion toward other people, different species, and Mother Earth. All articles and philosophy are directed for positives rather than against negatives. The whole tone is so much kinder and more healthy than anything in mainstream news. Reading it is uplifting rather than depressing, unkind, frightening, or frustrating.

I asked Ara, my python spirit guide, to help me with the depression and negativity I was feeling. A short time later a woman called about an injured nuthatch who had flown into her window. I thought of suggesting she keep it for a while, but instead asked her to bring it to me. She lives fairly close and we have had superficial contact a number of times for several years. I was unable to find any injuries I could help with so put the tiny bird in a safe, quiet place, hoping it would recover on its own. Later that evening it appeared to want out rather than huddling in a corner. I considered releasing it here because other nuthatches do well around our place, but instead felt I should take it back to its home.

We released the little bird near the deck where it had been injured. It immediately flew to a tree, one I'm sure was familiar to it. Then the woman and I began to visit. I learned she has many of the same concerns and problems as I with negative politics, disasters, distorted news, and cruel treatment of animals and people. She recommended a book, *Winter World* by Bernd Heinrich, which I ordered and read.

The next day an elderly neighbor called for help with her old dog who was doing poorly. The woman did not want to put her friend through a lot of tests or give her drugs, so she preferred not to call a veterinarian. She's a bit uncomfortable with telepathic communication, but still wanted me to talk with the dog in case it might help. I was able to feel an area of discomfort which could have made it painful for the dog to eat. We got her some softer food and a tube of Nutrical (a high calorie supplement containing minerals and vitamins).

I didn't feel the dog was ready to go yet and told the woman she would probably know when it was time to help her pass. My suggestion was to let the dog eat whatever she wanted, help her get up when she became stuck, and just love her as long as she wanted to stay. Both of them seemed to feel better, as did I. It is common for people to find it easier to communicate with animals with whom they have no emotional bond. This reinforced my left brain knowledge that I am able to use my right brain telepathic skills when I get out of my own way. Thankfully, knowing that on an emotional level, stopping myself from questioning what I hear or feel from the animals, was becoming easier for me.

Within that same few days, a taxidermist, with whom I had had a conversation about bison skeletons some months before, called. He had cleaned bones from two buffalos for a man who is building a visitor center on a Montana Indian reservation, and was looking for someone who would put the bones together for a skeleton display. I know the anatomy and have articulated a number of skeletons, the largest being a young cow moose and the smallest a mouse. However, making them stable enough to be transported many miles would require a lot of rods, bolts, and strong glue. I would want them to be museum quality with few of the metal parts showing, as well as sturdy enough to transport. I decided I would assist in the work if I could find someone who is mechanically inclined, attentive to detail, and willing to learn from me about placement of the bones. So, I had something to think about other than Tisha's and my issues.

I'm grateful to Ara for facilitating all this due to my asking her for assistance. Each incident made me feel a bit better, increasing my motivation to focus on positives, including healthier reading material, thus further improving my mood. As explained in the movie and book *The Secret* by Rhonda Byrne, first we must ask for what we want – and then we must pay attention to what appears and act on it. Every time I do that, something positive happens.

By Thanksgiving things seemed to have settled a bit. I had begun to lock the birds in cages during the day, with wood chunks, egg cartons, and other toys available; music or TV provided further entertainment for them. Again I explained that keeping them in cages was not punishment and promised to let them out in the evening to interact with each other and us, especially Don. I decided I would not interfere if they screamed at each other unless someone was actually being injured, which had not happened. I kept the bathroom door closed when they were out, as well as placing pieces of plywood across doors in areas where they had caused damage. This gave me some peaceful time, greatly improving my mood.

Tisha was still biting herself, with small red spots on her back as though she was plucking new feathers before they even erupted through the skin, but I found no drops of blood anywhere. Don was able to drip some emu oil near the back edge of her wings, which would hopefully spread to the bigger wounds underneath. I no longer grabbed her to medicate those areas, because I feared the stress was worse than any possible benefit. She appeared healthy, acted calmer, and ate well.

CHAPTER 58

Sadly, we had another crisis toward the end of December in that I found a few drops of blood on the floor of Tisha's cage. She was then cooperative about going into her cage every night at my request, appearing more calm and relaxed, no longer screaming when anyone but Don approached her. She was still eating well with no sign of illness or lethargy. However, I was concerned about that extent of self-mutilation so asked Lyn to talk with her. She suggested a shamanic journey first and then a communication. I agreed with her recommendation.

Shamanic Journey for Tisha with Lyn - 1/3/10

Intentions:

1) Heal the undersides of Tisha's wings so they don't bleed and will grow feathers.

2) Heal mental and spiritual planes for her physical place in captivity.

3) Help build confidence for dealing with changes as her life progresses.

4) Remove blocks that are keeping her from developing strong, trusting, healthy, and rewarding relationships and provide the qualities that will enhance her relationships with others in her home.

Lyn's spirit guides, other compassionate, healing spirits, and some of Tisha's ancestors participated in the journey into non-ordinary reality with Lyn and Tisha. The spirits told Tisha her fears had been melted away and her ancestors gave her gifts of unconditional love and protection against all fears. They retrieved two soul parts, one from when she was taken away from her mother and the other from the trauma of her first home. She was

337

given a large dose of confidence and blocks to developing healthy relationships were removed. Tisha and Lyn's spirits returned to ordinary reality and the circle was closed.

Just before Tisha went to bed the night of her journey, I changed the newspapers on the bottom of her cage. It was a great relief to find no blood spots the next morning and she seemed to feel comfortable. I was so happy Tisha was behaving toward me more as she had before all this began. She quit screaming when I looked at or approached her, and even let me pet her sometimes. It felt so good to think we may be able to redevelop a close relationship.

When Tisha was out of her cage in the evening, she would sit on the heating vent by Don's chair while the forced-air furnace was running. Hot, dry air blowing on her belly and chest didn't seem like it could be good for her damaged skin. I had put a damp washcloth over the vent she preferred, hoping the heat would still appeal to her with the advantage of adding moisture. Apparently it wasn't as good, because she simply chose a different vent.

I was spritzing Tisha with aloe juice in water daily. She squawked a bit in complaint, but did not scream or struggle. The redness in some areas seemed to be decreasing and she continued acting toward me more as she had before all this began. As a follow-up to her journey, I again asked Lyn to talk with Tisha, which she did on 1/14/10.

Lyn: Tisha, this is Lyn. Are you wanting to talk with me?

Tisha: Yes, Lyn. Thanks for coming! The journey was good, so good I want to ask Adele to have one. It did things for me that nothing else could.

Lyn: Okay. I'll pass it on. Adele has ordered an essential oil spray called Thieves Oil™ [Young Living brand, a combination of essential oils with antiseptic properties]. It is all natural and will protect you from infection. It should arrive in a few days. Adele wants to know if you prefer being in or out of the cage?

Tisha: The spray will be good. I like being in the cage, but I get cold, especially down on the floor of my cage. When I'm out, I like the heat vents. They feel the best. You know, in the tropics where I come from it is often 80 degrees and with high humidity. The air here is really dry and I get cold.

Lyn: Adele says she can put a heating pad under your cage floor so it is warmer.

Tisha: That would be good. Warmer would be a lot better!

A heating pad taped under the floor of Tisha's cage warmed that area in case she wanted to sit there, but kept electrical parts away from her toenails and beak. I placed a small space heater next to her, aiming it across the front of her cage rather than directly toward her, again thinking hot, dry air could be harmful to her healing skin. Moving a misting humidifier much closer to her cage helped moisten the area. My skin certainly is less dry when I am in a damper environment.

Around that time, I bought a book called *Healing Anxiety and Depression* by Daniel G. Amen. A self-administered test showed I was depressed. Big surprise. Some homeopathic and western medicine remedies and drugs were discussed. I bought one of the supplements, after finding my brother David stocked it in his health food store. It increases production of serotonin, a natural neurochemical which causes a feeling of well-being. I noticed a great improvement after taking it for only a few days. I began feeling more energetic, more like living rather than simply hiding in escape fiction, and much less focused on unpleasant thoughts. I even seemed able to make decisions more easily.

I now believe at least part of my improvements were due to having worked through some major energy changes, both in adjusting to my spiritual evolution and involving a shift in energy frequencies on the planet. Lots of people whose work I've read and listened to since 2002 explain these difficult periods of time, some even calling it the dark night of the soul. This somehow feels right to me in that I have experienced a major shift in my awareness and continue to feel more grounded and stable than I was during the few months prior to this. Making decisions and dealing with any difficulties all became much easier for me and have remained so, even during the following month when I experienced a great loss.

CHAPTER 59

I scheduled a shamanic journey for myself on February 1 after emailing Carla Meeske, Lyn's shamanism teacher. Lyn is qualified to facilitate journeys for people, but prefers to work primarily with animals. I told Tisha when I would have the journey, with great hope that she would continue healing. A friend who hadn't seen her for a couple weeks remarked that Tisha appeared more calm. I envisioned her with healthy skin covered with beautiful feathers, being her former cheerful, busy self. Sadly, this was not to be.

About a week later, Tisha dripped blood two nights in a row, so I knew I had to do something directly with her. I again considered a plastic collar around her neck and even leaving her with Linda for a week, but decided I couldn't stress Tisha to that degree. I researched self-mutilation in parrots – again – and this time found an article about putting a sock over the body as protection from the beak.

I couldn't do that alone so took Tisha to Judy, who is highly creative about ways to help wild birds and animals. I washed a couple of Don's clean, nearly new, cotton socks in hot water and Thieves Oil, drying them in the clothes dryer. I drove Tisha, the socks, emu oil, and Peace and Calming essential oil to Judy's place. I held Tisha while Judy examined and cleaned her injuries, put emu oil on them, and then cut and put on her sock. It covered her body, including wings, leaving head, legs, and tail free. We made sure she could walk comfortably and eliminate without soiling the sock.

Tisha squawked a few times, of course, but fortunately there was no extended screaming like before. I'd have released her immediately if she had appeared that stressed. She sat in her carrier on the passenger seat during the drive both ways with no fussing, appearing calm and comfortable. I stopped at Linda's place on the way home for antibiotics, because Judy said there was an infected area under the left wing that did not look good. Judy told me later that she was concerned we might have to euthanize Tisha if this didn't work to help her heal.

When we arrived home, I put the carrier on the floor near Don's chair and opened the door. Tisha stepped out and marched across the room, climbing into her cage and up to her perch. I had thought she might not be able to do that and hoped she would stay on the floor, because being unable to use her wings might make it hard for her to balance till she grew accustomed to the sock.

However, Tisha had other plans and she did remain balanced. She would not eat or drink anything. Her only objective was to get rid of that sock. Within a couple of hours she had torn several large holes in it. I knew as soon as she joined the holes, the whole thing would fall off. I picked her up, Don cut through the last couple of strips with scissors, I gave her antibiotics, dripped more emu oil on her skin where the sock had touched, and put her back in her cage. She drank a lot of water and ate well before climbing out of her cage and settling in her favorite place near Don. She seemed perfectly content the rest of the evening, with no apparent hard feelings toward me.

I talked with my friend Mary Wolf, who has done parrot rescue, including dealing with self-mutilation. With all I learned and all I thought about, I came to the conclusion the best I could do for Tisha, if she didn't start improving soon, would be to euthanize her. No matter how I thought about it, I didn't believe she would be better off anywhere else or continuing to struggle with this forever, even if she could be kept alive. Quality of life just wasn't there. So I told Tisha that night what I was thinking, saying she needed to show me she wanted to continue this life. The only way she could do that was to quit hurting herself. I said I would do everything I could to help her and certainly hoped she would choose to live, but I wouldn't continue using force with her just to keep her alive.

Two days later, she had not hurt herself further, and her skin was healing remarkably well in most areas. I was still concerned about a couple spots, but with the progress she made in such a short time, I was hopeful.

Tisha was eating well and seemed calm about my handling her once she was wrapped in the towel, even taking a treat from me as soon as I put her back on the floor. Being picked up was unpleasant for her, but that only took a second. She was mostly quiet while I worked with her, too. All of this was a huge relief for me and, no doubt, for her.

I later learned Don and Judy both had told Tisha she had to stop hurting herself or she wouldn't survive. I praised and thanked her frequently for doing so well, asking Mikey and Simon to help her, too. I was optimistic that, unless she had abscesses I couldn't see and that wouldn't heal without some other treatment, Tisha would be okay. She continued to seem calm, no longer exhibiting abnormal behaviors like rocking or stretching or screaming without an apparent threat to her, all of which she had done before.

Lyn told me she had never found threats of euthanasia to change any behavior in an animal. She believed Tisha was responding to the improvements in my frame of mind, feeling like I was again well enough to be able to take care of her. I was so glad she was letting me do things with her rather than screaming every time I approached her!

Later that month (January) Tisha dripped blood on the floor of her cage again. Her right wing and back were much better; she no longer had injuries on her back and was even letting some feathers grow. However, the area under her left wing was a mess and she was on her second round of oral antibiotics. At this point I was still spritzing her with aloe vera juice, hoping to reduce inflammation and irritation during healing. I thought if only the injuries could heal once she might not damage herself again.

I decided to keep Tisha in my bed at night to prevent her from biting herself, hoping to give her time to heal. She didn't seem to do it during the day. I didn't get much sleep because it was necessary to be aware of her, both to avoid harming her and to touch her if she started picking at her skin. Tisha seemed to enjoy sleeping with me, even to the extent of cuddling next to my hand. I rolled up two small towels, putting her between them and using the towels to keep bedding from resting directly on her. I made sure there was a tunnel to the outside, allowing fresh air flow to her nest. Then I lay on my side between her and the edge of the bed. She let me put my hand over her back or next to her face. Of course I rested the weight of my hand on the towels, not on her. She mostly slept quietly, without seeming to be itchy or restless.

During the day Tisha liked sitting under a towel on Don's lap while he read and watched TV. She still ate well, but began to seem unhappy and even apathetic, seldom interested in chewing up egg cartons, pieces of wood, and rolled up newspapers stuffed through cage bars, which she had enjoyed before.

CHAPTER 60

My shamanic journey with Carla Meeske on February 1, 2010, was fascinating and helpful. Intentions for the journey were to increase the balance between my left and right brain (the rational/logical and the intuitive/creative sides) and to help with any negativity that might be interfering with Tisha's healing. Carla's brief explanation about what she was doing was beneficial because I didn't understand much about shamanic journeys at the time.

Carla talks on the phone while she is doing the journey, describing everything that is happening and recording it as she goes. She then makes it available for download as well as mailing a CD to her client. I greatly appreciated the recording and, in fact, learned more when I transcribed it. I was to simply relax and listen, without analyzing or interrupting. It would even be fine if I drifted off and missed part of it because I could hear it again later. My summary of her description follows, with direct quotes marked.

The shaman uses rhythm from a handheld drum and sometimes rattles to enter the shamanic state of consciousness, a form of light trance. Shamans have learned to connect directly with spirits, who use the shaman's imagination and sensory ability to communicate with them. Participating spirits have connections with the shaman and the client, including but not limited to spirit guides, power animals, ancestors of either or both, always with the condition they be compassionate, healing spirits. The messages and information that come in can be as surprising to the shaman as when a friend says something unexpected and astonishing.

Carla said, "The power of the work is that I, as a shamanic healer, will be bringing your spirit with me into a sacred healing place in non-ordinary reality where we will be surrounded by compassionate spirits who will work with you. They'll actually work on the energetic flow between your hemispheres and your left and right side." The spirits find things that need to be shifted and changed or removed, such as stuck energies or blockages, also retrieving soul parts which may have separated during past traumatic events. Shamans are facilitators, observers, and participants, with the direction of the spirits.

After her explanation, Carla began drumming, continuing this throughout the journey, which lasted nearly an hour. It reads like a story in a mythology text, but a number of details Carla did not know would resonate with my life came up throughout, making it all completely believable. At one point she asked the spirits if I needed a power animal retrieval and they said no because I had a lot of power animals.

A white buffalo calf volunteered as one of my spirits. Later in the journey she became a white buffalo cow, as she integrated with me to continue helping me. More than three years later, during the summer of 2013, I had the opportunity to see a group of magnificent white buffalos, including cows, calves, and bulls.

Carla described a Peruvian shaman with a multicolored, flowing robe as my teacher, who came to help with the journey. A year or two earlier, my friend Sarah Monson had seen someone like this near me, who identified himself as my spirit guide. Another friend, Anna, also had the experience of seeing a spirit fitting this description when I was in her home. None of the three women knew anything about the experiences of the others, and Anna's and Sarah's sightings were before I had any knowledge of Carla or shamanic journeys.

Then another amazing being joined the journey. The following is what Carla, who knew nothing of Ara or my living with snakes, said about her:

"Interesting! A snake comes to take the intrusion [something negative the spirits had removed from me]. A giant snake, like this goddess snake! Wow! I've never seen this animal. I've never seen this goddess before. And she pulls the intrusion down like Morpheus' egg, eats it, and goes into the ground. Thank you, Snake."

Later in the journey Carla said, "I see the snake again and she turns into an infinity sign and she goes plooooom! And explodes outward into light. Then she comes back again as the snake and she winks and nods. She says, 'I am the master of your ceremonies. I have everything you need. I have fear, keeps you

346

sharp; I have magic, keeps you active; I have definity, I can be a straight line; I have infinity, find me anyone else who can become an infinity sign; I have transfiguration. Remember me when you see the worm in the apple. He is my friendly self.' And then she makes a hoop around you and you stand tall within the hoop of the snake."

I was able to take some classes in shamanism with Marge Hulburt, a knowledgeable and gifted shamanic healer and shamanism teacher, in Missoula during the end of 2013 and the beginning of 2014, so I better understand what Carla was doing and describing. The Peruvian shaman showed himself to me during the first journey I facilitated for myself with Marge's help, though I haven't yet seen the white buffalo or Ara in journeys. When classmates practiced with me, they said they saw many different animals around me, providing further validation. How awesome and exciting to participate on the level of Spirit with this much awareness!

CHAPTER 61

After sleeping with me for five or six nights, Tisha seemed
so much better I decided after the shamanic journey to try letting her
sleep in her cage again. I could still see some dry blood under her
left wing when she raised it a bit, but she seemed better otherwise.
For 10 days there was no more blood on the floor of her cage;
then, on the morning of February 9, I found more drops. I picked
Tisha up, put her on her back on a towel and really examined the
area under her wings. The wounds looked mostly like abrasions
covered with dry scabs. However, whenever she spread her wings
at all, the scabs tore open and bled. Wounds in areas where skin
moves as the body part moves are difficult to heal because of this,
especially with birds whose skin is so thin and fragile.

I decided to use more emu oil under Tisha's wings, hoping
it would keep the scabs softer so they wouldn't tear or crack. The
aloe vera juice is soothing, but dries quickly. I also slept with her
again. This time, unlike before, she seemed restless, as though her
skin was itchy or perhaps burning. I was unable to keep her from
picking at it, even with her in my bed. I gave her a tiny bit of
an over-the-counter children's allergy medicine, which she licked
from a spoon; it helped her rest more quietly, both because it has a
sedative effect and it may also have decreased irritation.

Then, when I looked into her eyes on February 12, 2010,
Tisha seemed totally miserable, more unhappy than I'd ever seen
her. I felt she was done – that she simply didn't want to go on.
I picked her up in a small towel and hugged her under my chin,
telling her I loved her and would help her leave her body. She was
calm, seeming at ease with the decision and to enjoy the close
contact. I gave her some of the allergy medicine, as much as she
would take voluntarily, hoping it would be an overdose and she
would peacefully drift away. She did get sleepy, but it wasn't
enough. So I took her to Judy, who had an injectable drug for
euthanizing wild birds.

Judy's home is a half-hour drive from here. I tucked Tisha,
wrapped in the little towel, into my jacket, keeping her next to my
body under my chin. She remained there quietly through the trip,

349

sometimes nuzzling me with her beak, and I continued talking with her the whole time. I felt she knew exactly what was happening and it was what she chose for herself. Judy looked carefully at her injuries, agreeing that Tisha wasn't healing and suggesting she might even have cancer. She carefully injected the medicine into Tisha's chest. Tisha didn't fuss at all, as though she was ready, or perhaps the allergy medicine also relieved any discomfort or anxiety.

I snuggled Tisha under my chin with both hands around her, sending her love and light. I told her telepathically that she could let go now and later pick a different life in which she could be a mom in a more healthy, normal, rewarding environment. My thumb was against her chest so I felt her great heart beating in a steady, gentle rhythm for a couple minutes. Then it stuttered once and stopped, and my beautiful little Tisha gently flew free of her damaged body.

I tried to control my emotions somewhat, but a few tears slipped down my cheeks before I could leave. Judy was concerned about my ability to drive safely, wanting me to stay for a while. I just wanted go home and be alone with the pain. Don was playing bridge that afternoon so Mikey and Simon were the only ones there. They watched quietly as I wrapped Tisha's body and put it in the freezer. I was definitely not ready for a necropsy, but wanted to keep it in case I decided to have one done later. It's still there – and I'm still not ready for a necropsy. Somehow it just doesn't seem important. One of these days I'll get around to burying the body, though that also seems unimportant because Tisha isn't there.

Simon and Mikey were subdued, but I felt they were more concerned about me than about losing Tisha. That would make sense, since they knew they hadn't really lost her anyway. I also think they knew it was her choice and her time, so they were probably happy for her. Because they were no longer able to upset Tisha, I let them stay out of their cages nearly all the time. Simon soon went back to wandering around the house, seeming more cheerful than he had been for quite a while. Mikey also was doing more of his goofy stuff that always made me smile or laugh. The

350

atmosphere had apparently been quite heavy and sad for them as well. All this supported my decision to help Tisha leave her body.

CHAPTER 62

My philosophy about keeping animals in captivity before learning about telepathic animal communication can be summarized as follows: When we put an animal in a cage, as is essentially the case with domestic animals as well as captive wild ones, we take away its ability to care for itself in a natural way. We are therefore obligated to fill as many of its needs as we can, though identifying all their needs is challenging. Since I began interacting with them more on the level of Spirit, my philosophy has shifted and deepened. I now experience them more as equals.

Domestic animals are defined as those species that have lived with us for many generations and have thus adapted genetically to our way of life. In captive breeding programs, we select animals with desired characteristics of behavior as well as physical qualities, so the animals become quite different from their wild ancestors. For example, dogs who are friendly or easily trained are more likely to be chosen as breeders than those who are perhaps less friendly or harder to train. The intention, of course, is to produce puppies with more of the desired personality traits. When this is done through a number of generations, we find certain breeds are known for specific characteristics.

Because of this, domesticated animals are easier to live with and care for than their wild ancestors. We know more about them, for one thing, and many books and experts are available to teach us about their care, training, and medical needs. They also accept captive conditions much better than wild animals, most of which are not amenable to being caged. I don't consider exotic birds (parrots, emus, etc.), snakes, wallabies, or zoo animals to be domestic, even when they were born in captivity, because they haven't lived with us through enough generations to be significantly changed genetically. Frankly, I hope they never are and that normal populations are allowed to live as their ancestors did.

Keeping animals in small cages without a variety of stimuli or others of their kind is unfair to the animals and a risk to people when the animal is potentially dangerous (e.g., big cats, elephants, etc.). Even animals as primitive as snakes are curious and can become lethargic due to boredom. Some captive animals become highly aggressive or exhibit strange, repetitive behaviors which indicate emotional problems. Just filling the physical needs of appropriate shelter, temperature, humidity, and food is insufficient. As Tisha (parrot) and Toby (wallaby) said, animals may choose to die early when conditions are too disturbing for them, as they may be if their needs are not met.

I am so glad many zoos now provide more natural habitats and are becoming aware of emotional and social needs of animals in their care. Some put food in many different places around an enclosure, hiding it to give captives the experience of searching for their food or coming upon surprise tidbits. Also, scents of other animals may be placed in pens to provide interesting stimuli. Avoiding stressful stimuli is important; what is stressful depends on the species of animal and often the individual. Some sounds, scents, movements, or lighting can be torturous to individual animals, the equivalent of scratching fingernails on a chalkboard or repetitive, high-pitched sounds for us. The scent of a predator in the area would be terrifying to a small, nervous prey animal. Careful observation is necessary to determine what is stressful for each individual.

Zoos also often develop captive breeding programs which can be beneficial for several reasons. For one, fewer animals are caught in the wild then because captive-born ones can be shared with other zoos. Also, many animals will not breed in captivity until conditions are suitable, thus giving people more incentive to learn their needs and provide more complete and comfortable living conditions.

My advice to anyone thinking about living with any species of animal is to learn as much about its nature as possible and be objective when deciding whether its needs, both when healthy and when ill or injured, can be met in that environment. Keep in mind that every animal, like every person, is an individual, so filling the needs of one will probably be somewhat different from others even of the same species. A good animal communicator, as well as a knowledgeable veterinarian, can be helpful, both before and after taking an animal home. Many animals actually arrange to present themselves to people they choose to be with (e.g., Ross, the raven and Clover, the dog), so those who feel drawn to a particular animal may be responding to a telepathic or Spirit message. In these cases, living with that person is apparently part of the path of the animal and its human companion.

It is encouraging that more people are becoming aware of the messages animals can give us as communication with them is more widely accepted. On one level, people can learn how to better fill the physical and emotional needs of animals by paying more attention and by listening to them. This alone is of great value. Most people who live with and love an animal know it can read their moods and respond accordingly. They also realize they respond to the animal as if it is telling them something, though they may not know it actually is sending them telepathic messages. Increasing awareness of this aspect of living with animals is a huge gift, to both the animals and their human companions, and greatly enhances the experience for all concerned.

However, after living with parrots, learning about telepathic communication, and taking care of wild animals, I now seriously question any attempt to keep exotic birds and animals in captivity in any capacity, from private homes to zoos to experimental laboratories. Captive breeding programs to help avoid extinction and animals kept in more natural housing in order to educate people may be exceptions, though I wonder whether either is truly kind. I know I won't participate in any of it anymore, beyond giving the exotics we have as good a life as we can until they're ready to pass.

CHAPTER 63

After Tisha died, Simon and Mikey began interacting more with each other, sometimes even taking turns grooming and feeding each other. They seemed to be developing a friendship, which pleased me. Perhaps with no female parrot in the house, rivalry was eliminated. Simon and Tisha had never groomed each other, though Simon did feed her at times. I had kept Tisha's cage and Simon's, storing Mikey's because it was lower and therefore less appealing to them. I would have removed the nest box but Mikey spent quite a lot of time in it, maybe instinctive behavior in case a female appeared or he just liked a place to escape for a while.

During this time I began talking with some other people who were far more knowledgeable than I about spirituality from a non-religious perspective. I continued learning about properties of crystals and gemstones, and how some talented people, like my dear friend Sarah Monson, are able to feel energy in and around beings, living and non-living (as in rocks). They are then able to influence that energy to flow in more healthy ways, helping people and animals to feel better and even be physically healthier. I bought books and collected more rocks, greatly increasing my knowledge of these fascinating aspects of life. The expanding awareness is wonderful; I doubt I would have been open to it without confirmation from animals through telepathic communication.

Lyn and I also began talking on the phone more regularly, simply for the pleasure of sharing thoughts and new knowledge rather than more formally about animal communications. We both found few others who were interested in these topics, so it was always a special treat to spend some time with her, even if only on the phone.

Then, on March 30, about six weeks after she passed, Tisha gave me a phenomenal gift! I was preparing to feed Simon and Mikey in the morning, not really thinking of anything as I completed this mundane task. My daily routine was to take the food and water dishes, which were on top of Tisha's cage, into the kitchen to wash and refill them. Simon was on top of his cage to the left of the dishes; Mikey was on the perch on top of Tisha's cage to the right of the food and water. As I reached for the dishes, an African grey parrot slid down the bars in front of me, swinging inside the cage to stand on the perch. I picked up the bowls and turned toward the kitchen before realizing that was one too many birds! As I looked over my shoulder to see the empty cage, I heard Tisha laugh. Even then, it took a moment to understand what had just happened.

Sometimes, when she was standing on the kitchen counter sharing a meal with me, Tisha would lunge at my hand, as though to bite me, sometimes even thumping a finger with the top of her beak, when I reached toward our plate for another piece of food. Naturally I would jump and she would laugh as if to say, "Ha, ha! I gotcha!" Tisha's laugh that morning, weeks after she passed, was the one she used when she had tricked me during her happy times. I knew she was showing me she was fine and all was well. I so appreciated her kindness and still am deeply touched every time I think about her amazing gift to me. I thanked her and continued my day wearing a big smile. I now include her in my list of spirit guides, still feeling her presence on occasion, but without seeing her again.

In May, I felt Simon wanted to talk with Lyn. He had begun pulling more feathers from his chest, after letting them grow again for some time. He was still eating well, active with bright eyes, no other changes, but I've learned when I think they want to talk with her, it's because they are telling me they do. No doubt they first try to tell me what is bothering them. Then, when I don't get it, they resort to different behavior, at the same time telling me to call Lyn. Finally, at the end of May, I asked her to speak with both Simon and Mikey. She had time on June 2, with the following communications as a result.

> Simon: Hello, Lyn. It's me, Simon. Thanks for coming to talk with me – and thank Adele for calling you! She is so great to honor me by listening. I have been wanting to tell her I think it is time for her to find me a new home. I've been doubting my feelings because I think I'm crazy

sometimes for wanting to leave. But it's not that I want to leave. It's that I know I will go to another home someday and I think now is best, when Adele can find someone she believes will be really good to me. Tisha feels it is the right time, too! It involves more than just Adele; it involves catching an opening into the right home for me – one that may outlive me – so it's not like I think Adele will die next year. I hope she understands I don't want to ever leave, just like Tisha, but sometimes it is best to go with the right timing for best long-term results.

Lyn: I understand, Simon, and I think Adele will, too. Is that why you have been plucking your feathers? Do you feel caught between two choices, neither to your liking?

Simon: Yes! That's it exactly. I don't feel good about myself.

Lyn: It's important to realize that having to make difficult decisions does not mean we have failed in any way. It's important for you to see past the pain in your heart and see that you are doing the best for you and Adele and your new people, when you find them.

Simon: Yes, it is hard to see past my pain, but I do believe I have a good future ahead and so does Adele. Thanks so much!

Lyn: You are welcome! How do you feel about Mikey?

Simon: He's okay. Cheery guy! Doesn't take anything from me. That's how I lost my feathers on my head. He and I could both use some companionship with female parrots. I hope Adele can find me a home with a female parrot. I miss Tisha. And yes, I like men, but parrots live with both sexes and that is what I miss.

Lyn: Okay. I'll tell her. Do you have anything else you want to say?

Simon: Just be sure she knows how much she means to me, how much I hate that we must part, and how grateful I am for this wonderful home she has provided for us here!

Lyn: I'll do that. Take care!

Mikey: Hey, Lyn! Simon has made me a bit crazy lately, worrying about a new home, and how Adele will take it. That boy really worries! Now, as for me, I'm enjoying my new home! It's the best one I've had and I don't want to move on now. I want to stay here and enjoy Adele and Don for quite some time. When they say it's necessary, well, then I'll move on, but why leave a good thing? It doesn't make sense to me so I will just keep grounded and focused on staying here and let Simon move on.

Now, as for female parrots, I'm okay with or without. I'm real happy here and even Tisha rejecting me and leaving didn't bother me much. That's 'cause I know a good thing when I see it (if you know what I mean). I know Tisha and Simon had it rough before coming here, but they don't know the half of it. I know this is a great place and I don't intend to leave until I have to. Do you understand what I mean?

Lyn: Yes, I do, Mikey. I'm glad you are so happy! I'll tell Adele.

Mikey: You do that, Chicky, and thank Adele. I'm just good to go!

Lyn said she would be offended at being called Chicky by most beings, but with Mikey it seemed a term of endearment with no disrespect intended. He was such a funny guy – and Simon was such a worrier and a sweetheart, concerned about hurting my feelings or scaring me into thinking he might want to leave because I wasn't going to live much longer. That actually didn't cross my mind and isn't something that disturbs me.

CHAPTER 64

I had been procrastinating on the project of finding a long-term home for Simon. Clearly it was time to change that. I agreed to let Mikey stay as long as we could and went to work on finding a special place for Simon. I was glad, though not surprised, to hear they were still connected with Tisha. From her new perspective, she was probably in a better position to help with my project.

I had tried to find a private home for Simon but found I wasn't comfortable about transferring him to another family where all the same issues as our place would apply. So I went back to researching parrot rescue places, expanding my search to neighboring states, concentrating on the Pacific Northwest because it would be easier to take Simon there. I would not consider putting him on a plane or any other form of public transport. Sadly, the vast majority of parrot rescue places are run like dog and cat shelters in that the animals are taken in, cared for, and then adopted out. They provide an important service, no doubt rescuing many birds from bad situations, but that wasn't what I wanted for Simon. He was already in a better place than many, if not most, captive parrots.

Then I found a sanctuary just north of Spokane, Washington, only about a six-hour drive from here. The birds are not adopted out, but are expected to stay for the rest of their lives. They are not allowed to make babies, so avoid creating more captive parrots, which is great! A project for building an aviary where the birds could fly was in the works. All birds had relatively large cages and were frequently allowed out of them. The stated philosophy and intentions were definitely good. I emailed the owner, asking some questions, and then made arrangements to visit the place.

The facilities were clean and cheerful, with the birds in large parrot cages. Macaws especially had much bigger cages than could be maintained in most homes. There is enough property for a huge building containing aviaries, but some expected funding was either delayed or perhaps no longer available, so that project was on hold. Without expansion, they were at nearly maximum occupancy.

The owner had help, necessary with that many parrots, in the form of a couple who lived in a guest house on the property. I was a bit concerned about whether adequate provisions had been made for the birds in the event of the owner's death or incapacitation. She was working on that, being aware of the necessity. Another disadvantage was that she had no other Congo African greys and only one Timneh (a smaller variety), so Simon would have had no others of his kind to bond with. The bottom line is that it was close to what I wanted for Simon, but didn't feel quite right. Also, with limited space, it would be unfair to increase their load with a bird who already had an acceptable home. So my search continued.

On the way home, I intended to drive through Spokane, find an easily accessible motel in a small town or outlying area, and drive home the next day. However, wildlife rehabilitation got in the way. Just after I left the parrot refuge, a rehabber in our valley who works with raptors but wasn't available called my cell phone about an injured hawk. Judy, the main rehabber, was in Yellowstone National Park so she also couldn't care for the bird. In fact, Don was already babysitting a few little critters of hers, including a cute, orphaned baby skunk and a couple of small owls.

I called the people with the hawk, arranging for them to take it to Don. He would provide it with food and water in a safe place for the night. After I had prepared Don for this, I received another call saying the hawk had flown out of the cardboard box and away. I suspect it was a youngster who was still learning to be afraid of humans. It is easier to take off from a high position than from the ground, so it often appears they are unable to fly when the problem is simply inexperience or perhaps being temporarily too full to lift themselves off the ground after a big meal.

Then a game warden called about an owl who had been hit by a car. So much for staying overnight. I arrived home safely at about midnight, after some unpleasant stretches of construction which are more difficult to traverse in the dark.

The next morning someone called about five orphaned finch eggs, the mom having been killed by her dog. I quickly set up an incubator near Simon's area, without much hope for the babies because the mother had died at least 24 hours before. Especially during early stages of incubation, which these were, being cold for that long is usually fatal. Judy was to return home later that day, a relief for me. The young owl, a fledgling great horned, had a broken wing I wanted her to check. I also had a cedar waxwing with some apparent neurological damage. At least the hawk had taken care of himself.

Simon was, as always, interested in the wild birds, especially eggs in the incubator or babies. I felt he wanted to help them, but wouldn't let him actually touch any of them for several reasons. First, I wasn't entirely sure his interest was benign or helpful and wanted to avoid an injury. Also, the wild ones do have parasites, viruses, and bacteria, some of which could be harmful to the parrots. So I showed them to him from a distance, inviting him to look in the incubator when I turned eggs.

I asked Lyn to talk with Simon again, which she did on 6/12/10. I had explained to him, with attempts at telepathically sending him pictures, what I had seen and learned at the parrot sanctuary. I'm sure Tisha was there as well, having no doubt told Simon more than I could. However, I wanted Lyn to ask Simon for his input and whether he wanted me to do anything further at that time.

Simon: Hello, Lyn! Awk! Awk! Hello, Lyn! Great of you to talk with me again. I need to take a leadership role, ay? Tell Adele how much I appreciated that she would go see the Washington parrot refuge. Well, it didn't live up to my expectations so I'm glad I'm not going there. An aviary is still my first choice – not a zoo and not a half-way house to a new home and owner, but a real, fly-in-the-trees-no-cages aviary, permanent home!

Please ask Adele to keep looking. Tisha tells me there are some good places out there and that Adele and I must remain focused and she must keep actively seeking the right place for me. In this way Tisha says the right place will suddenly appear! (This is me taking the leadership role, Lyn. See? I'm really doing it!)

I continued looking on the Internet for sanctuaries. I had come across the website of a parrot refuge on Vancouver Island, British Columbia, but hadn't explored it well. It is farther from here than I had hoped and I was concerned about the procedures for taking animals across an international border. I looked more for a place in the U.S., expanding the search range with no success.

CHAPTER 65

So I roamed through the large, informative website for the World Parrot Refuge in Canada, which includes lots of YouTube videos and stories about different rescued birds. Their philosophy is the same as the Washington sanctuary, with no babies, no adoptions, and lifelong care. A special area houses birds with medical needs, avian veterinary care is available, employees and volunteers help with maintenance and cleaning, food consists of fresh fruits, vegetables, seeds, and nuts, and the birds are fed three times daily.

Especially great is they have a huge building filled with aviaries, some even big enough for macaws, extra large parrots, to be able to fly. One area is just for African grey parrots and a lot of them live there. The birds have tall trees, many branches at different levels, windows, and room to fly. Outdoor aviaries were being built for summer weather.

I began an email dialogue with Wendy, the owner of the place, and loved everything she said. Her knowledge and concern for the birds came through loud and clear. Legal and financial arrangements have been made to continue the sanctuary should something happen to Wendy and her husband, Horst. I began to think both Simon and Mikey would be much better off in this place than any other.

Wendy said they do have parrots from the U.S. as well as Canada. I researched transporting pets into Canada and found getting them in required limited formal paperwork, with a health certificate being most important. Bringing them back through U.S. customs had more requirements, but I would not be doing that, so remained unconcerned. My passport, all I needed to cross the border, was still valid from my trip to Africa.

I asked Lyn for input from Simon and Mikey before I made a final decision or went further with plans.

Simon: Hello, Lyn! Simon here!

Mikey: Ado, Ado - Mikey, too! [Adieu or ado or just

rhyming?

Lyn: Hello, fellows! How are you today?

Mikey: Oh, we're peachy keen – peachy keen! Whale says you need to rattle and 'om' for us now so we can get in touch with our Records. That's what Whale says!

Lyn: Okay, here goes! (Rattle and 'ooommm')

Simon: That's it! Did you get it, Lyn? We are to go to the sanctuary in order to fulfill our destiny to live as wild parrots – even though we won't live in the wild. [singing] Back to the Wild! Back to the Wild! Awk! Awk! A hunting we will go! Back to the Wild! Back to the Wild! Got it?

Lyn: Yes, I do.

Simon: I am leading, Lyn. Do you see? Tisha started this. She started all of this by stopping living. Never think that stopping is bad! Good can come from anything, if you can see it! Tell Adele she needed to see clearly that Mikey must go, too, and that she would never be happy with us in private homes.

Mikey saw clearly during the rattling that he has managed to keep a wonderful attitude through many bad situations and the Universe is rewarding him with a return to an almost wild state. Same for me. I've come a long way and forgiven myself a lot (thanks to Adele and you), so I am being allowed into an almost wild bird state, because I've completed my business here on this planet. Now I can help Adele with hers by leading her to the sanctuary in B.C.

Tell Adele to get in touch with Whale for her records. Life will be easier for her if she does!

Lyn: Thank you! Anything else from anyone?

Mikey: Lyn, Chicky Pea, tell Adele how sad I am to leave such a great home, but how great it will be to fly to a tree top and chat with birds and fly and peck and fly and fly and fly! Tell her she's the greatest to do this for us! We will be indebted and we will stay in touch forever – but wheelchair people come close to knowing how we feel about not being able to fly!

Simon: We are forever indebted to Adele for this – for giving us the freedom to fly again. We will always be One and there for her! Tisha, too, is truly a remarkable soul. She gave her life that we might know flight before we die. Tisha is delighted and sends her heart-felt thanks to Adele, too! When the slaves get their freedom and the blind man sees and the crippled walk – they are the ones who know how we feel now!

I didn't understand Mikey's use of the word ado so I looked it up. According to dictionary.com, it can mean excitement and activity, either positive or negative, definitely appropriate from Mikey's point of view in this communication. Also, of course, it rhymes with too in his greeting, consistent with his way of talking.

When Simon and Mikey compared their lives as pets to those of slaves and people unable to walk, it brought tears to my eyes. I know many people they referred to have rich, rewarding lives in spite of, and perhaps in part because of, their circumstances. However, they are physically less free than others, just as captive parrots, even those in loving, respectful homes, have relatively limited freedom due to their inability to fly free in their natural environment with many options for food, friends, mates, and raising families.

So the decision was made, including to get on with it and go as soon as possible. Don had some dental procedures to complete which would be easier for him if I was home, so it was important to finish that first. Fortunately, I had received no injured or orphaned fawns (*not* a coincidence, I'm sure!) so it would be unnecessary for Don and Tom to care for them. Judy would take over with any birds that showed up.

On June 21, I had an interesting energy session with my dear friend Sarah. She is an amazing woman whose knowledge and skills, including psychic abilities, are apparently growing rapidly. Actually, I think it's also that she is trusting them more due to positive experiences and feedback from others, as well as continuing formal education in these fields. I didn't understand then much about what she does, but have since learned a lot more.

After the energy work, I felt much better in several ways. During the two or three months prior to this session, I'd had some upper abdominal discomfort three or four times, usually at night, which I was unable to relate to anything specific or any other symptoms. Following my usual pattern, I researched some possible diagnoses, this time without definitive results. I had also recently made the mistake of lifting something much too heavy for me and was still feeling the effects in my abdomen of that bit of stubbornness.

After the session with Sarah, I better understood the abdominal problem, which has not recurred after several years. I was much more comfortable from the lifting injury, healing from it quickly and completely. I also felt more energized and confident about the trip to B.C. with Simon and Mikey. I was unconcerned about finding someone to go with me, in fact thinking it might be better with just the birds. I was ready to go, however it worked out.

Sarah said what I do in my work with the animals is a bit like plugging in a lamp. The spiritual part of my association with them is far more significant than the physical, even though I've been less aware of it. Her work with people is like that as well, with her connecting with Spirit and the energy of unconditional love which surrounds us all. I already did that, but needed to do so with more awareness, as the animals had been saying.

I decided to leave here with Simon and Mikey on Saturday, July 10. Wendy said she would be at the refuge on the weekend, so would be able to take them whenever I arrived. In an attempt to minimize stress for the birds, I chose to drive almost to Vancouver,

B.C. that day, so made motel reservations near there. It would be acceptable for me to take the birds into the room with me, an important requirement due to cool night temperatures as well as my unwillingness to leave them alone or locked in small carriers that long. The next day we would cross on a ferry to Nanaimo on Vancouver Island, with a short drive from there to the sanctuary.

After settling Simon and Mikey, I planned to drive down to Victoria, where I would meet my friends Ed and Anna. Ed would be attending a seminar in Seattle that weekend and Anna would drive up from their home outside of Portland, Oregon, to meet him on Sunday. We would spend a couple days in Victoria, visiting the Butterfly Gardens and Butchart Gardens, with a whale-watching trip in there somewhere.

I emailed my plans to Wendy, receiving a great reply from her. I had asked if she wanted to read Lyn's last communication with the birds; not only was she interested, she told me birds sometimes talk to her telepathically. Wendy also explains to the birds what is to be done if they have to be handled or treated medically, saying they already know because she has been thinking about it. Another great reason to feel good about taking them to her sanctuary and trusting her to treat them with kindness, dignity, and respect!

One of the reasons I had thought about keeping Mikey, other than his saying he wanted to stay, was that I didn't feel he was as uncomfortable as Simon about captivity, since he was in an acceptable home. The refuge is a non-profit organization with huge expenses for keeping so many birds, so I thought it might be better to avoid adding birds who are doing well. However, when I told Wendy I would be taking Mikey as well as Simon, she thought it was great, saying they were already the start of a flock so it would be unkind to separate them. At the refuge, they would simply befriend more birds to create a more normal-sized flock. Wendy is one of those people who expects to have enough for all, doing whatever needs to be done to provide for them. I didn't talk with her about manifesting, as described in the movie *The Secret*, but she appears to be doing it, with or without awareness.

It seemed everything was flowing even better than I had hoped, indicating the Universe was in accord with my plans. This continued until I actually tried to cross the border. Then all my plans fell apart.

CHAPTER 66

I reached the border on Interstate 5 around 8:00 p.m. that Saturday evening, after a pleasant and peaceful drive. Simon and Mikey were in individual cat carriers on the back seat, each with his own seatbelt through the handle of the crate. I gave them water, grapes, and juice through the front bars every time I stopped; they each had a chunk of wood to chew on, as well as parrot food always available. Most of the time they stood at the front looking out, seeming curious without being nervous. I had some homeopathic drops for reducing travel stress in pets. Simon took some; Mikey was more interested in biting off the top of the plastic dropper bottle.

At the border, I handed over my passport, telling the guard I was going to Vancouver and then to Vancouver Island and Victoria to meet friends from Oregon. He asked why I wasn't traveling with them (I had, after all, just driven through Seattle, where Ed and Anna were.) He seemed to be quite suspicious – and then he saw the carriers in the back seat. I told him the parrots were my pets, giving him the health certificate from Linda, but he was uncomfortable about just accepting that, telling me to park the car and go inside.

After more than an hour of looking up regulations and asking questions, a border officer told me I would have to go back. He called the U.S. officials and held my passport until my car was headed directly toward the U.S. border crossing. One of those officials met me with some paperwork about transporting pets, including relevant names and phone numbers. He suggested I go to Sumas, Washington, a smaller border crossing a few miles to the east, and talk with some officials there. They would not be available till Monday morning, but he thought they may have some suggestions about taking the birds into Canada.

I was exhausted and frazzled. By that time it was nearly 10:00 p.m. and dark. I had watched guards arrest one man inside the building, and my car was parked next to one they were dismantling, presumably looking for drugs. The birds had been in the car alone for at least an hour and the terrifying possibility of confiscation had been mentioned. I drove back toward Seattle, pulling off the freeway where I saw some motels to find a room where I could let the birds out of carriers for a while. My plan was to sleep for a few hours before making my way to Sumas in the daylight.

A sign at the first motel said pets were allowed for a $10 fee, which was fine with me. However, when I told the clerk about Simon and Mikey, I was informed they do not allow birds in the rooms. I went to the next place, only to find the same rules. I decided I'd have to leave them in the car and get some rest. I hoped they would sleep, as they usually do at night, and that it wouldn't be too cold for them.

I called Ed and the motel in Canada where I had reservations. The person at the latter was nice, not even charging me a fee after I explained what had happened. I still thought I might be able to cross the border on Monday. Ed found the phone number for a motel in Sumas where the manager told me the parrots could stay in the room with me. What a relief! I could spend Sunday there with Simon and Mikey out of carriers and call officials Monday morning.

Needless to say, I did not sleep well or long that night; I was back in the car with Simon and Mikey at daylight. They appeared fine and the car thermometer said it was 60 degrees – colder than they were used to, but not dangerously so. Sumas was only about 30 miles away and I had no idea what I would do until check-in time. However, I wanted to be out of the high population area. I followed a map, traveling on narrow rural roads, much less stressful than freeways, to reach the tiny town.

Sumas has one main street leading directly to the border crossing with a few short side streets. The motel, where I stopped just in case they would let me have the room early, is on the main street within sight of the border. I met the manager, a pleasant, friendly man who told me the room was available. What a relief! I immediately took in the birds and their paraphernalia, plus my bag. Then I walked across the street to a small grocery store, stocked up on a few supplies, and went back to the room.

Birds are messy. Not only do they poop a lot, flapping their wings causes seeds and small feathers to fly around. They are also inclined to chew and they prefer the highest perch in the area. I spread a blanket and some towels from home on the floor to protect the carpet and reduce time I would have to spend cleaning. When I set the carriers on a table with doors open, Mikey immediately walked out and flew up onto the curtain rod, scattering seeds and shells all over the floor. Simon soon followed and both had a great time flying around. So much for keeping the mess in a small area. They seemed so happy, crawling around on the floor cleaning up after them for an hour or more was worth it.

I kept the curtains closed and lighting dim, hoping to reduce their activity and especially their noise. They did squawk occasionally, but not much and only during the day. I know they were audible to others because I could easily hear people in the hall and other rooms. Nobody complained to me, though, and the manager was still friendly when I saw him again. I read and napped and waited till Monday.

At 8:00 that morning I began making phone calls. Two U.S. departments and two Canadian ones are involved in transporting exotic animals and/or livestock across the border. Domestic pets may be included in this as well, especially if they are to be left in Canada. I explained to each official that I was trying to take the parrots to the sanctuary. No money was changing hands, the birds would never be sold, the breeder who sold them to me was willing to talk with them on the phone, I did have a health certificate from my veterinarian, who had known the birds as long as I had. No one was remotely inclined to give an inch. I would have to go home and apply for import and export permits, even though they were not relevant to this situation.

I let everyone know (Ed and Anna, Wendy, Don, hotel) that all was canceled and began the long trip home.

The drive was relatively easy. Construction caused two-lane freeway with close oncoming traffic between 50 and 75 miles from home, which we reached after dark. Simon and Mikey had been mostly quiet the whole trip, seeming unconcerned and often watching through the wire doors of their carriers. However, when I was tense driving through the construction, they began to vocalize. The sounds didn't include words, instead seeming rhythmic and soothing, almost like singing. I tried copying their sounds and they repeated them. Their voices were clear, with no raspy squawking. I felt they were helping to distract and relax me as I drove in the uncomfortable conditions. When roads returned to normal, they again were mostly quiet. I thanked them for their help and told them we'd be home soon. We arrived safely about midnight and Simon and Mikey settled easily into their familiar surroundings, seemingly with no ill effects from the unusual few days.

CHAPTER 67

The next morning I started collecting relevant forms. I was able to download the CITES* application for transporting exotics across borders through the U.S. Fish and Wildlife website. Both this form and the health certificate require some type of identification for each animal, proving they are the ones on the forms. Bands had been put on Simon and Mikey years before, but had been cut off because they can be uncomfortable and even dangerous for birds if they rub the leg or get caught on something. I was given their bands by the woman who sold them to me, but there was no way to prove which was which. The breeder gave me a statement saying they were born there and that she had sold them to me for $800 each. When I thought I had everything, I sent it to the appropriate U.S. Fish and Wildlife office and began waiting.

*(CITES: Convention on International Trade in Endangered Species of Wild Fauna and Flora, an international agreement between governments)

The Department of Agriculture required Linda, as my veterinarian, to request the health certificate form instead of me. It was designed for poultry, so much of the information was irrelevant to parrots, but I couldn't cross the border without it. The health examination was to be done within a month of travel so it had to wait till I knew when I could go.

Two Canadian departments are also involved in importing animals into Canada. They have different names but are similar to the two U.S. departments. It turned out Wendy needed to obtain permission from them since she was technically the importer. They required an import date and the export number from the CITES permit, so she would be unable to start her application before I received my permit.

Wendy expected mine to take about a month, with hers another two weeks. Since this was mid-July, I was concerned about the approaching winter. I definitely wanted to avoid the possibility of driving in or after snow storms. They usually start in the fall here and most of the trip is north of our area. I also thought it was important to transfer Simon and Mikey before the following spring. I believe this is why the birds were so anxious to go quickly. If I had delayed the first trip, during which I learned what was required, we would have been unable to go before winter.

I would have to make an appointment with a U.S. Department of Agriculture official, who would meet me during business hours at the border to sign off on the health certificate before I could cross into Canada. Requirements continued to become even more complicated. Wendy had to make an appointment for a Canadian official to see the birds and sign off on her paperwork, too.

Then Wendy was told the birds would have to be quarantined in Canada for at least 45 days before they could go to the sanctuary – and Canada has no quarantine facilities specifically for parrots. That could have ended the whole plan. There is no way I would have allowed them to be housed in a facility with other animals, cared for by people who didn't know much about parrots. Fortunately Wendy was able to convince officials to agree to let Simon and Mikey stay with a friend of hers not far from the refuge. They would have to be in parrot cages (not little carriers), but would be in the home of a kind person who had direct access to Wendy's knowledge. An official would check the birds shortly after they arrived and again before they were released to the sanctuary.

The plan was for me to drive to Sumas, Washington, check into the motel where the birds could get out of carriers, then go to the border the next morning to meet with all the officials. Wendy and her husband Horst would connect with me after I crossed into Canada, where we would complete the Canadian paperwork and transfer the birds. Then I would turn around and drive home. That sounds a lot quicker and easier than it was, though the first part, waiting for the permit, was the most frustrating.

On August 23, a month after I mailed the forms, I received a call from a woman who processes CITES applications. She had questions about the leg bands because they were ones breeders use for babies, not official identification, and she needed to know which Port of Entry I would use, a question I had missed on the form. The woman said a senior biologist still needed to review the applications and may not get to it for a week or two. I was encouraged that there seemed to be no problems and expected everything to be finished so we could go during the middle of September. That turned out to be overly optimistic.

When I still had no permit by September 20, I decided to follow Lyn's suggestion to have another shamanic journey with Carla; my intention was to clear negativity surrounding the paperwork. The following is a summary of the journey:

Shamanic Journey for Adele, 9/22/10

[Drumming begins and continues throughout the session.] This is a session for Adele, to clear her and the parrots of energy that is disagreeable and fearful and creating blockages toward the smooth passage of the birds to their new forever home and to bring the spirits to bear to lubricate right passage for the birds so that everyone who touches anything to do with them smiles and is compelled to hustle this along, because it's such a neat idea.

Simon and Mikey joined Carla and me and said they wanted to stay together. I told them they would. They were somewhat apprehensive due to the major changes, but were excited as well. They said they had tried to calm my fears on the last trip. The spirits did some things to help me with my concerns for the birds and for missing them, which I knew would happen. They also helped all of us release old fear, anger, and resentment, and shielded us from absorbing any negative energy from others.

Then we were taken to some spirits who work with the government to lubricate the flow of documents. The papers were laid out and the proper stamp chosen. Then a wallaby appeared and stamped all the papers. Carla did not know about our wallabies nor had she ever seen one in a journey before. As with Ara (python) appearing in my first journey, this added validation to what Carla was describing.

379

We went to another one of Carla's teachers for further support with government procedures. He checked the energy around Simon, Mikey, and me, saying we were all good to go. An Ebony Egret volunteered to be a power animal for the Canada trip, overseeing everything and sheltering us from negativity.

The most interesting and exciting part about this journey was that I received the CITES permit several days later – and it had been approved September 23, the day after my shamanic journey. I contacted Wendy and we agreed that Wednesday, October 6, would work for both of us. She could pick up the import permit on the way to Sumas, her friend was ready for Simon and Mikey to stay through the quarantine period, appointments were made with officials on both sides of the border, and all was good. My friend Sandy was free to go with me this time, so she and I would drive to Sumas on Tuesday, planning to cross the border the next morning. Everything worked, with Simon and Mikey safely transferred to Wendy and Horst, but not without a few more trials.

CHAPTER 68

All went well on the way to Sumas, a more pleasant trip than before with Sandy as a companion. We both enjoy looking at the scenery and visiting; Simon and Mikey remained peaceful and calm. In the motel, Simon flew onto the bed next to Sandy, seeming to like being close, though she hadn't been around birds much. His behavior was unusual for him; I hadn't seen him approach a woman voluntarily before. Apparently he had picked up good feelings from Sandy during the drive. She didn't try to touch him, but was comfortable letting him stay beside her for a while.

The next morning I left Sandy and the birds in my car when I went inside to connect with the USDA official. He was stationed at a different office so he drove to this one, parking right next to my car shortly after we arrived. He saw the pet carriers and identified himself to Sandy, who let him look at the birds. I was really glad he didn't have to handle them and hoped no one else would, either, because that would have been quite stressful for Simon and Mikey. The official found me inside, looked over the papers, stamped the health certificate, processed the $250 fee, and I was ready to cross the border. I drove to one of the booths, told the officer I had an appointment with the Canadian official, and was directed to a parking area.

I again left Sandy, this time taking the birds to the office where I met Wendy. The Canadian official was not happy that the birds had no bands or marks, saying the official who would examine them at the quarantine place would be unable to tell they were the same ones. He directed me to carry them back to the first office where I asked that official to lock their carriers with numbered metal strips and add that information to the paperwork. We went back to Canada, paid $150 to their official, and were finally cleared.

I thought. It turned out we still hadn't been through customs, a necessary step before the birds were free to go.

Wendy and I carried Simon and Mikey to a customs official, who asked what the birds were worth. We said they were not being sold nor would they be because they were going to a permanent sanctuary, so there really was no monetary value. Things got a bit tense for a few minutes, so Wendy sat down with the parrots while I talked with the official. Because of the receipt showing I had paid $800 each for them, the man was able to determine a customs fee for importing them. When I gave him my credit card, he asked why I was paying it rather than Wendy. I again explained what was happening. He still had to charge me (more than $100) but he kindly gave me a form I could use to request a refund, if I chose. I thanked him for the form but never completed it. I was more than ready to be finished with government organizations and forms!

What a huge relief! This whole process had taken hours, with Sandy sitting patiently in the car the whole time, though she usually doesn't sit still for long. Fortunately she had a book, which she finished while she was waiting. Sandy, Wendy, and I went to a café while Horst took care of some business. Then I said goodbye to Simon and Mikey, who seemed fairly calm about everything, and Sandy and I came home.

A few days later, I received an email from Wendy saying the birds were settled in a big cage and doing well. They had had to stay in the carriers for more than a day till the official came to check them and cut the metal strips, but all of that was done. Finally! Now they simply had to wait till the quarantine was finished before they could fly. I asked Lyn to talk with them, both to find out how they felt and also to explain more completely what was happening. This time she didn't do a formal communication so her email about them is as follows:

> Simon is happy and seems to be saying over and over "just six more weeks until I fly!" He is so glad to be this far on his path to flying that he seems quite unconcerned about the wait. Mikey feels the same way. He told me that since he has waited all of his life for this, waiting six more weeks seems of no consequence. Both of them said they will really miss you, but since you can't stay with them as long as they live, they are glad to be going to live where there are other parrots and are mostly focused on their upcoming freedom.

Nicki said he has always been a happy bird, much happier than either Simon or Mikey, but now he is even happier since they are gone. He liked them, but he likes the idea of not having to share you with so many others. He is aware that he is not going to be sent away.

The six weeks turned out to be closer to eight, but they finally did get to the sanctuary. They stayed first in regular parrot cages in the hall next to the African grey compound; then, when they seemed ready, Simon and Mikey were released into the aviary with the flock. A month or so later, after they had time to settle, I asked Lyn to talk with them again, which she did on 1/5/11.

Simon: How are you, Lyn?

Mikey: Howdy, howdy, howdy!

Lyn: I am well! How are both of you?

Simon: Great! Terrific! Marvelous! I'm flying and I have new friends!

Mikey: Me, too! It is just Chicky-poo-poo-poo everywhere and it is so great! You humans won't understand, but lots of birds (and poo) are just so normal, natural – like coming home. It is way better than I hoped or imagined! I've got several girl friends. We sit together and nuzzle and coo and oh! It is so sweet! Chicky-poo!

Simon: I have some men friends. We don't do like Mikey and his girls! We hang together and chat as we walk across the wire on top. It is so cool, 'cause women, females, just never understand the male-bonding thing. [Lyn glanced at JoJo, her male dog who prefers the company of men] Yeah! JoJo knows. It's cool – real cool. And I love to fly. I'm good. I wasn't, but I learned fast, huh, Mikey?

Mikey: Oh, he did learn quickly! He's an amazing flyer. All the parrots think so! I fly, but girls are my thing! And not just one girl. I like lots at one time. Chicky-poo! Chicky-poo! [singing in time with his special, head-bobbing, cool-guy walk]

Lyn: Do you guys need anything from Adele or the people at the sanctuary?

Simon: No, not at all!

Mikey: Heck no! I've got food and gals and they are good here. Some birds like people and hang out with the caretakers, but we don't! We were born to be Free-ee-ee-ee! I've got my gal and I've got two and three - Whee-ee-ee! We are good to go – good-to-go – good-to-go! See-ee-ee! [more singing]

Simon: Yeah, Lyn, tell Adele we're good, really good. Except for living out of doors, we've got it all and we know it is too cold for us to do that here, so this is great – and we're glad we don't have to leave! Tell Adele we want her to come see us. We'll know her, even if she doesn't recognize us. Tell her to step in, be quiet, and call us, and we'll come to her. We won't go to just anybody. We know she won't take us home with her. We want her to see what she has done for us! That is the best gift we can give her!

Mikey: You bet your bootie, gal! Tell Adele to come see us and we'll come to her. I'll leave my gals to say Hi to her. She rescued me from that bad lady for her darlin' Tisha and then she found me this forever home where I can have my gals and fly, too! You bet your bootie, we'll find her if she comes to see us. Tell her thanks so much. Thankee! Thankee! Thankee! We're happy to be here and grateful! So much Grateful!

Lyn: Do you have anything else to say to Adele?

Mikey: We love her - Yes, indeedy! Yes, indeedy!

Simon: Absolutely! We send our best to her and Don, Nicki, and all the rest! We miss them, but like it here much better!

Their happiness made all the difficulty and expense worthwhile. I am thrilled I was able to find this home for them. And I did get to see them later that year.

CHAPTER 69

I began to plan a driving trip for the end of June and first part of July 2011; it included seeing Simon and Mikey at the parrot refuge on Vancouver Island, attending a Flower of Life workshop in Puyallup, Washington, and visiting friends in Oregon. Then what seemed to be a crisis with Nicki, the parrot who was always healthy and happy, almost kept me home.

During the early part of June, I noticed Nicki seemed a bit more clumsy when he was climbing around in his cage. I assumed his toenails were too long, getting caught on the branches and wire, so I trimmed them. However, that didn't seem to help as it usually did. Then I noticed his right foot was not opening when he ran around on the floor. He was walking on his fist (closed foot) rather than normally with his toes spread. He was able to push his toes against a round perch like my finger or a branch and then grip, but he was unable to open that foot with his muscles.

As usual, I began trying to figure out what could be wrong, researching on the Internet, calling Linda, our veterinarian, wondering whether he had hurt himself or if I was feeding him the wrong things. I was concerned about being away from home in case this was the beginning of a serious medical problem. Linda suggested I leave him at a veterinary clinic in Missoula for ultra sound and possibly an abdominal scope exam to determine what was wrong. I knew I wouldn't do that to Nicki; he would be totally traumatized just by being left in a strange place, let alone being handled by strangers and given drugs.

Sarah came over to do some energy work with him (without touching him) and suggested some gemstones for the bottom of his sleeping cage. I started giving him alkaline water and some homeopathic products, thinking he may have systemic gout because I gave him more protein than his suggested diet includes.

Another friend, Karey, who does different energy healing techniques, offered to teach me some Reiki so I could use it with him before I left. She said I could learn more about Reiki from her when I returned home. I saw no change from any of what I tried, so, as Nicki said, I finally asked Lyn to check with him. Duh! His communication on 6/18/11 is pure Nicki. He is such a character!

Nicki: Lyn, Lyn, Lyn! It's not a sin - to talk to Lyn! Adele, Adele, Adele! She's doing Well, Well, Well! Nicki, Nicki, Nicki! It's fun to see and be like Nicki!

Ha! Ha! Ha! I'm a poet and Don't I Know It! (Lots of laughter! He's feeling good and happy - Lyn)

Hi, Lyn! Long time, no talk! Thank Adele for listening to me! And thanks for doing this! I'm so proud of Adele for F I N A L L Y (very slow and drawn out - Lyn) thinking to ask me what I was feeling! That is so great! She tends to run off on that vet-talk-track and it's hard to get her back on line – with us – with Spirit (all One, don't we know. Hee! hee!). You are doing great yourself.

Here! Feel my toe!

Lyn: (focusing on my feet) I don't feel anything, Nicki.

Nicki: (laughing hard) I know! It doesn't hurt! I'm standing on the stones! Hooray! [Sarah had put a crystal cluster under the towel in Nicki's sleeping cage and I later put two other gemstones there as well.]

Now feel it! (Lyn said, "I could feel a throb in my small toe.") See. It can hurt, but Adele knows how to fix things! She's so good! She's great! Tell her, Lyn, that I have no plans to call her home early. I think she needs to do all that stuff, too, especially the seminar. Simon and Mikey are fine. She doesn't need to do that [go to Canada to visit them]. But tell her all of her animal friends are behind her new growth spurt [spiritual growth] and we wouldn't think of messing that up. So tell Adele I'm fine with the trip and Don and her treatment of me and to go and have a great and wonderful time – but don't forget to trust Spirit for Everything!until there is a reason not to do that!

Whee - ee - ee! It's me! I'm swinging in a tree! (Looking at me upside down - Lyn) [hanging upside down from the top of his cage, as he does frequently - Adele]

I'm so free! Can't you see! It's me! Nicki-i-i!
Little Red Nicki! High in a tree! Oh, I can see! See! SEE!
Won't you come with me! I'm a Lory! Sweet as can be!
Hear me! Hear me! I'm a Chattering Be - Bee - Beee!

Oh, I'm so great! That's just some of what I can do. Impressed?

Lyn: Yes, very impressed!

Nicki: Good. We're done now! Thanks so much!

Lyn said she understood Nicki uses singing and rhyming in his head to entertain himself much of the time. I still laugh when I think of or read this communication, both because Nicki is so cheerful and because of the way he critiques my behavior. I relaxed and quit worrying about leaving him. Of course he was fine when I returned home, though he was still unable to open his foot with his muscles four years later. He also was no worse, and just as busy, cheerful, and demanding as before, showing no evidence of discomfort. I'm glad I didn't traumatize him physically and emotionally with all the diagnostic tests.

CHAPTER 70

This trip was great in a number of ways. I decided to use some of what I'd been learning about energy, Spirit, and metaphysics by asking Archangels Michael and Raphael to travel with me, keeping me alert and aware as I drove and helping me avoid problems. According to author Doreen Virtue, among others, archangels are beings of energy/light; therefore they can be many places at once with no diminution of their powers. They are unable to interfere in our lives without invitation, but are happy to provide help when we ask for it.

I was amazed how relieved I felt on the trip due to this simple act of faith. I noticed more beauty as I drove, was more relaxed and comfortable, and yet maintained a high level of energy and awareness. When I started to feel tired or distracted, I asked Michael for more energy – and it was there. I still ask for their presence and assistance when I travel and often consult Doreen Virtue's Archangel Oracle Cards. I ask a question, then draw one or more cards, usually with appropriate and helpful results.

As a hypnotherapist, I know some of my improved travel experiences could be from my subconscious mind taking in my suggestions. However, the more I learn about Spirit and quantum physics, the more sure I am that I have outside help when I ask for it, which I greatly appreciate. I now believe the subconscious mind, though powerful in itself, is much more so through its greater awareness of our connection to Spirit, with access to everything there such as archangels, spirit guides, power animals, ancestors, Akashic records. We truly are never alone, even when we are unaware of spirits and, if we ask, they help us be present and aware in order to receive gifts and to avoid difficulties. I've found them to be great companions – on trips and while living each day.

The first night of my trip, I stayed in a motel near the Washington/Canada border, crossing the next morning with no difficulties or delays (and no parrots). I drove through Vancouver to a ferry which took me to Nanaimo on Vancouver Island using a new GPS navigator, which I found helpful though not infallible.

I reached the World Parrot Refuge that afternoon with plenty of time to see Simon and Mikey.

Lyn had briefly told them I'd be visiting; they were so excited and pleased that I would take the time to do so. I also let them know I was on the way and when I expected to be there. I found Wendy who took me into the African greys' compound, even though she was busy caring for special-needs birds. We visited there for a few minutes before she needed to return to her patients. She, of course, didn't know which birds were Simon and Mikey. She knows the ones who require special care or become more attached to humans, but there are so many birds she can't possibly keep track of all those like Simon and Mikey, who are healthy and independent. I am happy to say she does not band or mark them in any way, either.

The aviary was a bit overwhelming at first, with African grey parrots all around me and a Macaw enclosure, also containing many noisy, busy birds, just across a hall. Most of the inside walls consisted of chain link fencing, so there was no sound buffering. I'd been offered ear plugs and, though I chose not to use them, I could certainly understand why the noise might bother some folks.

There were lots of branches in each enclosure, with places to hide and feeding stations containing fresh fruits, veggies, seeds, and nuts in several places, including on the chain link sides, the floor, and hanging from chain link panels on top. Some birds were flying, others walking on the floor, many sitting quietly on branches, some climbing and hanging on the chain link panels, both sides and top. Sliding glass doors allowing sunlight, outside views, and access to outside flight pens were in each enclosure. Large, long-handled brushes and hoses were strategically placed, and floors were smooth cement with drains for ease of cleaning, a constant and unrewarding task with that many birds.

After Wendy left, I stood in the center of the enclosure, turning slowly around, trying to look carefully at a bunch of constantly moving birds, hoping to recognize two. When I finally gave up and asked Simon to show me where he was, something I should have done first, I noticed one bird climbing down the chain link fence toward a food tray. I looked more closely and recognized Simon by an unusual pattern of feathers caused from plucking them in the past. He was still missing some feathers, but fewer than before, and he looked healthy. I moved closer to him and he said, "Whaaat?" in a distinctly deep tone of voice, so I would know for sure it was Simon. He climbed back up the fence to a branch after I thanked him for letting me see him.

I then asked Simon to show me where Mikey was. He is noticeably larger than Simon (as were some other birds) with no identifying markings. I had watched parrots on the floor, trying to spot Mikey's distinctive macho-guy walk, without success. Simon again moved off his branch onto the chain link panel, but this time he climbed up and, hanging upside down from the top, 'walked' over toward a large parrot who was sitting on top of a branch. Simon stopped, looked down at me, looked toward the other bird and then looked at me again. When I thanked him for showing Mikey to me, Simon turned around and went back to his perch.

Mikey flew down to the floor and, making sure I was watching him, pointedly executed his macho walk. He also showed me some of his ladies, appearing completely at ease in his home. I talked briefly with him, then went back toward Simon and asked him to come down again. He did, stopping about the level of my face. I asked if he would let me pet his back, as he sometimes did when he lived with us, and he carefully held still for me while I touched him. That is hard for Simon to do, something he wasn't able to tolerate till he'd been in our home a number of years, so I greatly appreciated his allowing it after nearly a year away from me.

I'm glad I went to see Simon and Mikey and so grateful to them for helping me recognize them. I have no need to go again, feeling confident they have the best home I could provide under the circumstances. As with the wild ones I release, I assume they are living – or not – as they choose.

CHAPTER 71

The Flower of Life workshop was amazing and wonderful, greatly increasing my understanding and awareness of my connection to Spirit. I learned the MerKaBa meditation, something I practiced almost daily for a year and occasionally after that. It is being taught by a number of different people including Maureen St. Germain and Drunvalo Melchizedek. Both have websites and books readily available.

Briefly, the MerKaBa meditation involves imagining oneself sitting or standing in a star tetrahedron and following specific steps in order to activate a light body around our physical body. Once learned, it only takes a few minutes. I always feel renewed when I do it, though I more often use other meditations now. We began learning about sacred geometry, superficially the energy associated with different geometric shapes, and participated in several activities to show us we could all access unseen energies with positive results. I found it fun and exciting, well worthwhile.

One workshop exercise involved using dowsing rods to find the edge of the energy field around a person. Nancy made them using slender brass rods from a hardware store. They are bent into an elongated L shape; the short section is covered with a loose piece of clear plastic tubing, allowing the rod to swing easily when gently held. The person holding the rods, one in each hand, would walk toward someone who was standing still. When the energy field was reached, the rods would swing outward or cross inward.

This works with plants, too, and also when someone walks toward the rod-holder. The distance the edge of an energy field is from a person varies between individuals and also at different times, partly depending on how that person feels. More energetic, outgoing people showed a wider field, as did those who had recently completed the MerKaBa meditation. Someone who is depressed or withdrawn may have a narrower field.

I became friends with Nancy McMillan, the workshop facilitator and have since attended several more of her workshops, including one in 2014. Nancy introduced me to valuable and fascinating Internet material from several people, e.g.,Tom Kenyon who channels the Hathors, and my favorite still, Lee Harris, an energy intuitive who channels entities he calls the Zs (Zachary, Ziadora, and Zapharia). Later Sarah and other friends attended Flower of Life workshops facilitated by Nancy, as did my husband Don.

I was able to practice my newly acquired Reiki techniques on three friends while I was in Oregon during this trip, with interesting results. One had a bad headache till I requested help with the energy around her head. Another was coming down with a nasty cold. His fever broke shortly after I shared the Reiki energy with him and he felt a lot better the next day. The third had ear pain due to congestion which released and drained almost immediately after she was exposed to the Reiki energy. I was at least as surprised as anyone else, looking for other reasons and thinking the improvements could be coincidence, though that would have been more believable if only one person had responded. It was a good start for me, because it wasn't long before I learned about another form of energy healing I find even more amazing (Reconnective Healing taught by Eric Pearl) .

By this time I could no longer call myself an atheist. I finally understood my options were not limited to either being scientific and an atheist or believing in some organized religion. If those really were the only options, I'd still choose atheism, gladly. In fact, I missed that philosophy occasionally for a while. It had been pleasant and comfortable to think I had an understandable and acceptable view of life – a belief system that worked for me – and friends who agreed and/or understood. As an atheist, there were still many amazing places to see, people to meet, and subjects to learn without including spirituality in any form.

Now, however, I was beginning to grasp the immensity of my new understanding, which was somewhat overwhelming, though fascinating and awesome, too. The bottom line in all the new information I was learning is that Spirit is unconditional love, which completely excludes judgment, punishment, exclusivity, jealousy, control – all the negatives that had bothered me about religions for years.

Reincarnation, with each of us choosing our own path and learning experiences, makes so much more sense to me and simply feels right. It is kind and empowering, logical from the perspective of unconditional love and free will. Recycling energy seems much more reasonable than one lifetime per soul followed by eternal reward or punishment. Mother Nature is not wasteful. What we learn in each lifetime adds to collective knowledge and experience. Even without conscious awareness, old souls retain information from previous lifetimes. Just as early classes in school provide basic information, allowing students to learn subjects in greater depth from later, more advanced classes, so we humans are able to progress further toward conscious enlightenment with multiple lives.

From the perspective of Energy, the basic building block of everything in the universe, we truly are all one. Each of us is a part of Source, Creator, Universe, Great Spirit, God (the name we give it is irrelevant), no matter what we believe or do. This includes humans, plants, animals, rocks, Mother Earth, and the Cosmos, for that matter. Each is a piece of the whole and therefore important.

I have continued to listen to Lee Harris and his team, whom I greatly respect and appreciate. I am so glad my friend Nancy forwarded one of Lee's YouTube Energy Forecasts to me after my first Flower of Life workshop! One of my major criteria in choosing whose material to take in is that their information must be compassionate and based on love, not fear. Lee epitomizes that. He also often reminds us he is not suggesting we follow him. Instead, we should notice our own reactions to any new information and respond accordingly. His objective seems to be to help people become more self-sufficient about spiritual and Energy matters, recognizing there is no one right way for everyone.

I've purchased many of Lee's MP3s (recordings of his talks and channels) and always find them uplifting and helpful, as are his monthly and annual Energy Forecasts, available free on YouTube. I also receive his Facebook posts. I joined Lee's online group, The Portal, which provides more of a forum for him plus association with other people who appreciate his energy and information. He presents experts in appropriate fields each month, who often have free gifts for Portal members. I was able to meet Lee briefly when I attended a weekend workshop in which he was a presenter, and found him to be the same kind, down-to-earth person as he appears online.

I had a personal energy reading session with Lee around the beginning of 2013, which was interesting and helpful, well worth the fee. During an hour-long phone conversation, Lee talked as he read my energy field, explaining what he intuited about me. He felt my main focus would be on sharing with people what I've learned about animals, including telepathically communicating with them. I hadn't told him I had started a book or about my association with Lyn or my beginning animal communication training. He thought I would expand greatly during the next year or year and a half, which I did and have continued doing. He also made sure there was time for me to ask questions. His sessions are recorded and I have listened to mine several times, gaining more insight each time.

As consciousness is raised on our planet, more and more people are providing information for those who are seeking further enlightenment. Many seem to be saying similar things, though with different presenting styles and, of course, personalities. I don't try to keep up with more than a few of them, but am so glad they are available. Anyone who is seeking spiritual awareness should be able to find some who appeal to them.

CHAPTER 72

Before the trip that included seeing Simon and Mikey, attending the Flower of Life workshop, and visiting friends in Oregon, I had watched a documentary with Sarah called *The Living Matrix, a Film on the New Science of Healing*. The first part of it involves Dr. Eric Pearl, a chiropractor, and his work with a little Greek boy who has cerebral palsy. Then, on my trip to Oregon, I met a woman who is a Reiki master. She saw me reading a Reiki book and asked if I had heard of Eric Pearl. I'd forgotten his name so didn't connect him then with the story about the little boy, but she gave me the name of his book, *The Reconnection: Heal Others, Heal Yourself*. Of course I had to buy it, though I didn't read it for some time after I returned home. Little did I know that Sarah and I would experience The Reconnection and eventually become Reconnective Healing facilitators.

After reading Dr. Pearl's book, I found his website (see References) and then checked the practitioner listing for someone in Montana who had attended his seminars. I was pleased to find one near Helena, only a few hours' drive from here. The woman and I emailed and talked on the phone before I asked her to schedule a Reconnective Healing session from a distance for me.

Just before the session, we spoke for a few minutes on the phone without my saying anything about any health issues. I was to rest quietly in a place where I could avoid being disturbed (my home office) and she would call me back to ask about my experiences after she finished in 20 to 30 minutes. I did my best to remain open to anything, believing intellectually that sharing energy from a distance is possible, and interested in what I might experience to create an emotional knowing as well.

I sat in the recliner I use for hypnotherapy clients, putting myself into a pleasant state of relaxation (light hypnosis). Soon one of my hands began to move slowly and somewhat jerkily, indicating the movement was generated by my subconscious mind. I noticed and simply observed from a distance, wondering where my hand would go. It lifted off the arm of my chair till my whole arm was free-floating, though no effort was involved.

In fact, I didn't feel like I was controlling it at all. After moving slowly across my body, my arm went limp and flopped onto my abdomen where it rested.

Then the other hand started twitching, with the same results over a period of time. This hand flopped against my chest where it came to rest. I could have stopped the movement of my hands and arms, of course, but chose to continue relaxing and observing. I had experienced something similar in a cranio-sacral therapy session, during which the practitioner and I were in the same room where she worked around me as I lay on a massage table. Both sessions were amazing to me and left me with a sense of having released old tensions and negativity. I definitely knew something energetic had happened without involving direct touching.

Dr. Pearl suggested one to three Reconnective Healing sessions no matter what issues are involved, saying what is supposed to happen will at least begin in that amount of time. Of course, more sessions are appropriate if something new happens later. People experience physical, mental, emotional, and/or spiritual changes, always positive, from Reconnective Healing. The changes may be immediate and dramatic, slower over a period of time, or more subtle. I chose to just have the one session at that time.

When she had finished, the practitioner explained a bit about The Reconnection, as opposed to the Reconnective Healing session I had undergone. Dr. Pearl experienced a form of this a short time before he began feeling and sharing these amazing healing frequencies, as he explains in his book. Briefly, it involves connecting our energy lines with those continuing out into the cosmos (axiatonal lines). For more complete information about this, see Dr. Pearl's books and website.

After Sarah read the Reconnective Healing book, she and I decided to go to Helena to experience The Reconnection. It is a one-time procedure involving two consecutive sessions, half an hour to 45 minutes in length. These are to be done in person (not from a distance) with one or two nights between, so we stayed overnight in Helena.

This was the first time Sarah and I traveled together, but fortunately not the last. We can always find subjects to discuss for hours and interesting things to see wherever we are, so she's a great traveling companion for me. On the way to Helena, she told me she had problems with snoring and hoped I'd be able to sleep, since we would share a motel room. Our sessions were in the practitioner's home, where we took turns lying on a massage table in a private room. We both experienced events unusual in ordinary circumstances, but described by other people when they have a Reconnection session.

Sarah and I felt good after our experience, though somewhat ungrounded for a short time. We checked into a motel, ate dinner, and then relaxed in the room before going to sleep. The next morning Sarah asked whether I'd been disturbed by her snoring. I told her I hadn't noticed any snoring, that I heard her breathing deeply, as we do when we're asleep, but nothing other than that. She then told me she had had sleep apnea for years, and it was apparently always a problem. However, since that first session of her Reconnection, she no longer experiences it. Sarah and I have both felt a greater sense of peace and I've been opening more to higher levels of consciousness than I did before. There have been a number of internal changes which greatly improved my life, though outwardly all is much the same.

The following year circumstances came together perfectly to allow Sarah and me to attend Eric Pearl's Level I/II seminar, qualifying us to be Reconnective Healing facilitators. We flew to Phoenix the end of March 2012, for the Friday evening lecture and all day Saturday and Sunday workshop. Eric and several of his teaching assistants were there to make sure all 200 students received some personal attention as we practiced what we learned on each other using 50 massage tables. It was an intense time, with noticeably high energy levels in the room. Everyone seemed happy and enthusiastic as we experienced the frequencies and learned more about this new healing modality.

Sarah and I were so pleased with what we had learned that we later decided to carry our training further in order to facilitate The Reconnection (Level III) as well as Reconnective Healing. We were happy we had had our Reconnection done before, because experiencing it is a requirement before learning how to do it.

We chose to accomplish our Level III training in a small group with one of the teaching assistants, Renee, who lives in Phoenix. She also teaches Reconnective Healing with Animals, a workshop she scheduled the day before she started the Level III classes, so Sarah and I signed up for both. That was a full and intense three days! Part of the animal workshop was held outside at a sanctuary for abused, unwanted, or abandoned farm animals such as horses, donkeys, sheep, goats, and even a pig. There were also quite a few dogs, though I don't know their history.

Sarah was able to schedule some extra vacation time so we decided to drive this time, a full two days from Montana. The end of June is perhaps not the best time for traveling through the red rock country of Utah and into Arizona because it is so hot. We had a great time, though, seeing new sights and enjoying the companionship. We even took an extra day to drive home so we could do more tourist things. We went to Sedona, checked out one of the portals, drove through Arches State Park, bought some new stones, and saw lots of fantastic scenery.

CHAPTER 73

Sarah and I found a number of opportunities to share Reconnective Healing (RH) frequencies, she mostly with friends and family members, I mostly with animals, of course. I've had some amazing experiences with it, as well as some in which I was unable to notice any changes specifically related to it. As I continue to learn more about Spirit and individual paths, this makes perfect sense to me.

One morning not long after we attended the first Reconnective Healing seminars, Don asked me to check Aten, our male emu, because he was in sleeping or incubating position (legs folded under him, chest resting on the ground) and didn't want to stand up, unusual for him during the day. Don knew Aten wasn't sitting on eggs so was concerned. When I felt around under him, I noticed the area around his vent appeared to be swollen, dry, and tight. I tried to insert a small tube on a syringe with the intention of squirting some olive oil into his cloaca, hoping that would make passage of anything inside it easier. However, the opening was so tight it may as well have been sealed with super glue.

Birds, as well as reptiles and amphibians, have a single opening (the vent) for passing urine and feces, and for reproduction in the form of insemination and egg laying. The cloaca, similar to the rectum in mammals, is just inside the body where it holds material to be eliminated through the vent.

As usual in an attempt to diagnose his problem, I thought of as many possibilities as I could imagine: something he had eaten obstructing his cloaca from inside; an abscess or tumor blocking the vent; injury causing swelling of the phallus, which is located inside the cloaca. I had been offering him and Ara knapweed as I pulled it from the wallaby pen for a couple days, and was afraid he had eaten a piece his body couldn't break down. The plant is fibrous and tough, especially older ones with a large taproot.

I called our friend from the local emu ranch, but she had not experienced this problem with any of their birds. Linda, the veterinarian, suggested x-rays and possible internal examination by inserting a scope into the cloaca. This would require transport to a clinic in Missoula and anesthesia for western medicine procedures to which I was unwilling to subject him. She also suggested swelling might be decreased if I put a hemorrhoid cream on the area. Then I called Lyn and Aten talked with her briefly.

> Aten: Lyn! Thank you! Thank Adele for calling you! I am fine – truly. Just slightly out of balance from the knapweed. Perhaps Adele could balance all of my organs with her Reconnective Healing energy. No, there isn't much pain but discomfort, yes. Tight, needing to go and can't. That kind of discomfort – but no pain. Tell Adele, no, I did not injure myself. Tell her to play with the energy all over my body. She must gain more faith in the unseen for healing! Tell her I'm here for her. Tell her to take a deep breath and relax. I'm really fine, Lyn! (He smiled!) Send love to Adele!

I did relax a bit and started using Reconnective Healing energy with him. The first session was early in the morning while Aten was standing next to a white wall at the back of our house. When I stood beside him, the morning sun was behind me, projecting our shadows onto the wall.

I began feeling the energy frequencies in my hands, as happens whenever I intend to do a Reconnective Healing session. I was sharing them with Aten's energy field, when I suddenly noticed what appeared to be shadows of heat waves on the white wall above the shadows of my hands. They were eight to ten inches high and moved with my hands. I played with them for a while before deciding to step aside and see whether they were visible above Aten's back. They were not so I moved next to him again, and again energy waves were visible above my hands. Then I noticed they were also above my head, even higher than those above my hands. I was unable to see them when I looked directly at my hands, only when I looked at the shadows on the wall. The same thing happened the next morning. I thanked Aten for providing the opportunity for such an awesome experience. Within a few days Aten was eliminating normally and has remained healthy.

A young great horned owl (Jedidiah) Lyn talked with after I learned Reconnective Healing was found at the bottom of a power pole with a wet spot on his head. I drove to a farm to pick him up after the people called about him. He appeared disoriented, though with no obvious fractures; the dampness on his head was not blood and I was concerned he may have been electrocuted. I took him home, shared the RH frequencies with him, and called Lyn.

Jed: Lyn, how nice! Oh, say, you girls do a lot for us. I'm so appreciative of Adele's care. Something could've eaten me! I ran into the pole. (St. Francis said no electrocution). I'm out of balance and that energy stuff [Reconnective Healing] was nice. I'm feeling some better. Oh, and I do have a message for both of you. I'm told to say, "Let go – fly high! Quit acting like your wings are clipped! Spirit will be the breeze beneath your wings. Really let go of your fears and you will soar! Patience and stamina are yours for the asking. Drop the illusion that you can't fly and take off into the wind. Stretch out your arms and wind (Spirit) will do the rest."

Tee hee! We're all in the same boat – can't fly – need to make changes and get rid of the illusions. See the humor? I'm a bird, you're humans – all of us in the same boat – all of us are One! Many thanks, Adele, Lyn! We'll fly together!

This cheerful young owl soon recovered and was released near where he was found. Hopefully his parents were still there to help him become a proficient hunter. His messages are ones we can all apply to our lives.

Later that summer I went to Oregon to visit friends, where an accident forced a longer trip than I had intended. My first stop was in Portland at the home of Patrizia Mastne, a dear friend I met in a Comparative Vertebrate Anatomy class at Portland State University many years ago. She and her family remain special people in my life. As always, we had a great visit and wonderful Italian food.

Then I drove to Ed and Anna's place near McMinnville, south of Portland. I had also met Ed when we were students at Portland State University (in a Herpetology class, which he now teaches) about the same time I met Patrizia. After he and Anna married years later, they came to our place in Montana, where she and I quickly became close friends as well.

To Ed and Anna's horror, I fell within a few hours of arriving at their home, causing a pelvic fracture. I was extremely fortunate in many ways and consider this injury a valuable gift. Anna works as a nurse in a hospital near their home. She and Ed were able to safely help me into the car and take me to ER. The fracture was simple (one small break, not displaced, supported by the rest of the pelvis) so I only had to stay overnight in the hospital, use a walker for a few weeks, a cane for a while longer, and make sure I didn't fall again until it healed.

I called Sarah, who did three distance Reconnective Healing sessions for me, one while I was in the ER and two more in the next few days. Ed and Anna remained with me while I waited to be taken to a room. I was comfortable as long as I didn't move much so we were able to visit. All of a sudden Anna said, "Adele, I can see energy waves coming off your knee!" She is quite psychic and sometimes sees auras, so I wasn't surprised. I just told her Sarah must be sharing the Reconnective Healing frequencies with me at that time.

Ed and Anna graciously disrupted their household and their summer vacation for more than two weeks, while I rested and healed. They prepared a bedroom on the first floor because I was unable to walk up or down stairs. Luckily there is a bathroom on that floor, but it doesn't have shower facilities. They took me to locker rooms (a public swimming pool and the college where Ed teaches) to shower a few times. Otherwise, Anna helped me stay clean.

I felt riding in a car would be easier for me than dealing with a walker in airports and planes, and I didn't want to leave my car in Oregon; however, I didn't think I should drive yet, especially not that far (about 600 miles). Ed kindly drove me home, a trip we made in one day because low doses of pain medication allowed me to remain comfortable. He stayed overnight with us and flew back to Portland the next day.

We had planned to remodel the bathroom, including adding a walk-in shower, before I went to Oregon so Don made sure it was installed before I came home. It seemed such a luxury! I was unable to get into or out of a tub and even needed my walker in the shower for a few days after returning home. I love that shower to this day!

Don and our friend Tom continued feeding the six fawns we had at the time, because I couldn't risk being pushed or head-butted by them. In less than seven weeks from the fall, I had no more discomfort or impairment and was walking normally without needing even a cane.

Perhaps the best result of the accident was that I decided I don't want to be that helpless again. Ed, who teaches Human Anatomy and Physiology as well as Biology and Herpetology, suggested walking as a way to improve strength, balance, and bone density. Shortly before the discomfort from the injury disappeared, Don and I bought a used treadmill and I started exercising, something I've never done regularly before. I could only walk about half a mile at first, at one mile per hour, but I soon increased both distance and speed. A year and a half later, I was walking four miles at three mph five to seven days a week, and still continue to do so.

I also decided to pay attention to my diet, another healthy practice I had never bothered with before, eating mostly what was easy and readily available. I'd already gradually reduced my intake of meat, mostly because of my closer association with animals. It becomes harder to eat something when I think of it as an individual, sentient being with whom I can communicate.

I read a book (*The Raw Food Detox Diet*) I heard about through an on-line interview with the author, Natalia Rose; following some of her suggestions, I bought a blender, juicer, and food processor. I became familiar with the organic produce section in a local grocery store, where I was pleasantly surprised to find a wide variety of healthy-looking, fresh produce. It now comprises the majority of my diet and I rarely use a microwave or stove.

I feel much better now, healthier, better balance, with more energy and stamina, as though I'm younger. I've also lost the weight I gained after quitting smoking almost four years before the accident. It is always possible to find something positive in any situation, though it may not appear to overshadow the negatives. In this case, the positive results of the pelvic fracture are easy to see and far outweigh any negatives.

Another great horned owl with whom I shared Reconnective Healing frequencies surprised me by recovering quickly from what I had thought was a leg fracture. He was unable to use the lower part of one leg and palpation showed what felt like a break just above his knee. Because of the location (difficult to splint in birds) and my being unsure of his injury, I took him to Judy the next day, after two short (10 minutes) Reconnective Healing sessions. He still wasn't using his foot and Judy could feel some swelling above his knee, but she didn't think there was a fracture. He completely recovered the use of his leg and was released. Of course I can't prove he'd had a fracture, but I wouldn't be surprised if he did and it healed within a few days without a splint, due to Reconnective Healing energy.

We were quite concerned about a different great horned owl, who had been found hanging by one foot from a net on a baseball field. A game warden had to cut the net to release the foot, which had been tightly bound. No one knew how long he'd been hanging there. The foot remained closed even after he was freed, so we thought it may have had insufficient blood circulation for too long, causing tissue death. He could also have torn tendons and nerves in his upper leg during his struggles, possibly causing paralysis. Some birds seem to get along well in the wild with only one working foot, though probably not raptors. They need all possible tools to survive as predators.

Lyn: (Adele called about this owl who had been caught in a net on a baseball field and I presented it to St. Francis for healing in alignment with the owl's highest good. St.

408

Francis said to talk with him when I had time.)

Owl: Hallooo Lyn! I'm honored! Thank you for coming!
Please thank Adele for all she is doing for me! I'm
grateful to be here! The raptors sing her praises and I
do see why. How silly of me to get caught in that net.
I was so excited about my dinner that I didn't even see
it. And, of course, dinner got away and I'm just glad
I didn't get eaten. I guess this is one way to seek new life
experiences, but it wasn't what I really had in mind.
But – ahem! – I'm off track. You have come to see if I
have anything I need or want to say. Well – I do.
Tell Adele she needs to assert her viewpoint, seek new
teachers, and venture forth in search of her answers.
So, there, now, I'm looking forward to being released, but
I'm certainly glad I've made your acquaintance and
Adele's. I will be singing your praises when I get out of
here.

I kept him in a small carrier in the house, tube-fed him
electrolytes with calcium/phosphorus and bioplasma, did a
Reconnective Healing session, and gave him mice. The foot was
still clenched the next morning, though he seemed to have recovered
well from the shock of his terrifying and painful experience. I did
a couple more Reconnective Healing sessions over the next two
days with no noticeable results. Then, on the third morning, his
foot was open and he appeared to stand and walk normally. I put
him in our owl flight room to make sure he could fly and would
find and pick up his mice even when they were scattered in various
places. He reached the higher perches, possible only by flying,
landed well, and the mice disappeared. The game warden picked
him up to transport him back to his home area.

409

CHAPTER 74

When we humans use poisons or other toxic materials, we often find they cause unexpected problems. Some of these are intended to poison what we consider to be pests, but also harm animals we like, or even people. Unfortunately, as a wildlife rehabilitator, I often see unpleasant results of our behavior.

One May evening I received a call from a game warden asking if he could bring a bald eagle in need of help. He was not optimistic as the bird was in poor condition, but wanted to try to save him. From the description, the eagle was more likely sick than injured because he could still fly and there were no obvious wounds or broken bones. He was seen lying on his chest in a field with his head down, beak touching the ground, a highly abnormal position for an adult bird. Wild animals typically hide if they are unable to present an appearance of health and strength. Showing obvious signs of weakness in the open is dangerous for them.

People were able to walk within a few feet of the eagle when he unexpectedly gathered enough strength to fly for some distance just above the ground before falling. This happened a couple of times, with him crashing into a tree once, until he landed in a river where the game warden was able to catch him in a net.

The only enclosure available for transporting a bird that large was a wire carrier in the back of the game warden's pickup. Wire cages can be dangerous for birds because they often fight to escape, seriously damaging their flight feathers in the process. This can render them unable to fly until their next molt, possibly many months in the future. To protect the eagle, duct tape was used to trap his wings against his body and to cover his talons, usually the most dangerous weapon for a bird of prey.

While I waited for the game warden to arrive, I prepared a carrier and a work space on our deck and mixed electrolytes and cell salts in water. I also called my friend Sarah, asking her to help by working with the bird's energy field and possibly also for telepathic and/or psychic information. Fortunately she was able to come over; I know from experience how helpful Sarah can be.

411

The first eagle Sarah worked with, a mature female bald eagle with a drooping wing, was brought by a deputy sheriff after he waded into the river to catch her. The eagle was unable to fly, but I found no sign of a fracture or other injury. Sarah helped soothe her while we placed her into a carrier for transport to Judy, who has larger flight pens and more experience with eagles than I do. When we were able to release the eagle on the ground in Judy's large enclosure, Sarah moved slowly toward her, sending calming energy. I was several feet away when I felt my muscles relax so much I had to brace myself with my hand for a moment. I knew that relaxing energy was coming from Sarah when I saw her squat next to this huge wild bird who could certainly run away even though she was unable to fly.

In a short time, Sarah was able to hold her hand a couple inches above the feathers, sensing and soothing the bird's aura (energy field). She felt a problem in the shoulder involving a lot of pain. Judy could find no shoulder injury and was afraid the eagle had been electrocuted when a wing or foot touched a bare wire as she landed on a power pole. One foot and the opposite wing are usually damaged when this happens, and the tissue in both eventually dies. It may be several days before the wing is rendered completely immobile and, during that time, the bird may not appear seriously injured, though it is unable to fly. Eventually, as the tissue dies, fly eggs hatch and maggots begin feeding on it.

The decision for this magnificent bird was to provide protection and supportive care at least through the night, hoping for improvement rather than deterioration. If it became apparent electrocution had occurred or the injury was too great for any possibility of release into the wild, the bird would be euthanized to prevent further suffering. The great eagle took matters into her own hands, however, tearing her shoulder apart with her beak and bleeding to death during the night.

When I called her about this new eagle, Sarah agreed to cancel her other plans for the evening and come over to help. The game warden arrived shortly before she did, bringing a mature male bald eagle with white head and tail. He appeared terribly ill,

412

hardly able to hold his head up. A murky liquid dripped from his beak when his head was hanging below his crop, which felt empty of food.

I found no obvious injuries and the flight muscles on his chest were full and firm, indicating he was well nourished and therefore had been ill only a short time. His tail feathers were somewhat soiled, probably from diarrhea, and several of them were broken. We thought he may have eaten poisoned ground squirrels or some other wild animals considered to be a nuisance by people. I gave him electrolytes and cell salts through a tube before leaving him with Don and the game warden.

I then called Lyn, hoping she could talk with him and possibly do a shamanic journey if she thought it appropriate. Sarah arrived during that call, immediately going to the deck to help the bird. I explained to Lyn what was going on and she agreed to ask Eagle what he would prefer. I found out later that he had a lot to say. Lyn spoke and worked with him for more than 30 minutes, finishing shortly after we put Eagle into a large dog crate for the night.

At first Don was holding Eagle. His legs hung down loosely, as did his head unless it was supported on Don's arm. When I finished talking with Lyn, I took him, sitting in a chair with Eagle on my lap while Sarah connected with his energy. She felt he had an injury on his chest which was painful, and having tape on his feet and around his body was uncomfortable. Slowly, carefully, Sarah peeled and cut tape and some feathers, doing her best to avoid damaging flight feathers or causing pain.

While Sarah and I were working with Eagle, removing tape, tubing him with electrolytes, cell salts, etc., and checking him for injuries, he didn't flinch or struggle. In fact, he seemed nearly lifeless in my arms, though I could feel him breathing. Much of the time his eyes were closed and he seemed unable to hold up his head. I hadn't much hope for him because he appeared so ill.

When the tape was off, he suddenly appeared more alert, lifting his head and moving his legs. We put him on a towel on his back to examine him and found an abraded, bruised place on his chest, probably from crashing into the tree and the ground when trying to escape capture. We rinsed it with electrolytes and cell salts and were fortunately unable to find any deep cuts or puncture wounds. Eagle's feet were also damaged in several places. This often happens when male eagles grab each other's feet while fighting in the air. None of the wounds appeared serious so we covered them and the chest wound with emu oil. By this time Eagle had regained enough of his strength that Don had to hold him while I again put a tube down his esophagus to give him more fluids from a syringe before putting him in a carrier for the night. He thrashed around a bit in the crate until he was left alone with Sarah, who was able to calm him.

Just after we finished working with Eagle, Lyn called to tell us about her connection with him. She said Eagle had jumped right in, quite anxious to talk with her. The following is a transcript of their communication:

> Eagle: I am here, Lyn! Thank you! Great Spirit has sent
> me to speak to you, Adele, Sarah, and all who will listen.
> Yes, I am dealing with poison. The stones are so helpful!
> Thank them! [I had put a few crystals and gemstones near
> the eagle with the intention of bringing comfort and
> healing, and removing anxiety and negativity] They,
> Adele and Sarah, need to know that there will be many
> more animals, not all eagles, who will need their gift of
> using the Creative Force – Energy – to heal. This is good!
> They must continue. Tell them "Thank you" for me.
>
> Lyn, I'd like to stay in my body, but the poison is in all
> my cells. Talk to the cells, Lyn, and tell them what to do.
> I am too weak! Thank you!
>
> (Lyn perceived his cells as being covered with a sticky,
> smog-like substance. Many of them seemed nearly dead.
> She did a shamanic journey for Eagle, calling in his
> ancestors, her spirit guides, and other kind and
> compassionate spirits. They came and began cleaning

each cell, purifying and rejuvenating it. One of Lyn's spirit guides told her, "The work will continue all night.")

Lyn: (Eagle's will is to live, if possible. He promised me he would not hurt Sarah or Adele with his beak, wings, or talons as he starts to move and feel better. He said he was now able to feel his wing tips and feet.)
[Sarah was removing the tape while Lyn was talking with Eagle. He probably began regaining feeling as it came off. During that time he did not try to hurt us.]

Eagle: Lyn, whether I live or die, these ladies must continue to work with Spirit to help others and so must you. I didn't expect to feel any better and I do, so tell them. This work they do is important. Lyn, tell them to send love to those who don't know or care to see that the ground squirrels are Great Spirit's creation just as we all are. Hate and anger brings more ground squirrel haters. Love smooths the way.

The journey spirits are doing well for me. Thank you.

Ah! That is better! I'm so grateful! [Lyn said: Eagle's body is starting to relax and he is smiling.] You three work well together, each with your own gifts. Together what you do is greatly magnified. Wow! Great Spirit has need of all of you working together. This change will not come about by words. It will come from the faith each of you has shown by using what you know to heal others. Those that poisoned the ground squirrels need you healers the most. Use meditation to forgive and heal those who would harm others. That is my message from Great Spirit!

I'm to end the talking now and the journey will continue as long as need be. St. Francis is here – one of the head healers. Thank you all so much! Tell Adele and Sarah to leave the stones around me. Sarah can return home and do what she has been doing for me mentally from there. It will be as powerful. Adele just needs to let me rest now and give me appropriate liquids through the night. I'll see you in the morning.

When I looked at him before going to bed, Eagle was lying on his chest with his beak touching hay on the floor of his crate, the position he had assumed while in the field before being caught. He was still in that position when I checked him at 11:00 p.m., but was strong enough to refuse electrolytes through a tube. I gave him a shallow dish of them in case he wanted to drink and went to bed. At 2:00 a.m. he was much more alert, holding his head up though not yet standing. I couldn't tell whether he had taken any water, but he seemed aware enough to drink if he so chose.

After daylight Eagle was more alert, even standing in the crate, and seemed ready for more space. Don and I transferred him to the sheltered chain link pen we use for new fawns, but he fought the cage, risking feather damage in his efforts to escape. I decided he needed to go to a flight area without fence wire so we put him back in the crate, no longer an easy task. While Don was holding his feet, I carelessly reached in front of Eagle to fold his wing and safely push it through the cage door. Being unhappy and stressed about the handling, he quickly bit my little finger, peeling off some skin without creating a deep wound. Once he was safe, I washed my hand and bandaged the finger to stop the bleeding. It healed easily, leaving only a small scar. I certainly didn't blame him for biting me in the heat of the moment, even though he had promised Lyn he wouldn't.

I transported him to Judy, who had safer facilities (we now have flight rooms, but didn't at that time). I told Eagle what was happening and put a towel over the door of the carrier, making it seem more enclosed. He rode quietly in the car during the half-hour trip. He was much stronger and more difficult to handle by then, giving me great hope for his survival.

Judy thought Eagle should remain in captivity for a while due to his broken tail feathers; he would be unable to control his landings and flight maneuvers well before most of them regrew.

416

She planned to pull a couple of them at a time to stimulate growth of new feathers without waiting for a molt. Judy, who has handled a lot of eagles, said he was the strongest one she had ever handled – only one day after he was so sick I expected him to die.

More than a week later, I learned from Judy that Eagle was not settling down in her flight room. He attacked bars on the window, seeming frantic to escape. I asked Lyn to find out what he was experiencing. She had planned to go on a shopping trip, but had felt, before I called, that she should put it off. If she had gone as planned, she would not have been available to talk with Eagle that morning.

> Eagle: Lyn! Oh, man! I'm so glad to talk with you! I've got to get out of here! Can you help me?

> Lyn: Yes. Adele says that your tail feathers haven't grown in yet, so you may have difficulty flying but rather than have you injure yourself or worse, they will honor your wishes!

> Eagle: Oh! Great! When?

> Lyn: Adele can do it today, but Sarah would like to be present and has asked Adele if she could see you Wednesday evening, two days from now, after work.

> Eagle: Oh, man! I can't wait! I'm being called! There are those who need me now. Tell Sarah I'm honored that she wants to be present, but if I can go today, I must! I appreciate all Sarah did for me! Tell Adele I'll be calm in the crate, if she takes me today. I'll be calm for her – yes, even on the car ride. Oh, I'm so glad she will take me back where I came from. I'm really needed! Tell her thanks so much for me in advance! And you and Sarah, too! Thank you! I'll be fine! I will fly well. She'll see. All three of you will have your names written in the sky by

me for all to see. All the animals and birds will know of your greatness. I'm honored to have been healed by you.

Eagle seemed so frantic I hurried to Judy's place. He was a bit difficult for her to catch, but once he was in the dog carrier, he settled right down. It was about an hour-long drive to his home. I heard him rustling around a few times, but more as though he was rearranging his feathers after being handled than struggling to escape the small space.

A place to pull some distance off the highway was near where Eagle had been caught. From there he would easily recognize the area as soon as he flew above the trees. After setting the carrier on the ground and removing the cover, I opened the door, stepping back to allow him to walk out without my being in his personal space. By then Eagle was definitely moving and ready to go! He stepped out immediately, looked around briefly, and then flew close to the ground to the base of a tree next to a hill not far away.

Eagle sat there for a couple of minutes, making me a bit anxious because I'd be unable to catch him again even if he couldn't fly well. Then he stepped up onto a downed log, looked around carefully and, to my huge relief, spread his great wings and took off, still flying low but moving steadily up the hill. I saw flashes of his white tail through the trees as he flew toward the top of a much larger hill – and then he began soaring into the sky. First he made small circles, but as they expanded he flew over me, still circling and rising high into the sky, perhaps "writing our names for all to see," as he promised. I watched until he appeared about the size of a blackbird above me, sending him wishes for a good life, and then I came home.

Eagle told Lyn we could call him Cinco de Mayo (the date he came to me), but only after he was released. We shortened it to Cinco and all of us who were honored to meet him think of him now and then. He apparently still sends other injured wild ones to us as well.

CHAPTER 75

Lead poisoning is another problem many animals experience due to their proximity to us. A mature female bald eagle suffering from this condition was brought to me by a game warden after being found in a pasture unable to fly. She was too thin and sometimes exhibited symptoms of neurologic damage in the form of repeatedly stretching and contracting her neck, looking like she was trying to regurgitate but without opening her beak or vomiting. She was standing, but appeared disoriented and I felt she was seriously ill. Lyn talked with her and did what she could to help.

> Eagle: Wow! Lyn! Cinco! Adele! I've heard of all of you! Am I dreaming?
>
> Lyn: No, you're not. I'm here, as is Cinco, to find out what your will is and to help as much as we can along those lines. Adele will be helping you to survive, if possible, but she also wants to know what you desire.
>
> Eagle: I'm honored! I fly high. I see a lot. I have been dreaming of the Other Side. I see I can change my dream and stay and fly high. Cinco is saying it is my choice right now. It's not too late. I haven't seen much of this kind of behavior on this side of the planet. [Lyn said Eagle was referring to people helping animals and each other.] Cinco says I'm still needed. Okay! Yes! I'd like all of you to help me stay. This world needs all the high fliers it can get!
>
> Lyn: I'm going to have my guides do a shamanic journey for you now, intending to get your cells to reject the poison. The poison will be extracted and eliminated from your body. It is your job to dream yourself well while this is going on.

Eagle: Yes, I'll do that. Thank you. Is this what you did for Cinco?

Lyn: Yes, it's similar.

Lyn: Cinco steps in to help Bald Eagle by helping her mind stay focused on the dream of health. Cinco's spirit leads Bald Eagle from her body and they soar into the air, flying to the shamanic healing. This is equally true for all of us here. We must dream ourselves well before we can be well. It is time we all utilize our power to heal ourselves.

Then Cinco and Bald Eagle return. The shamanic journey is done. Bald Eagle returns to her body and thanks Cinco. Cinco winks at her and me and leaves, saying to Bald Eagle, "You're in good hands!"

Bald Eagle nods and asks that we help her dream herself well. She wants all the help she can get. I send her our best thoughts for dreaming herself well. We are again reminded that all of us can dream ourselves well!

I had hoped she would respond as Cinco had, but unlike him, she was no better the next morning. Sometimes continuing to live is apparently not part of the path of an individual, so shamanic journeys and other alternative healing modalities may simply make passing easier or help the animal or person feel at peace. However, to give Eagle every chance I could, I decided to take her to the Montana Wildlife Center in Helena, where they provide veterinary care. Sadly, she died a few hours after arriving there. A lab test of her blood showed high levels of lead, accounting for her symptoms.

Lead poisoning is not an easy or quick way to die. The metal accumulates in the body over time, creating increasingly more serious health and reproductive problems before they are bad enough to cause death. Eagle was hungry, but had difficulty swallowing. Her digestive system was no longer functioning so food rotted in her crop, giving her a terrible odor and causing great discomfort. Her heart and liver were enlarged. Stress from being handled often caused her to gasp for breath. Even though she was so ill, she instinctively tried to escape the game warden and the rest of us who were there to help her. Handling these magnificent wild beings is terrifying to them, greatly adding to their discomfort.

Eagle had not been shot, but some of her food animals (e.g., ground squirrels, game animals, other birds) had been. Her condition was a result of ingesting pieces of lead ammunition, as happens to many predators and scavengers. The lead is absorbed into the body instead of being eliminated. When an animal dies from lead poisoning, whatever scavenger eats it increases its own lead levels, thus continuing the cycle. This vicious circle will end only when we no longer use lead ammunition.

People often fail to realize they create unintended victims when they leave bodies or offal behind after shooting or poisoning one kind of animal. Pet dogs and cats, foxes, bobcats, cougars, and many other animals, as well as birds, are harmed by this. Even humans can ingest lead when eating meat of an animal shot with lead bullets, which often shatter, scattering tiny pieces of lead through meat. According to doctors, no level of lead in the body is safe, especially in children or pregnant mothers.

Eagles and other birds often land on the ground to feed. However, most birds, especially birds of prey, neither lie down on the ground nor allow humans to get close to them. They also seldom stay in one place on the ground for long. If an eagle, hawk, or owl is acting as though it might be ill, it is best to report it to a game warden or wildlife rehabilitator. They can probably tell if the bird really needs help. Unfortunately the birds must be extremely ill before they allow themselves to be caught. Sometimes they can be saved and returned to the wild, so it is worth the effort.

CHAPTER 76

One spring I received a call about a baby great horned owl, who was on the ground under his nest tree bleeding. The people were unable to bring him to me so I went to him. When I was almost to that place, I received another call about an injured young great horned owl a few miles farther north. Spring is a busy time for wildlife rehabilitators.

The first little owl was standing on the ground between branches of his nest tree, a tall, beautiful spruce. He was still covered with grey down and appeared somewhat forlorn. He snapped his beak at me, making a popping sound, but remained calm with no attempt to escape. The beak snapping is a warning many owls use to intimidate predators, though it is seldom followed by actual biting in my experience, especially with babies. I picked the little guy up, controlling his taloned feet, placed him on his back on a towel, and examined him. Damp blood was all over his abdominal and upper leg pinfeathers and down, but I could find no sign of injury. His skin appeared undamaged, as did his feathers.

At his age (around three weeks old), feathers other than baby down contain blood vessels because they are still growing. In fact, his were mostly pinfeathers, the sheathed, developing feathers. I thought enough of them had been scraped as he fell from his nest to be the source of blood and hoped it would stop seeping by the time I got home. Even if it did, he would need to be raised by us because we couldn't put him back in his nest high in the tree. I settled him in a small carrier and drove to the other owl.

The second one was older, fully feathered with only a small amount of down on her head. She had apparently been flying, possibly even her first flight, when she hit a guy wire on a power pole. She was lying flat on the ground, looking nearly dead, with an obviously injured eye. When I picked her up, she opened her other eye, but made no attempt to struggle and was nearly limp. I was afraid she was too seriously injured to recover, but took her home to try.

I tube fed both owls electrolytes, put gemstones and essential oils in their crates, shared Reconnective Healing frequencies with them, cleaned the injured eye on the big one and put some ophthalmic ointment in it, and powdered the little one with cornstarch, hoping it would help with clotting. However, blood kept seeping, with small drops on the towel wherever the owl stood, and on the tops of his feathered feet.

Even after a more thorough examination, I was unable to find a specific source of the blood; it just seemed to be oozing out of his feathers. I frequently gave him electrolytes in an attempt to keep him hydrated and fed him bloody mouse organs, easy to digest and containing nutrients he needed to replace the blood he was losing. This continued through the night, at least every two hours, with more applications of cornstarch and flour, all to no avail. The blood seemed to be getting lighter in color; I was amazed he was still alive and standing.

Finally the next morning it occurred to me he must have eaten rodents poisoned with warfarin or something similar. It is the main ingredient used in many poisons intended for killing squirrels, rats, and mice; warfarin and similar chemicals interfere with their clotting mechanisms, causing them to bleed to death as the little owl was doing. This is a slow death involving progressive weakness, so poisoned animals become easy prey for the many birds and animals who eat them, including some of our pets. I'm sure this little owl's parents were happy to find it easier than usual to catch food for their babies and themselves, not realizing the danger.

I immediately called Linda who researched the problem on her veterinary Internet site. Fortunately she had what was suggested so I rushed to her place for injectable Vitamin K. About 10 hours after the first of two doses, the bleeding finally stopped. I continued giving the little owl electrolytes and mouse organs frequently for a couple days till I thought he was safe.

The big owl was standing the next day, having recovered from shock. She ate mice I handed to her with forceps, though was still too dizzy from the head injury to bend over and pick up her food. Both owls drank electrolytes from a syringe when I dripped it on their beaks, easier for them and me than pushing a tube down their throats, and they were alert enough by then to decide how much they needed.

By the time the big owl was picking up her own mice, Judy was able to free a flight room for her and another great horned owl. Her eye looked better, but we were unable to tell how well she could see with it. The pupil wasn't completely round and a spot of blood was visible between the cornea and iris. Judy was later able to tell she could fly, land on perches, and find mice in a larger area, indicating she was releasable. She returned her to the area where she was found, hoping she would reconnect with her family.

When the little owl was noticeably growing, I called a reporter about putting his story in the local newspaper, hoping to educate people about some unintended consequences of using poisons. Many folks enjoy and appreciate owls and other birds of prey and wouldn't knowingly hurt them. I don't know for sure what happened to the parents or sibling(s) of this owl, but it's possible they all died. This is counterproductive because they eat a lot of the rodents people want to eliminate. When the predator/prey ratio is allowed to balance naturally, neither is a serious problem, as Don and I learned by experience later.

I named this little guy Star after his story was in two local newspapers. He was such a sweet, entertaining fellow after he recovered from the poisons. When I cleaned his carrier or gave him fresh water, he would grab my hand with a foot. The first time this happened I was startled and concerned because his needle-sharp talons were already nearly an inch long. I knew better than to jerk away from him, potentially causing damage to both of us, and was pleasantly surprised to find he was so gentle his grip was hardly noticeable. He easily released my hand when I was ready. Then he grabbed my finger with his beak, with the same results – gentle with no pressure. I'm sure he was showing me I could trust him.

After that I let him hold my hand or groom my skin whenever I opened his crate. The only time a talon poked me was when I put him on my arm to be photographed. Star had never been carried that way and felt unstable enough to grip harder, causing a slight scratch on my arm. He chirped whenever he saw me, as though he was greeting me. Babies and their parents groom and vocalize with each other so it was natural for him to do so with me.

A short time before I got Star Owl, Judy had also received a baby great horned owl. His nest tree had caught fire when someone was burning dry grass nearby, a common practice here in the spring. His sibling died, but this little guy was rescued by people who thought he was a baby eagle. Judy didn't pay much attention to his appearance at first, assuming the people had seen his parents, and simply concentrated on treating his dehydration and singed pinfeathers. The delicate skin on his eyelids and other places was bright red from heat, but fortunately Judy found no blisters. A couple days later she realized he was an owl when she noticed the shape of his head. She began calling him Eagly Owl.

Eagly seemed somewhat older than Star, but they were close enough in age to be siblings. When Star was ready to move around more and learn to use his wings, we remodeled one of our outbuildings as a flight room for Star and Eagly. Judy's flight rooms were full so bringing Eagly here worked well for her. Being with another young owl was great for both of them, too, giving them someone to play with and the opportunity to interact with their own kind. Eagly was as tame as Star and soon accepted me as he had Judy. So I had two young owls, nearly as big as adults by then, wanting to hold my hand and groom me. It wasn't long before they were full-grown and flying up to perches in the flight room.

Then they began landing on my shoulders or back when I bent over to clean or fill water and food dishes. I became concerned when they did that with Don as well, thinking they might try it with other people after their release. No matter how benign and friendly the owls' intentions, most people would be startled, to say the least, if an unfamiliar bird of prey with a four to five-foot wingspan flew at them. Judy's neighbors are a bit farther from her so I took both young owls there when she had an available flight room. She kept them till weather cooled before releasing them at her place. Most of those she had released before stayed near her for a while, accepting mice from her till they were more proficient at hunting. Eagly and Star, however, took off immediately and she hasn't seen them since. They could still return, even in a few years, as others have done.

One great horned owl Judy had raised and released would land on her deck and knock on the back door with his beak when he was hungry. Once he perfected his flying and hunting skills he moved on and she no longer saw him. Then, several years later, Judy heard someone knocking on her back door. It was dark outside and that door is not even visible from the driveway; it isn't a place people go when they approach the house, especially at night. When Judy looked out the window, she thought no one was there, but the knocking occurred again. Of course she found the owl at her feet when she opened the door. He was quite thin with a heavy infestation of lice after apparently having a hard time finding food. Judy took him in, sprinkled some poultry lice powder on his feathers and under his wings, and gave him mice. He soon recovered and went on his way again.

One October I picked up an adult great horned owl who was suffering from contact with another of our poisonous materials. His feathers were soaked in dark oil and plastered to his body. He had been like that at least overnight so was shivering and miserable. October nights are cold here and feathers are only insulating when they are clean, dry, and fluffy. His skin was red, probably stinging, though I didn't find any raw or bloody spots. I bathed him twice that day, keeping him inside where it was warm.

Owl told Lyn he had seen a mouse swimming in what he thought was water but, when he tried to grab the mouse, he became trapped in oil. Someone had pulled him out before he drowned in it, but only set him on the ground, even though he was unable to fly with oil-soaked feathers. He wandered to another place where he was seen by the people who called me. I suspect someone was using a barrel without a lid to hold dirty oil from cars or farm equipment. I hope they started covering it or disposing of the oil more safely after finding an owl in it.

Sarah came over the next day and we bathed Owl again, with me holding him and Sarah working dishwashing detergent into his matted feathers. Each time we rinsed him, more oil came off – but there was still more left. The next day another friend came over with Sarah and the three of us washed him. We found a large bruise on one wing, fortunately with no evidence of a fracture or wound. Perhaps he had hit it on the barrel edge when frantically trying to escape the oil.

Owl's feathers fluffed up when he dried and his skin was the normal whitish-pink by then. I put him in a bigger carrier on our deck, thinking his feathers were clean enough to provide insulation. He ate well all the time he was here, seeming alert and healthy. Unfortunately, I could again see oily feathers the next day.

I took him to Judy, who would provide a flight room till the bruise healed enough so he could fly well. Judy kept him in her house for a while because his feathers still weren't clean enough. Apparently down next to his skin was full of the stuff, which spread to outer feathers as they dried. Judy worked corn meal into the downy feathers to absorb more oil, but thought he was going to need another bath before he could be released. He ate well for her and was able to fly. A female great horned owl was brought in so Judy put them together in a flight room. They got along well and were released sometime later, after Owl had been bathed at least once more.

This experience causes me to wonder about how long birds caught in oil spills are kept and whether they are bathed more than once. We spent quite a lot of time with this owl whenever we washed him, though being handled was stressful for him. Even so, his feathers contained still more oil, which was only apparent after a few days. I suspect he'd have been unable to survive if we had released him the first few times he seemed free of oil.

CHAPTER 77

The reintroduction of wolves into Yellowstone National Park in the 1990s provides an excellent example of the value of native predators in an ecosystem. In a beautiful YouTube video called *How Wolves Change Rivers*, David Attenborough explains in only four and a half minutes some of the improvements that occurred within a few years of bringing wolves back to the park. The changes came about partly because wolf behavior affected elk behavior, causing them to move more often and to different areas, as well as somewhat reducing their numbers. This allowed vegetation in valleys and near rivers to grow better, providing more feed and shelter for a number of other animals and birds whose populations then increased. It also reduced erosion, thus positively affecting streams and rivers.

In addition, wolves killed some of the coyotes, whose high population had reduced the numbers of rabbits and mice, normal prey for hawks and other animals as well as coyotes. Leftovers from wolf kills provided additional food for bears, eagles, ravens, and other scavengers, allowing their populations to increase as well. The result is a far more balanced ecosystem, with native wild animals, birds, and plants returning to an earlier and more natural lifestyle. Elk and deer populations are also healthy.

Unfortunately many people are angry about returning wolves to some of their former ranges, giving several main reasons for wanting to again destroy them. Their animosity seems excessive to me, based more on some undefined fear than reality. I feel sorry for those who are so disturbed by these amazing animals and hope their distress begins to fade as what they fear fails to materialize.

One major issue involves the concern from hunters who believe wolves so seriously reduce elk numbers that few, if any, will be available for humans to kill. Aside from the obvious discrepancy (clearly their concern is not for the elk), populations of predators and their prey naturally fluctuate. When one goes up, the other goes down, and vice versa. In a normal wild situation, (i.e., not confined in an enclosure) predators other than humans are unable to kill a dangerously high percentage of available prey animals. Humans, on the other hand, have caused the extinction of many animals and plants, and continue to do so at an alarming rate.

Life as a predator is not easy, especially when the prey is as large as deer, elk, moose, and bison, all of which wolves eat (as well as mice and squirrels). Hunting requires a great deal of energy and frequently ends in failure. If they are unsuccessful too often, predators have insufficient energy to hunt effectively, so they starve. When prey numbers decrease, predators are less successful at finding and killing food animals. They then reduce the numbers of young they have or raise; also older animals may die sooner than usual, and some younger animals leave to find a different pack or territory.

As predator numbers decrease in a given area, prey populations begin to increase again. This cycle is normal and has been happening between predators and prey of all kinds for millennia. The bottom line is that wolves are not able to kill enough elk to put their populations at risk. In order to adjust to wolf predation, elk become more difficult to kill by moving around more and being more wary and protective. This prey behavior limits the number of wolves who can survive in any given area.

Another strong complaint I've heard from wolf haters is that wolves are cruel, often maiming and torturing their prey before killing them. It's true that predators are not kind to their prey, but they are neither malicious nor intentionally (or even knowingly) cruel about it. Their objective is to survive and raise their young, hopefully without injury to themselves or pack members. Their behavior is recognized as reasonable when one considers their only chance for survival is to run down and/or corner these large animals before killing them with their teeth. If they can quickly get close enough to bite, causing the animal to grow weaker from blood loss and/or reduced mobility, the wolves may be safer during the process of killing. A wolf with broken ribs, jaw, or leg, or a concussion from being kicked can suffer a slow, painful death due to being unable to hunt or eat. Wolves, like people, will often provide food for an injured pack member for a while, but they must first care for themselves and their young. If conditions are too difficult, the injured animal may starve before its injuries can heal.

I seriously doubt any modern humans would consider hunting and killing in the manner necessary for wolves because of the risk of injury. If any did choose to hunt only with a knife instead of killing safely from a distance, they probably wouldn't worry about causing discomfort for their prey while trying to kill it. Guns and especially arrows certainly cause pain and suffering, even when death is fairly quick. Sadly, many wounded game animals escape death for a time, dying later from blood loss, incapacitation, or infection. Humans have more difficulty finding wounded animals than wolves do, and many give up more quickly.

In comparison to wolf behavior, we should consider what we routinely do to our livestock for the purpose of making a living and providing food, entertainment, or information for people. Practices like castration, tail docking, beak cutting, dehorning, branding, confining animals in tiny enclosures, using them in scientific experiments, rodeo activities, etc., all come to mind. Though most people don't intend to be cruel, none of these practices is kind to any of the animals involved and would be considered felony torture if children and even pets were the victims rather than livestock. We justify it by believing we are more important than animals and that treating them that way is necessary for our well-being and comfort. I find it interesting when people expect or demand kinder behavior from animals such as wolves than from themselves.

Other complaints are that wolves kill livestock and that they kill more than they can eat. We create part of these problems when we kill wolves. Too often alpha adults are the ones who are killed; they are also the wolves who keep the rest of the pack in line and teach the young ones appropriate behavior. Younger wolves may become too excited when vulnerable animals (such as livestock surrounded by fences or game animals incapacitated by deep snow) are available, killing more than they can eat.

An article (*Effects of Wolf Mortality on Livestock Depredations*) in the December 3, 2014, issue of PLOS (Public

431

Library of Science) One Journal, a scientific, peer-reviewed publication, describes this behavior. Authors Robert B. Wielgus, Kaylie A. Peebles found more livestock were killed by wolves in areas where they were hunted, until a threshold number of wolves are killed.

I doubt any human adults would want to leave our teenagers completely unsupervised or consider they know all they need to know in order to be productive members of our society. In fact, recently there have been several examples in Montana of humans, adults as well as teens, slaughtering and wounding many elk indiscriminately by shooting repeatedly into a herd. Game wardens had to kill some of the wounded ones and didn't know how many had escaped only to die later.

Hunting is not a sport for adult wolves; it is essential for their survival. Most American hunters do not truly need wild game in order to feed their families, including those who do eat the meat. If they didn't love hunting, they wouldn't do it. Many kill primarily for trophies and bragging rights, the size of the animal being more important than the quality of the meat. I find it sad many people still teach children that killing magnificent wild animals is an acceptable source of pride and pleasure. I so hope more children begin making different choices and prefer to simply watch and/or photograph wildlife.

The fear that wolves would begin killing people in the United States has not materialized since they were reintroduced, though some still seem to expect it and even claim it has happened. The truth is that far more of us are injured or killed by pet dogs than have been killed by any wild animals. And far more people have been injured or killed by bears, moose, bison, and even deer than wolves in North America. Yet the phobia about wolves seems to persist. There are now hundreds of wild wolves in a few states where many people spend a lot of time in wild areas. The wolves are extremely aware of us and more likely to see us than we are to see them in the woods. Thus, they have had many opportunities to harm people without doing so, even though they have suffered horribly because of our cruelty.

Human-caused decimation of wild animal populations, whether intentionally as with wolves, or inadvertently due to lack of knowledge and concern (e.g., passenger pigeons, dodo birds, and unfortunately many more all the time) is sad, unnecessary, and a great loss to us and our planet. Ecosystems evolved with many interacting organisms, from microscopic, single-celled ones to the largest plants and animals. So many variables are involved in this balance, we don't even know the majority of them. Thus, when we try to change things to better suit ourselves, we cause unexpected and sometimes disastrous problems for other living beings and usually for ourselves, too.

Animal communicators have asked wolves and other wild animals to protect themselves by avoiding people, domestic animals, and crops. Some of them have said they are living close to human settlements and causing problems, including preying on livestock, as a way of forcing us to consider better ways of living with them and the rest of the natural environment. These animals know they may be killed or trapped and moved and are willing to put themselves in this position in an attempt to increase human awareness and to encourage us to develop other solutions for living with our wild neighbors.

CHAPTER 78

Don and I had a more personal experience with predator/ prey balances on our place the summer my pelvis was injured. We always have a lot of feed here for wallabies, emus, chickens, wild birds, and fawns. Of course it attracts mice, chipmunks, and squirrels, all of which we saw frequently. I wondered why we didn't see more raptors when rodent numbers seemed excessive. At night we often hear coyotes, who prey on these animals, too.

However, when looking out the kitchen window during the day, I frequently saw 10 to 12 chipmunks and even several mice, though usually they only come out at night. I didn't consider it a problem until we began finding evidence, including chewed wires, of them in our cars. I asked mice and chipmunks to stay out of them, to no avail, so I turned to Lyn.

Groups of beings can have sort of an overseer, called a Deva, who can be contacted when an issue has to do with the group instead of an individual. Lyn connected with mouse and chipmunk devas in her attempt to resolve our problem.

Devas: Lyn, this is Mouse Deva! Hi! I'm the Chipmunk Deva! Now, what can we do for you?

Lyn: Adele has asked me to talk with you about their cars. It seems some small rodent has chewed through the wires (strings) in their cars. This keeps the cars from moving, which is a great inconvenience to them. It is also a drain on their food supplies because the means of purchasing food now has to be used to fix the cars. Adele has talked with you and asked you not to do this. She doesn't know why you are ignoring her respectful requests. She doesn't want to put out traps or bring in cats or hawks, but having these wires (strings) chewed up is unacceptable. She will have to do something more to stop you if you don't willingly and respectfully leave her cars and house completely alone!

Devas: We honor you and your requests.

Lyn: (Both bowed) (deep, dark, quiet time) Then they told me they had gone to hear what the mice and the chipmunks at your place had to say.

Devas: We've spoken with all concerned. This is their reply. (Both Devas) Things – energy – are out of balance here. We know there are too many of us for this area, but the food supply is plentiful! Everything needs balance. We feel the imbalance and we get a little crazy and we chew wires. We also don't listen to the humans. They are out of balance, too.

Now, we suggest energy balancing for everything. The land – feng shui works well. The animals – too many – all need energy balance or more space – area – humans need more balance. We suggest they get cats – feral cats. Cats win – we win – only strongest and smartest survive and balance is restored. Traps won't work well to balance anything. Will make us – everything – crazier! Hawks don't like the closed-in feeling under the trees. Won't come. Cats best solution. We operate on survival law – very balanced – no hard feelings. We chew to balance ourselves and to communicate to you that all is out of balance and needs balancing. Universe says can't save everything! Must have balance – give-and-take – can't save everything always – very bad! Done now. We thank you for listening.

Well, this was not what I expected, nor was it as easy as I had hoped, though it certainly made sense. In thinking about the situation, it also occurred to me that one of the programs I set for a surrogate MerKaBa (light body) surrounding our property was that all living beings on our place be safe and comfortable. From the perspective of predator/prey balances, that seemed poorly worded! It is extremely important to thoroughly think through

436

intentions and state them clearly!

So I re-worded my MerKaBa program before my next meditation, and began thinking about correcting my imbalances. I had another shamanic journey with the intention of creating better balance in myself and our property. I called the couple who operate Feral Cat Rescue (a non-profit service in our valley to help cats and people), asking if they had two semi-feral cats who would be comfortable here, live mostly outside, and help with our rodent problem.

The cat rescue people (Tami and Chris) were great – helpful and thorough. They maintain as many as 40 cats in their home, while looking for permanent places for most of them. They came here, found a good enclosure to keep cats long enough to familiarize them with us and our place (the owl flight room which contained no owls), and brought two spayed female cats.

The younger one, Pika, was feral, hiding and wanting no contact with me. She was a climber, running up posts in the room, seeming almost as agile as a squirrel. She managed to push a small board out from under the eaves of the owl room and escape. I kept watching for her, but assumed she had gone elsewhere. Terri and Chris came to look for her as well, but she didn't show herself to them, either. A couple weeks later Don spotted her in his workshop, which is in another outbuilding. He spends time there every day, but it has lots of hiding places for a small, secretive cat. Pika had apparently slipped through the door when he left it open.

Don put food and a litter pan in the workshop, which he keeps heated in the winter, and talked to Pika while he was repairing air purifiers. Eventually she would allow him to see her and finally, after some liver treats and a lot of patience, she adopted him as her person. She even jumps on his lap for pets, something she is unable to tolerate for long. Pika still won't let me touch her, though she sometimes comes fairly close to me now. She spends a lot of time outside, hunting and climbing, seeming completely at home.

The older cat, Gwennie, really liked Tami, but continued to avoid me when I fed and visited them in the flight room. She seemed quite unhappy to me, so I asked Tami and Chris to come back for her. She was obviously happy to see them, 'talking' to them and asking to be touched, so I knew this was not the right place for her.

A few days later Tami called about another cat they had just taken in. This one, Kali, wasn't feral but had apparently been abandoned when her family moved. She only stayed in the flight room for two days before I decided she was happy here and let her out. She made herself at home on our deck, often asking to come in the house. Kali ended up being my cat, living mostly in the house and sleeping on my bed.

A yellow cat, Tansy, appeared on our deck around that time, too, eating food I put out for Kali. She is somewhat feral, not completely trustworthy, though she comes in the house once in a while and rubs against our legs when we go outside. It wasn't long before we saw fewer chipmunks and no mice during the day, though some of both are still here. We also quit finding chewed wires or other evidence of rodents in our vehicles.

Poor Clover and Eden, the dogs! They were great about all the strange beings in and around their home, learning to live in peace even with natural rivals or what they were bred to hunt (game birds of various kinds). Deer, chickens, and wild turkeys walked around them on our place, somehow knowing they were safe, though they avoid other dogs. The only things Clover and Eden were allowed to chase were squirrels (when outside, not patients in cages) and cats when they came on our property, neither of which they caught. Then we betrayed them to the extent of bringing cats here, with Don telling them not to chase them, either. Perhaps the worst of it was when Clover and Eden had to tolerate them in Don's workshop and eventually in the house. There were a number of eye-rolls and long-suffering groans, but no violence or even chases.

Our difficulties were not over for that year, however. Before my pelvis was completely healed, a forest fire started on the mountain next to us, the bottom of which is half a mile from our home. At one point, flames were only about 500 yards from here, the closest we've been to a wildfire, although we have watched several from our house over the years. We were under evacuation warning so I felt wallabies and emus, the most difficult of our animals to transport or house, should be moved. We took Casey and Jordan (Toby and Cricket had passed by then) to Linda's place because she had a suitable enclosure for wallabies and was willing to look after them. Our friends who own an emu ranch about 10 miles from our place came for Aten and Ara with their custom trailer, so they also were safe. Fawns could be released through a gate and hopefully would run toward the river if fire reached our place. They were nearly weaned, too big to transport or confine safely by then.

I packed photos and important papers in my car and even took Nicki downtown to stay with me at my mother's place one night. Don stayed home, getting up several times during the night to walk the property looking for embers. Helicopters used to drop water on the fires were based in a field across the road from us. The fire camp, where firefighters slept, showered, and ate, was just north of that, so we were in the best possible position. However, embers can fly quite far when burning trees explode or wind is blowing. Some people found warm, burned sticks a mile or more from the actual fire. The firefighters did a great job, losing only one small shed on the side of the mountain, even though lots of people live near the fire. We were able to bring our animals home in a couple weeks and all went back to normal.

Then I received another message through Lyn from an owl, giving me more insights and encouraging me to make further changes.

> Lyn: (Adele received an adult male Saw Whet Owl whose left wing was injured but not broken, as far as she could tell. I presented the owl for healing to St. Francis, who suggested I talk with him.)

> Owl: Hi, Lyn! Thanks so much to Adele and the others for taking me in while my wing heals. I think it will be fine soon. I'm glad to know that when I can fly, I can be free again. My message for you, Adele, is to speak of grounding and maintaining a steady pace rather than a

fast one. Recently, you received a message to balance yourself and the land you own and all the animals on it and then the evacuation notices started arriving and perhaps you are wondering how the forest fire ties in with all of this, for Mother Earth is certainly aware of all of these things.

Fire is one of the ways in which Earth balances herself, particularly when people get out of balance. The shamanic journey you had with Carla was helpful and timely and she (Earth) thanks you. Since you deal with so many animals who are out of balance, she wants you to put most of your thoughts and energy into balance in order to be a help to her. She sees that you focus on my wing and fixing it and that is good. However, she wants you to see that I was out of balance or I wouldn't have had this injury – just as you and your surroundings were out of balance enough to allow you to injure yourself. The problem was not the broken pelvis but the imbalance within your energy field. So she asks you to please look at all the hurt animals first with an eye to bring back complete balance and then do what is needed for the problem or injury. She has high praise for your dedication and service. She sends her best to you and all who revolve around you! Bye now!

It felt to me that I'd moved more toward balance of my physical self and surroundings, but I decided to be even more aware of balance and healing frequencies. I hadn't thought to use Reconnective Healing with this owl before his communication, but did so afterward. He soon regained use of his wing and was released. I can't prove he recovered more quickly because of energy healing or wouldn't have recovered without it, just as I can't prove my pelvis healed more quickly because of Sarah's distance sessions for me. However, I do believe it helped and there are many examples of scientific experiments showing the efficacy of Reconnective Healing, as well as other energy healing modalities. (See References for web addresses and books).

CHAPTER 79

Many wild animals are hit by cars, sometimes resulting in injuries from which they can recover if they have help. Fortunately, some people stop when they see hurt ones next to roads, even if they don't initially know who to call or what to do for an injured animal. It can be especially difficult when the animal is potentially dangerous, as when some people found a golden eagle who had been hit by a car.

A lot of animals (eagles, vultures, crows, ravens, coyotes, etc.) take advantage of road kills in their search for food. Sometimes they fly or run in the wrong direction when a car approaches and are then also hit. A road-killed deer was off the road where this eagle was found so she was probably feeding on it. She may have been too heavy from her meal to lift off as high and fast as usual, a reason she was unable to avoid the vehicle.

The people in a following car (not the one that hit her) found her lying on her back in the middle of a winding, two-lane highway. At first they thought she was dead and were simply going to move her off the road, but she responded when they turned her over. Because she was still limp, a passenger decided to hold her with the intention of continuing into town where help could be found. However, they soon correctly decided that was unsafe when she began to move more purposefully. A strong, wild bird with inch-long talons, a huge beak, and a six-foot wingspan isn't a good travel companion!

The rescuers left her on the ground at a pull-out, contacted a friend in the area to watch her so she didn't stumble into the road, and then continued on as they looked for someone who could care for her. Cell service in that area is sporadic, but they were eventually given my phone number. From their description, we knew exactly where the eagle was, so Don and I put a carrier in his truck and went to retrieve her.

The eagle was standing when we arrived. I was able to walk to her, cover her with a large towel, and grasp her lower legs from behind, pinning her wings to her body with the towel and my arms. Then I picked her up and carried her to the crate on the pickup tailgate. She was aware, but fortunately didn't struggle with me or in the crate.

I decided she should stay in the house that night because it's harder to regulate temperature when in shock and it was cold outside. One eye was closed most of the time, but I saw no swelling, disturbed feathers, or blood. She could use both feet and held her wings in normal position. I gave her the usual electrolytes, but offered no food till the next day, thinking she first needed water and quiet time. She was in good flesh, heavy and with full chest muscles.

The next day I fixed a bigger enclosure in the house where she could move around more. A couple days later she was ready for the outside flight area. It works well for owls and hawks, but isn't big enough for eagles to take flight so she stayed on the straw-covered floor.

Until I told her she would have to move around more before I could feel comfortable about releasing her, she remained in the same place on the floor. The next few times I checked she was in different places, and seemed much more energetic. A week after she arrived, I opened the door and watched to see whether she would fly. If she did, it would indicate she was able to care for herself. If not, it would be easy to put her back into the room. I didn't want to keep her longer than necessary and felt she wanted to leave.

She did take off, but flew only a short distance before landing in a nearby pine tree. She stayed there most of the day before she flew again, this time apparently leaving the area. When she was ready to fly high, she would get her bearings and be able to go back home, if she chose to do so.

Another animal I received after being injured by a car was a newborn white-tailed deer. She was brought to me by Tori, the woman who reported the young moose with West Nile virus and who sent reports on Solo from the Stock Farm when he was visiting there. Tori was following a car when it hit and killed a pregnant deer. She saw the fawn ejected from the doe's womb onto the road. Tori did what she could for the baby and then brought her here, still wet from birth fluids.

Once the fawn, whom we called Sophia (a name that came to Sarah when she was here to help), was settled in the playpen, I located some frozen goat colostrum and drove to get it. At first Sophia didn't try to stand, but I thought it was because of the traumatic birth. She did suckle so enthusiastically took the colostrum. I was concerned about its value because it was about a year old; Linda had told me antibodies may only be effective up to three months when kept in home freezers.

When Sophia started acting like she wanted to stand, I noticed a bone (the femur) in one back leg was broken. It appeared to be a simple fracture with no wounds, but it did require a splint, which my friend Mary Wolf (the retired rehabber who is a close friend) helped me apply. When I then helped Sophia stand up, I found her feet were also in an abnormal position in that they folded backward, causing her to stand on the tops. She didn't appear premature nor did her feet seem injured, but they had to be splinted as well. I believe the fracture was due to her impact with the car before birth, but the abnormal position of her feet could have been from birth defects. If she had been born normally in the wild, she would not have been able to follow her mother well, even if she could have learned to stand and walk.

Unfortunately, Sophia was unable to get up onto her feet, though she tried. She also was unable to stand when I lifted and braced her, even with all the splints supporting feet and fractured leg. Of course she had never learned how to get up or stand or walk. I made a sling with holes for her legs from an old sheet, which hung from the corners of the playpen. I put her in it several times daily, hoping she would begin using her legs, perhaps standing on her own and trying to walk.

Mary took her to her place after a week or so to do physical therapy on her feet, working them several times daily to stretch ligaments or tendons, because they seemed to not straighten normally even with splints. In addition to therapy in Mary's lap, they also went for outdoor walks. Finally, Sophia had good use of three legs, with only one foot still folding. When Mary brought her back, I was able to put her in the deer pen with other fawns. By then, Sophia was able to straighten that foot, too, though it folded sometimes at first. When even the last foot was almost always in a nearly normal position, she was able to run and jump with the others.

Sophia usually ate well, but she sometimes had diarrhea for no apparent reason. I was concerned about her abnormal birth, lack of appropriate colostrum, and birth defects. Her feet seemed to be fine, but she could have had some internal problems about which I was unaware. Sadly, when she was between three and four weeks old, Sophia suddenly refused bottles and mostly refused to stand up. I did everything I could think of to help her but, 15 hours after she refused her first bottle, Sophia quietly died. On necropsy, Judy found her chest to be full of bloody fluid; I don't know what caused it.

CHAPTER 80

Most of the birds and animals who come to us for help have been harmed in some way by their close association with humans. The following are brief stories about some of them.

This Eurasian Dove flew into a window of a home in town. Her message through Lyn follows.

> Dove: Hi, Ms. Lyn. I'm called Dovey by my friends. Tell Adele she can call me that. She's my friend now. Contrary Swan is right. I do need grounding. I've been walking about a lot to help me do that. I'll also try not to visit the Dreamtime unless I'm still. Tell Adele I have been eating. Food's great! Thank her for me. I'm grateful! One minute I was flying and the last thing I remember was hitting something hard and falling. What was it?

> Lyn: It could have been a window. Houses have windows so we can see out, but you can also see in or worse, get a reflection of the out-of-doors. Many birds die from hitting windows. You were lucky!

> Dove: I guess so! Humans are progressing and that is so great! It's all the talk now! I'll keep trying to fly. I'm so glad I can go back to where I was. Tell all the people who have helped me thanks! Bye!

Dovey had bruised the flight muscles on her breast, causing her to be unable to fly for a while. She soon recovered and was released. Some birds, woodpeckers especially in my experience, are more likely to break their neck or back when they hit a window. Some suffer serious head injuries. Those who just bruise chest muscles are lucky.

Late one fall, I received a great horned owl whose head was injured when she flew into a window. The man who found her in his yard thought at first that she was dead because she was lying flat on the ground with her wings spread. She revived somewhat

447

after he brought her to me, though clearly still didn't feel well. I gave her electrolytes and asked Sarah to come help her. Sarah didn't understand why she felt hawk energy more than owl energy, but Jasmine, a name that came to Sarah, explains it by saying she was flying during the day, indicating she was confused, since owls usually don't fly then. I hadn't known she had hit the window during daylight hours.

I suggested Sarah put on a welder's glove before reaching for Jasmine, because I wasn't sure how the owl would react. She appeared defensive at first, but as soon as the glove was removed, Jasmine quieted and let Sarah continue working with her energy safely, though well within reach of talons and beak. Sarah felt the glove was scary because Jasmine knew it was hiding something – a human hand. I've often noticed animals respond with fear when someone is trying to deceive them in order to get closer. They can tell the difference in our thoughts and behavior and respond accordingly.

Unfortunately, the head injury didn't heal well. Jasmine sometimes walked in a tight circle, even falling occasionally. I took her to Judy, who gave her an injectable drug which helps some birds with brain damage, but it didn't work for her. When Jasmine later began having convulsions, as well as circling and falling, Judy decided to euthanize her. Jasmine was apparently ready to move on.

Windows, especially those with reflective surfaces, mirror the surrounding area. Therefore, birds see vegetation or open skies rather than a window, house, or what is inside the house. When something dangerous appears, such as a hawk, cat, or human, instincts tell birds to instantly fly away. Often a window looks like an escape route. I've heard people call them stupid, an inaccurate evaluation of their behavior. We would walk into a reflective sheet of glass if the reflection looked like a continuation of a path we were following. Many times people bump into a clean glass door, thinking it is open.

Some people hang decorations or even see-through curtains inside windows, intending to provide a visible barrier. Unfortunately birds may not see them through the window because of the reflection. A fine net (such as those used to protect fruit trees from birds) hanging outside the house several inches or even a foot away from windows may be a good solution. Birds will usually see and avoid the net. Some may hit it, but will safely bounce back. If it's too close to the window, they still may be hurt. We are easily able to see through these nets so they don't interfere with our view.

Often our pets attack wild birds and animals, usually with poor results for the wild ones. Late one fall some people who have a pond on their land called me about an injured Canada goose. They had no means of catching her to bring her here so Don and I drove to their place, about half an hour away. Goose had lost part of a wing in what the people thought was an attack by a neighbor's dogs. She was with a small flock of other wild geese, including her mate, but they would soon have to leave for the winter. The pond, at a higher elevation than our place, would freeze, snow would be deep, and the people also planned to leave for the winter, so this goose had no chance to survive there. Don and I were able to catch her with a large fishing net. We planned to ask permission to release her at a pond in the valley where other geese and ducks live through the winter. They are fed by people who own the pond and by those who come to see the birds. Lyn helped by explaining our intentions and asking Goose what she wanted.

> Goose: Oh, Lyn, thanks so much for connecting me once again to Mother Earth. I have been wondering whether to continue my life on the ground without my mate, or to leave my body. I feel that Mother Earth has given me my answer by saying I am to stay grounded – figuratively and literally – in a place where people come to see us. Now I feel my life has purpose and meaning, even if I can't fly. I've told my mate he is free to go and that I am in good hands. He was stressed when they caught me. Sarah is helpful with her immense peace and calming. (They tried to bottle her - but it's not anywhere near as good! Inside joke between us!). [Peace and

Calming is the name of an essential oil mixture, Young Living brand]

Geese mate for life when possible. I was concerned about her mate, hoping he wouldn't stay too long waiting for her to come back, something she would be unable to do. I was glad to hear she had told him to leave and that she understood she still has a purpose, even though it is different from her former one. Goose bumped the end of the damaged wing when we caught her, causing it to bleed a little. I put emu oil on it and it healed within a few days. We then released her at the pond with others.

A baby fox squirrel was brought to me late one September night after being taken out of a gentle dog's mouth by a person in whose yard he was born. They tried to find his mother, but were sure she must be dead since she wasn't trying to help her baby. His eyes were open but hadn't been for long. He was not yet weaned, definitely too young to be out of the nest.

I agreed to take care of him because the people wanted to release him at their place in town, saying they would help him survive the winter. We usually don't raise non-native species of animals or birds, like fox squirrels, starlings, and house sparrows. They can be a threat to native species and our time and funds are limited; we prefer to use them to help natives. There are no regulations about keeping them, though, and the native squirrels mostly live out of town. I told the people the little squirrel would be better off living free in their yard rather than as a pet. They agreed. Lyn talked with him the next morning.

Squirrel: Hi, Lyn! I'm Baby Fox Squirrel. I was told I'm in shock. I need to be kept warmer and given a drop of electrolytes about three times an hour. Nothing else until I show signs of appetite. St. Francis is here doing a journey for my lost soul parts. I lost my mother right before my eyes and then a dog almost ate me! Thank this kind woman. I'll give it my best shot to live. Blessings to you all. I'll carry back a good report if I leave my body. Thanks!

I had thought he would be warm enough curled up in a receiving blanket and towels in the house, but he still was quite listless the next morning. As soon as I heard Lyn's communication with him, I put a heating pad under his 10-gallon terrarium. I did continue to give him electrolytes and offered drops of warm goat milk with whipping cream in it. By the next day he was sucking on a syringe containing goat milk, cream, and oatmeal baby food. He continued to improve that week and began eating his milk mixture from a tiny bowl. He became much more active so I gave him grains and fruit after putting him in a bigger cage.

When Squirrel was ready to go outside, I had the people pick him up. I suggested they put a wood nest box filled with cotton batting in a wire cage, attaching both to a fork in one of their trees. That way he could begin to adjust to outside conditions without actually being free and threatened by predators while he learned. They could continue to provide his food.

I later learned they had been too afraid for him to release him so built a bigger cage and kept him inside as a pet. I would not have made that choice for him, but know their intentions were good and they did the best for him they could. Sometime later his teeth had to be ground down by a veterinarian. Rodent teeth continue growing because they wear off through natural gnawing behavior. This squirrel didn't need to gnaw on anything, so overgrown teeth became a problem for him. He passed in 2013, after a couple years of being well-loved.

CHAPTER 81

Sometimes wild ones develop illnesses not necessarily attributable to us. One winter day, a small bird known as a Common Redpoll showed up at my neighbor's place, making himself known by first landing on Tom's knee as he sat on his front porch. Tom was concerned because, though the Redpoll hopped around pecking at seeds on the ground, his feathers were ruffled, usually an indication they are cold and possibly ill. Also, approaching Tom was abnormal behavior. The outside temperature was above freezing with clear skies, so he should have been comfortable. I took over a small net with which Tom was able to catch the small bird. I was unable to find any injuries and he could fly. At home, I placed him in a terrarium with food and water and called Lyn. She presented him to St. Francis and talked with him later that day.

> Redpoll: Hi! Lyn. Wow! I didn't know I'd get to talk to you! The word's out about you and Adele and Sarah. I was so glad to meet Adele and have her help me that I didn't expect to get to talk to you, too! I'm to remember I have a message for Adele. She is to be on the look-out for omens and messages from Great Spirit! They can come from anywhere or anyone. Tell Adele to look for the Oneness. She is me and I am her! St. Francis says I can go fly tomorrow!

Redpoll appeared to be eating and drinking here, and his feathers looked more smooth as though being warmer helped. However, he was extremely thin and his eating behavior seemed somewhat frantic. When I opened his mouth I found it full of a cheesy material indicating a fungal infection. I found him sleeping with ruffled feathers in the middle of the night, and he died before morning. My first thought was that St. Francis had meant he could fly free of this life instead of being released as we had assumed. I didn't tell Lyn he had passed but she told me later that he had come to her with that message.

453

Late one May I took in a male Evening Grosbeak who was obviously extremely ill. He was emaciated and too weak to stand, though no injuries were apparent. I gave him electrolytes, made a soft bed with support for his head, shared Reconnective Healing frequencies with him, and hoped for the best. I felt this bird wanted to talk with Lyn. She was busy so checked with St. Francis about it and was told she could talk with Grosbeak later. Grosbeak left his body that night, but Lyn was able to connect with him as spirit in the morning, with the following results:

> Grosbeak: Miss Lyn! How do you do? I'm Professor Grosbeak, at your service and Adele's. Adele was good to me and I do appreciate all of her care! I was planning to leave my body when I was asked if I could hang on long enough to deliver a message for Great Spirit. It is for both of you and I do encourage you both to take it to heart. Life is short – see! Particularly now that everyone needs to raise their frequencies, it is important to meditate on the various qualities of movement in your world. Decide which are appropriate and which are not 'growing grass.' Ask your guides all of the questions you have in order to figure out what is best at this time! There! I delivered my message, my life is completed and I'm quite happy to be on my way! Thanks for the chat! Toodle-oo!

As always, I appreciated the message delivered by Grosbeak. Raising frequencies by meditating, learning, and being more positive, compassionate, and aware of Spirit is becoming easier all the time on our planet, and perhaps more important as we move out of third dimension duality into higher, more peaceful, magical dimensions. It is an amazing time to be alive, though sometimes difficult, especially if we struggle against the changes. Grosbeak demonstrates the concept that death is simply a transition, not something to be feared. He still exists and is, in fact, in a more comfortable place.

The only baby beaver I've cared for so far was brought by a man named Cliff, who rescued her after his dogs found her huddled on the bank of the Bitterroot River near his home south of Darby. Cliff knew of no other beavers in the immediate area so thought she must have been swept away from her home somewhere upstream. She was definitely too young to be on her own.

The beaver was quite thin and had a problem with vertigo. She would fall onto her side after walking a few steps, and tip over backward when she stood up on her hind legs, though she should have been able to easily maintain that position. Vertigo consists of dizziness, sometimes with nausea, often related to position or head movements. It can be due to a number of different problems including head injury, inner ear inflammation or infection, a protozoan parasite, tick paralysis, or chemical poisoning. I made some phone calls to ask for suggestions about caring for her.

Judy had raised two younger beavers, but they were healthy. She suggested trying some homeopathic remedies (cell salts, electrolytes, and MSM), and believed the problem was caused by pesticide exposure. Linda (veterinarian) said it could be due to a head injury, though I found no evidence of that, and offered to prescribe medications that may help control vertigo but don't necessarily fix the problem. Raccoons are susceptible to a protozoan parasite that can cause balance difficulties, but she didn't know whether beavers could be infected by it. Beavers are rodents and raccoons are carnivores (according to scientific classification); they may be too distantly related to share most illnesses or parasites.

One of the game wardens who had raised and released a baby beaver suggested I try feeding her dog biscuits as well as willows and other plants and fruits. He said she would urinate and defecate whenever I put her in water, which makes keeping them clean easier. When they're that young, they are buoyant, like little corks, only able to swim on top of the water.

I called her Bonnie and kept her in a large plastic tub with towels for bedding. She would stand up on her hind legs and tip over, bumping her head against the side of the tub. I didn't want to put her in something with hard or inflexible sides, nor did I want her to be able to fall on food and water dishes. I gave her the homeopathic remedies and frequently offered water without leaving it in her tub. She ate well (puppy chow, emu pellets, grapes, willows), easily finding her food on the towels, and she drank an amazing amount of water. At first she didn't appear to be in pain.

Bonnie was a sweet little creature. She would lie on her back in my arms when sleepy, though preferred to be down when she was more awake. She never tried to bite or scratch, seeming completely unafraid. Bonnie slept a lot, especially during the day. At night, however, she was much more active; beavers are mostly nocturnal. That meant I had to listen for her, getting up to offer water two or three times during the night. The only time she cried was when she was thirsty. She seemed comfortable about sleeping alone, fortunately. Rodents eliminate frequently and copiously; I really didn't want to share my bed with her.

Lyn did a shamanic journey for Bonnie a couple days after she arrived here. She slept even more than usual that day, waking up thirsty and hungry in the evening. She was able to walk farther without tipping onto her side, and wandered around on the kitchen floor. Bonnie even sat up on her haunches to chew dog food, which she held in her hands. She had been eating only while standing on all four feet or lying on her belly. She mainly tipped over when she stood up too straight on her back legs. By the third day Bonnie had already gained weight; ribs and pelvic bones were no longer so noticeable when I touched her.

Bonnie had improved enough to need a bigger cage where she could have a water dish, so I took her to Judy. She fixed a padded enclosure with plenty of room for Bonnie to move around safely and continued treatment with homeopathic remedies. Unfortunately Bonnie took a turn for the worse about a week after Judy started caring for her. She slept all day and all night without eating or drinking. When Judy woke her, Bonnie tipped over more and was sometimes unable to right herself when she fell onto her back.

The worst new symptom was that she would curve her back downward with her tail and head up off the bedding, gritting her teeth as though she was in pain. These can be symptoms of some type of meningitis; treatment would require lab tests to determine antibiotics effective against the organism involved. Judy decided she didn't want her to suffer anymore, so Bonnie was euthanized.

On the last day of May, sometime after Cinco came to us, a woman brought me a young red fox who was terribly sick, with eye and nasal discharge, wheezing, and coughing. He was unable to breathe through his nose. If anything stressed him at all, he gasped for air and I could hear fluid gurgling in his chest. It appeared he had pneumonia, possibly due to our cold, wet spring. He was big enough to have been following his mom, so could easily have become wet and chilled when running through long grass. Little Fox was emaciated and weak, weighing only 2 pounds. His nose was long, indicating he was at least close to being weaned, but he still had baby teeth.

Fox was found in the middle of a road the night before by two kind women who were on their way home from a movie. Afraid he would be hit by a car, they walked toward him, expecting him to move off the road. When he didn't even stand or try to move away, they picked him up and took him home. The women put him in a small dog or cat carrier with towels and some milk. The next morning they thought he had eaten the milk, so they gave him a small amount of cooked hamburger before calling Judy, who referred them to me because I was closer. The women said he seemed more alert that morning.

I put Fox in a small carrier in our kitchen after giving him electrolytes, cell salts, and MSM in water, squirting it slowly into the back of his mouth so he wouldn't choke. He acted like he wanted it, though anxiety from being held made his breathing more difficult. Judy suggested I feed him mice and give him antibiotics. I called Lyn to ask St. Francis for help and then Linda for antibiotics. I put a couple of small mice in the carrier, spritzed Thieves Oil on his towel, put Peace and Calming essential oil on the doorway to the carrier, and covered the front with a towel. Then I left for just over an hour to do errands, including picking up antibiotics and some eucalyptus oil.

When I got home, I found Fox had not eaten his mice. I gave him the antibiotics (oral liquid) and more electrolytes, etc., cleaned and medicated his eyes, and put him back in the carrier while I fixed a dish of water containing a drop of Rescue Remedy for him. When I put the water in his crate, the two mice were gone. I covered the front of the carrier and left him alone to rest, digest, and hopefully begin healing.

Lyn wasn't planning to talk with Fox that morning; she just intended to present him to St. Francis. However, St. Francis told her she should talk with him right then.

> Fox: Are you Lyn? I've heard about you and Adele and Sarah. I asked for you. I don't feel well and Cinco de Mayo has said what marvelous healers you are. So can you help me?

> Lyn: We are doing all we can. I have given your name to St. Francis, the patron saint of animals, and he is working to heal you right now. Adele is seeing to it you get the physical care you need. Are you wanting to live?

> Fox: Oh, yes! I want to see my mom again. I could not keep up with her

> Lyn: When you are well, they will release you close to where they found you, so hopefully you'll find her.

> Fox: Oh, they are all so kind. Mom said people aren't to be trusted!

> Lyn: That is true about some people, but not all of them. It's best to not trust any because that will keep you safest, but you can tell your friends that not all people are the same.

> Fox: Oh, I will do that. I certainly will. Will you talk to my cells like you did for Cinco?

> Lyn: Yes, I'll do that now... All right. I've told them what

458

they are to do to get you well [return to functioning as they did in an optimum state of health]. Now I will ask my spirit guides to do a journey for you with your ancestors to help the process continue until you are well. They will also aid you in your highest purpose for this lifetime and give you a lot of immune protection so you will be stronger.

Fox: Oh, thank you! I'm to tell you something. Oh, yeah! Cinco said to tell you that he and his family are fine and he's grateful! He said you can all be trusted and that you are quite special. He said you are doing great work. Thanks and keep it up! He's telling all the animals. We are working for the continuation of Earth as it is now and has been, but there is still much to be done. He says I'm one of his messengers. Thank you! I'm grateful, too! I'm so glad you found me!

Sometimes the individual's path is not what we would choose, nor does healing happen in the way we expect. Little Fox's breathing continued to worsen. I even gave him oxygen for a while, but he died in my arms later that day. My thought was he could then run with his mom again and maybe choose a longer life in the future. By this time I was becoming much more aware of these experiences from the level of Spirit, rather than focusing completely in the duality of third dimension.

CHAPTER 82

The following are some communications and stories of wild ones who brought positive, informative, and loving messages when Cinco sent them to us for help:

2 Baby Canada Geese Communication

1st Gosling: Lyn, is that you? We've heard of you and Adele and Sarah! Cinco de Mayo wrote your names in the sky for all who needed help to contact you. It's taken awhile to get to you. Judy got the message that we wanted her to contact all three of you! She's good! Tell her thanks!

2nd Gosling: Yes! Tell her thanks and we've already benefitted from Sarah. Now you have contacted St. Francis and he's already talked with us. We are so grateful. We got hurt and we aren't feeling so good. St. Francis is doing a healing and he said you might do one, too. We need all the help we can get. We haven't had a normal beginning!

1st Gosling: That's right! We are emissaries from another planet and we needed to imprint with humans so we can work with them again when we are grown. We have major goals to accomplish for the people on earth so it's important that we live. It's also important that we go on record now, before we get older!

2nd Gosling: Lyn, can you help us heal faster so we can merge with the wild geese soon?

Lyn: I have some spirit guides who will journey for you to help speed the healing and tell your cells what to do to be well again. I'm telling them to return to how they were before you got hurt. I'm also telling your cells to encase

461

any toxins that are in your body and eliminate them and to increase your appetites for the foods that are best for your immediate growth! My spirit guides are doing a journey for you now as we talk. They will also include some help and protection for you so you will have an easier time of getting to your goals. Where are you from?

1st Gosling: We're from a planet in another solar system. Earth is getting a lot of extra help right now. Planets are sending extra helpers into most every species. The insects are going to be helpful, so be sure to ask them for assistance!

Lyn: I will! Thank you! Have you any messages for those of us who are helping you now?

2nd Gosling: It's important to broaden your perspectives. All of you are doing that, but we want to encourage you to do more thinking outside the box. The larger your perspective becomes, the easier it will be to stay on Earth and be of help. All of you have times when you are ready to leave and there will be more. However, you are still a minority in your thinking, so staying and sharing your perspectives will be most helpful. All of you, when you feel helpless, keep asking and pushing for more spirit guidance. Don't give up or quit!

Lyn: Is there anything else you'd like to say?

Both Goslings: Just - Thanks so much! All of you! You make a great team! So many abilities working together! We know you lack awareness of your greatness, which is good! Otherwise, you might all develop big heads! Ha! Ha! That's just a joke. Keep up the good work! And thanks so much for all the help!

These baby Canada geese were somehow separated from their family and kept for a while by well-intentioned people who didn't know what to feed them. When one became unable to walk, they turned the goslings over to Judy. The healthier one, a male, immediately started eating the Purina Game Bird Startena we use for baby chicks, ducks, geese, and other species with similar requirements. Often feed, even those intended for these babies, has insufficient protein and/or other nutrients to promote normal growth. This can result in bodies too heavy for bones, among other problems.

The little female was a major challenge for Judy, who had to tube feed her for quite some time before she started eating on her own. Her growth was significantly delayed and Judy was afraid she was going to have to euthanize her. However, she finally regained the ability to walk and grew rapidly after she recovered enough to eat well on her own.

The male was soon sufficiently strong and healthy to be released with a pair of wild geese, who raised him with their own youngsters. Sometime later, when the female was nearly full grown, Judy took her to a local wildlife refuge where there are ponds and wild geese. I assume these two beings continued their path of working to help us, as we continue to raise consciousness on our planet.

Lyn told about some of what the animals are doing for us when she explained Master Beings after her communication with Solo (Chapter 46). More can be found about concepts touched on by the little geese on the Internet (see References). It is tremendously exciting and encouraging to notice the increasing number of websites spreading positive philosophies and energy, as are books such as *Star Origins and Wisdom of Animals* by Jacquelin Smith and *Before We Leave You: Messages from the Great Whales and the Dolphin Beings* by Patricia Cori.

I especially remember a story in *Star Origins* about a butterfly whose soul was part of the author's soul, allowing her spirit to experience life in that form at the same time she was living as a human. This resonates with me as entirely possible, even logical, something I feel I've experienced. Most if not all of us have had the feeling of knowing a person we just met, which I believe to be spirit or soul recognition of someone we've known in other lives and on the Other Side. I feel that way about some individual animals, such as Solo, Ross, Nicki, Ara (python), and Cinco, as well as some species of animals, such as snakes, large pythons in particular, and lady bugs, many of whom appear in my office each spring. I can easily envision myself living in their bodies, probably because of soul memory of having done so.

The book *Before We Leave You* contains valuable insights and information from the whales and dolphins. The information given is loving, helpful, and uplifting, as messages from Wild Ones seem to be. Because they are eternal beings, as are we, their kindness and wisdom are never lost and are always accessible to us. Even so, I still prefer knowing they are living comfortably in our oceans. I envision clean water and earth, with an environment healthy and supportive of all life, as greater numbers of humans become more aware, enlightened, compassionate, peaceful – as we learn to live and love as the Wild Ones do. Sending them our gratitude greatly adds to the positive energy in the universe and helps them in their mission to bring enlightenment to us.

A western pond turtle with a damaged shell was another animal brought to me for care who had an interesting story. It is similar to some of the messages in *Star Origins* in that Turtle talks about coming here from a different planet and being somewhat unfamiliar with Earth and humans. I receive few reptiles for rehabilitation, but fortunately some people are willing to seek help when they find injured ones. I've even received some snakes, though injured turtles are more often brought to me.

Turtle shells are bone, actually fused ribs and vertebrae, so they contain living cells, blood vessels, and nerves. Scales covering the bone are modified skin, somewhat like fingernails on top of a sensitive bed of soft tissue, nerves, and blood vessels. When a shell is broken or perforated, the turtle's breathing is often impaired and internal organs can be exposed to infection. The recommended treatment is to realign the pieces as much as possible before creating a solid bandage using fiberglass cloth and epoxy.

464

When I was a child, there were quite a few western pond turtles in this Montana valley. We often saw them injured or dead on the main highway, which was built through wetlands in a few places. The highway is still there, but I never see turtles on the road anymore. I'm sure this is because so few survived rather than because they no longer try to cross. Some still live in more isolated ponds and wetlands, but those are often destroyed to make room for new homes, which is how this turtle was injured.

My brother Jim and I kept a couple of these turtles as pets, sadly with the cruel practice of drilling a hole in the edge of the shell. A wire was placed through the hole and attached to a peg on the bank of a small irrigation ditch in our front yard, so the turtle couldn't get away but could remain clean and feed itself. I saw that the hole bled a bit, but didn't think about how painful that must have been, not to mention the cruelty of taking away their freedom. Some who are confined this way struggle enough to break a piece out of the shell to escape, similar to trapped animals chewing off a body part to achieve freedom.

I took Turtle to Judy, holding it while she lifted shell pieces back into place with forceps, cleaned the outside of the shell, and glued a bandage over the damaged area. Linda calculated the dosage for an injectable antibiotic, which I picked up from her on the way home with the turtle. Sarah came over later to help with energy healing. We found Lyn's following communication interesting. It seems animals are saying more about metaphysical aspects of the universe as I learn enough to understand and be open to their messages. They are amazingly interested in helping us learn and grow!

> Turtle: Hi, Lyn! Wow! I'm really talking to a person who communicates with animals. Oh, yes, I know Adele and Sarah can communicate, too; sometimes they don't have enough confidence to receive, but they will. What they do for us animals is so wonderful, just like you! So, when will I be well and released?

> Lyn: Adele says about two weeks or 14 days and nights,

give or take some depending on how quickly your shell is ready to protect you again.

Turtle: Yes - they glued it and they gave me stuff so I don't get sick and then energy work took away the pain. I'm so grateful! Tell them all thank you for me!

Lyn: I will! What are your plans for this lifetime?

Turtle: Oh, I'm a sightseer! I'm just here to be a turtle and enjoy. I'm visiting from another planet – star, really – you call it a vacation, I believe. Anyway, this is one of those package deals where I get to travel and live free and do what I want, within the confines of the body I picked, of course. I didn't want to be noticeable, but I did want to meet some real people and I like them.

Lyn: Are all turtles from the same place?

Turtle: Oh, no. We come from all over the stars, but we make some great new friends that way. Of course, when a trip is really good and we go back home and tell our friends there, they often want to come do it, too, so some earth vehicles [bodies] get a bunch from the same place sometimes.

Lyn: Right! I know how that works. Is there anything else you'd like to say?

Turtle: Oh, Cinco was right about all of you being unusual humans and some of the best. Hope we can get a revolution going of your kind of people.

Turtle did not eat well while in captivity, no matter what I offered him. Most reptiles can survive amazingly long periods without food, but I still was concerned about his choice. As soon as his antibiotic regime was finished, I released him in a pond

466

which contains water all year, wishing him well during the rest of his time here and thanking him for his messages to us.

A young crow also gave us a brief but valuable message when he needed our help.

> Crow: Hi, Lyn! Kaw! Kaw! I was hoping I'd get to talk to you. Mom and Dad were, too! We think all of you bird people are great! Thank Adele for saving me and I won't be with you long. You'll see! Kaw! Kaw! A deformity is only a problem if you think it is. I don't know the word or meaning so I'm Perfect Crow! Kaw! Kaw! A short time is all I need. You'll see!

This little guy's legs were somewhat deformed, so I took him to Judy for splinting. After they straightened and became functional, when he was getting around well and finding food for himself, Judy released him. I assume he kept his bubbly, Perfect Crow personality.

The following young magpie was found on the ground in a parking lot, too young to get back into the nest tree on her own. Adult birds were there but it was dark when I picked her up, so I brought her home overnight and then took her back the next morning. Her parents were still around, letting me know they would finish raising her.

> Magpie: Hi, Lyn! We love all you bird people and we know all about all of you. Cinco made sure of that. I'm supposed to tell all of you to fly HIGH. Each of you will have to determine what that means to you. That message comes to all of you from all of us birds. Soar with the Eagles (in spirit, mainly) and Touch the Sun! We birds can lift you up out of the mud of third-dimension living. We are connected to higher levels and we can be of great help! Thanks so much to Adele for taking me in last night. My mom knows where I am and she is happy I'll be returning home. Thank you so much!

Her mention of lifting us out of the third dimension is interesting. Many people who are teaching about raising consciousness on the planet speak of moving into higher dimensions. The third dimension is described as being one of duality, meaning good/bad, positive/negative, right/wrong. In other words, there are a lot of rules, judgment, competition, and imbalance in third dimension, the one we're used to experiencing.

My understanding is that living in a physical body in third dimension allows many learning opportunities, some of which may be unpleasant, but provide important experiences. The fourth dimension, with few rules and more choices, is kind of a transition between the third and fifth dimension, where we reconnect with our higher selves with full awareness. This is a place of complete peace and non-judgment in which we more quickly manifest what we choose. There are also a number of even higher dimensions, but I'm still practicing with these so am not ready to learn much about them yet.

Author Jim Self is one of the people who describes the concept of moving back and forth between dimensions and teaches many skills for making the transitions easier. His books *The Shift: What it is, Why it's happening, How it's going to affect you*, and *What Do You Mean the Third Dimension Is Going Away?* are well worth reading. He also gives seminars and webinars, and provides a lot of information on his website (Mastering Alchemy). I was able to attend one of his seminars in Colorado and found it interesting and beneficial.

Messages from another Baby Magpie:

Magpie: Hey, Lyn! Thanks for coming to talk. Tell Adele thanks so much for helping me. Flying is harder than it looks. This is my first time as a bird. I've always admired birds and wanted to try flying. Guess I was too much in a hurry. I'm quite eager, you know! Say, all the stuff you guys are doing is great! Working together like you are really makes things go faster and better, for those who want to get well. Now, I'm not sick – just precocious.

Fly higher and see what we birds see. It's a whole different world up in a tree. Everyone on the ground runs around like ants. Up in the tree, we just enjoy the view and eat – gotta eat! But I don't like all that rushing around. Seems pointless! Fly high! All of you! Shake off your worries and cares and enjoy the day, the world, from a higher point of view. You'll find you relax more and smile more!

My, but I really rattled on, didn't I? Good talking to you! Tell Adele, Thanks so much! Have a great day! See ya! Fly Away!

As he said, this little magpie got out of his nest too early; he wasn't even able to balance on a branch, let alone fly. Judy raised him with some other magpies his age, releasing them all at her place when they were ready to go. I love his advice of looking at things from a higher perspective! When we ask ourselves what is truly important and what is best forgotten, we may find we can release a lot of unpleasantness.

CHAPTER 83

We can receive interesting and beneficial insights and knowledge from our pets as well as from wild animals. Their messages can be transmitted through a professional animal communicator or directly to us, if we learn to open ourselves to them. We also are able to share information with our pets, especially when we do it with conscious intent. Often speaking out loud helps because we are usually more focused when we think about stating vocally what we want to express. This reduces interference from mind chatter, making our intentions more clear.

The following is a communication I did with my brother and sister-in-law's dog, a sweet and gentle griffon named Cricket.

> Adele: Cricket, are you there? Will you talk with me this evening?
>
> Cricket: Hi, Adele. I'm here. [sounds listless]
>
> Adele: David and Diana are worried about you because you haven't been eating. What is going on?
>
> Cricket: They are afraid and that makes me afraid. What will happen to me if something happens to them? I'm filled with fears.
>
> Adele: David and Diana have been afraid and worried because Diana is having some unexpected health issues, but it looks like she will be fine and things will soon go back to normal. No matter what happens, you will still be loved and safe.
>
> Cricket: Are you sure? They've really been worried.
>
> Adele: I'm as sure as you can ever be. Check with Dave and Di right now and see how they feel.

Cricket: [pause] You're right. They do seem better! But now they're worried about me! [seems more energetic]

Adele: That's true. Can you relax and release your fears now and eat the treats Diana fixes for you?

Cricket: I'll try. I do feel better.

Adele: Did you know you will be going bird hunting with them the day after tomorrow? Two more nights at home and then you get to go.

Cricket: I did know, but I thought maybe I was mistaken since everyone has been so upset.

Adele: You're not mistaken. The trip is going to happen and you'll all have a good time.

Cricket: That's great! But what about Diana's illness?

Adele: She'll have some more procedures for a while, but then she'll be fine again. I think the worst is over because they now know what is going on and what they need to do to fix it.

Cricket: Oh, I am so relieved! Thanks, Adele. I can eat now.

Adele: Do you want me to send you some Reiki energy?

Cricket: Oh, yes! That would be great! Thank you!

I did do a distance Reiki session for Cricket. She perked up, began eating well again, and enjoyed her hunting trip with them.

When she was eight years old, Don took our sweet dog Clover to Linda for surgery to remove a tumor just below her right

472

elbow. It had grown rapidly and tested malignant. Linda didn't think she was able to excise the entire growth, because a lot of threads spread from the main mass. Clover recovered well, but it wasn't long before it was clearly observable again. The following communication occurred shortly after we first noticed return tumor growth.

> Clover: Hi, Lyn. Tell Adele I just want to leave my body, when the time comes – peacefully! Tell her there is a tightness in my leg when I move and, when I do too much, that tightness becomes pain in the stretched skin and muscles. It tells me to slow down. For the most part, the lump on my leg is not painful.
>
> Lyn: I could do a shamanic journey for you and ask your compassionate, loving ancestors to come in and do a healing.
>
> Clover: Oh! Could you? Would you? That would be so great! Please thank Adele and Don for calling you! I'm so grateful! When?
>
> Lyn: Now, if you are ready.
>
> Clover: Yes! Thank you!

Lyn did the journey for Clover with the intention of clearing her cells of cancer. She suggested my using some gem stones and essential oils for Clover as well, which I did for some time. However, the tumor continued to grow, leading me to believe Clover's path may not include eliminating cancer.

Clover had a second surgery about five months after the first, when the tumor was already larger than the other one had been. Amputating the affected leg was not an option. Linda said it would be difficult for her to adjust to losing it and, because of her size (around 90 pounds), her other front leg would suffer from carrying the extra weight.

During the surgery, Linda found another small mass on the shoulder of the same leg. She biopsied it with the report showing one malignant cell, not a good sign. We chose to give Clover a type of chemotherapy in pill form, with another capsule to help avoid stomach damage from that drug. She seemed to do well with it, feeling good and with no sign of tumor growth for most of a year, much longer than before.

Linda had said chemo probably wouldn't eliminate the cancer, but we were still disappointed when we could tell it was growing again. Before making any decisions, Linda suggested x-rays to determine whether there were any internal growths. When Don took her to the clinic, Clover began shaking with fear so badly she could hardly walk. At my request, Lyn asked her about her preferences with the following result:

Clover: Hello, Lyn! Nice to see you today! What brings you calling?

Lyn: Adele and Don wanted me give you some information about your health. They would like to know what decisions you would make.

Clover: Okay. So, I know I've had two surgeries. All of them had bad cells, so they have been giving me a pill they call chemo. What now?

Lyn: There is another tumor on your shoulder above the place that had the surgeries. It and the old one are growing rapidly, and they've been told by the veterinarian that another surgery to remove them before the get bigger and make you more uncomfortable would be recommended. However, the severe shaking they noticed the last two times you saw Linda makes them wonder how you would feel about another surgery. They will give you a pill that will relax you and make you sleepy before you go, if you decide you want to have the lumps removed. Do you want to tell me and them how you feel about another surgery?

Clover: What's the point of removing the tumors? A few more months and then another surgery? Don't get me wrong! I love them with all my heart, but I've been trying gently to let them know it is time for me to go! It is time for our relationship to change to a spiritual one!

Don and I are extremely close and as spirit, I can help him every moment of every day – if he will allow me to. That is what I want. Our connection is forever – not just for a few more months. There is no one who can help him as much as I can, because I love him most and he loves me most. I was sent here and I volunteered to come in order to be a bridge between the conscious and spirit world. Adele has many spirits who love and guide her already. So I am here for Don. He needs me more in spirit form now than in physical form. I am not in pain, but I will be if I have surgery! Every surgery has been painful and it is hard on me, because I have to be in a place where I don't feel connected to love. I really want to spend all my time with Don, loving him, and I want as little vet assistance as possible! I will welcome euthanasia when I'm in pain and unable to go with Don in this body.

I'm not needing extra weeks or months thanks to another surgery! I need to leave my body as easily and peacefully as possible in my own time frame. I will have to conjure up more cancer to get the job done, if need be, and that is not easy or fun. The important part of life is enjoying it and having fun. All this –"I've got to save you so you can live with me one more week, one more month, one more year" is not for me! Love and laughter, peace and joy, are ever so much more important – because they last for eternity! And Lyn, you are so kind to offer a Quantum Healing to me – I really do need to transition, so it wouldn't be helpful to mc – but thanks for the thought and the offer!

Now, Don, you would probably be amazed at the number of times we've been together, so I won't tell you, but you know me and, Dear Boy, that is never going to change! All that will change when I leave this Earth Plane is that you will have me as your constant guide and companion 24/7, and believe me! – that is no small thing or insignificant matter! Trust me! I love you more than you know, and I am asking that you stop trying to save me and just love me and all of our time together before I leave my body. This is as much or more for you as it is for me – even if you think you don't want it.

Oh, I shake at the sight of the vet because I can't stand the thought of one more medical procedure in the name of love. Believe me – torture by any other name is still torture! So, even in your pain, know that by following my wishes you have given me Joy! Thank you! Thank you! Thank you! Regardless, my love for you knows no limits! Oh, thanks, Adele, for everything! Love! Laughter! Joy! to you both!

We chose to honor Clover's wishes, avoiding further surgeries or medication other than for pain. Two years later, the masses were both larger than grapefruit, though Clover still seemed in good spirits without indication of much discomfort. She mostly preferred to stay in the house by then, except when she rode in the truck with Don. I gave her pain medication twice daily for many months. Not long after she was no longer able to get into Don's truck to ride with him, we released her great spirit.

CHAPTER 84

On the first day of June 2013, a game warden called to ask if I could care for a baby golden eagle who was on the ground at the base of his nest tree. After receiving directions from Wayne, one of the men who found the little eagle, I drove across the valley and up a narrow dirt road where the eagles had nested for at least several years. As soon as I pulled off the road, I saw an adorable, mostly down-covered, chicken-sized bird, with alert, dark eyes and a large, yellow beak, lying in the grass. He seemed comfortable, with no immediate evidence of injury from the fall. The nest tree was on the side of a hill some distance from the road, the nest about 50 feet up. Under the circumstances, taking him home seemed the best option for the little guy. He was relaxed and unafraid when I picked him up, remaining still and quiet in the carrier on the ride home.

I named him Spirit from the *Medicine Cards* book, which gives Spirit as the keyword for Eagle. According to a bird book (*Nests, Eggs and Nestlings of North American Birds* by Paul J. Bacchic and Colin J.O. Harrison), baby golden eagles are about a month old when dark feathers start appearing in the white down, a description allowing me to assume Spirit was between four and five weeks of age. I was surprised at how dense his down was. It reminded me of wool, much thicker and softer than I expected.

These babies grow amazingly fast. Spirit's head was already about the size of the egg from which he hatched; his body would be as big as that of his father by the time he was ready to fly at only 60 to 70 days old. Spirit was unable to walk or even stand at that time, though he could shuffle around on the lower part of his legs. He had huge, dangerous-looking black talons, but his bright yellow toes were usually limp, causing his talons to be completely harmless then.

A year or more earlier, I had watched videos of bald eagles in their nest. Babies, and often even their parents, kept their toes somewhat folded and limp when they moved around the nest. They (babies and parents) usually didn't stand up, either, walking instead on their ankles rather than on their feet. It seems they need to walk that way to avoid harming themselves or each other with their talons. Also, it's probably better to maintain a low center of gravity if you're born on a platform 50 feet from the ground in the often-windy air, at least until you have enough feathers, strength, and coordination to fly.

(Imagine a chicken leg. The drumstick is actually the part between the knee and ankle. What we think of as their foot consists only of toes. However, the first joint above toes, at the top of the scaly part of the leg (bottom of the drumstick), is analogous to our ankle. In birds, the whole lower section of the leg plus toes is a foot.)

In some species of birds, including golden eagles, it is common for an older or stronger sibling to push a smaller one out of the nest, which is probably what happened to Spirit. Mom usually begins sitting on her eggs after the first one is laid, rather than waiting till all eggs are in the nest several days later. The temperature is often still cold here when golden eagles lay in early spring. If the eggs were left exposed, embryos would likely die. Because fertilized eggs begin developing when incubation starts, the first egg hatches before others. That baby is then older so bigger and usually stronger than later ones. Even a few days makes a significant difference because they grow so fast. This seems cruel but is adaptive; the strongest one then has a better chance to survive. If food is scarce, this is more likely to happen, thus helping ensure at least one baby grows up.

When Spirit first came here, he stayed in the carrier on our dining room table, which holds birds and little animals more often than dishes and meals. Spirit seemed to have no fear of us, eating readily from forceps and even accepting a tube down his throat through which I gave him electrolytes for a day or two, making sure he was well hydrated. More detailed examination still didn't reveal any injuries and he was heavy for his size. I doubt he was on the ground long before being found. His parents may still have fed him sometimes when he called to them, but he was much more vulnerable to cold and predators there. His sibling in the nest was probably fed first.

Spirit ate four to eight mice at a time, five or six times daily. Feeding them meat alone is not adequate because they get a lot of nutrients from bones, organs, and even stomach and intestinal contents. He preferred his mice to be skinned, cut up, and handed to him. Parents feed their young that way at first, tearing off bits of meat and offering it to the babies. Indigestible parts such as hair, toenails, teeth, and some bones are clumped into what is called a pellet, which is periodically regurgitated. As babies grow bigger and more coordinated, parents leave larger pieces in the nest, encouraging them to pick up and tear apart their own food. Part of my responsibility as a wildlife rehabilitator was to help him learn those skills.

I soon moved Spirit to the floor with access to a larger carrier for sleeping. Our tile floor is slippery for youngsters learning to walk, so I put large towels down for Spirit to practice on. At first he still shuffled on his ankles, sometimes using his amazingly long wings for balance. He didn't go far that way and was unable to get in and out of the carrier, with a 2-inch lip, by himself. As he grew stronger, he moved more, sometimes even standing on his feet for short periods of time. I left the carrier open and, when he was more coordinated and walking, Spirit began stepping in and out as he chose. He slept in it at night, putting himself to bed before dark and sometimes also napping there during the day.

Birds eliminate frequently so the washer and dryer were in use every day. Baby birds naturally aim and squirt at the edge or off their nest, but it is difficult to determine where that is in unnatural surroundings like our house. Spirit mostly squirted on the sides of the carrier or out through the door. When he was bigger, he tried to direct it off the towels onto the floor, with moderate success. After he started hanging out by the sliding glass doors next to the deck, that's where he aimed his tail. There are still a couple of white streaks on the screen. Uric acid (the white part of bird and reptile feces, their form of urine) is hard to clean off of screens or anything else once it dries.

One of my spring projects involves pulling knapweed in the wallaby enclosure. I began taking Spirit with me to give him better footing on the ground as he practiced walking. He loved being outside! At first he would find a sheltered place among tall weeds to sit, remaining alert and always looking around. He was especially aware of the sky, something he couldn't see well when he was in the house. Later he explored more, walking, playing with pine cones, and attacking plants.

Once he started to scream, a sound I hadn't heard him make before, with his head tipped in a watching-the-sky position. I looked up to see a golden eagle flying west, toward the mountains. It apparently heard and/or saw Spirit, even though it was very high, because it turned around and circled us a few times before continuing on. I was so happy Spirit still recognized golden eagles and was able to call them in. This behavior is one part of what would be required to return him to his parents. It would also be necessary for his parents and sibling to still be at the nest site, and Spirit would have to be able to fly well enough to land safely on a branch.

When I went back to the nest area a couple weeks after picking up Spirit, I heard his sibling calling from the nest and saw both parents, giving me more hope he could go back with them. The parents are much better than we are at teaching youngsters what they need to know and supporting them while they learn. That was the best possible option for Spirit, allowing him to go free much sooner and under nearly ideal conditions.Perfectly ideal would have been to complete his growth in the nest with his family, of course.

After his first few days here, Spirit often chirped at me when I walked into the room, when he was hungry, or even just when he heard my voice. I was the only one who fed him, though other people were around occasionally for short periods of time. Our two dogs were often in the same room, ignoring him when possible and moving away if he approached them as he learned to use his legs and wings.

All this time, Spirit's feathers were growing longer and in more places on his body. After about three weeks, he began practicing with his wings, spreading and even sometimes flapping them when he stood up. I gave him sticks and pine cones as toys. At first he was unable to grab them with his feet, though he tried.

He was more successful with his beak but not much. He would reach toward the forceps for food only if he didn't have to bend over to take it with his beak. Even without standing up, his balance was still somewhat shaky.

Later, as he became more coordinated, he would be walking normally when he spotted a pine cone. Then, before I even knew he was going to grab it, he had jumped on it, gripped it in both feet, and was tearing it apart with his beak. He could also lean over from a standing position to pick up and swallow whole mice without losing his balance.

One day when he was outside with me, Spirit expressed great displeasure about going back in the house. He disliked being picked up (parents never lift them, of course), so I would put him in a shallow tub to carry him. He was fine with that initially, maybe because I only held the tub, not him. Also it was more like a nest, and he was used to looking down at the ground. This time, however, he screamed at me and kept getting out of the tub before I could pick it up. To prevent him from falling, I had to put a towel over his wings, grab his feet and tuck him under my arm to carry him back into the house.

Clearly it was time for Spirit to be outside, where he could see the sky and have more room to develop his eagle skills without needing to be carried. Don prepared a large woodshed for him in our back yard. It has perches at different levels, clean straw on the dirt floor, and white vinyl lattice covering most of one large wall, allowing sunlight to enter and giving him a floor-to-ceiling view of the sky and backyard. He also had more room to move, play, and spread his wings. There is no wire on which he could damage feathers or feet and the walking surface is not slippery.

By this time, Spirit was practicing a lot with his wings and was nearly as large as an adult golden eagle, whose wingspan is about seven feet, with females being somewhat larger than males. He flapped enough to lift a few inches above the floor and often used a hop/flap method of moving across the room, though he could walk well, too. The flight room isn't big enough for him to fly much, but he learned to flap up to perches and down onto the stump where I fed him. He was clearly at the stage where they at least hop around the nest tree from branch to branch, coordinated, balanced, and able to land purposefully and gracefully.

The weather was quite hot then, often with daytime temperatures in the 90s. Spirit had plenty of shade and air flowed through the flight shed, but it was still hot. He sometimes stood in his large water dish, wetting the down and growing feathers on his lower legs. I decided to splash water on him, thinking a shower might cool him. He loved it! He'd ruffle his feathers and preen. I was surprised to see how much brighter his feathers were after the shower.

Birds create a lot of dander, especially when they are growing new feathers. The sheath around developing feathers at first contains blood vessels to carry nutrients to them. As the feather becomes longer and more mature, the sheath begins to dry and flake (dander) as the blood supply decreases and then stops. Grooming with beak and toes is used to facilitate this flaking process. When Spirit was in the house, his towels, carrier, and the floor were always dusted with feather sheaths, from tiny particles to larger, clear, curled pieces. The fine, white dust coating his feathers washed off with his showers, allowing darker natural colors to show more.

Because birds are unable to groom their heads other than by scratching with their feet, they often help each other by gently picking at the pinfeathers in unreachable areas. Spirit would tip his head sideways, offering me his neck and head for grooming whenever I was close to him. As I scratched him, he changed position to help me reach all spots. My fingers are not nearly as good as their beaks at removing dry sheaths! He would also offer to groom me, sometimes pinching a piece of skin on my hand or arm. He wasn't quite as gentle about it as I would prefer; my skin contains nerves and doesn't flake properly like dry feather sheaths.

One time when I was sprinkling water on Spirit, I asked him if he wanted some under his wings. He immediately spread one wing and waited for me to splash water there. When he put that wing down, I asked if he wanted me to do the other wing – and he immediately opened it. Animals telepathically pick up so much of what we think, even when they don't directly understand our verbal languages.

We actually create images in our minds as we speak or think, so on that level, the level of telepathy, words are irrelevant. Lying to them is pointless; they respond to our thoughts and the energy we project rather than our words. When we are calm, patient, and loving, taking time to explain to them what we're doing and why, even wild ones are much more cooperative and easier to handle than one would expect.

When Spirit had been in the flight room for a couple weeks, Wayne (one of the men who found him) called to tell me his sibling was standing on a rock near the nest tree and both parents were circling overhead. I knew Spirit needed to go home before his sibling learned too much more about flying and while his parents were still there in caretaking mode. From his behavior here, I thought he would still recognize them and call for their attention. Spirit's best chance for learning the rest of what he needed to know was to go back with his family.

The next morning, I put Spirit in a carrier, and my friend (and hypnotherapy teacher) Roberta Swartz and I took him back to his nest area. The two men were there, as were his sibling and both parents. I took Spirit's water dish, a plastic bag of mice, and a gallon jug of water. We put the carrier in the shade under a tree, set out water and mice, and opened the door. Spirit did not care about shade, his supplies, or me. He just wanted to be free! He headed up the hill, using a combination of walking and hop/flapping. We watched till he stopped under a bush, resting in the shade nearly at the top of the large, steep hill.

When it appeared Spirit was going to stay there for a while, Roberta and I left, hoping his parents would soon land near him. Later that evening one of the men called to tell me Spirit had moved farther up the hill. He offered to take the water and mice up to him, which seemed like a good idea. He called later to say a couple of mostly-eaten fawn legs were under the first bush where Spirit had stopped, probably put there by his parents. Two days later, Roberta, her husband Tom, and I went back to the nest site, climbing the hill and calling for Spirit. We found his water dish and some of the mice but saw no eagles after climbing all the way to the top, nor did I hear one calling. If he had been hungry and able to hear me, Spirit would have called or come to me, since I had been feeding him for five weeks. I took it to be a good indication that he was fine.

Several days later, I told a psychic friend about Spirit and his release. She connected with the eagles telepathically and said his mom was so grateful we took care of him and then brought him back that she would send me a wonderful gift.

The next afternoon, Wayne called to tell me Spirit was sitting on an irrigation pipe in a field at the base of the hill where we released him. Wayne's wife had seen the young eagle there that morning, but he was gone when Wayne drove by a short time later. On his way home, Wayne saw the eagle was back. I grabbed some mice, jumped in the car, and drove over, telling Spirit I was on the way. He was still there, standing on one leg on a pipe in the middle of the field, completely at ease.

The gate was open, hay had been mowed, sprinklers were off, and I had already asked the owner for permission before we climbed the hill on their property. I slowly walked out into the field, asking Spirit if he was hungry, telling him I had mice for him. When I was within 20 feet of him, he put his other foot down and spread his wings, as he had done sometimes to greet me when he lived here. I continued walking slowly and talking. At 10 feet, he lowered his wings, calmly turned around with his back toward me, again opened his wings, and took off. Spirit flew perfectly, as though he'd been flying for years rather than just a few days. He made a big, graceful circle before landing in a tree near a creek some distance from me.

I thanked him and his mom for the wonderful gift of seeing him again to learn he was fine, no longer needing me. A couple weeks later I went back and was told the eagles were gone. They had probably reduced the nearby populations of ground squirrels and other prey by feeding themselves and their babies. Now the babies were grown and it was time for the family to move on, until they return to nest next year. Youngsters stay with their parents through the winter, going off on their own the next spring when the adults begin nesting again. They reach reproductive maturity at about four years of age.

I still think of Spirit now and then, as I do many of the others who were with me for a while, and believe he and they are living as they should be, either on the earth plane or in spirit. I also believe I will see them again on the Other Side, recognizing them by their individual energy. Perhaps we will decide to participate in each other's subsequent lives.

CHAPTER 85

My spiritual growth began when I decided as a child that religious beliefs of divine judgment and punishment seemed neither godlike nor loving. As a result, I rejected the entire concept of spirituality until I was nearly 60 years old. Then I began learning that being spiritual is possible without the precepts of organized religion. The metaphysics section of self-hypnosis classes introduced several new and fascinating subjects for me to explore along these lines. Working with wild animals, telepathic animal communication, and living with parrots further broadened my knowledge and awareness.

Though initially skeptical, I was unable to discredit Lyn's communications with animals. She had no other way of knowing at least part of what she said; furthermore, I found I could receive answers to questions by asking animals. I knew some answers hadn't come from me when what I heard from them would not have occurred to me. I've since learned from many different teachers in one form or another, but doubt I would have been open to their knowledge without corroboration in messages from animals.

Perhaps most instrumental in moving me from atheism to spiritualism was learning more about the philosophy of reincarnation. The form of it I came to believe, including unconditional love, non-judgment, and free will, is totally opposite of what disturbs me about religions. It somehow feels completely right. Awareness and trust in my own intuition, which I believe comes from Source/spirit guides/higher self, is one of the most valuable consequences of my spiritual journey. I now know I am never truly alone; unlimited information is available any time I ask; I am empowered rather than victimized or at the mercy of some external force.

A story I read in *The Complete Idiot's Guide to the Akashic Record* briefly but profoundly summarizes my reincarnation beliefs. When I find myself feeling disturbed about a situation, remembering it helps me avoid being judgmental or even seriously upset by the behavior and experiences of others. My interpretation and paraphrasing of the story is as follows:

Members of a soul group on the Other Side were discussing their roles in a next lifetime on earth. One soul chose to experience life as an abused child; others agreed to fill all supporting roles except one. Nobody wanted to be the abusive father. Finally, the oldest, gentlest soul came forward and volunteered. This unfathomable sacrifice in the name of love not only requires the behavior of abusing another; that individual also had to endure extreme abuse as a child. Child abusers were abused as children by someone. People who are psychologically healthy don't abuse others. Planning our roles on the Other Side must include what we experience in childhood to make us capable of our intended later behaviors.

This concept takes us beyond forgiveness, which to me is a form of judgment, implying someone did something wrong. Instead, it's entirely possible those who hurt us are among our best friends on the Other Side, making huge sacrifices out of love for us by living difficult roles. When we learn to see others as eternal souls in temporary physical bodies whose intentions are to help in some way, it becomes easier to release negative emotions when we have painful or unpleasant experiences.

I believe all of us, including abusers and victims, plan our roles before coming here, knowing we are perfect, eternal beings who experience life in physical bodies in order to learn, evolve, and share. This philosophy feels empowering, much more pleasant than judging or feeling victimized. Everyone is following a path, living on the Earth Plane in order to have firsthand knowledge of what can only be experienced in a physical body. All paths have a purpose and are equally important, from the most enlightened to the least.

People with other beliefs have told me they would not have chosen their most challenging and painful experiences. Of course this is true – from a conscious level in a physical body. However, part of being born here involves losing most of the memory of living on the Other Side, especially that of choosing experiences for this lifetime.

From our perspective on the Other Side, any lifetime here is no longer than the blink of an eye. Compared to eternity, it is much shorter than a vacation and, as with our vacations, we return Home when we're finished. Using life in a physical body to add information to the whole, especially with the possibility of helping other souls progress or to increase positive energy on our planet, makes even the least pleasant lives worthwhile. In looking at it that way, I can only thank all sides of any issue, focusing on peace, non-judgment, non-punishment – kindness and compassion to all rather than only to those with whom I agree.

I definitely do not mean we must continue living as victims or look the other way when someone is causing harm! Everything we notice or experience is an opportunity for us to choose a course of action. Our growth includes learning which actions make us feel better about ourselves and our choices. Our help in those situations could easily be part of our path and/or that of animals or other people involved.

I've found it is always possible find some positives in any situation, even though apparent negatives may greatly outweigh them from our perspective in this lifetime. An incident that tested integration of spiritual beliefs into my daily life occurred on October 30, 2008, the year Solo went on his first journeys.

Lily, Rosie, and Fancy, the three fawns I raised that summer, had been living outside our back yard and exploring the neighborhood for about four weeks. I quit giving them milk on October 10, but they continued coming for grain two or more times daily. They brought wild friends as well, so we frequently had up to six fawns in the front yard. Lily and Fancy were inseparable; Rosie sometimes wandered off on her own or with the wild ones.

That evening (October 30), I was reading in the bedroom with the window open. About dusk I heard a car drive by much too fast, the sound of a horn, and then a sickening thump. I immediately went to a window, but was no longer able to see headlights or hear the car. I told Don I was concerned about the fawns; I had seen them not far from the road 10 or 15 minutes before. Of course he went out to look for them.

Sadly, Lily and Rosie had both been hit. Lily (the oldest at five and a half months) was thrown off the road by the impact and died instantly. Rosie was lying in the road, still alive but unable to move. Don did not believe she could recover from her injuries, so he euthanized her to release her from the pain and fear. Fancy was nowhere to be seen, but had probably been with them.

My Earth Plane thoughts and feelings are all those expected. Then I reminded myself to ask the following questions related to both Earth and Spirit:

> Could I have done anything at the time to prevent the accident? No.

> If I had been able to prevent it and made a mistake, would self-judgment help the fawns or me or anyone else? No. Deciding how to better handle the situation in the future would be valuable, but guilt and self-punishment cause harm by increasing negativity in the world and reducing the ability to be helpful to others.

> Would I force the fawns to stay in a pen if I had it to do over again? No. They are native to this area and are not domestic animals. Locking them up would be unfair to them, not to mention illegal, and they would soon be able to jump our fences anyway.

> If I had known the outcome, would I have refused to care for them? No. They had a good life here, even though it was short, and I couldn't condemn them to death as infants when I had the ability to raise them.

> Does quickly releasing unhappy feelings as much as possible indicate coldness on my part? No. I certainly wish the accident hadn't happened, would have prevented it if possible, and think of and miss Lily and Rosie. They know my feelings and, from what many other animals have said, do not want me to feel sad or guilty.

Do I believe their spirits are still intact and are now in pure love and/or a new life? Yes. And even if their life forces were simply dissipated and incorporated into universal energy, they are certainly not in any kind of discomfort.

Do I believe their spirits chose this path, including the length of it? Yes. That makes sense to me and is what many animals tell us.

Do I believe they were victims? No. If the above is true, they simply took advantage of that particular car to take the next step on their path. I think about Rosie and Lily much as I do about Solo: they all have chosen to live away from me, so I am unable to be a physical part of their lives now.

Should I be angry with the people in the car? No. They are following their path, too. My being angry would add more negativity to the Universe without improving anything. As Cinco, the bald eagle, said about the people who poisoned the squirrels that almost killed him, "Send love to them. They need it most." Maybe the purpose was for someone in the car to learn something beneficial from the experience of killing fawns.

A much greater test of my developing philosophy came on January 14, 2015, when my brother David collapsed and died while playing basketball with friends less than two weeks before his 57th birthday. He had been in apparent good health so his passing was a shock to all who knew him.

If it was in my power, I would have given my brother another 30 to 40 good years with his loved ones. I was 11 years old when David was born so remember learning of his impending arrival, his birth, and much of his childhood. He was an adorable little guy, with curly, bright red hair and a temper to match. He lost most of his hair early, as did our dad and two other brothers, but some of his fiery personality remained. David was well-known and liked in our community; his funeral was packed with many who miss him.

I did not attend David's funeral, or our father's a few years earlier. I have never been to a funeral. My feelings about death, even of human loved ones, are different from those of many others. The loss of David, and my spiritual growth through the past few years, makes that difference more apparent. I now firmly believe David and Dad are in a place of universal, unconditional love. I don't call it heaven because to me that implies the existence of hell, in which I do not believe. All souls are perfect and go to the same place in Spirit when they leave a physical body.

Most people who have had much of an impact on me during this life are part of the same soul group as I am. This means we will see each other again if we choose, possibly to plan roles in another shared lifetime. David could be my wife or husband, mother or son, even my enemy or victim, in another life. Perhaps we have been all of those to each other in the past.

So, though I will expect to see David when I go places he would have been before he passed, and I will think of something I should ask him before remembering he is no longer here, I am not miserable about his passing. Death is a part of life; it is a transition from one form to another, as is birth. My little brother is fine. As with the fawns and other animals who have gone, my living in a perception of loss is not beneficial to anyone, here or on the Other Side. I feel sympathy for our mother and David's wife, daughters, sons-in-law, grandchildren, great grandchildren, because I know his passing is felt more painfully by them.

Funerals are not the only ceremonies I avoid. I also don't attend weddings, graduations, parties of any sort. Being that close to energy from so many people, especially in emotional situations, has always been uncomfortable for me. I even quit going to family gatherings, especially at holidays such as Christmas and Thanksgiving. I didn't enjoy them for most of my life, but still felt obligated to go until the last few years.

I've never really felt I fit in with my family, a condition that has increased since 2002, due primarily to my changes. We seldom have any conversation topics in common. I am more focused on the present than the past and unworried about the future. I don't care to discuss illnesses, accidents, personal problems, politics, economy, cruelties, wars, terrorism, religion, environmental damage, movies – any of the negatives people often discuss. Focusing on them gives them more power, improves nothing, and feels uncomfortable. I even find most comedies unpleasant because they seem to be about ridiculing people and/or their beliefs, something I consider unkind and therefore not funny.

Hunting and fishing stories, and photos of dead animals, are painful to me but important to my family. Either I have to listen to them without comment (and then release the negative energy later) or they have to curb their conversations around me. That might work if they liked to discuss subjects that interest me, but they don't. So, since I'm in the minority, it's more comfortable for all of us if I have only short, superficial contact with them.

I can, however, talk for days about animals, energy, Spirit, synchronicities, reincarnation, books, psychology, learning experiences, positive changes in our world, similarities in people no matter where they live – all discussions that increase positive energy in the universe. I am so fortunate to have a number of friends who share some or all of these interests. More people all the time are growing and evolving this way, greatly benefitting Mother Earth and all who live here.

I no longer believe it is helpful to anyone when I disrespect myself by doing what feels inappropriate. I certainly don't want others to do something disturbing to them in a misguided attempt to please or appease me. Instead, I speak my truth and do what feels right to me, regardless of the opinions of others, giving me a sense of internal peace. The following statement applies: "Your opinion of me is none of my business and doesn't change what I think of myself." The truth is, it is impossible to satisfy others; if we ask six different people what they think about any given belief or act, we may well receive six or even eight different answers. There are many acceptable ways to do most things, not just one, so each of us can decide what is appropriate.

I believe choosing to be born into this family was for the purpose of increasing my independence, perhaps making it more likely I would evolve in the ways I have. I am proud of my young self for recognizing, at such an early age, discrepancies between many religious teachings and what seemed more god-like and loving to me. I'm also proud of my adult self for being open-minded enough to put away my angry atheist philosophy, allowing me to learn, expand, grow, and evolve as I have these last few years.

Without the participation of others in our lives, we would be unable to learn what we intended on coming into this physical body. I'm grateful to my family for enacting the roles we agreed upon, even though at times it was difficult for me and perhaps continues to be for them. I look forward to seeing them on the Other Side and expect we'll be part of each other's lives again.

David would probably dislike much of this book. He would, however, have let me sell it in his health food store. That seeming contradiction epitomizes my relationship with the family into which I chose to be born. They are all good people – just different from me.

Due to what I've learned through the Flower of Life workshops and studying hypnotherapy, telepathic animal communication, sacred geometry, energetics, energy healing, quantum physics, shamanism, reading books about the energy changes on our planet since the Harmonic Convergence in 1987, I've come a huge distance on my spiritual path in slightly over a decade. My understanding is that many people are experiencing this shift toward enlightenment now and beneficial changes are occurring much faster than ever before. It is so encouraging to see how many books, web sites, YouTube videos, seminars, and workshops covering these subjects are readily accessible now. It seems more teachers and facilitators become available all the time, ensuring a wide selection from which to choose.

I believe we humans truly are moving toward a remarkably different, even more wonderful world, and that one day our planet will be free of wars and environmental destruction. I know many unpleasant, often tragic, incidents are occurring now, from extremes

494

of climate and other earth issues, to wars, terrorism, illnesses, fear, and anger. However, these problems are due at least in part to the reaction of those who feel and fear energy changes, as well as those who work to generate that fear in order to maintain their sense of power. The process of clearing us of negativity sometimes requires extremes: circumstances have to get worse before we're ready to make changes for the better.

Also, most of those problems have been happening somewhere on the planet for a long time; a difference now is that we are more aware of them and are no longer tolerating these harmful behaviors. People who feel and embrace the energy changes, avoiding fear and focusing on love, dilute the negativity. Sending love and thoughts of peace to disturbed areas really does help everyone. I choose to participate in that way rather than as an activist working against what I perceive as harmful to others and our planet.

The more I learn, the better I understand how much more there is to learn. When I was an atheist, I said this about biology and other fields of study that fascinated me, thinking I couldn't learn as much as I want to know even if I lived 400 years. At the time I had no idea how limited even those beliefs were. Now, with the help of many animal and human teachers, I've learned not only that the amount of information to be learned is far more vast than I had conceived but that I, as an eternal being with free will, have plenty of time and opportunity to absorb as much knowledge as I choose. What a priceless gift! Whenever I think about it, I am in awe and so filled with gratitude.

REFERENCES

WEB ADDRESSES

Benedict, Lyn J., Telepathic Animal Communicator
lynbenedict.org

Bitterroot Audubon Wildlife Rehabilitation Fund
tax deductible fund for wildlife care in the Bitterroot
Valley of Montana
Bitterroot Audubon WRF, Rocky Mountain Bank, 220
Main St., Stevensville, MT 59870

Cline, Foster, and Jim Fay. Parenting with Love and Logic
loveandlogic.com

Effects of Wolf Mortality on Livestock Depredations by Robert
B. Wielgus, Kaylie A. Peebles, December 3, 2014. PLOS
One Journal article at: http://www.plosone.org/article/
info%3Adoi%2F10.1371%2Fjournal.pone.0113505

Gabriel, Shanta: author, teacher, mystic, channels Archangel
Gabriel
shantagabriel.com

Harris, Lee, Energy Intuitive, Channel, Singer, Songwriter
leeharrisenergy.com

HeartMath Institutes
heartmath.org

Hoy, Judy, Wildlife Rehabilitator
westernwildlifeecology.org
bjhoy@localnet.com

Hulburt, Marge, Shamanic Healer, Shamanism Teacher, Author, Editor, Writing Coach
blueeaglewoman.com
gonewriting.com

Indigo, Crystal, Rainbow, and Star Children
http://www.mojan.com/content/indigo-crystal-rainbow-star-children

Institute of Science, Technology and Public Policy: lists studies on positive effects of group meditation
www.istpp.org

Koon, Becki, Intuitive Channel, Life Coach, Artist (channeled jewelry designed in partnership with your unique energetic signature)
beckikoon.com

Law of Attraction Radio
loaradionetwork.com

Meeske, Carla, Shamanic Healer, Shamanism Instructor
spirithealer.com

Monson, Sarah, Intuitive Counselor, Reconnection Facilitator, Bioenergy and Spiritual Healer, Owner - Reconnection in the Bitterroot
bitterrootreconnection.com

Self, Jim, Mastering Alchemy
masteringalchemy.com

Smith, Penelope, Telepathic Animal Communicator, Author, Instructor
animaltalk.net

The Spirit Science article 'Are Animals Psychic?'
http://thespiritscience.net/2014/10/25/are-animals-
psychic/

Swartz, Roberta A., Clinical Hypnotherapist, Hypnotherapy
Instructor, Author
hypnosis4yourlife.com

Species Link Journal, telepathic animal communication
specieslinkjournal.com

Walsch, Neale Donald, Author, Lecturer
nealedonaldwalsch.com

World Parrot Refuge
worldparrotrefuge.com

Young Living Essential Oils
youngliving.com

The following video and articles give more information about the
problems and incidence of lead poisoning in wildlife.

Toxic Harvest by The Peregrine Fund
http://www.youtube.com/watch?v=qHZGQ8i8AwI

Lead Concentrations in Bones and Feathers of the Spanish
Imperial Eagle. Science Direct. 2003.
http://www.vincenzopenteriani.org/publications_pdfs/
aquila_adalberti_biol_cons1.pdf

Get the Lead Out: How we needlessly poison ourselves and
wildlife. The Wildlife Center of Virginia.
http://www.adirondackwildlife.org/Lead_Poisoning_
Wildlife.html

Metals Toxicity Laboratory. Environment Canada. 2013. http://www.ec.gc.ca/faunescience-wildlifescience/default. asp?lang=En&n=5D89D9FF-1&xsl=privateArticles2,vie wfull&po=3DC71E17

BOOKS

Altea, Rosemary. *You Own The Power*. United States: Quill, Imprint of Harper Collins Publishers, 2000.

Altea, Rosemary. *Proud Spirit*. United States: Warner Vision Books, 1995.

Altea, Rosemary. *Soul Signs*. United States: Rodale, Inc., 2004.

Altea, Rosemary. *Give The Gift of Healing*. United States: Quill, Imprint of Harper Collins, 1997.

Amen, M.D., Daniel G. and Lisa C. Routh, M.D. *Healing Anxiety and Depression*. New York: Berkeley Books, 2003.

Anderson, George, and Andrew Barone. *Walking in the Garden of Souls*. New York: Berkeley Publishing Group, 2001.

Andrews, N.D., Synthia. *Complete Idiot's Guide to The Akashic Record*. United States: Alpha Books, 2010.

Andrews, Ted. *Animal Speak, The Spiritual and Magical Powers of Creatures Great and Small*. St. Paul, Minnesota: Llewellyn Publications, 1993.

Beck, Martha. *Finding Your Way in a Wild New World*. New York: Free Press, 2012.

Bird, Joan. *Montana UFOs and Extraterrestrials*. United States: Riverbend Publishing, 2013.

Bittner, Mark. *The Wild Parrots of Telegraph Hill*. New York: Three Rivers Press, 2004

Browne, Sylvia. *Past Lives, Future Healing*. New York: New American Library, 2002.

Browne, Sylvia. *Book of Dreams*. New York: New American Library, 2003.

Browne, Sylvia. *Visits From The Afterlife*. New York: New American Library, 2003.

Browne, Sylvia. *Phenomenon*. New York: New American Library, 2005.

Browne, Sylvia. *If You Could See What I See*. United States: Hay House, Inc., 2006.

Browne, Sylvia. *Life on the Other Side*. New York: New American Library, 2000.

Browne, Sylvia. *End of Days*. New York: New American Library, 2008.

Browne, Sylvia. *All Pets Go To Heaven*. New York: Pocket Books, 2009.

Browne, Sylvia. *Contacting Your Spirit Guide*. New York: Hay House, Inc., 2005.

Browne, Sylvia. *Psychic Healing*. New York: Hay House, Inc., 2009.

Browne, Sylvia. *Temples on the Other Side*. New York: Hay House, Inc., 2008.

Browne, Sylvia. *The Other Side and Back*. New York: New American Library, 2000.

Bruce, Robert. *Astral Dynamics*. Charlottsville, VA: Hampton Roads Publishing Co., 2009.

Bruce, Robert. *Mastering Astral Projection*. Woodbury, Minnesota: Llewellyn Publications, 2004.

Byrne, Rhonda. *The Secret*. New York: Atria Books, 2006.

Byrne, Rhonda. *The Power*. Audiobook. Making Good LLC, 2010.

Cameron, Julia. *The Artist's Way, A Spiritual Path to Higher Creativity*. New York: Jeremy P. Tarcher/Putnam, 1992.

Canfield, Jack. *Chicken Soup for the Pet Lover's Soul*. Deerfield Beach, Florida: Health Communications, Inc., 1998.

Canfield, Jack. *Chicken Soup for the Nature Lover's Soul*. Deerfield Beach, Florida: Health Communications, Inc., 2004.

Carroll, Lee and Jan Tober. *The Indigo Children*. United States: Hay House, Inc., 1999.

Carroll, Lee and Jan Tober, *The Indigo Children Ten Years Later*. United States: Hay House, Inc., 2008.

Carroll, Lee. *Kryon Book One, The End Times*. Del Mar, CA: The Kryon Writings, 1993.

Carroll, Lee. *Kryon Book Two, Don't Think Like A Human*. Del Mar, CA: The Kryon Writings, 1994.

Carroll, Lee. *Kryon Book Three, Alchemy of the Human Spirit*: Del Mar, CA: The Kryon Writings, 1995.

Carroll, Lee. *Kryon Book Four, Parables*. United States: Hay House, Inc., 1996.

Carroll, Lee. *Kryon Book Five, The Journey Home*. United States: Hay House, Inc. 1997.

Carroll, Lee. *Kryon Book Six, Partnering With God*. Del Mar, CA: The Kryon Writings, 1997.

Carroll, Lee. *Kryon Book Seven, Letters From Home*. Del Mar, CA: The Kryon Writings, 1999.

Carroll, Lee. *Kryon Book Eight, Passing the Marker*. Del Mar, CA: The Kryon Writings, 2000.

Carroll, Lee. *Kryon Book Nine, The New Beginning*. Del Mar, CA: The Kryon Writings, 2002.

Childre, Doc and Howard Martin. *The Heartmath Solution*. New York: HarperCollins, 1999.

Chopra, M.D., Deepak. *Seven Spiritual Laws of Success*. United States: Amber-Allen Publishing, 1993.

Chopra, M.D., Deepak. *Quantum Healing*. United States: Bantam Books, 1989.

Chopra, M.D., Deepak. *The Future of God*. New York: Harmony Books, 2014.

Cline, Foster and Jim Fay. *Parenting with Love and Logic*. United States: NavPress, 1990 and 2006.

Cori, Patricia. *Before We Leave You, Messages from the Great Whales and the Dolphin Beings.* Berkeley, CA: North Atlantic Books, 2011.

Daniels, Don. *Evolution Through Contact.* United States: Etc. Books, 2012.

Emoto, Masaru. *The Hidden Messages in Water.* Hillsboro, OR: Beyond Words Publishing, 2004.

Fulton, Elizabeth and Kathleen Prasad. *Animal Reiki.* Berkeley, CA: Ulysses Press, 2006.

Green, Ruth Hurmence. *The Born Again Skeptic's Guide to the Bible.* Madison, Wisconsin: Freedom From Religion Foundation, 1979.

Green, Susie. *Animal Wisdom.* London: Cico Books, 2005.

Greer, PhD, PsyD, Carl. *Change Your Story, Change Your Life: Using Shamanic and Jungian Tools to Achieve Personal Transformation.* Scotland: Findhorn Press, 2014.

Gurney, Carol. *7 Steps to Communicating With Animals.* New York: Bantam-Dell Publishing, 2001.

Hall, Judy. *The Crystal Bible, A Definitive Guide to Crystals.* Cincinnati, OH: Walking Stick Press, 2003.

Harris, Lee. *Energy Speaks, Channeled Guidance for Personal Transformation.* Berkshire, England: Lee Harris Energy, 2012.

Harris, Lee. *Energy Speaks, Volume Two, Channeled Guidance for Personal Transformation.* Berkshire, England: Lee Harris Energy, 2014.

Hart, Francene. *Sacred Geometry Oracle Deck.* Vermont: Bear & Company, 2001.

Hauck, Dennis William. *The Emerald Tablet, Alchemy for Personal Transformation.* New York: Penguin Compass, 1999.

Hulburt, Marge. *Finding Eagle: A Journey into Modern-Day Shamanism.* Missoula, Montana: Gone Writing, 2011.

Hurtak, J.J. *The Book of Knowledge: The Keys of Enoch.* Los Gatos, CA: The Academy for Future Science, 1977.

Kagan, Annie. *The Afterlife of Billy Fingers.* United States: Hampton Roads Publishing, 2013.

Kenyon, Tom, and Virginia Essene. *The Hathor Material.* Santa Clara, CA: Spiritual Education Endeavors, 1996.

King, Scott Alexander. *Animal Messenger.* Australia: New Holland Publishers, 2006.

Lester, Meera. *The Everything Law of Attraction Book.* Avon, Massachusetts: Adams Media, 2008.

Lipton, Ph.D.,Bruce H. *The Biology of Belief.* United States: Hay House, Inc., 2008.

MacLeod, Ainslie. *The Instruction.* Boulder, CO: Sounds True, Inc., 2007.

McArthur, David, and Bruce McArthur. *The Intelligent Heart: Transform Your Life with the Laws of Love.* Virginia Beach, Virginia: ARE Press, 1997.

McTaggart, Lynne. *The Field, The Quest for the Secret Force of the Universe.* United States: Harper, 2008.

McTaggart, Lynne. *The Intention Experiment, Using Your Thoughts to Change Your Live and the World.* New York: Free Press, 2007.

McTaggart, Lynne. *The Bond, How to Fix Your Falling-Down World.* New York: Free Press, 2011.

Medicine Eagle, Brooke. *Buffalo Woman Comes Singing.* New York: Ballantine Books, 1991.

Melchizedek, Drunvalo. *The Ancient Secret of the Flower of Life Vol 1.* Flagstaff, AZ: Light Technology Publishing, 1990.

Melchizedek, Drunvalo. *The Ancient Secret of the Flower of Life Vol 2.* Flagstaff, AZ: Light Technology Publishing, 2000.

Melchizedek, Drunvalo. *Serpent of Light Beyond 2012.* San Francisco: Red Wheel/Weiser, LLC, 2008.

Melchizedek, Drunvalo. *Living in the Heart.* Flagstaff, AZ: Light Technology Publishing, 2003.

Monroe, Robert A. *Journeys Out of the Body.* New York: Doubleday, 1971.

Morgan, Marlo. *Mutant Message Down Under.* United States: Harper, 1991.

Morgan, Marlo. *Mutant Message From Forever.* United States: Harper Perennial, 1999.

Moorjani, Anita. *Dying to Be Me.* United States: Hay House, Inc., 2012.

Myss, Ph.D.,Caroline. *Why People Don't Heal & How They Can.* New York: Three Rivers Press, 1997.

Myss, Ph.D., Caroline. *Anatomy of the Spirit*. New York: Three Rivers Press, 1996

Narby, Jeremy. *The Cosmic Serpent*. New York: Jeremy P. Tarcher/Putnam, 1998.

Pert, Ph.D., Candace B. *Molecules of Emotion*. New York: Scribner, 1997.

Newton, Ph.D.,Michael. *Journey of Souls, Case Studies of Life Between Lives*. Woodbury, MN: Llewellyn Publications, 1996.

Newton, Ph.D., Michael. *Destiny of Souls*. Woodbury, MN: Llewellyn Publications, 2000.

Newton, Ph.D., Michael. *Life Between Lives*. Woodbury, MN: Llewellyn Publications, 2004.

Orloff, M.D., Judith. *Positive Energy*. New York: Three Rivers Press, 2004.

Patent, Dorothy Hinshaw. *Alex and Friends*. Minneapolis: Lerner Publications Company, 1998.

Pearl, Eric. *The Reconnection, Heal Others, Heal Yourself*. United States: Hay House, Inc., 2001.

Pearl, Eric, and Frederick Ponzlov. *Solomon Speaks on Reconnecting Your Life*. United States: Hay House, Inc., 2013.

Pepperberg, Irene. *The Alex Studies*. Cambridge and London, England: Harvard University Press, 1999.

Peschek-Bohmer, Dr. Flora, and Gisela Schreiber. *Healing Crystals and Gemstones from Amethyst to Zircon*. Old Saybrook, CT: Konecky & Konecky, 2002.

Pope, Raphaela, and Elizabeth Morrison. *Wisdom Of The Animals, Communication Between Animals and the People Who Love Them*. Holbrook, MA: Adams Media Corporation, 2001.

Pradervand, Pierre. *The Gentle Art of Blessing*. United States: Atria Paperback, 2009.

Redfield, James. *The Celestine Prophecy*. New York. Grand Central Publishing, 1993.

Redfield, James. *The Celestine Vision*. New York. Grand Central Publishing, 1997.

Redfield, James. *The Tenth Insight*. New York. Grand Central Publishing, 1996.

Redfield, James. *The Secret of Shambhala*. New York. Grand Central Publishing, 1999.

Redfield, James. *The Twelfth Insight*. New York. Grand Central Publishing, 2011.

Roberts, Jane. *Seth Speaks*. United States: Bantam Books, 1972.

Rose, Natalia. *The Raw Food Detox Diet*. New York: HarperCollins Publishers, 2005.

Rose, Natalia. *The New Energy Body*. New York: Natalia Rose, 2007.

St. Germain, Maureen J. *Beyond the Flower of Life*. New York: Phoenix Rising Publishing, 2009.

St. Germain, Maureen J. *Reweaving the Fabric of Your Reality.* New York: Phoenix Rising Publishing, 2010.

Sams, Jamie. *Dancing the Dream.* United States: HarperCollins, 1998.

Sams, Jamie. *Sacred Path Workbook.* United States: HarperCollins, 1991.

Sams, Jamie. *Sacred Path Cards.* United States: HarperCollins, 1990.

Sams, Jamie and David Carson. *Medicine Cards.* Revised expanded edition. New York: 1999.

Sarno, M.D. John E. *Healing Back Pain.* New York: Warner Books, 1991.

Schaefer, Carol. *Grandmothers Counsel the World.* Boston: Trumpeter, 2006.

Schnaubelt, Ph.D., Kurt. *The Healing Intelligence of Essential Oils.* Rochester, Vermont: Healing Arts Press, 2011.

Self, Jim, and Roxanne Burnett. *What Do You Mean the Third Dimension is Going Away?* Scottsdale, AZ: Inner Sight Press, 2013.

Self, Jim, and Roxanne Burnett. *The Shift. What it is. Why it's happening. How it's going to affect you.* E-book. 36 pages.

Simmerman, Tim. *Medical Hypnotherapy Vol. One.* Santa Fe, NM: Peaceful Planet Press, 2007.

Smith, Jacquelin. *Star Origins and Wisdom of Animals, Talks with Animal Souls*. Bloomington, IN: Author House, 2010.

Smith, Penelope. *When Animals Speak*. Hillsboro, OR: Beyond Words Publishing, Inc., 1999.

Stibal, Vianna. *Theta Healing*. United States: Hay House, Inc., 2006.

Swartz, Roberta A. *Me, Myself and Mind: Reclaim Your Self, Your Health and Your Life*. United States: Hypnotism Center of Western Montana, 2011.

Vallee, Martine. *The Great Shift, Co-Creating a New World for 2012 and Beyond*. San Francisco: Red Wheel/Weiser, LLC, 2009.

Vallee, Martine. *Transition Now, Redefining Duality, 2012 and Beyond*. San Francisco: Red Wheel/Weiser, 2010.

Virtue, Doreen. *Archangel Oracle Cards*. United States: Hay House, Inc., 2004.

Walsch, Neale Donald. *Conversations With God, Vol. 1*. New York: Putnam and Sons, 1996.

Walsch, Neale Donald. *Conversations With God, Vol. 2*. Charlottsville, VA: Hampton Roads, 1997.

Walsch, Neale Donald. *Conversations With God, Vol. 3*. Charlottsville, VA: Hampton Roads, 1998.

Zukkav, Gary. *The Dancing Wu Li Masters*. New York: Perennial Classics, 1979.

VIDEOS

2012, The Prophecies From The Heart. Drunvalo Melchizedek. Spiritual Planet Publishing Group, LLC, 2009.

Awakening to Zero Point: The Collective Initiation. Gregg Braden. Sacred Spaces/Ancient Wisdom, 1995.

Conversations With God. Neale Donald Walsch. CWG Films, LLC, 2006.

Extraterrestrial Realities. J.J. Hurtak, Ph.D. The Academy for Future Science, 1993.

Home, A Stunning Visual Portrayal of Earth. Yann Arthus-Bertrand. Europacorp - Elzevir Films. 2009.

How Wolves Change Rivers. Sustainable Human. Short video narrated by George Monblot, 2014. https://www.youtube.com/watch?v=ysa5OBhXz-Q&feature=youtu.be

I Am. Tom Shadyac. Shady Acres, Inc., 2011.

Infinity, The Ultimate Trip. Jay Weidner. Sacred Mysteries Productions, 2009. www.sacredmysteries.com

Merkabah, Voyage of a Star Seed. J.J. Hurtak and Jean-Luc Bozzoli. The Academy for Future Science, 1998.

Something Unknown Is Doing We Don't Know What... Renee Sheltema. Telekan, 2009. www.somethingunknown.com

"The Living Matrix. A Film on the New Science of Healing. The Living Matrix, LTD, and Becker Massey LLC, 2009.

"The Message of the Keys of Enoch." J.J. Hurtak. The Academy for Future Science, 1993.

"The Quantum Activist." Amit Goswami, Ph.D. Blue Dot Productions, 2009. www.quantumactivist.com

"The Secret." Rhonda Byrne. TS Production, LLC, 2006.

"Thrive, What On Earth Will It Take?" Clear Compass Media, 2011. www.thrivemovement.com

"What the Bleep!? Down the Rabbit Hole." Captured Light and Lord of the Wind Films, 2004.

Made in the USA
San Bernardino, CA
21 August 2015